THE FORMATION OF ENGLISH

NEO-CLASSICAL THOUGHT

THE FORMATION OF ENGLISH NEO-CLASSICAL THOUGHT

BY JAMES WILLIAM JOHNSON

PRINCETON, NEW JERSEY

PRINCETON UNIVERSITY PRESS

1967

PR
441
J6
1967

820.9
J634

FOR NAN

γυνή τ᾽ ἀρίστη τῶν ὑφ᾽ ἡλίῳ μακρῷ

Preface

Since its establishment in the eighteenth century as a significant variety of literary activity, criticism in English has tended to employ certain basic approaches in a more or less sequential pattern. In the period between the Restoration of Charles and the Regency of Prince George, the space of about 160 years, critics developed most of the stances that have since become basic: the impressionist, the historical, the editorial, the contextual, the syncretistic, and so on. Moreover, the sequential development of criticism between 1660 and 1820 is an imperfect but workable paradigm of the manner in which a body of literature, accepted or rejected in its own day on the basis of its emotional validity or "truth" for its contemporaries, undergoes a series of reappraisals as time and change alter the circumstances which originally helped to produce it.

Another period of 160 years has passed since the literature of English classicism became overbalanced by literature composed in accordance with nonclassical assumptions and a critical rationale was developed to justify that literature even though critical modes remained the established ones. In that time, critics have been refining their equipment as they have been examining the works of Dryden, Swift, Pope, and Johnson—the great tetrad of classical literature—and making successive syntheses to explain their comprehension of the nature of the literature and mentality they have come to call "classical," "Neo-Classical," or "Augustan." Today, it might superficially appear that modern scholarship, somewhat like Browning's grammarian, has succeeded in settling Neo-Classicism's business.

Certainly our own understanding of Restoration and eighteenth century literature is more comprehensive and accurate than that of our predecessors in the critical procession. We have largely succeeded in slipping off the narrow, pejorative impressions of the "romantic" critic. We have managed to

Preface

place the moral as well as the aesthetic reactions of the early Victorian critics into perspective. We have benefited from the efforts at historical and contextual criticism by such later Victorians as Elton, Gosse, and Stephen. And we profit enormously from contemporary financial and technological conditions that enable several scholars to complete in a few years editorial chores that formerly would have occupied the lifetime of a solitary Bentley or Johnson.

Today, the student of late seventeenth and eighteenth century English literature may view with satisfaction the authoritative editions produced in the twentieth century: of Rochester, Dennis, Prior, Swift, Pope, Gray, Johnson, and Gibbon. He confidently anticipates the completion of editions of Dryden, Addison, Goldsmith, Walpole, Burke, and Boswell. The increasing number of reprint societies make easily available to him works also accessible in a number of excellent, special library collections. As far as primary materials are concerned, the modern scholar has far more numerous and accurate sources than his critical forebears did.

Not surprisingly, the number of secondary critical works has increased in direct ratio to the availability of these primary materials, as a glance at annual bibliographies for 1920 and 1960 shows. Critical projects have dealt with problems as specific as Swift's correspondence with his Irish printer or as general as the evolution of the "classical" outlook into the "romantic" one during the eighteenth century. Critical works of varying persuasions—the critical biography, the history of ideas, the investigation of sources and analogues, the methodological, the interpretive—make accessible to the reader the dimensions of English classical thought in terms usually cogent and illuminating.

As a result, the student can get a great deal of information about the literature of the English classicists by reading twentieth century criticism. He can readily acquire a clear idea of the working hypotheses of their writing: a concern with "correctness," "rules," and "decorum"; the desire to imitate the

viii

Preface

styles of Horace and Virgil; an admiration for the critical
dicta of Longinus; enthusiasm for personification; distaste for
elaborate conceits; a reliance on the concept of "nature," and
so on. Moreover, twentieth century critics have carefully de-
lineated many of the preoccupations of the English classicists:
their admiration for the literature of the Greco-Roman world;
their implicitly Christian theological bias; their inclination to
favor the aristocratic, the urban, and the institutional; their
presuppositions about "taste" and moral responsibility; their
insistence on applicability and practicality. These and other
ideological boundaries of the classicists' frame of mind have
been lucidly marked.

Nevertheless, there are aspects of English classical literature
that have been slighted, taken for granted, and totally ignored,
just as there are writers and thinkers whose productions have
not been edited and who are but sparingly treated in modern
critical works. Swift and Pope have been edited, but what of
Steele, Gay, and Bolingbroke? Can any examination of the
"Augustan" mind afford to dismiss lightly the works of
Arbuthnot or Shaftesbury, to mention the obvious? Defoe's
London Review essays are now becoming available, but many
of the works listed in Harry T. Moore's bibliography of Defoe
continue to be unobtainable in an easy way. And what of the
social and political pamphlets of Dennis and Mandeville,
which certainly were an important part of the intellectual currency of the age of Swift and Pope? One is forced to question
whether any modern, critical synthesis that discusses the
"Augustan" state of mind or canon of literature can be very
complete if it fails to take into account writers of the second
and third magnitudes. There are, to be sure, formerly dark
critical spaces that are slowly being illuminated—the work
on Defoe by J. R. Sutherland and Maximillian Novak is a
worthy instance—but far too much primary material remains
unexamined in library stacks to permit us to feel we have
mastered the study of English classicism. The modern scholar
must perforce admit his finite comprehension of the purview

ix

and the literature of Neo-Classicism as he carries on his research and editing chores, modifying his conceptual synthesis as he goes.

This book is an attempt to formulate my own modifications of the prevailing twentieth century critical understanding of English Neo-Classicism. The investigative process that led to its writing began over ten years ago when I became curious about the volumes listed in eighteenth century library catalogues and started reading some of those arcane works as background for a study of Jonathan Swift. Some of these—by Thomas Burnet and Bishop Steno, for example—have been examined by other critics and their relevance to Neo-Classical thought explicated in separate studies. Other works—the writings of Synesius are an instance—have been critically related to English Renaissance literature but have been ignored by commentators on Restoration and eighteenth century literature. Still others—notably the *Catonic Distiches*—appear to have escaped the notice of previous critics, despite their obvious relevance to Neo-Classical literature. Finally, many works of interest to the English classicists are presently acknowledged to have exerted influence somehow or other, but no one has bothered to go beyond a simple assertion of influence or a foreshortened study of a single idea. Herodotus' *Histories* have met the first treatment, and Polybius' theory of Balanced Government the second.

As I read my way through various categories of literature, I found my understanding of Neo-Classical thought constantly being altered and modified by seeing it within the contexts assumed and identified by the English classicists themselves. Dryden's *Annus Mirabilis* expanded through its references to Diodorus Siculus, and so did Pope's *Dunciad* and Swift's *Gulliver's Travels*. Steele's *The Christian Hero*, when seen as an adaptation of Sallust, took on added significance, and the irony of Steele's critics—Theobald and Arbuthnot among them—became keener to the mind. The multifaceted brilliance of Swift's parodies grew more lustrous when placed beside the essays of Photius and J. J. Scaliger that helped to provoke them. Addison's familiar essays and numismatic interests assumed a greater proportion when juxtaposed with the writings of Erycius Puteanus and Thomas Erpenius. And the defenses of the Christian religion undertaken by Defoe, Addison, and Mandeville, not to mention Swift's scathing *Argument,* acquired important associations when placed beside Grotius' tract or the editions of Minucius Felix, Tertullian, Origen, and other patristic apologists that were being published in the same decades that the English apologists wrote.

Even more interesting I found the explanation for apparent contradictions in the Neo-Classical outlook to be the result of critical données that were originally made within an assumed context but later were removed from that context in such a way as to be separated from each other and so form implicit contradictions. That Neo-Classical thought was based on a reverence for classical civilization has been a critical truism for almost two hundred years. But why, if the classical world was venerated in its entirety, did eighteenth century England become identified almost exclusively with Roman civilization, specifically the Augustan Age of Rome? How is the supposed English admiration for Roman Augustanism to be reconciled with the Britons' choice of Roman heroes—Anthony, Cato, Pompey, Cicero—nearly all of them Republicans who died resisting the advent of imperialism? Could a Christian nation and age really accept as a model a pagan nation distinguished for its persecution of Christians, and could such a devout Christian as Addison seriously hold up a Cato as an archetype of human achievement? The Christian bias of writers from Dryden to Johnson, with a few exceptions, is indisputable, prima facie. What were the sources of their belief and how did they reconcile spiritual Christianity and secular classicism? Furthermore, if the Greek heritage played little part in English Augustanism, how can the Neo-Classicists' absorption with tragedy, that peculiarly Greek form, be explained in an age that habitually found Shakespeare, their other tragic model, wanting in vital ways?

Such antinomies as these would be less troublesome if it

were not for two factors: they are not the result of inherent intellectual weakness or limitation in the Neo-Classical point of view so much as the result of critical emphases; and they are sometimes made the point of attack by critics who wish to derogate English classical literature. Any congeries of beliefs—whether in the individual or collective mind—necessarily contains some contradictions. But for a purview such as the Neo-Classical, which purported to assimilate and reconcile disparities through the use of learning and common sense, to be guilty of the ignorance or the dogmatism necessary for overlooking contradictions would be damning indeed. Detractors of Neo-Classical literature have damned it for just such lack of logic and arbitrariness; and its defenders, in concentrating on specialized aspects of Neo-Classical literature, have seldom argued for its inclusiveness, its comprehensiveness, or its synthetic profundity.

The answer to the problem of how Neo-Classical thought could lay claim to comprehensive synthesis on the one hand and on the other could contain posits that appear contradictory today may be largely solved, as it seems to me, by returning to the intellectual heritage the classicists assumed to be valid and eternal: the literature of the past. Christopher Dawson has summed up the relationship between Neo-Classical culture and its inheritance in this way: "that culture was itself the product of . . . the tradition of the classical world transmitted through medieval Christendom and reinforced by the Humanism of the seventeenth and eighteenth centuries. . . ." In other words, to comprehend the intensity and scope of Neo-Classicism, one must have a minimal knowledge of the cultural bequests preserved in the literature of more than twenty centuries.

This is by no means to say that modern readers cannot understand the individual literary artifacts of Neo-Classicism without having read scores of works in mediaeval Latin and Byzantine Greek. *An Essay on Man* or *Rasselas*—or most of the other masterworks of English classicism—can be read, comprehended, and judged satisfactorily as self-contained entities. The internalist schools of modern criticism, including practitioners whose chief interest is Restoration and eighteenth century literature, may see no reason to go beyond the chef d'oeuvres themselves. But it seems to me that the modern reader necessarily straitens his appreciation as well as his understanding of much Neo-Classical literature if he refuses to admit the relevance of the intellectual and literary traditions that the English classicists constantly referred to and consciously drew upon. Perhaps the most tendentious modern critic will grant the usefulness of knowing something about classical and Renaissance literature to enhance one's understanding of the works of Pound, Yeats, Eliot, or Joyce. Is it not equally possible that the works of the classicists become more enhanced the greater the reader's knowledge of the classics?

I do not presume, in the present study, to claim that my excursions through the literary backgrounds of Neo-Classical thought have led me to read and ponder every possible source that may have effected the classicists' outlook. The reader can see from my bibliography the works that I drew upon directly in reaching the conclusions presented in the chapters ahead. I have also read, but frequently not itemized, the classics whose influence on English thought is traced in other critical works: for example, Longinus, Epictetus, Virgil, Horace, Juvenal, *et al.* The items listed in the bibliography have furnished the data for my comments or else they contain additional data and supplementary opinions. Quantitative criteria are always suspect and often ludicrous. I do not intend to suggest that I have read *more* background material than previous commentators, for I may well have read a good deal less. Nor do I claim that my reading has been more selective or profitable than theirs. I merely urge that the emphases suggested to me by my investigations provide some dimensions of pleasure and understanding beyond those established in other critical works.

It is not my intention to refute or even amend very much the assumptions underlying such excellent studies of Neo-Classicism as those by George Sherburn, Walter J. Bate, Francis Gallaway, W. P. Ker, J.A.K. Thomson, Sherard Vines,

Preface

Sir Herbert Grierson, R. F. Jones, and Geoffrey Tillotson, to name only a few of the leading authorities in the field. As I said earlier, I think the majority of scholarship and criticism regarding English classical literature illuminating and generally incisive. I do believe, however, that certain canards have sprung up as a result of standard emphases. In developing its own position, my thesis points out and attempts to dispose of these.

The most insidious of the canards seem to me to be these: English classicism between 1660 and 1800 was almost purely a literary phenomenon. Its modes were Latinate and imitative; its focus was preemptively stylistic. Its data, as well as its attitudes, were Roman in cast; Greek culture was barely known and imperfectly understood. Not only was it Roman; Restoration and eighteenth century literature was deliberately imitative of a slect few Latin poets and satirists of the Augustan Age of Rome and it scorned the achievements of other classical eras. Insofar as it embodied Christian materials or viewpoints, Neo-Classical literature derived these solely from Protestant sources, chiefly the Anglican tracts of the seventeenth century. It was ignorant about and scornful of mediaeval Latin and Greek literature. Although its critical precepts were a narrowing and rigidifying of Renaissance principles and its frame of mind a modification of Humanism, English Neo-Classicism actually repudiated Renaissance learning as outmoded and theoretical pedantry. It was an insular product with very few continental ties. And it lacked both a sense of history and of tragedy.

These truisms are untrue, I believe. Discerning critics of English classicism, George Sherburn chief among them, have constantly warned against facile generalizations about literature of the period 1660 to 1800 (see *A Literary History of England*, pp. 823-24). Yet generalizations are a useful form of understanding so long as they are based on a range of pertinent facts. This book tries to marshal sufficient facts and show their relevance to Neo-Classical thought so that critical opinion about the era can rely on referents rather than truisms.

Preface

Organizing my material led originally to some difficulties. There are already in existence some fine surveys of classical influences through the centuries and a few specific studies of Greco-Roman literary influences on eighteenth century English writing: J. E. Sandys' three volume *A History of Classical Scholarship* is itself a monument of scholarship, and J.A.K. Thomson has helpfully listed in two companion volumes the sources and analogues in Classical and Neo-Classical literature. There is also a more superficial study by Gilbert Highet. These surveys are helpful source books or reference works but they are by no means inclusive nor do they do much more than suggest literary parallels. In treating such largely ignored background areas as patristic, Byzantine, and continental Latin writing, I was at first tempted to imitate the cataloging techniques of Sandys and Thomson but with unsatisfactory results. In my desire to acquaint the reader with the writers and works I had discovered, I had to sacrifice cogency and focus. When this was charitably but pointedly remarked by others, I decided to leave epic lists to Homer and the Library of Congress.

The other possible technique of organization was to select a theme, or cluster of themes, to trace in their mutations down through the centuries; in brief, to write a limited history of ideas. Or, perhaps, I could select a defined group of works—such as R. S. Crane has done with logic texts and Philip Harth with Anglican apologetics—and profitably relate these thematically and rhetorically to a limited group of Neo-Classical *opera*. To do so, I at last decided, would restrict once again the critical approach in such a fashion as to obviate a depiction of the synthetic scope of the Neo-Classical outlook.

In its present form, therefore, this study is a combination of various techniques: the survey, the history of ideas, the study of influences, and the analytical, among them. My central purpose is to cast light on previously slighted aspects of Neo-Classical ideology by examining a reasonably broad range of background materials and by tracing themes and posits in a fairly widespread sample of English classical literature. Frequently this literature is not the canonized "masterpiece" or the standard anthology selection. In some instances, the lesser known work is a better example of the point to be made than a more famous one; but more relevantly to my purpose, the fullest meanings of the familiar work often are made accessible by the explication of the forgotten one. Everyone is familiar with the acerbic attack on religious enthusiasts in Swift's *A Tale of a Tub*; but few people are acquainted with Meric Casaubon's *A Treatise Concerning Enthusiasm*, the far more comprehensive and detailed attack from which Swift may have derived his premises.

The organization of my essay is closely bound to six related groups of background materials chosen from those twenty centuries of literary heritage. My first chapter, a discussion of the descriptive terms evolved by critics of the last two hundred years to characterize English thought and literature between 1660 and 1800, attempts two things: the clarification of several nebulous phrases ("classicism," "Neo-Classical," "Augustan," et cetera) , and a revelation of how the terms developed in such a manner as to foster current critical truisms. A portion of the material in this chapter originally appeared in a different context in my article, "The Meaning of Augustan" (*Journal of the History of Ideas*, October 1958). My extended tracing of key critical terms in the present book is, I believe, justified by the lack of such information elsewhere and by the necessity of exorcising prevalent critical assumptions implicit in some terms.

Once terms are clarified and definitions established, the next six chapters take up Neo-Classical thought and its relationship to these antecedent literary contexts: historiography, classical Greek literature in general, the legend of Cato, the patristic writings of the Ante- and Post-Nicene eras, Byzantine literature, and the continental Latin scholarship of the Renaissance. These chapters follow an approximately chronological order corresponding to historical and literary sequence. The works treated are illustrative of eclecticism rather than exhaustiveness.

Preface

Chapter 2, "The Role of Historiography," discusses the importance of classical history and its derivatives in forming basic Neo-Classical concerns and beliefs. It tries to show that Neo-Classicism was not simply a "literary" (that is, fictive) preoccupation but a world-view, an encompassing perspective. It surveys historical theory in the period before Hume and Gibbon, indicates the source of popular historical assumptions, and outlines the ideological effects of the study of history on the minds and works of a number of English classicists.

Chapter 3, "Greece," tests the proposition that English classicism was entirely Latinate and Roman by examining the literary evidence of English Hellenism between 1660 and 1750. Other studies have amassed much convincing proof of such Hellenism in travel and art books of the period. This chapter surveys scholarly interests in Greek literature, publication records, and public entertainments before 1750 for additional proof. It summarizes the Hellenic interests of a half-dozen literary figures. It educes evidence of Greek influence and identifies the Hellenic nucleus of some outstanding literary cruces of the early eighteenth century. The chapter intends to show that the modern opinion of English Neo-Classicism as "Roman" is too gross a simplification to retain.

Chapter 4, "Rome," similarly questions the proposition that the neo-Roman element in England was commensurate with "Augustanism" (the self-identification by English classicists with the literary and political elements of Augustan Rome). It does so by a close inspection of the treatment of Cato in eighteenth century literature. Cato, the symbol of Republicanism, is discussed for those qualities that English classicists found in him and chose him to exemplify: his public as well as private roles. Addison's *Cato* and other works are discussed to show that the historic Cato underwent Protean alterations to suit a very selective British notion of what was Roman. And the extent to which Catonism could exert psychological influence is demonstrated by his place in the life of Swift. By the use of a limited aspect of Roman tradition, the chapter tries to qualify the concept of English neo-Romanisn and Augustanism.

The fifth chapter, "Carthage, Alexandria, Nicaea," explores the extent to which patristic literature was known to and utilized by the Christian exponents of the Neo-Classical school. It briefly surveys the presence of patristic works in England following the Restoration, cites English works that drew from it or referred to it, and suggests the chief ways the Fathers supplied materials and attitudes for several Neo-Classicists. It also indicates ways in which patristic writers facilitated the reconciliation of spiritual Christianity and secular classicism. The chapter as a whole tries to emphasize the significance of Catholic Christian literature in the shaping of the ideology of Neo-Classicism.

Chapter 6, "Byzantium," undertakes to give evidence of the importance of mediaeval Greek study in England after 1660 and to identify the chief ways that Byzantine literature affected English writers; in their use of aphorisms, their conceptions of history and chronology, and their concern with literary criticism. This essay does not—and cannot—do more than scratch the surface of a topic so universally (if unjustly) ignored by literary scholars. Intellectual and literary Byzantinism may have been a limited influence on English classicism; but it was there and it ought not to be dismissed summarily.

Chapter 7, "Holland," looks at that vast body of ecumenical Latin scholarship of the fifteenth, sixteenth, and seventeenth centuries in the light of its effects on Neo-Classical thinking. Critics have perennially been burdened with linking late seventeenth and eighteenth century literary practice to that of Renaissance England. By investigating the Neo-Classicists' attitudes toward the Humanists and their works, this chapter propounds a direct connection between Neo-Classicism and continental Humanism as it was centered in Holland in the fifteenth century and later. The chapter proposes that certain data, themes, and genres—as well as theories—were the direct bequest to English classicism by Dutch polymaths.

The two final chapters are concerned with the Neo-Classical

synthesis of all these elements taken from the past and how it resulted in the vitiation of one form of literature in the eighteenth century and the vitalization of another. Chapter 8, "Neo-Classicism and the Tragic Drama," discusses the Neo-Classical theories of tragic drama, shows how their constituent elements were dependent on posits taken from the ancients, the Fathers, and others, and how these conjoined to subvert the essential nature of dramatic tragedy. It seeks to explain the failure of Neo-Classical tragic drama as a result of the intellectual constructs shown in previous chapters.

The final chapter, "Gibbon," takes up the man and the work that virtually embody the personal and ideological assumptions of the Neo-Classical viewpoint. The chapter is divided into two sections. "The Road to Rome" sees Gibbon's education as typical of that of English classicists of the era; it traces the classical elements in his reading as vital in the formation of his mind. The ultimate configuration of Gibbon's intellect is archetypical of the Neo-Classical "set." The second section, "Decline and Fall," discusses Gibbon's masterpiece as the triumphant synthesis of elements in English classical thought suggested in my earlier chapters. The intellectual constructs derived from the Classical-mediaeval-Humanist tradition by English Neo-Classicism fuse in such a way as to make *The History of the Decline and Fall of the Roman Empire* both a successful new genre—the "cultural history"—and perhaps the most complete statement of the Neo-Classical worldview. If the Gibbonian synthesis is not a total one, it encompasses most of the aspects of eighteenth century classicism that critics have slighted.

Such is the schema of the present study. Its method is syncretistic, its mode, contextualism. Whether its materials and its thesis are viable, I leave to the scholar's judgment. I realize that my effort does not strengthen very appreciably the case for the profundity of Neo-Classical insight nor does it succeed in making a transcendent critical synthesis. Yet, if it manages to expand the acknowledged scope of the English classical outlook and glimpse the inner consistencies of its posits, that is all I desired for it to attain. If it further manages to extend for the reader the dimensions of his understanding of Neo-Classical thought as it is preserved in Restoration and eighteenth century literature, I am entirely content.

ACKNOWLEDGMENTS

No one who has read Swift's merciless parodies of dedicatory rhetoric can feel very easy in composing formal thanks to those in whose debt he finds himself, however deep and real that debt. And if the grateful author manages to avoid the fatuous and effusive phrase, he still risks implicating in his failures those he would thank. In spite of these risks, however, I owe debts of gratitude which I cannot discharge by a public acknowledgment but can merely own.

The University of Rochester has made possible much of the research and writing behind this book through its administrative encouragement and financial aid. The Folger Shakespeare Library further helped me with a Fellowship that permitted me to use its facilities under perfect conditions.

The staff members of several libraries have eased my research with their kind, expert cooperation: the Widener and Houghton Libraries at Harvard University, the British Museum, the Folger, and the University of Rochester. Marian Allen and her staff at Rochester have helped me on many occasions when I must have tried their patience to the utmost with niggling requests.

The editors of the *Journal of the History of Ideas, History and Theory,* and *The Journal of British Studies* have been gracious in their permission for me to use materials that originally appeared in those publications. Jonathan Cape Limited has generously permitted me to adapt materials from Geoffrey Keynes' *The Library of Edward Gibbon* in the Appendix to the present work.

The labor involved in preparing manuscripts has been greatly lightened by the cheerful, intelligent efficiency of Marian McClintock and her staff, as well as that of Amelia Hicks and Natalie Tarbet.

Acknowledgments

To the editorial staff of the Princeton University Press, I am indebted not only for their expertise but for their steady encouragement.

Finally, there are the men and women whose kindness to me cannot be reckoned, certainly not in words. Only they know the nature and extent of my debt to them; but by setting down their names here, I may at least let them know that I am aware of it—Cecil Abernethy, Monroe K. Spears, James R. Sutherland, Kathrine Koller, Bernard Schilling, George H. Ford, Louis Landa, H. T. Swedenberg, Marjorie Nicolson. I am grateful to them for small favors and large.

To prevent those named above from suffering guilt by association, I respectfully remind the reader who may find this work an ill-favored thing, it is entirely mine own.

J. W. J.

Rochester, New York
April 1966

Contents

THE FORMATION OF ENGLISH
NEO-CLASSICAL THOUGHT

1 · Some Terms and Their Uses

Every age is one of complexity and conflict to the men who inhabit it; but later generations, who possess the seeming wisdom of hindsight, tend to equate understanding of the past with formulation. Whether from ignorance, nostalgia, or self-satisfaction, the living are inclined to see bygone social and intellectual issues in the simple terms of their resolution, theoretical or historical, and so to reduce a past age to its most obvious elements or the elements most relevant to the concerns of the present. Irrelevancies and contradictions are conveniently forgotten by retrospective commentators; thus a tumultuous, confused, and variegated period of human activity is tidily encapsuled by truisms. At last a label is attached, and comprehension of the past is made possible simply by sacrificing understanding.

English culture between 1660 and 1800 has undergone such a critical truncation during the last century and a half. Intellectually heterodox though it was, the period has challenged its commentators as often to generalizations as to detailed insights; and, ironically enough, it has acquired so many labels purporting to summarize its character that confusion has been compounded and the quintessence of the era, if there is any such thing, has remained an elusive unknown. The critics are persistent, however, and continue to submit phrases they hope will describe the age with the formality and succinctness of a Pope couplet. "The Age of Elegance," "Age of Reason," "Age of the Enlightenment"—these have been used in application to the period as a whole. Historians have contributed a number of other tags: the "Restoration," the "Queen Anne Period," the "Hanoverian Age." Finally, literary critics have concocted designatory phrases based on figures, themes, genres, and times.

3

Confronted with so great an accumulation of terminological debris, the commentator on English literature of the decades between 1660 and 1800 has an initial obligation to define his terms. An examination of the most popular phrases employed by literary critics may serve to discard the least helpful and to reconfirm the accuracy of familiar terms that have fallen into careless commonplaces.

Among the superficial titles for the 140 years of political and literary activity that seem to constitute a coherent phase is the "Age of Elegance."[1] Seldom used as a literary term, this phrase is sometimes flourished by a critic anxious to characterize the qualities of Addison's prose style or to pinpoint the social cabbalism of Lord Chesterfield. Generally, however, the "Age of Elegance" connotes the artistic and societal modes of the period. It refers to the visually stylized: the Adam decor, the Gainsborough portrait, the Wedgwood urn. Or it implies the mannered rituals reflected in the drawing room scenes of Congreve and Sheridan. It is a "texture" phrase that tries to embody the peculiarly refined, luxurious, formalized sensuality of the era. As a literary term it is largely useless, though euphonious. As a description of the cultural scene, it is inexact and oversimplified, omitting as it does any reference to the gross textures of Gin Lane, Medmenham, Grub Street, Bedlam, and other vital elements in the life of the times.

Less superficial and more ideologically precise a phrase is the "Age of Reason."[2] Originated by philosophical historians, it has been fitfully used by literary historians as well, though its inappropriateness in characterizing the precepts of such works as *Religio Laici*, *Gulliver's Travels*, and *Rasselas*, to name but a few, is all too obvious. Even as a label for the intellectual tradition of Hobbes, Locke, Hume, and other philosophers, the "Age of Reason" is liable to misuse. When applied to the conceptual bases of most Restoration and eighteenth century prose, it is grossly inappropriate. Dryden, Swift, Pope, Addison, Steele, Johnson, Goldsmith were all cautious in their reliance on the ratiocinative faculties of the human mind as the agency of truth; and all of them stood in con-

4

scious opposition to the philosophical school of Rationalists. Similarly, it is unwise to term the literary epoch between 1660 and 1800 the "Age of the Enlightenment," since this is still another phrase devised to describe the philosophical currents of the age. Most men of letters swam angrily against those currents; a few, like Swift and Johnson, considered the philosophical innovations of their century anything but enlightenment.

Somewhat more useful, but still limited as terms of literary criticism, are the phrases established on the basis of chronological classification. "The Restoration Period" is a well established and handy way to designate the decades from 1660 to 1700; historically, it coincides with the return of Charles II to the throne and the terminal date is close to the advent of Queen Anne. Literarily, it coincides with Dryden's career, his first poem of any note having appeared in 1659 and his death occurring in 1700. Unfortunately, the tidiness of historical and literary dates from 1660 to 1700 is not maintained after the reign of Queen Anne. Such apparently utilitarian phrases as the "Queen Anne Period" of literature or the "Queen Anne wits" verge on the meaningless when one considers the actual literary output from 1700 to 1714. *A Tale of a Tub* was composed seven or eight years before its appearance in 1704, and Swift's only other compositions during the "Queen Anne Period" were *The Examiner* papers and the *Journal to Stella*. Apart from a few attempts at pastorals, Pope produced nothing of note. *The Tatler* and *The Spectator* appeared during this time. But aside from these obvious exceptions, the masterworks of the first half of the eighteenth century were not composed until after the end of the reign of Anne. Then, the successive periods of George I and George II fail to correlate literary events in an illuminating manner. Monarchic designations, though helpful in establishing chronological sequence, are generally deficient as literary guideposts separating Dryden and Johnson.

The use of a dominant literary figure to name an era is a common technique employed by literary historians, but with the period in question, certain ludicrous problems arise. Is one truly justified in calling the decades that witnessed the publication of *Paradise Lost, Paradise Regained,* and *Samson Agonistes* the "Age of Dryden"? Dryden more obviously set the tone for the time than Milton, however, whatever his relative literary stature. And should the decades between 1700 and 1750 be called the "Age of Swift" or the "Age of Pope"? Historically, the most suitable term might be the "Age of Addison"; but Addison died in 1718, long before *Gulliver's Travels, An Essay on Man, The Beggar's Opera,* and many other major works had appeared. The problem of whether to establish an era on the basis of a writer's lifespan or his productive years or his influence not only is relative to naming the first half of the eighteenth century but to the last half as well. Does the "Age of Johnson" end with the death of the great Lexiphanes in 1784, before the publication of Boswell's *Life?* Should it extend to that publication in 1792? Or does the influence of Johnson meet its most telling line of demarcation in 1798 with the publication of the *Lyrical Ballads?*

One might think all such questions a "perfect Cavil," to use Swift's phrase, if it were not for the fact that commentators on literature presumably use designatory terms to clarify periods and works of literature; such clarification is illusory unless the terms are precise and meaningful. Though it is true that terms are useful as long as their general meanings are clear—that a literary critic can use any term he likes to designate an age so long as he defines his term and it corresponds to the perceptible, traditional characteristics of that age—it is not true that charismatic terms are therefore the best or most accurate terms. The modern habit of referring to the period 1660 to 1800 as "the Eighteenth Century" is evidence enough of the inaccuracy of a phrase possessing great usefulness and appeal. The intellectual benefit accruing from a phrase that not only oversimplifies but commits a blatant anachronism is dubious. Unfortunately, many of the critical designations for aspects of literary history between 1660 and 1800 do one or both of these.

6

Some Terms and Their Uses

Still another limitation of the literary label is that it can conceal erroneous critical judgment or shield a narrow taste. The "Age of Prose" was the term often used in nineteenth century England to describe the literature of the previous century. Seemingly innocuous and apparently accurate in its estimate of the preeminence of brilliant prosewriters in the Stuart-Hanover decades, it nonetheless judges the poetry of the period and finds it wanting. As an encompassing term, the "Age of Prose" implicitly supports Matthew Arnold's contention that Pope and Dryden wrote prose in verse, that there was nothing worthy of the name of poetry in a time that produced Dryden, Rochester, Dorset, Sedley, Prior, Swift, Pope, Thomson, Collins, Gray, Cowper, Crabbe, Johnson, Goldsmith, and a score of others. This astigmatic purview has long been revealed, but the term subsuming it is still used by literary commentators.

None of the terms dealt with so far, then—the modal, dogmatic, chronological, influential, or generic—seems a very revealing way to epitomize a collation of literature that not only has been treated traditionally as a recognizable *corpus,* but which acknowledged its own entity and deliberately preserved it. Writers from 1660 to 1800 fostered common intellectual and literary bonds; they documented their dependence upon one another in private correspondence as well as public acknowledgment. Surely, then, it must be possible to formulate the nature of their ideological and literary interdependence in a summarizing phrase? This has been done, of course, by the men themselves. It is significant that the terms still useful today were formulated by the writers to whom we apply them. The associations, however, have altered considerably.

When, in the latter half of the seventeenth century spokesmen for the new era sought to encourage political consolidation, they enlisted the support of literary men, who promptly clarioned catchwords to serve as standards or goals for Restoration England. This was to be the "new" classical age, the time of a renewed "Augustan" literature and society.[3] The phrases that resulted—"classick," "classical," "Augustan"—became a permanent part of the English literary vocabulary. But what began as a terminology of aspiration, in time turned into one of assessment, then disillusionment, derogation, and at last in our own time, seemingly judicious evaluation. A review of the history of usage of these terms discloses not only a considerable complexity in eighteenth century thought but also reveals some errors in modern critical judgment.[4]

The English meanings of "classical" ultimately derive from the Latin, *classicus*, "of first rank, importance; best." The literary connotations of *classicus* to the ancient world may be seen in the comment of Aulus Gellius on an author as "classicus . . . scriptor, non proletarius"; that is, he was a first rate, or first class, writer as opposed to a poor or lesser one. The *Oxford English Dictionary* cites Sir Edwin Sandys' *Europae speculum* (1599) as the first use of the word "classical" in the sense "Of first rank or authority" and Edward Topsell's *The historie of fourefootid beastes* (1607) as the first use of "classical" in the sense "Of the standard Greek and Latin writers." These two basic meanings of the adjective have persisted through the centuries, often being used interchangeably. Bishop Hall, in his *Epistles* (1608-11) used "classical" to mean "first rank"; but it was not until 1613 that the adjective "classick" was employed by Robert Cawdrey in the *Table Alphabet* in the same sense. From that time on in the seventeenth century, "classical" and "classic" were used to mean, variously, of first rank and authority and of the Greek and Latin writers.

In 1700, with the publication of the translation into English of Jean Le Clerc's *Parrhasiana*, the rationale of classicism found one of its earliest expressions. Though he has been condemned by classical scholars of later centuries as something of an upstart, nevertheless Le Clerc's statement about "Humane Learning" and his estimate of the role of what he himself calls the "Humanists" is fundamental to the intellectual position of eighteenth century defenders of the "Ancients" or Greek and Latin writers:

Some Terms and Their Uses

'Tho properly speaking, Humane Learning includes only the Knowledge of ancient Languages, and what is necessary to know Antiquity; yet it puts us in a condition of knowing things themselves, by furnishing us with the means of Conversing, as it were, with a great many learned Men, both Heathen and Christians. So that it has a strict Connexion with all the Knowledge we can get by the reading of ancient Authors: And the Desire of Knowing what they, who lived before us, believed, said, or did, as much as it can be Known, cannot be satisfied without such a Learning. The Knowledge of Dead Languages is, as it were, an Interpreter, whom we carry along with us, to Travel, if I may say so, in an *Intelligible* World [Le Clerc's italics], which exists only in Books written in Languages, that are not spoken at present. Without such an Interpreter, 'tis impossible to know what past in it . . . we must keep up that Knowledge, and make it common, as it can possibly be; unless we give over the Thoughts of knowing what past in former Times. (pp. 190-91)

Here are the seeds of the configuration of beliefs that has since come to be called "classicism." Starting from the assumption that language is the instrument to knowledge, Le Clerc posits the "intelligible world, which exists only in books"; it is a complete, coherent, fulfilled world of experience which has value for the present because it shows the causes and consequences of actions in lucid terms and because human experience is universally the same. Le Clerc, speaking for the humanists of the seventeenth century, has found the answer to the question that so troubled the thinkers of the Middle Ages: *ubi sunt qui ante nos fuerunt?* They continue to exist in their suspended world of books written in dead languages; and if the man of today wishes to benefit from their wisdom and experience, if he wants to affirm his own "humane" condition, he must master the languages that will give him entry into that world. In time, his knowledge of that world will give him an understanding of "things themselves," that is, ultimate reality or truth.

9

The sense of immediacy and relevance in classical literature is vividly present in Addison's letters from Italy. In his earlier, academic period he was able to write in *A Discourse on Ancient and Modern Learning,* "Now the proper Names of a Latin or Greek Author have the same Effect upon us as those of a Romance, because we meet with 'em no where else but in Books." In "A Letter from Italy," however, he found himself overwhelmed by the living presence of the literature of antiquity—"I seem to tread on Classick Ground"—and he finds the degenerate Italians a reproach to the heroic Romans of the past. It is Addison who is credited with using the adjective "classic" (or "classick") for the first time in reference to the standard authors of Greek and Latin literature, a shortening of the established "classical" that was to become widely used in the eighteenth century.

In 1711 H. Felton produced his *Dissertation on Reading the Classics,* where he used "classics" as a noun referring to Greco-Roman literature; and Sir Richard Steele referred to "pretty Classical Scholars" in *The Spectator* Number 147, "Classical" meaning "versed in the classics (Greek and Latin literature)." This new version of an old word became popular with English men of letters in the years following. In 1726 Swift wrote, "If clergymen to shew their wit/ Praise classicks more than holy writ." In 1737, Pope in the *Epistles,* ii.1.56, gave the noun "classic" a wider meaning: "Who lasts a century can have no flaw;/ I hold that wit a classic, good in law." Also, in 1737, Edward Manwaring published his *Historical and Critical Account of Classic Authors,* with its extensive comments on leading Greek and Latin authors. By 1748 Chesterfield was commenting on the then firmly established enthusiasm for the masterworks of the ancients. He wrote to his son, "Others to shew their learning . . . are always talking of the ancients. . . . They are never without a classic or two in their pocket." Then again in 1748, "Classical knowledge, that is Greek and Latin, is absolutely necessary for everybody; because everybody has agreed to think and call it so. And the word ILLITERATE in its common acceptance, means a man who is ignorant of these two languages."

As in so many other matters, Dr. Samuel Johnson gave the final word on the eighteenth century meanings of "classical" and "classic." In the *Dictionary* he wrote:

> Classical   Adj. from the Latin *classicus*
> Classick
> 1. Relating to antique authors; relating to literature (A citation from Addison)
> 2. Of the first order or rank (citation from Arbuthnot)
> Classick, noun   An author of the first rank: usually taken for ancient authors.

Significantly, Johnson did not include the word, "classicism," in his dictionary. This was a term developed in the nineteenth century as a pejorative way of referring to the then unfashionable literature and literary principles of the eighteenth century.

The mutations of "classic" and "classical" produced in the century following Johnson's simple definitions reveal a great deal about nineteenth century prejudices and their aftereffects. In 1802 Dibdin used "classical" as Steele had done: to refer to persons versed in Greek and Latin literature; and he was imitated by other critics through the first half of the century. But in casting about for suitable ways to describe eighteenth century literature and subsequent reactions to it, the editors of the *Monthly Review*, LXXXIX (1819), 336, spoke of "an affectation of classicality." Unhappily, "classicality" became a term of opprobrious laughter toward those who professed admiration for the writers of the ancient past. Gleefully, anonymous reviewers for the monthlies used the word to heap scorn on their victims. In 1827 the *Foreign Quarterly Review* sneered at "a display of this scrap of classicality he had just acquired." In 1831 *Blackwood's Magazine* hooted at "the land . . . of clouds and classicality." And in 1856 the *Saturday Review* jeered at "small classicalities."

For a time, even the most voluble defenders of the past used

11

variants of "classical" to refer to the intellectual propensities developed in the eighteenth century. Byron, in his *Letter to Goethe* (1820), used "classical" in speaking of a style conforming to the practice of ancient authors. Byron's approval of such conformity was later reenforced by Matthew Arnold, writing in *Cornhill's Magazine* in 1864; but a review of Arnold's position toward ancient literature (in *The Spectator*, August 20, 1864) once again sounded the note of contumely; Arnold's "classical" views were a "self-satisfied equanimity." In 1840, Arnold had tried coining the word, "classicalism," as a synonym for the synthesis of attitudes attendant upon admiration of Greek and Roman literature; but in spite of the efforts of Ruskin, who habitually spoke of "classicalists" and "classicalism," the terms never achieved a firm footing.

The term that did survive—"classicism"—was used as early as 1837 by Carlyle, who contemptuously wrote in his *Essay on the French Revolution*: "Catholicism, Classicism, Sentimentalism, Cannibalism: all isms that make up Man in France. . . ." In 1840 John Stuart Mill set up the theoretical antithesis that has since become a commonplace: "This insurrection against the old traditions of classicism was called romanticism." From that time on, "classicism" was used in its modern sense, a veneration for the literature of the ancient world and an adoption of its precepts, though during the period between 1870 and 1880, the word was employed to mean "a classic idiom." Earle, Saintsbury, and Lowell used it in this meaning.

"Classicist"—one who upholds classic style or form, or one who advocates school study of Greek and Latin classics—came into use about 1839. In that year *Blackwood's Magazine* employed the term in a nonpejorative sense. By 1867 *Macmillan's Magazine* could make this succinct statement in the November issue: "The classicist says . . . that if you would cultivate the mind, you must imbue it with good literature." The influence of Arnold is manifest. Thus by the centenary of Johnson's death, the words "classicist" and "classicism" had come into common use in speaking of the Victorian appraisal of eighteenth century attitudes toward Greek and Latin literature.

In the last quarter of the nineteenth century, academic critical terminology was surprisingly consistent, despite small variations. The Victorian distaste for eighteenth century literature, while somewhat lessened, was still apparent, however. Saintsbury chose to use terms other than "classicism" and "classical," as will be seen later; but his opinion of the literature of the previous century resembled that of the *Spectator* critic who castigated Arnold. According to Saintsbury, the critical outlook of the eighteenth century started with "a not altogether intelligent adoration of the classics" which resulted in a "comfortable, somewhat obtuse" disposition. Leslie Stephen was more objective in his comments on Pope but continued to use the faintly acrid term, "classicalism," in application to that master's cast of mind. Sir Edmund Gosse, in the 1885 survey, *From Shakespeare to Pope*, remarked with unjustified confidence:

> The time seems to have arrived at last, when we may contemplate without passion that precise, mundane, and rhetorical order of poetry which is mainly identified in our minds with the names and practice of Dryden, of Pope, and of Johnson. The school of writers who cultivated this order . . . have commonly been described as the classical, because their early leaders claimed to emulate and restore the grace and precision of the poets of antiquity, to write in English as Horace and Ovid were then supposed to have written in Latin,—that is to say, with a polished and eclectic elegance.

It is worth noting that Gosse is narrowing the sense of "classicism" to the literary in general and the stylistic and prosodic in particular. His emphasis on Horace, Ovid, and their imitators in the eighteenth century anticipates the later critical concentration on style as the essence of English classicism, though in fact literary style was but one aspect of that classical purview. In *The Augustan Ages* (1899), Oliver Elton presented what was probably the most favorable exegesis of eighteenth

13

century literature made after the start of the nineteenth century. Of classicism, he wrote, "[It] is and always must be a beacon . . . because, as its name implies, it drew inspiration, powerful if limited, from the ancient writings."

As Elton and others used the term, "classicism" had come to mean something more than the literary phenomenon of the eighteenth century. Classicism to him was the state of mind, the frame of knowledge produced in anyone in any age by an education in Greek and Latin literature. In speaking of the literature of the period between 1660 and 1740, Elton used another term, "Augustan," to indicate the eighteenth century version of classicism. After all, by 1900, ancient literature had been rediscovered and reinterpreted by such varied intellects as those of Shelley, Keats, Byron, Landor, Arnold, Tennyson, Ruskin, Pater, Swinburne, and Gilbert Murray. The peculiar cast of classicism in the poetry of the so-called "Romantics" was not that of Dryden or Pope or Johnson. And Victorian classicism was something else again. What had been minted as a term characterizing a specific period of literary thought needed expansion to cover other periods; thus "classicism" became generic by 1900 and the problem arose of how to differentiate its manifestations.

For the first two decades of the twentieth century, critics in both England and America toyed with the phrase "pseudo-classic" in dealing with literature between 1660 and 1800. This term was so derogatory in connotation, however, that its critical use by admirers of eighteenth century literature was virtually impossible. It still savored of Victorian contempt for the "false" standards of Pope and Johnson as it dismissed for hypocrisy and self-deception anything they had appreciated for its classical qualities. J.A.K. Thomson has since scored the unfairness involved in calling such writers as Dryden, Swift, and Johnson "pseudo-classical." These men after all believed they *were* classical; they were not pretending at being classical, in their own minds. Since every age identifies itself with the characteristics it envisions in the classical world, and each age thinks it alone has identified the essence of classicism, no one age is more to be censured than another. If Pope's Homer was "a pretty poem" but not Homer, then *Sejanus* was not Seneca, *Samson Agonistes* was not Sophocles, *Prometheus Unbound* was not Aeschylus, and Richmond Lattimore's Homer is not Homer either. Restoration and Eighteenth Century literature is no more "pseudo" classical than nineteenth or twentieth century literature.

Yet, some term *was* and *is* necessary to distinguish the characteristic form of classicism prevalent in the age commencing with Dryden and ending with Johnson's circle. So in academic parlance in the 1920s in America, these men came to be termed the "neoclassicists," or the "new classicists" of the seventeenth and eighteenth centuries, as distinguished from the "Humanists" of the sixteenth and seventeenth centuries and the "Hellenists" of the nineteenth, as well as from the "classicists" of all periods. The vagueness attached to all of these terms was at least partially dispatched by studies published in American journals during the twenties.

Typical of the studies of the day was Paul S. Wood's "Native Elements in English Neo-Classicism," published in 1926 in *Modern Philology*, xxiv, 201. Wood wrote:

As a result of Renaissance extravagance and the undisciplined individualism of the first part of the seventeenth century, English literature needed restriction, reform; it needed purging of excess and return to the normal, the healthy, the sane. It needed order, decorum, measure, respect for the general sense, precisely as England everywhere needed these same qualities. In the effort to obtain them, it appealed to authority and tradition on the one hand and to reason and expediency on the other, precisely as the same appeals were made elsewhere. The resultant movement in literature we call "neo-Classicism" [sic]; but in constitutional, ecclesiastical, or social history we call it "good sense," "conservatism," "moderation," the "British national temper," or the "spirit of the age."

The relation of these ideals to Jonsonian classicism is evi-

dent. They represent the old principles developed logically
and affected by the events of the intervening years. Their
chief addition is in the increased respect paid the general
sense and in the corresponding discredit of Renaissance individualism, in so far as the latter tended toward singularity. Jonson's respect for authority, for reason, and for measure had been extending their influence over the land. And
when there was added to these the one classical quality in
which Jonson had been deficient, the way was made ready
for the literature of the new age.

In another, companion piece, Wood gives further characteristics of "neo-classicism" [sic]: its "classical ideals were social
and therefore predominantly urban"; it was "the arbitrament
of the general sense," using "as its standards the language
and manners of the court." Wood cites the erroneous opinions
of the German critic, P. Hamelius, whose work is "a striking
example of literary criticism" that assumes the "romantic" to be
good and "whatever is called classic or 'pseudo-classic' must
be bad."

As a supplement to these pronouncements stands George
Sherburn's discussion of "The Restoration and Eighteenth
Century" in *A Literary History of England*. There, he equated
"neo-classicism" with "Neo-Augustanism"; that is, the identification of the Restoration writers with writers of the Augustan
Age of Rome and the restoration of Charles II with the accession of Octavius to the Roman throne after the civil wars. Sherburn used the term as a description of a literary state of mind,
asserting that it was based on "a veneration for the Roman
classics, thought, and way of life" which produced a literature
with nobility of tone, dignity, and stateliness. It was these
qualities that "we [the academicians] had in mind in calling
the age "neo-classical."

Sherburn's terse, encyclopedic account of the origin of the
term, "Augustan," and his efforts to identify it entirely with
the state of mind termed "neo-classical" is the nearest thing
to a fusion of those two phrases yet effected. But the fusion was

16

not complete. As a specifically literary designation, "Augustan" has an even longer existence than "classical" in reference to the period between 1660 and 1800. It is still commonly used in British criticism, where the American neologism of "Neo-Classical" (or "neo-classical") has not been countenanced. "Augustan" has had as many obfuscations and misuses as "classical"; but the two terms are not equatable, as an examination of the development of the term, "Augustan," shows.

"Augustan" is, of course, the English adjective form of the Latin, *augustus*, "majestic," "venerable," "worthy of honor." The English adjective, "august," is the direct denotative version of the Latin *augustus*; but connotatively, "Augustan" has historical associations that "august" has not. Octavius Caesar, later titled "Augustus," the nephew of Julius Caesar, emerged from the power struggles of the Second Triumvirate as undisputed master of Roman politics and culture in 27 B.C. For the next forty years, Rome attained an unprecedented political and literary magnificence. Not even the austere virtues of the vanished Roman Republic could compete in the eyes of later historians with the diplomacy of peace, the scintillating letters, and the patronage of literature by politics in the Augustan Age. The Emperor and his close friend, Maecenas, cultivated men of genius partly from a genuine admiration for their work and partly to secure their pens in the Augustan cause. For whatever reason, the age produced a spectacular array of literary talent: Virgil, Horace, Ovid, Propertius, Tibullus, Livy, Diodorus Siculus, Dionysius of Halicarnassus, Trogus Pompeius, Hyginus, and many others.

Though such Augustan writers as Livy persisted in pointing out the defects of the age, it was the panegyrics of Virgil, that master publicist, which cast the image for future times. E. K. Rand has traced the development of the Augustan myth to some extent in his study, *The Building of Eternal Rome,* and one can find evidence everywhere in Latin literature of that myth. Post-Augustan historians were an especially interesting and important agency for perpetuating the Augustan ideal. Though Livy declined to engage in fulsome praise of

Augustus, his disciple Florus eagerly lauded everything about the Emperor and his reign. Augustus "by his wisdom and skill restored order in the body of the empire," which desperately needed the "coherence and harmony" resulting from "the will of a single ruler" (*Histories*, II.13.3). Florus carefully washed out the blots on Augustus' pure white, homespun toga by acquitting him of all crimes committed by the Triumvirate, including the death of Cicero, and left him so spotless a ruler as to become a model for all time. Historians living under later emperors sought to encourage them into virtue (or literary patronage) by citing the exemplary Augustus. Thus Appian in his *Civil Wars* (I.2) exhorted Trajan; Dio Cassius cajoled Commodus (*Fragments*, XLVII) ; and Eutropius encouraged Valens (*Roman History*, VII.8-9).

With the rediscovery of Latin literature by Renaissance scholars, the Augustan myth was resuscitated. First the poets, Virgil and Horace, became sources of authority for the literary glories of Augustan literature. Ben Jonson, among others, cited the linguistic and literary beauties of the Augustan Age in his *Discoveries*. Then Latin historians gained greater circulation, and such writers as Florus were used as school texts for aspiring young classicists. Striking as the effects of classical history were on Elizabethan dramatists, they continued to grow as Roman history gained wider usage. The intellectual lacuna in literature caused by the Civil Wars and Interregnum in England was actually a germinal period during which young scholars like Cowley and Dryden were absorbing precepts and historical analogies from Livy, Diodorus, Dionysius, and Florus. Still later, during the Restoration era, youths like Addison, Swift, Congreve, and Richard Bentley were feeding on the historians of Rome, making excerpted lists and gaining, as they believed, a knowledge of an "Intelligible World."

Under such circumstances, and given the facts of English history, it was unavoidable that analogies be drawn between the course of Roman history and that of England. Despite time gaps and variant conditions, the age of Elizabeth I was akin to the Roman Republic after the Third Punic War:

Carthage (Spain) was defeated and national power and wealth reached a new height with expanding commerce. The Cromwellian Wars were the internecine struggles between Marius and Sulla or Caesar and Pompey. Quite obviously, to the English classicist, an Augustus had to emerge to settle the world and throw open permanently the gates to the temple of peace.

Somewhat prematurely, Edmund Waller bestowed the laurels on Cromwell. About 1654, Waller wrote in "A Panegyric to my Lord Protector":

> As the vexed world, to find repose, at last
> Itself into Augustus' arms did cast;
> So England now does with like toil oppressed,
> Her weary head upon your bosom rest.

When, distressingly, Cromwell turned out to be more a Marius than an Augustus, the analogy was once more open for exploitation. John Dryden availed himself of the chance when Charles II assumed his rightful place on the English throne. The "Astraea Redux," published in 1660, carefully established the analogy between the return of Justice to the world following the restoration of the golden age of mythology and the return of justice to England; then for good measure, Dryden compared Charles to Jove, David, Adam, and other heroes, concluding with Augustus:

> Oh Happy Age! Oh times like those alone,
> By Fate reserv'd for great Augustus throne!
> When the joint growth of Arms and Arts forshew,
> The World a Monarch, and that *Monarch* You!

Dryden's obvious plea to Charles to prove himself an Augustus in literary patronage as well as military and political matters is a *ficelle* of long standing. In Dryden's case, it worked most successfully—so well, indeed, that when Charles died, Dryden refurbished the Augustan analogy in the "Threnodia Augustalis."

The first known use of the word "Augustan" (or "Augustean") came in 1690 in the Preface to *The Second Part of Mr.*

Waller's Poems. There, an anonymous writer, commonly identified to be Francis Atterbury, wrote of the English language: "... I question whether in *Charles* the Second's Reign, English did not come to its full perfection; and whether it has not had its *Augustean Age,* as well as the Latin." Atterbury's association of "Augustan" with the literary qualities of Latin was an important one, for it established one clear element of what has come to be called Augustanism or the Augustan Age of English literature. The concern of writers with the English language especially in the period from 1660 to 1715 was reflected in their estimates of Latin style in the time of Augustus. Dryden, in the Preface to his translation of Ovid, Thomas Rymer, John Dennis, William Wotton, and many others, admired the archetypal Latin of Augustus' time. Temple, it is true, thought the style of Augustan Latin already corrupted by the interfusion of foreign languages after the conquests, but he was in a minority. Wotton's appraisal, in the 1694 edition of *Reflections upon Ancient and Modern Learning,* demonstrates the daring of Atterbury in going counter to popular opinion. Wotton found English "terse" and "harsh" in comparison with the "regal, majestic gravity" of Latin. Atterbury's use of "Augustan" to describe the state of English was certainly innovational; but it ought to be pointed out that this linguistic analogy was only one of several. The political analogy was already important; in time, the historical and social were to become paramount.

The hope of literary men for a royal patron led to the continued use of the Augustan analogy after Charles' death in 1685. James' reign was too turbulent to permit even the most tendentious poet to compare him with Augustus; but in 1693, Thomas Rymer was willing to imply an analogy if not state it overtly. To the Earl of Dorset, he wrote in the Preface to *A Short View of Tragedy:*

> Contemplation and Action have their different Seasons. It
> was after the defeat of *Anthony,* and the business of the
> World pretty well over, when *Virgil* and *Horace* came to be

so distinguished at Court. . . . . When once again the business of the World is over, Now my Lord, that the *Muses* Commonweal is become your Province, what may we not expect? This I say, not with intent to apply that of *Quintilian* on *Augustus Caesar, Parum Diis visum est esse eum Maximus Poetarum*: that were a Common Topick. . . .

Then he went on to comment on the English language, which fermented in the time of Elizabeth but "did not shine and sparkle until Mr. Waller set it a running." Indeed, Waller's poetry was among the very best "upwards to *Horace* and *Virgil*." Rymer also spoke of Horace's praise of Augustus and referred to "Roman Mettle" and the fact that "their Stomach [was] not so very fierce, in Augustus' time." Evidently, Rymer longed to think a new Augustan Age had come, but hesitated to term a Prince of Orange the new "Augustus."

Addison was less hesitant. In a Latin composition of 1697, *Pax Gulielmi Auspiciis Europae Reditta*, he addressed William III as "Caesar" and his careful use of the historical role of Augustus as military man and patron of the arts makes clear that William is to consider himself a Caesar Augustus, even though the word "Augustus" is not used. Addison says, ". . . aspice, Caesare, Quae tibi soliciti, turba importuna, Poetae / Munera deducunt. . . ." Apparently, William was less susceptible to classical flattery than Charles II, since Addison had to wait for George I to honor his literary talent with a political office.

Swift, also a disappointed candidate for the patronage of William III, was reluctant to admit that the restoration of the Stuarts had issued in a new Augustan Age. He wrote in his *Thoughts on Various Subjects*:

> The Epicureans began to spread at Rome in the empire of Augustus, as the Socinians, and even the Epicureans too, did in England toward the end of King Charles the Second's reign; which is reckoned, though very absurdly, our Augustan Age.

Formation of English Neo-Classical Thought

Though the precise date of this Thought is not known, it probably was set down sometime between 1690 and 1715. A date somewhere within the decade of Anne's reign is likely, since the term "Augustan Age" seems thoroughly settled on, and its associations are clearly social and political rather than literary, within the context of Swift's remark.

In 1704 Nicholas Rowe continued the tradition of Dryden, Rymer, and Addison in hoping for an age of Augustan literary patronage. To Lord Godolphin, he wrote in the Preface to *Ulysses*:

> "[Poetry] has miserably languish'd and been despis'd, for want of that Favor and Protection which is found in the famous Augustin [sic] Age. Since then, it may be asserted, without any Partiality to the present Time, it never had a fairer Prospect of lifting up its Head, and returning to its former Reputation, than now; And the best Reason can be given for it, is, that it seems to have a particular Hope from, and Dependance [sic] upon Your Lordship. . . ."

After him, a number of works published in the era of Queen Anne leaned heavily on analogies with the Augustan Age of Rome. In 1706 Matthew Prior's "An Ode, Humbly Inscrib'd to the Queen," suggested political and literary parallels between the ages of Augustus and Anne. In 1708 Thomas Hearne published an edition of Livy with a dedication to James, Count Salisbury, that praised the Romans as a people, *augustissimi*, to be read of, admired, and emulated as patterns of conduct. In 1711 Richard Bentley, the great classical scholar of the age, dedicated his new edition of Horace to the Tory minister, Robert Harley, the Earl of Oxford, identifying himself as a former Whig but reminding Harley that Maecenas did not like Horace any the less for having sided with Brutus at Philippi. Again in 1714, Hearne dwelled lovingly on the reign of Augustus as a golden literary period, famous for its numerous writers.

Apparently the first specific reference to an "Augustan Age" of English literature as a whole was that in John Oldmixon's

Some Terms and Their Uses

Reflections on Dr. Swift's Letter in 1712. In it, he stated that Charles II's reign marked "the Augustan Age of English Poetry," a view which Swift disagreed with, as we know. But if Oldmixon found in the rule of Charles the British equivalent of an age in which political might and literary preeminence met, other writers failed to concur. In 1715, when George I became king, an anonymous Whig pamphlet hailed him as an heroic Augustus come to save the nation from the infamous intrigues of the banished Tories. And the banished Tories retaliated by declaring, as John Gay did in 1720, that George I was no Augustus from the literary standpoint: Gay wrote, in his *Fourth Epistle, to the Right Honourable Paul Methuen, Esq.*:

> Why flourished verse in great Augustus' reign?
> He and Maecenas lov'd the Muse's strain.
> But now that wight in poverty must mourn
> Who was (O cruel stars!) a Poet born.

In 1721 a major development in the history of "Augustan" as a literary description came. In the Preface to an edition of Addison's poems, Thomas Tickell discussed Addison's career as a Latinist and correlated Latin and English poetry according to the "Augustan" standards of "good breeding," "gracefulness," "correctness," "propriety of thought," and "chastity of style." Of Addison he wrote:

> He employed his first years in the study of the old *Greek* and *Roman* writers; whose language and manner he caught at that time of life, as strongly as other young people gain a *French* accent. An early acquaintance with the Classics is what may be called the good-breeding of Poetry, as it gives a certain gracefulness which never forsakes a mind, that contracted it in youth. . . . He first distinguished himself by his *Latin* compositions . . . and was admired as one of the best authors since the Augustan age. . . .

And he cited Boileau's praise of Addison both for his classicism and his country "that possessed the *Roman* genius in so eminent a degree."

23

Just as "Augustan" seemed to be settled as an honorific literary designation, suggesting grace, high style, urbanity of tone, meticulousness of form, and morality of theme, when applied to Addison and his circle, events changed it into a derogatory political term. In 1726 George II ascended the throne, thereby confirming the Whig supremacy over the Tories for several more decades at the least. Those Tories had not been silent between 1714 and 1726, however. They had been carefully identifying George I with Julius Caesar in his suppression of individual freedoms. Gay, for instance, had described a "Happy Augusta" (England) where "tyranny ne'er lifts her purple hand," and Swift, in the *Drapier Letters* of 1724, had unflatteringly spoken of George I as a tyrannic Caesar. Tory attacks were so frequent and numerous that as early as 1722, John Dennis, a whole-hearted Whig, had composed an essay absolving Caesar of the charge of suppressing Roman liberty in answer to a piece in the *London Journal* that compared the first Hanover and the first Caesar. George II, christened George Augustus, irresistibly tempted the Tories to take the Whig title of "Augustus" and subvert it to their own malicious ends.

Eagerly, the Tories scanned Roman history for evidence of the sins of the Roman Augustus in order to lay them at the door of the British one. In *Gulliver's Travels* (1726), Swift had Gulliver meet a Roman seaman who told of venery and corruption at the court of Augustus, thereby causing Gulliver to draw parallels between Rome and England. In 1727 Pope wrote to Swift: "Horace might keep his Coach in Augustus' time, if he pleased, but I won't in the time of our Augustus" (October 22, 1727). Pope's attacks on George II and his ironic "Epistle to Augustus" caused the Whigs to react in bristling anger. M. Concanen (?) wrote:

> The Name of Augustus has been generally used with more Decency and Respect by our Poets, and they have a better reason for doing so now than ever. If any Prophecy can be shewn, or any Allusion to the Classicks proved to justify

24

the Use of this Word in this Place, I will allow it may have no Malignance in it. . . .

The Tories merely redoubled their attack after drawing blood. Dr. Arbuthnot made ironic comparison between Rome and England in *Mr. John Ginglicutt's Treatise* (1731), and the *Critical Remarks on Gulliver's Travels* (1730), attributed to Arbuthnot, ruined any possible favorable analogies between George II and Augustus:

> From the Time of *Augustus Caesar, Rome* was evidently in a declining Condition. The Number of her *Patriots* was very small, and the Wisdom of her Senate extreamly decreased. Her *Consuls* were more remarkable for Intemperance, Oppression, and Avarice, than for military Virtue abroad, or an exact Distribution of Justice at home.

Of course, there continued to be trite references to the Augustan Age of literature, and a few hopeful writers identified it with the present age. William Stukeley declared in the Preface to his *Paleographia Sacra* (1736), a fatuous performance that made Horace's Ode XIX a hymn to Jehovah:

> We might well think this the Augustan age reviv'd; among other reasons, because our poet Horace is in every hand. He is thought unpolite and out of fashion that has not a taste for his beauties.

Any hopes of revitalizing the literary associations of "Augustan" and applying them to the period from 1720 to 1750 were effectively crushed under the massively ironic uses of the word to describe the political affairs of the era. In 1738 Bolingbroke's *The Craftsman* (August 26) piously deplored the example of the Roman Augustus in permitting gambling; it had led to moral decline. And elsewhere in his periodical, Bolingbroke lost no chance of ranging up a list of Augustan sins. In 1740 George Turnbull published a translation of the Abbe de Vertot's *Characters of Augustus, Horace, and Agrippa,* in which he made the following notation:

However fashionable it is now to speak of the Age of *Alexander* the Great, and the *Augustan* Age, that was not the ancient style. Philosophy and the Arts are said by the Ancients to have been at their Height in *Greece, circa Socratis tempora*; and in Rome, *circa tempora Ciceronis*.

By midcentury, the comparison between England and Rome, Augustus and George Augustus, was so thoroughly unfavorable as to deny further use of "Augustan" as a political accolade. In 1747 Dr. Conyers Middleton published his *Treatise on the Roman Senate*, with a dedication to Lord Hervey, who had anxiously been consulting Roman history to see how the suppression of freedom came about. According to Middleton, Augustus had been the agent of complete extinction of liberty in the Empire. The implied comparison was obvious. Later, Hervey himself wrote:

> Not that there was any similitude between the two princes who presided in the Roman and English Augustan ages besides their names, for George Augustus neither loved learning nor encouraged men of letters, nor were there any Maecenases about him.

In 1754 Henry Fielding, in *An Epistle to The Right Honourable George Dodington, Esq.*, published in his *Miscellanies,* sounded once again the note struck by Gay twenty-five years earlier:

> To you! who in this *Gothick* Leaden Age,
> When Wit is banish'd from the Press and Stage,
> When Fools to greater Folly make Pretence,
> And those who have it, seem asham'd of sense . . .
> You for their Sakes with Fashion dare engage,
> Maecenas you in no *Augustan Age.*

Probably the single writer most responsible for the popularity of "Augustan" as a phrase describing the literature of eighteenth century England was Oliver Goldsmith. A popular writer, widely read and admired for his learning, Goldsmith followed Tickell in making the decades between 1700 and 1740 the English "Augustan Age," which he compared with the Roman Augustan Age and the "Augustan" period of France under Louis XIV. In *The Bee*, Goldsmith set forth the analogy that he fully developed in *An Enquiry into the Present State of Polite Learning in Europe* (1759). Goldsmith's exaltation of the age of Addison, Swift, and Pope into a literary period of Augustan dimensions may have been partly due to his anxiety about the condition of literature in his own day; he feared that the non-Maecenean example of "a certain minister" (Walpole) had led England into a permanent state of literary decline. In any case, Goldsmith made "Augustan" a term with social and political connotations, as well as linguistic and literary ones, when he applied the epithet to the first three or four decades of the century. It is interesting that Dr. Johnson failed to include "Augustan" in his *Dictionary*, though he did give "august" and its Latin derivation.

In the fifty years after Goldsmith's formalization of "Augustan" in the sense originally imparted to it by Tickell, the term appears to have sunk into desuetude. Since it was conceived as a term honorific in both a political and literary sense, and because it lost most of its favorable political connotations during the age that acknowledged its own Augustanism, only the honorific literary connotations were bequeathed to a critical posterity. That posterity, intent on repudiating the "classicality" of its fathers, disdained the use of a phrase held in such esteem by those parent writers. It was not until the last half of the nineteenth century that critics revived the term and then with emendations that somewhat distorted its original meaning. The *Oxford English Dictionary* gives only two citations of uses of "Augustan": one that of Rowe in 1704 and the other of a writer in *The Athenaeum*, No. 2874 (November 25, 1882). *The Athenaeum* reviewer spoke of the writers of the Queen Anne period as the "later" Augustans, a designation that might have had some usefulness if the critic had made clear who the earlier Augustans were and why all of them were "Augustan." In 1889 Oliver Elton's

The Augustan Ages scrupulously maintained the definition of "Augustan" given by Goldsmith and applied it to the period of Louis XV in France and Queen Anne in England. George Saintsbury, in *The Peace of the Augustans,* enlarged the term to include Dryden and all writers through Johnson in the eighteenth century.

In the present century, English critics almost unanimously have used "Augustan" rather than "Neo-Classical" as the epithet for English literature of the Restoration and eighteenth century. In doing so, they have copied the nineteenth century critics who enlarged and consequently blurred the meaning of the term. Today most English commentators use "Augustan" as a synonym for "classical" and "Augustanism" for "classicism." A. R. Humphrey's *The Augustan World* includes everything from 1660 to 1800, and Geoffrey Tillotson similarly includes commentaries on Dryden and Johnson in his *Augustan Studies.* Ian Jack narrows the "Augustan Age" down somewhat in his *Augustan Satire, 1660-1750.* But only John Butt has questioned the Victorian inclusive use of "Augustan" in any detail. He has written in various places: "In 1697, before the Augustans had really begun to be Augustan . . ."; "The Augustan Age used to be called the Age of Prose but really excludes 'the Age of Johnson' "; at last he sets 1760 as the terminal date for the English Augustan Age. Butt, therefore, limits the Augustan period to the dates 1697-1760, though no other critics consistently subscribe to so brief a span of time.

Confronted with the mutations outlined above, the student of Restoration and eighteenth century English literature may well wonder how many contemporary critical usages obtain. The basic significations of such terms as "classic," "classical," and "Augustan" are approximately the same in eighteenth and twentieth century usage, but the associations differ. It would seem that the English classicists of the period after 1660 and modern literary critics allude to somewhat different intellectual posits when they employ identical terms.

There is legitimate question whether the men of an age are better qualified than those of a later time to see themselves within the fullest context. In the case of the English classicists, however, their context was the "intelligible world" contained in Greek and Latin literature; and the connotations attached to their terminology were meaningful largely within that context. Unfortunately, the modern man is too often ignorant of classical contexts and he judges his classicist-predecessors too frequently by impertinent frames of reference. If the shoe is put on the other foot and modern critical usage judged by the classicists' standards, twentieth century understanding appears rather narrow, inexact, over-simplified, and vague.

Between 1660 and 1800, a "classicist" was the man who saw within preserved Greco-Roman literature a total and applicable world. He was concerned with *all* of that literature as manifestation of a total world, geography as well as epic, history and philosophy as well as satire. His fundamental introit was through the study of syntax and etymology, but once inside classical literature, the scholar's frame of mind was not simply "literary" but utilitarian. In time, a "classic" came to mean a masterwork of any period, though usually an ancient one, which exerted a cultural influence or which contained permanent, archetypal qualities. The "realities" of the contemporary world—whether social, political, military, literary, or moral—became more attainable through reading the "classics."

It was this preoccupation with the "truth" or "reality" of their own world that led English classicists to scan ancient literature for analogues or significant precedents. The "Augustan" emphasis was the result. The analogy between England and Rome—politically, historically, linguistically, literarily—was never without its detractors, but it was popularized by the pamphleteers of Charles II's reign and accretions of attitudes preserved it through the eighteenth century. Augustanism was but one aspect of Restoration and eighteenth century classicism, however, despite the dogmatic generalizations of the Victorians. It should be viewed as a voluble but limited stress on the similarity between politics in Rome between 60 B.C. and A.D. 40 and England from 1660 to 1750 and a deliberate cultivation of resemblances between English and Roman public poetry of those eras.

The term which has come to vie with "Augustanism" as the inclusive critical epithet, "Neo-Classicism," is a latter-day coinage, but it may well prove the more useful, once it loses its ersatz connotations. Nowadays, "classicism" can be conveniently defined as the intellectual disposition to find in ancient culture, particularly Greek and Roman, the values which recurrently appear in human experience. "Neo-Classicism" may be concomitantly designated that variation of classicism characteristic of English thought and literature between 1660 and 1800. It is temporally and ideologically differentiated from the earlier "Humanism" and the later "Romantic classicism" (often identified with Romantic Hellenism). Its characteristics have been enunciated in a number of scholarly studies.[5] It is the concern of the chapters following to supplement previous commentaries by examining some elements of Neo-Classical thought not emphasized elsewhere.

It may seem at times to the reader that tracing a theme through several centuries or inspecting in detail background materials and obscure prefaces is a devious way to confront the reasonably apparent symmetry of Neo-Classical literature. But the traveller to ancient Athens or Rome, excited by his first prospect of the Acropolis or the Capitoline, found that he had to wind his way through a multitude of sidestreets and alleyways to reach his goal. By the time he stood on the point where he could survey the cityscape about him, he had already learned it at close range. Similarly, if we wish to know well the intellectual geography of the Neo-Classical *polis*, we must explore some literary sidestreets. When we come finally to the *agora* of English classical thought and view one of its monuments, hopefully our excursion will have made our outlook both wider and more acute.

2 · The Role
of Historiography

No aspect of classical thought in England from the end of
the Cromwell era to the reign of George III has been so
ignored as its historiographical basis. It is difficult to read even
the slightest part of the works by a major writer of the time
and not encounter references to historians from Herodotus to
Clarendon. Yet critics have customarily dismissed the omni-
present references as trite usage, empty homage to an ideal,
or an affected display of knowledge. Those who have taken
the phenomenon seriously, like Paul Hazard and several
others, have contented themselves with remarking that the
study of ancient history was an important part of the public
school curriculum of the day, that classical scholars looked to
the past for answers to current problems, or that Roman people and events were more real than his own contemporaries
to the classicist.

The unwillingness of critics to deal with the role historiography had in seventeenth and eighteenth century classicism
can be attributed to several causes. In the last two hundred
years, theories of historiography have taken the work of Gibbon as a starting point. Consequently, the significance of pre-
Gibbon historiography has been diminished to such an extent
that its part in the thought of Swift or Johnson may appear
unimportant. If the classicists of the eighteenth century knew
only "inferior" historical writing, can that writing be a useful
means to studying their thought? The answer is yes, but the
implications of modern historical theory are the opposite.
Furthermore, students of the classics did express their views
of history in very much the same phrases, taken from classical
history, so it is all too easy to make them out truisms or

clichés. Additionally, to study the influence of historiography on a literary tradition is to cut across academic disciplines. Literary critics often hesitate to do this, and with good cause. Many of the histories read by English classicists were in Greek and Latin and have not yet been translated into other languages. There are, in short, valid reasons for commentators to avoid the study of historiographical antecedents of classicism. But this neglect flies in the face of an obvious preoccupation by Neo-Classical men of letters with the theory and practice of history.

Although they were divided on nearly every other question, writers from Hobbes to Burke agreed on one thing: the educated man must have an intimate knowledge of history. One of their authorities for this belief was Jean Bodin, whose *Method for the Easy Comprehension of History* was written in 1566. There were other influential texts at later periods—Gerard Johann Voss's *The Historic Art* in 1623, for instance—but Bodin's comprehensive survey of historical writing and historiographical theory remained a popular and important work. In it Bodin said history was "the master of life" and "the whole life of man ought to be shaped according to the sacred laws of history." Philosophy was meaningless "unless all sayings, deeds, and plans are considered in relation to the account of days long past. From these not only are present-day affairs readily interpreted but also future events are inferred, and we may acquire reliable maxims for what we should seek and avoid."[1]

After the Restoration, when editions of classical historians were being printed in huge lots by the presses of Holland and Switzerland and men like Burnet, Clarendon, Sprat, Evelyn, and Laurence Eachard were adding to the volume of historical writing, the enthusiasm for history grew greater. It was indeed unanimous. Thomas Hobbes, iconoclastic in other matters, wrote in the *Leviathan* that prudence results from knowledge of past actions, that the wisest man is he who knows the greatest number of past actions from reading history, and that such knowledge helps one to anticipate the future. Sir William

The Role of Historiography

Temple declared that an acquaintance with history permits the wise man to apply to himself and his own times the lessons learned in the past. John Locke, in his essay on education, said the perusal of history was absolutely necessary for the well educated man since an insight into public affairs could best be learned only through experience or the records of the past. Addison praised history for conferring immortality on the worthiest and best men, who could thus be used as patterns of conduct; history, moreover, permits future generations to benefit from the wisdom of the present. Henry St. John, Viscount Bolingbroke, in his extensive *Letters on the Study and Use of History*, emphasized the peculiar advantages of history: its examples are complete and comprehensive, thereby presenting all aspects and conclusions of any given situation or set of conditions. "Mere sons of earth, if they have experience without any knowledge of the history of the world, are but half scholars in the science of mankind." Bolingbroke also made a point cited by other apologists for historiography:

> I think that history is philosophy teaching by examples. . . . Such is the imperfection of human understanding, such is the frail temper of our minds, that abstract or general propositions, though ever so true, appear obscure or doubtful to us very often, till they are explained by examples.[2]

History thus is the concrete embodiment of general truths applicable to all mankind. In Bolingbroke, as in other classicist defenders of history, the doctrine of "Uniformitarianism" (men are the same in all times and places) is fundamental.

Jonathan Swift, among his many other commendations of history, held that it provided a thorough understanding of human affairs. Lord Chesterfield assured his son that the truly wise politician and thinker must have a complete knowledge of history in order to comprehend the issues involved in present events. Dr. Johnson told Boswell that historical events were comparable to daily affairs in that each illuminated the other and that both were readily ascertainable and provable by reason. And he had Imlac say, in *Rasselas*, "If we act only for ourselves, to neglect the study of history is not prudent; if we are entrusted with the care of others, it is not just." In like aphoristic form, Edmund Burke wrote: "In history a great volume is unrolled for our instruction, drawing the materials of future wisdom from the past errors and infirmities of mankind." Even the ladies lauded the salutary effects of studying history. Lady Mary Wortley Montagu, surfeited with French romances, slipped off to her father's library to read Greek and Latin historians for five or six hours a day, by her admission. And Hannah More, in her *Hints towards Forming the Character of a Young Princess*, said:

> [Historians who] unfold the internal principles of action, and dissect the hearts and minds of their personages, who develop complicated circumstances, furnish a clue to trace the labyrinth of causes and effects, and assign to every incident its proper motive will be eminently useful.[3]

Reasons for reading history were systematically collected and expanded in at least half a dozen treatises during the first half of the eighteenth century. Each decade saw the publication of a lengthy tract, commenting on the nature of history, its practice, and its uses. As a body of opinion, these tracts indicate a whole-hearted interest in history as well as a sincere desire to define and limit its characteristics meaningfully and precisely. Their enthusiasm for the benefits of reading history, to man and nation, was vast. From Jean Le Clerc's *Of History and the Difference between the Modern and Ancient Historians* to Peter Whalley's *Essay on the Manner of Writing History*, admirers of historical literature were developing the rationale of its place in classicism.

In 1700 Le Clerc set up the prerequisites of a good historian, stipulating objectivity, accuracy, and polylingualism; and he noted that most historical writing was worthless, since no "ordinary Man" is capable of writing history. Unless the "Springs and Motives" of actions are given, "History will resemble a Body without a Soul." The historian must go back to the most remote sources to learn the causes of action. According to Le Clerc, Greek and Roman historians were more objective than contemporary ones; the "moderns" were too involved in current events and too bent on self-aggrandizement to qualify as respectable, trustworthy, useful writers.[4]

In 1714 Thomas Hearne, a respected antiquarian and historian, published his *Ductor Historicus: Or, A Short System of Universal History, And An Introduction to the Study of it*. In it, he gave a concise description of history:

> History is a Narration of the more Remarkable Actions and Events in general Order, illustrated with the Reasons of Actions, the Characters of Great Men; and occasionally, with the Descriptions of Places, Customs, Governments, Armies, Order of Battle, Encampments, Methods of Fortifying and Attacking, &c together sometimes with the Writer's Judgment upon Actions and Persons.

Then Hearne listed his own requirements for the historian and noted that all modern history was somewhat suspect, especially when it confuted Scripture or ancient historians. The great advantages of history were that: it makes us coeval with the celebrated heroes of the past and exhorts us to emulation of them; stirs up our natural affections for our families, ancestors, and nations; provides agreeable diversion and delightful pastime; instructs professional men in their several sciences; provides examples for every type of virtue; incites us to hate and condemn vice of all sorts; makes a proper study for gentlemen; and shows us how God manifests himself in human affairs.[5]

In 1728 Richard Rawlinson produced *A New Method of Studying History* in two volumes. In it he stated his variations of the basic themes; history improves thinking and provides models of conduct, both positive and negative. Himself a man of vast reading, if not erudition—his personal library contained 10,000 volumes including a vast assortment of classical historians, more Latin than Greek—he emphasized the quasi-historical writings of the chronologers and the use of history as a scheme of universal knowledge.

Formation of English Neo-Classical Thought

In 1734 an English translation appeared of Charles Rollin's *Method of Teaching and Studying the Belles Lettres,* a pedagogical work composed to help frustrated schoolmasters impart the beauties of Greek and Latin to their young scholars. Rollin peremptorily dismissed the idea of teaching French history in the schools—there was barely enough time to deal thoroughly with Greek and Roman history. Classical history, however, was the chief branch of learning:

> It is not without reason that History has been ever look'd upon as the light of ages, the depository of events, the faithful witness of truth, the source of prudence and good counsel, and the rule of conduct and manners. Confined without it to the bounds of the age and country wherein we live, and shut up in the narrow circle of such branches of knowledge as are peculiar to us, and with the limits of our own private reflexions, we remain ever in a kind of infancy, which leaves us strangers to the rest of the world, and profoundly ignorant of all that has gone before us, or even now surrounds us.

Furthermore,

> History may properly be called the common school of mankind, equally open to both great and small, to princes and subjects, and still more necessary to princes and great men than to all the world besides.

Dividing history into the sacred, or ecclesiastical, and the secular, or profane, Rollin carefully outlined certain "Rules and principles for the study of Profane History":

> These principles may be reduced to six or seven: To reduce this study to order and method: To observe what relates to usages and customs; Principally to enquire after the Truth; To endeavour to find out the causes of the rise and fall of empires, the victory or loss of battles, and events of the like nature: To study the character of the people and great men mentioned in history: To attend to such instructions as con-

cern manners and the conduct of life: And, lastly, carefully
to take notice of everything that relates to religion.[6]

Bolingbroke's *Letters on the Study and Use of History*, written
in 1735, discarded the notion of reading history to gain insight into the workings of Providence, but he retained the
other reasons embraced by his predecessors.

> The love of history seems inseparable from human nature,
> because it seems inseparable from self-love. The same princi-
> ple in this instance carries us forward and backward, to fu-
> ture and to past ages. We imagine the things which affect
> us, must affect posterity: this sentiment runs through man-
> kind, from Caesar down to the parish-clerk in Pope's
> Miscellany.

To Bolingbroke history had all the drama of a Greek tragedy.
He wrote of it in Aristotelian terms: it has a beginning, middle, and end; "errors in judgment" produce historical catas-
trophes; there is a "continuous progression" in the movement
of events. In general, he felt ancient history suspect and he
openly derided sacred history; but his summarizing sentiment
had a familiar ring: ". . . the study of history seems to me, of
all other, the most proper to train us up to private and public
virtue."[7]

Though Bolingbroke's Letters were not generally known
until some years later, another extensive treatise on history
appeared in the 1730s: Edward Manwaring's *Historical and
Critical Account Of the most Eminent Classic Authors in
Poetry and History*. This three-part examination of Greek and
Latin literature, published in 1737, set forth the customary
number of aphoristic assertions: "History is a faithful Exposition of past Transactions. . . ."; "The End of History is Instruction and Knowledge. History instructs us by Example,
by moral Philosophy and Precepts"; "The Parts of History are
the Beginning and the Narration; for History admits of no
Epilogue." Then Manwaring stated the prevalent view of his
era toward the body of historical writing:

Antient History is equally excellent [in pleasing and improving the reader's knowledge]; not so much for the Narrations, as the Causes, Councils, Maxims, Descriptions, Characters and Harangues, which are very instructive. . . . I mention this, to persuade the Moderns to a strict and constant Study of the Antients; for our Modern History, and political Tracts have not that Erudition and Learning we find in the Antients.[8]

The state of historiographical theory by midcentury is aptly revealed in Peter Whalley's *An Essay on the Manner of Writing History* (1746). Whalley paid routine service to the maxims of his topic: the end of history is "Improvement and Instruction"; "The *Statesman* travels in the Field of History, to enrich himself with Maxims of *Prudence*, and civil *Policy*"; the historian must give not events alone but "Motives, Actors, and Consequences." But Whalley also had some innovational remarks to make. Contrary to popular belief, history is not supposed to "please." This false conception had led to the inclusion of fabulous elements in otherwise creditable historians. The "only Scope of History, is *Utility*, which can be attained by nothing else but a religious Regard to Truth." Readers have a right to expect the historian "to be exact, honest, and impartial" and his style to be "easy, elegant, and agreeable." Examining several sacrosanct classic historians by this yardstick, Whalley found Florus too full of wit and fancy, Tacitus overly moralistic, and Dio Cassius and Velleius Paterculus suspect of bias. Sincerity is "the Soul of History" and the characteristic enthusiasm of Poetry is inimical to the sobriety of history. Whalley is one of the first theorists to declare that history and poetry are irreconcilable perspectives. Though he did not specifically rank the two, his preference is nonetheless clear:

Of all the Compositions of the human Mind, *History* is allowed to be the noblest, and most deserving of our serious Attention. . . . It may be needless to enlarge on the Usefulness of this Study, as the united Testimony of the Wisest in all Times giveth it the highest Rank of Praise, and sets it above all others.[9]

Thus only a decade or two before Gibbon, history was universally praised as the source of greatest knowledge by poets, statesmen, literary savants, even clergymen. From a general, vague enthusiasm for history begun in the early seventeenth century and continued through the Restoration period, a specific, reasonably thorough and coherent theory of historiography emerged in the first half of the eighteenth century.

Because the tradition of distrust for nonclassical historians has continued from the eighteenth century to the present day, it is difficult even now to evaluate fairly the prejudice of the eighteenth century against "modern" historians. Certainly, historians from Bede to Burnet were known and commonly read between 1660 and 1800. The library catalogues of the day substantiate the evidence in private correspondence that the eighteenth century man of affairs knew English and continental historians of the period from, roughly, the eighth century to the eighteenth. The range of reading by such a man as Swift is representative of the time. He knew more than a score of the early British historians, including the major Elizabethan and Jacobean writers, as well as many ecclesiastical chroniclers.[10] Temple, in *An Introduction to the History of England*, complained that England had no good national historian comparable to those of other nations: Mezeray, de Mexia, *et al.* Indeed, England had

> such mean and vulgar authors, so tedious in their relations or rather collections, so injudicious in the choice of what was fit to be told, or to be let alone, with so little order, and in so wretched a style, that . . . it is hardly worth the time or pains to be informed. . . .[11]

Temple, however, thought England had some acceptable fragmentary historical writers: More, Francis Bacon, Herbert, Haywood, Camden, and Polydore.

The general dissatisfaction with English historians touched

many leading writers. Dryden was unhappy with the dearth of competent British histories; Milton assayed his own history to fill the breach. Laurence Eacherd's history of England was one of many tried by those discontented with the situation; Swift and Goldsmith also made attempts at comprehensive surveys, though Swift never got beyond making notes. Addison deplored the paucity of histories in *The Freeholder*, No. 35. And finally, the disgruntlement led to criticism of all "modern history," continental and English. The distrust of Le Clerc, Hearne, Rollin, Manwaring, and Whalley for everything but Greek and Latin historiographers was the prevalent feeling of the age.

Twentieth century surveyors of the tradition of historiography are inclined to agree. Eduard Fueter has written in his compendious *Geschichte der Neueren Historiographie* of the bulk of sixteenth and seventeenth century "royal chronologies": "Die meisten sind gar keine eigentlichen Geschichtswerke, sondern rohe Kompilationen, Fabrikate für den Massengebrauch, wie sie den auch vielfach nicht von Schriftstellern von Beruf, sondern Buchändlern verfertigt worden sind."[12] The objection of the classicists themselves to modern historical literature was most pungently expressed by Swift in his famous account of Gulliver's encounter with the spirits of historians on his third voyage:

> I was chiefly disgusted with modern History. For having strictly examined all the Persons of the greatest Name in the Courts of Princes for an Hundred Years past, I found how the World had been misled by prostitute Writers, to ascribe the greatest Exploits in War to Cowards, the wisest Counsel to Fools, Sincerity to Flatterers, *Roman* Virtue to Betrayers of their Country, Piety to Atheists, Chastity to Sodomites, Truth to Informers. . . . Here I discovered the Roguery and Ignorance of those who pretend to write *Anecdotes*, or secret History. . . . How a Whore can govern the Back-stairs, the Back-stairs a Council, and the Council a Senate. . . . I had often read of some great Services done to Princes and States,

and desired to see the Persons by whom these Services were performed. Upon Enquiry I was told, that their Names were to be found on no Record, except a few of them whom History hath represented as the vilest Rogues and Traitors. . . .[13]

This appraisal is not a mere statement of Swift's disenchantment with the court of Queen Anne but an indictment of modern history made by Whig and Tory alike.

If, then, history was the source of wisdom, the storehouse of experience, but "modern" history was suspect and corrupted, where was the seeker after truth to turn? Where indeed? The classicist had a ready answer, painstakingly presented in reading list after reading list in Guides, Introductions, Accounts, and Examinations. Thomas Hearne's recommendations in the *Ductor Historicus* are representative.

Starting with the assumption that "sacred history" (that is, the Bible) must be the foundation block of all truth, historical and otherwise, Hearne went on to recommend a few overall surveys of world history that confirmed or supplemented the Bible: Josephus' *History of the Jews*, Sir Walter Raleigh's *History of the World*, and Sir John Marsham's *Chronicus Canon Aegypticus Ebraicus Graecus & Disquisitiones*. Then he drew up a reading list of Greek and Latin historians that would give the reader the best and fullest understanding of history. These works were to be read in their original languages; some of them were translated by 1714 and most of them had appeared in new editions during the fifteenth and sixteenth or seventeenth centuries. Deploring the loss of the invaluable works of Ctesias, Megasthenes, and Berosus, whose fragments were preserved in the compilations of several later historiographers, Hearne placed Justin first on his list, Justin's abridgment of the world history of Trogus Pompeius covering the period from Ninus of Assyria to Augustus. Then in an order approximating their span of historical coverage, Hearne put Herodotus, Thucydides, Xenophon, Diodorus Siculus, Arrian, Quintus Curtius, Plutarch, Cornelius Nepos, Polybius, L. Annaeus Florus, Dionysius of Halicarnassus, Appian, Sallust, Julius Caesar, Dio Cassius, Velleius Paterculus, Suetonius, Tacitus, the Scriptores Historiae Augustae, Herodian, Aurelius Victor, Eutropius, Zosimus, Eusebius, and Ammianus Marcellinus.

Hearne's list is interesting for several reasons. In itself, it is not surprisingly innovational. In 1678 a translation of Francis La Mothe le Vayer's *Notitia Historicorum Selectorum, or Animadversions upon the Antient and Famous Greek and Latin Historians* was published. It contained more or less the same list with evaluations and comments. In 1684 Charles Blount published his reader's pocket guide to history, the *Janua Scientiarum*, with capsule comments on the Greek and Latin Historians. And there were others. But Hearne included long selections of criticism from earlier authorities on historiography, including le Vayer; he quoted at length from both classical and Renaissance sources. Thus the *Ductor Historicus* was a sort of index to all of historiographical practice and historical theory from Herodotus to the eighteenth century. For instance, Hearne might list the name of Diodorus Siculus, give biographical information about him, catalogue his work and its editions, appraise his content and style, then quote the remarks of Eusebius and Photius about him. Among the chief modern commentators cited in the *Ductor Historicus* were Rapin, Le Mothe le Vayer, and Dacier. Hearne's encyclopedia is thus a convenient guide to eighteenth century English usages of classical, Renaissance, and continental historical writing.

The surprising thing about such historical guide lists as those published in Le Mothe le Vayer and Hearne is that they read, title for title, like the catalogues of many private libraries in the years from 1660 to 1800. A number of sales catalogues exist, including those for Thomas Hearne and Richard Rawlinson among the self-professed experts on historiography, and for such literary luminaries as William Congreve, Joseph Addison, Jonathan Swift, David Garrick, and Samuel Johnson. Unfortunately, the catalogue for Garrick's library does not contain the titles of his vast collection of the classics; this had been bequeathed to a relative and never was itemized.

But the libraries of the other men show an amazing correspondence between popular notions of what good classicists should read and what they actually did read. That the volumes were read is indicated by notations in margins as well as by confirmatory references in other writings.[14]

If the twentieth century reader follows Hearne's recommendations and reads historians from Herodotus to Ammianus Marcellinus inclusively, he will discover the origin of the classicist's emphasis on history. He had imbibed it in his study of Greek and Latin historians, all of whom had propagated the idea of history as the record of exemplary conduct. One need look no further than Herodotus to find the notion in full-blown form. Herodotus repeatedly insisted that he was recording the events of the past so that his reader might gain insight into the ever-changing nature of human affairs and use his knowledge to guide his life. Thucydides and Xenophon followed suit.[15]

Abundant evidence could be cited of the prevalence in ancient historiography of the opinion that history is the means of seeing "the changeless patterns and structures which underlie the world of change." One or two classic sources may stand for all, however. Polybius, who was praised by Dryden and who exerted the strongest of influences on political theory in the period after 1660, had this to say:

> For there are two ways by which men can reform themselves, the one through their own mischances, the other through those of others, and of these the former is the more impressive, but the latter the less hurtful. . . . Reflecting on this we should regard as best discipline for actual life the experience that accrues from serious history; for this alone makes us, without inflicting any harm on us, the most competent judges of what is best at every time and in every circumstance.[16]

Diodorus Siculus, another influential historian in the earlier decades of the new English classicism, amended this view somewhat in his Augustan *Library of History*:

For it is an excellent thing to be able to use the ignorant mistakes of others as warning examples for the correction of error, and, when we confront the varied vicissitudes of life, instead of having to investigate what is being done now, to be able to imitate the successes of the past . . . it is a fact that such experience is so far surpassed by the understanding which is gained from history, as history excels, as we know, in the multitude of facts at its disposal. For this reason, one may hold that the acquisition of knowledge of history is of the greatest utility for every conceivable circumstance of life.[17]

Here in embryonic form is the utilitarian theory of history that was employed by classical historians, refurbished during the Renaissance, adopted by historians from Polydore Vergil to Clarendon, and finally made the basic tenet of eighteenth century historical opinion. The important difference between the use of this theory in earlier ages and in the period from 1660 to 1800 is that in the latter time it was the opinion of all educated men, not historians alone, and that it was formally expounded in essays about historiography, not histories only. Furthermore, in the era of enthusiasm for the classics in preference to succeeding literature, the theory had the weight of authority coming from classical *ipse dixit*.

It may seem contradictory for such conservative Christians as Dryden, Swift, and Johnson to have espoused classicism and put their confidence in pagan historians. It had not always been possible for Christians to accept the revelations of heathen writers, but the classicists managed it, though on several occasions Swift denounced pagan knowledge as inferior to Christian revelation and Johnson willingly discarded classical learning whenever he had to choose between it and Christian doctrine. Ancient history was easier for the eighteenth century classicist to justify than pagan mythology had been for classicists of earlier centuries, however. In Christian belief, human events followed a divinely ordained and executed plan. The kinetic movement of history, therefore, revealed the Hand of

God moving the universe, whether the recording historian was pagan or Christian. Indeed, even the pagan historians had testified to the providential direction of history. The classicist was thus exonerated in using ancient historiography, since its ultimate use was for Christian purposes. Tertullian, Orosius, even Augustine had read pagan historians for their own purposes; the English Christian who was also classicist in sympathies did the same.[18]

All scruples being appeased, admirers of ancient historians read them to find precepts and examples of use in private and public affairs. The innumerable precepts discovered—the analogies, quotations, maxims, and citations—threatened to become a literary Babel constructed of classical bricks sometimes. The practice continued, nevertheless, in an earnest belief that the solution to all problems besetting the present age might be found buried deep in the pages of Thucydides, Polybius, Plutarch, or perhaps Xiphilinus' collection of the fragments of Dio Cassius. The abuses of dilettante classicists and the pontifications of pedants occasionally drove Swift or Addison to insist a "nice Judgment" was essential in selecting from history the proper circumstances to illuminate the complexities of the present.[19] But they never doubted a nice judgment could do just that. *The Tatler* and *The Examiner* are striking evidence of the trust Addison and Swift put in historical analogies.

Did the classicist find in ancient historiography the truths he wanted to serve as a guide for life? He found a great many, to his view. For the sake of convenience, historiographically inculcated "truths" may be separated into categories corresponding to the three broad areas of historical concern, as defined by eighteenth century theorists: those of Causes, Actions, and Consequences.[20] Though the terms are by no means precise, they are workable classifications, and they have the merit of reflecting popular historical opinion. If classes can be set up to accommodate the "useful knowledge" contained in the *res gestae* of the past, those of Causes, Actions, and Consequences are as apt as any.

The first Cause for events in history was, quite naturally,

God or God's will. The Christian classicist was forced to start with this premise. He found it substantiated in Greek and Latin history, so much so that he could forgive the polytheistic errors of his beloved authorities in their profuse evidence of providential ordination of history. Though a few classical historians, notably Thucydides and Livy, put more a pragmatic than a theological face on things, most of them attested to the divine manipulation of human affairs.

Herodotus, for instance, habitually referred to divine wrath or *theou nemesis* as the cause of kingly downfall or providential ordination (*theie pompe*) of defeat in war (1.34; 1.62; 1.86ff). In the *Memorabilia* (1.1), Xenophon reported with care Socrates' opinions of divine presence in all events and his belief that "the Universal disposes all things to its pleasure." Dionysius of Halicarnassus wrote (11.68) that history shows the gods' constant supervision of human actions and their reward or punishment of men. Similar instances of divine control or intervention were given by Diodorus Siculus (xi.12), Appian (vii.8; xi.11), Florus (1.7), Plutarch (*Romulus* xxviii), and Livy (1.Pref.). Like Herodotus, Florus held that Nemesis was the historical manifestation of God's immediate direction of worldly events. Of course, the premise of God as the first Cause in history became the transcendent, if not the sole, consideration in the historical views of the Church Fathers and chronologers.

Once the Supernatural Causes in classical history were clearly perceived, the classicist was free to search for physical or Natural Causes. There were two main ones: Time and Climate. The conceptualizations of Time in the ancient historiographical tradition are so involved that they cannot be more than mentioned here. Fortunately, several full-scale studies have already been made.[21] In general, however, it can be said that Augustine's synthesis of Time and Mind of God in his *Confessions* and his treatment of Time as the embodiment of divine will was the most abstract depiction of Time in the ancient world. The mythic personification of Time in Chronos, Saturn, and later Tempus was not used by historians. Herodotus, Diodorus, and Dionysius of Halicarnassus were especially interested in the nature of time; but they usually treated it less as a manifestation of God than as an innate property of matter.[22] The image of the rotting seed was widely used. The depiction of time as a prime historic Cause did not achieve real importance until the efforts of Orosius, Cyprian, and Augustine forced it to, however.

To the historian, Climate was a far more fascinating Natural Cause. Even in pre-historic thought, climatic influence on human affairs was emphasized in myths about the Sky Father and Earth Mother; the creation accounts in Greek and Babylonian as well as Hebrew legend; the anthropomorphic pantheon created by the Greeks to explain sun, wind, rain, earthquakes, soil, temperature, and seasons. The "father of historians," Herodotus, countenanced many of the old legends and made them accredited history. He told of peoples "sprung from the soil"; spoke of the Ethiopians and their skulls which thickened "by exposure to the sun"; asserted that Africans had sensual, passionate natures because of their hot climate.[23] Later, Hippocrates in his semi-historical, semi-scientific *Airs, Waters, Places* (XII-XIII) amassed the folklore of his day about the effects of climatic factors on plants, animals, and human physique and intelligence. Subsequent historiographers dutifully followed Herodotus and confirmed his opinions and those of Hippocrates as historically verifiable.

Some of the results were weird and wonderful. Diodorus described the generation of animals from the mud of the Nile Delta (I.10), mentioned that the Arabian sun "bred" peculiar creatures like strutho-cameli (ostriches) as well as precious stones (II.51-52), and contrasted the antipodal Ethiopians and Scythians (III.34). Dionysius said climate was responsible for Ethiopians living to be 120 and Hyperboreans (Britons), 1,000 (IV.7). Livy's image of transplanted seeds losing their "virtue" (XXXVIII.17) was adapted by Florus to show why the Gallo-Greeks had changed in character after settling in Macedonia (I.27.11). Polybius remarked the national characteristics produced by climate (III.73; IX.11); as did Livy (XXIX.23), Justin (ii.2), Appian (vi.9), and Dio Cassius (li). In short, Greco-Roman history developed the theory that climate was a Natural Cause responsible for human body type, intelligence, personal disposition, national character, standards of morality, and the properties of plants and animals as well.

Climatic causation was believed by writers from Isidore of Seville to Jean Bodin; but with the reinfusion of classical history into the mainstream of thought in seventeenth century England, the theory gained fresh impetus. It was held in France by Chardin and Montesquieu, whose use of it in political theory is the *locus classicus*. Sir William Temple was its foremost advocate in England during the Restoration, though he had plenty of company. Milton thought the sun ripened wits as well as fruits; and he feared, with Lord Clarendon, that the cold English climate was inimical to the development of political arts. Thomas Rymer and John Dennis thought the inhospitable climate of Britain had prevented the flowering of true tragedy there: Athens was the proper "soyle" for tragedy. Dryden, Defoe, Swift, and Addison believed the climate to be a Natural Cause for the tendency of the English language to fall into harsh, unmusical barbarisms. Dr. Arbuthnot's scientific *Essay on the Effects of Air* collected the medical lore of climate contained in the ancient historians. Dryden used poetically many of the climatic notions of Diodorus, notably in *Annus Mirabilis* and *Religio Laici*, and Pope reflected them in the *Dunciad* and *An Essay on Criticism*. After midcentury less credence was put in climatic causation—Dr. Johnson snorted at the idea and Hume wrily dismissed it—though Goldsmith's *History of the World* was permeated with it, and Boswell and Burke still believed it.[24]

A third Cause universally cited by ancient historians was Luxury. Sometimes conjoined to ideas of climate, "luxury" meant economic prosperity and cultural affluence. As usual, Herodotus began the tradition: "Soft lands breed soft warriors; wondrous fruits of the earth and valiant warriors grow not from the same soil" (ix.122). It was sustained by Livy (vii.32), Florus (1.38), and Appian (iii.1; iv.7). Nearly without exception,

Greco-Roman history propagated the paradigm of rise and fall: need engenders virtue and courage; courage results in aggression, leading to success and prosperity; prosperity leads to the self-indulgences of luxury, eventual enervation, and final defeat. Historiographers documented the theory with examples culled from the past: Xenophon (*Mem.* III.5), Strabo (*Geo.* VII.3), Varro (1.13), Diodorus (V.41; VII.12), Justin (1.7; XXXVI.4), and Dio Cassius (IX). It was appropriated by Augustan and post-Augustan satirists and exaggerated into vehement social criticism by Horace (*Sat.* II, *Epis.* 1), Juvenal (*Sat.* VI, XI), Persius (*Sat.* II, V), and Martial (*Epig.* VIII). The chimaera of Luxury, elaborately styled by history and passed on to Roman satirists, in turn became a horrendous specter to English classicists, historian and man of letters alike.

The fondness for imitations of Roman satire in the period between 1660 and 1800 was in large part attributable to the revived interest in classical history during the same period. The reasoning of the classicist may have been tautological when he found Luxury a threat in his day by reading ancient history and then tried to arrest it by imitating classical attempts; but his conviction was an intense one. Analogies drawn between Rome and England often depended on social similarities, so it was natural for the great Social Cause in history to be emphasized. Already generations of English historiographers had drawn comparisons between Roman and British history and had warned against Luxury: Polydore Vergil and others had prepared the way. Temple, Clarendon, and Milton followed.[25]

Clarendon thought the moral and political decay of the Restoration period the result of "plenty, pride, and excess." Gilbert Burnet was so struck with the pernicious omnipresence of Luxury that he tried to substitute it for Original Sin in some of his theological and ethical tracts. Temple saw all of English history as the cycle of poverty–courage–conquest–prosperity–luxury–decline. So did Defoe, in his Explanatory Preface to *The True-Born Englishman* in 1703. The companionate Rymer and Dennis, the latter in particular, thought Luxury a chief cause for the decline of the arts in England.

Addison allegorically condemned Luxury in No. 55 of *The Spectator.* In all his works, Swift blamed Luxury for many ills, his castigation reaching its height in the works of the 1720s: the *Drapier Letters, Gulliver's Travels,* and *A Modest Proposal.* Even Pope, who subscribed to the Mandevillian thesis of luxury as economically stimulating, attacked excessive ostentation in dress, furnishings, and horticulture. And though in the later decades of the eighteenth century, Luxury lost some of its chimaerical fascination, it still stalked like an ominous threat in personified form through the poems of Gray, Goldsmith, and Cowper. Much of the popularity of the rustic and graveyard poetry of midcentury came from its counterthrusts at Luxury and its heaped shrines.

With his knowledge of historical Causes neatly arrayed in tripartite form—Supernatural (God), Natural (Time, Climate), and Social (Luxury) —the classicist approached the matter of Actions. The wisdom of the ancient historians about Actions seemed to be military, political, social, and personal.

In the sphere of military actions, a few tendentious classicists of the Restoration era followed the practice of Milton, who had educated his nephews in strategy by reading Polyaenus. The Leyden edition of Polyaenus (1690) was widely used and it even found its way into Swift's library. During the first part of the seventeenth century, some strategic excerpts from Aelian's histories ran through several editions under the title, *Aelian's Tactics*; and Procopius and Thucydides were also read for their campaign accounts. All three were still consulted after Charles II had returned to England and the domestic battles had ceased.

The wing-chair strategists of the eighteenth century were mocked by Abel Boyer in *The English Theophrastus* (1702) ; he scorned the classicists for their knowledge of ancient battles and their total ignorance of modern ones as well as their inability to see contemporary military events in any perspective at all. Variations of the satire on the theoretical military man were numerous long before Gilbert's modern Major General boasted of his knowledge of the details of Caractacus' uniform: Tristram Shandy's Uncle Toby was one specimen of the type.

Customarily, however, men of letters avoided strategy; and *The Freeholder* and *The Englishman* contented themselves with comparisons of the characters of ancient and modern military men—the model of Cornelius Nepos or Plutarch being ever present. Swift's famous comparison of the Duke of Marlborough to Crassus is an instance, and there were many more. But there is no evidence that Marlborough patterned his strategy at Blenheim on Crassus' campaigns against the Parthians—quite the contrary, in fact—and poetic military analogies like those of Dryden in *Annus Mirabilis* and Addison in *Pax Gulielmi* were safely *post facto*.

In a matter of military policy, however, ancient historians were often cited: the question of standing armies was a notable case in point. Most Roman historians stoutly distrusted mercenaries and standing armies. Polybius, a former general, well knew the role the revolt of the Carthaginian mercenaries had played in the Punic Wars and was anxious that Rome avoid a like fate (1.43, 66, 81). Diodorus, Justin, and Appian recorded examples of the corruption and venery of standing armies, expressing their historiographical disapproval all the while. In England such recent events as the Civil Wars, the tyranny of Cromwell and the Puritan Army, the defection of General Monck, and the insurrection of the Duke of Monmouth conjoined to produce a nervous distrust of armies and mercenaries in the public mind. Milton used Polybius to confirm his dislike of standing armies. Temple urged the use of levied citizens' armies in eternal preference to permanent, employed forces. In 1697 Prior took the opposite view in his verse, "A New Answer to An Argument against a Standing Army." Swift held standing armies to be a very font of pernicious practice; see *The Examiner*, No. 20, for instance. And if Swift's opinions were politically biased, Defoe's were free of political prejudice though not of meretriciousness. In 1703 Defoe reprinted in a volume of his writings *An Argument, shewing, that a Standing Army, with Consent of Parliament, is not Inconsistent with a Free Government &c.* Then in 1715, in *An Account of the Conduct of Robert Earl of Oxford,* he unqualifiedly condemned standing armies as a threat to liberty. Pro or con, opinions of standing armies were heavily redolent of classical historians.

Another body of Actions available to readers of history was the political. One tradition of ancient historiography, Polybian "balanced government," and its ramifications in seventeenth and eighteenth century thought is already fully explored.[26] Other political wisdom from the ancient past has received less scrutiny: for example, the nature of ambition in rulers, the king as example to his people, political faction and its effects.

Regarding the role and desirable character of monarchs, Greco-Roman history was even more explicit than classical political theorists such as Plato, Aristotle, and Cicero. At least, it was explicit to the classicist who valued examples over philosophy. No matter how severely Plato might warn of hypothetical abuses by tyrants, he was eclipsed by Herodotus' portrayal of Deioces, Dionysius on Tarquin Superbus, Suetonius on Caligula and Tiberius, Tacitus on Nero, and the Scriptores Augustae on Commodus, Pertinax, and Caracalla. No classicist was left unmoved by Xenophon's appraisals of Critias and Alcibiades or the horrible actions of the Sicilian tyrant, Phalaris, as recorded by several historians. The crimes of ambition committed by Julius Caesar were enumerated by historians from Livy to Lucan to Eutropius. Moralistically, ancient historians reproved their tyrannical subjects for their pride, ambition and hubris: Polybius (VI.7), Dionysius (IV.74), Florus (1.57), Dio Cassius (VIII), and the rest.

Concomitantly, classical history developed the ideal role of the king and illustrated it by striking examples. Several historical rulers were praised for their approximation of this ideal—Solon, Lycurgus, Pericles, and of course Caesar Augustus were favorites—but on occasion the historian predicated an ideal monarchy in some actual culture and described his utopia as though it were historical fact. The most significant account of this type was Diodorus' history of the Egyptians in the *Library*, 1.70. According to Diodorus, the Egyptian kings were exemplary in their lives; their piety, sobriety, justice, magnanimity, self-control, truthfulness, generosity, and asceticism were daily extolled by their priests and revered by their subjects. The priests read aloud the lives of virtuous men of the past so the king could emulate them. So successful was this program of royal tutelage and conduct that, said Diodorus, Egypt enjoyed "a most felicitous life [with an] orderly civil government"; it dominated more nations than any power before it; and the Egyptians "adorned their lands with monuments and buildings never to be surpassed" (1.71).

English fondness for admonishing the monarch was no less pronounced in the eighteenth century than it is today or was in the sixteenth century. It differed mostly in its reliance on models of kingly behavior drawn from ancient history—as in the Augustan usage seen earlier—and in the variety of literary genres cyropaedaic in tone. The classicist came habitually to relate his topic to the proper behavior of kings, whether he wrote prose essays, heroic dramas, verse essays, allegorical travels, or translations of classical history. The reader may find Temple lapsing from a discussion of gardening into a comparative analysis of Caligula and Augustus (*Upon the Gardens of Epicurus*); Dryden spending whole passages of dramatic rant on hints to kings (*The Conquest of Granada and Aureng-Zebe*, as elsewhere); Pope versifying the maxims of historiography in couplet form (*An Essay on Man* and the *Epistle to Augustus*); Swift incorporating whole sections of regal behavior from Diodorus' account of the Egyptians into his voyage to Lilliput (*Gulliver's Travels*, 1); Gay writing Aesopian *Fables* to teach the king and court right principles; and many translators—Laurence Eacherd, Conyers Middleton, George Turnbull, *et al.*—declaring their labors designed to acquaint modern statesmen with the examples of virtuous and vicious governance in the past. From the periodical essayists to Bolingbroke, in *The Idea of A Patriot King*, classicists used ancient reflections to burnish their own mirror for magistrates.

The corollary view of the ruler as a model for his people led, in the first years of the eighteenth century, to a serious proposal for the establishment of the post of Censor in England. The Romans' reliance on the official censor to regulate their conduct and forestall "luxurious" excesses was related by almost all historians of Rome: Dionysius (IV.24), Livy (IV.8), and Plutarch (*Cato*, XV-XVII) gave thorough accounts of the history and exercise of the office, expressing their approval of it, and the prominence of the Censor in the time of Augustus was noted by later historians. The hedonistic practices of the Restoration era in England helped produce a moralistic reaction in the reign of Anne that, innately classical as it was, soon led to sincere suggestions that a British censorship be instituted. Addison treated the whole notion with tongue in cheek merriment in *The Tatler*, No. 162 (April 1710), but other moralists were more somber. In *An Essay upon Publick Spirit* (1711), John Dennis urged the passing of sumptuary laws on the Roman order to combat British luxury; and Swift, first in *A Project for the Advancement of Religion* (1709) then in *The History of the Last Four Years of the Queen* (1713), championed sumptuary laws and censorship as the best way to purge the Augean conditions of the time.

The knowledge of Greco-Roman historiography also explains the horror of "parties" and "faction" evident among the Tories in that period. The works of Polybius and Diodorus were full of instances of political division and conflict that were bound to raise hackles in a nation so fresh from civil war. Livy and the post-Augustan historians indicted factionalism for many evils from the Marius–Sulla embroilment to the violence of the Gracchian Reforms and so to the pre-Augustan civil wars. In the histories of Florus, factionalism was incessantly blamed for most of the wrongs committed in the course of Roman history; and the dire consequences of "party" interests were organized at last into a paradigm of decline and fall. With classical historians as his guide, the Englishman of the eighteenth century could hardly avoid his distrust of party politics.

The Role of Historiography

In the realm of social Actions, the wisdom of ancient writers was no less disheartening. Most of the social concerns of the era from 1660 to 1800 were in some measure the apprehensions of classicists brought up on the fatalistic lessons of history. The licentiousness and silly ornateness of the British theater not only offended such puritans as Jeremy Collier. They appalled the urbane Addison, who well knew that theatrical displays of that sort had marked the worst times of Roman corruption: Livy (VII.2), Suetonius (*Caligula*), Aelius Lampridius (*Heliogabalus*), and others had shown him so. Before him, Dryden had uneasily pandered to lewd public taste and regretted it when he grew old. Swift thought the theater a sink of depravity and blamed the love of it for the sorrows of England and Ireland. Johnson's famous castigations of the theater and its provocative actresses may have been less historiographical than personal in source; but the defenders of the theater, Colley Cibber and Garrick among them, appealed to the glories of ancient dramatists and cited philosophical benefits to counteract the moral disadvantages catalogued by ancient historians and embraced by Tertullian (in the *De Spectaculis*).

In matters of clothing as well, the classicists saw the present with the eyes of ancient history. Augustan historians universally deplored the oriental fabrics introduced into Rome in their day: Augustus' overt use of homespun for his togas, the passing of sumptuary laws to prevent wearing of silk, and the correlation between immorality and dress were grist to the historiographer. Such anecdotal writers as Suetonius and Lampridius reported the luxurious, effeminate clothing of Tiberius, Nero, and Commodus. Tacitus contrasted the hardy, virile clothing of the Germans with the decadent dress of the Romans. The tradition grew until at last love of rich, elaborate clothing was thought to be a prime cause and symptom of cultural decline. Swift's papers on Irish manufacture and Addison's remarks on ladies' hair styles show the range of influence exerted by historians on the subject of clothing.

In the marginal area of thinking where social and personal behavior merge, the effect of historiographically recorded

Actions is conjectural but there are strong implications. It was in the first quarter of the eighteenth century that walking became the fashionable exercise, for instance. The reasons were multiple. Still, in Gay's *Trivia*, which formulated the "art" of walking, classical examples of walkers are surprisingly accurate and consistent; and Swift's *Journal*, which at times reads like an exercise manual, exhorts the hapless Stella to historically heroic efforts. The emergent code of personal conduct in the period, that now thought typically "British," seems amusingly dependent upon models from the classical past. The growing emphasis on Spartan eating habits, walking as exercise, "sensible" clothing, the endurance of cold, all smack strongly of the historiographically contained accounts of Epaminondas, Socrates, Leonidas, Cincinnatus, the assorted Catoes, and other heroes of the classicist.

Whether he consciously developed his private behavior from historical precedents or not, the educated Englishman of the Neo-Classical period was following a logical plan to put his overall view of history into daily perspective. To develop one's health by exercise, to take an avid interest in politics and eschew factionalism, to experience gloom upon contemplating the contemporary scene, to seek historical analogies as a solution to current dilemmas: these were all dependent upon the transcendent view of history contained in classical historiography. From Polybius to Eutropius, historians of Rome conspired to inculcate a paradigmatic overview of the course of human events. This view, eventually apotheosized in Gibbon's *Decline and Fall of the Roman Empire*, was the bone and marrow of much classicist literature.

The homunculus of historical determinism contained in Roman history was the metaphor of the body politic, probably most anciently contained in Aesop's fable of the Belly and the members. Aesop's rudimentary trope was popular with the Greek writers of political theory—Plato and Aristotle both referred to it—and it was subsequently borrowed by Roman historiographers. Polybius had covertly suggested in his *History* that the growth of Rome to its present vantage point was like

56

the development of an organism that would subsequently decline in its vigor and faculties. In the Augustan Age, historians used the body-state analogy specifically. Both Dionysius (VI.86) and Livy (II.32) made a great deal of the similarity between a human body and the corporate nature of the state, Livy actually using the fable of the Belly and the members for illustration. The abridgment by Florus gave it great prominence (I.17.23). Even as late as Dio Cassius, historical writers were finding the Aesop fable useful in depicting the birth and growth cycle of the body politic; see *Frag.* IV, for example. An extended passage from Florus shows the historiographical consequences of taking a metaphor over-literally:

> If anyone were to contemplate the Roman people as he would a single individual and review its whole life, how it began, how it grew up, how it arrived at what may be called the maturity of its manhood, and how it subsequently reached old age, as it were, he will find that it progressed through four stages. The first period, under the rule of the kings, lasted almost four hundred years, during which it struggled against its neighbors in the vicinity of the capitol. This period will be its infancy. The next period extends . . . a space of one hundred and fifty years, during which the Roman people subjugated Italy. It was an age of great activity for its soldiers and arms and may thus be called its youth. The next period is the hundred and fifty years down to the time of Augustus Caesar, during which it spread peace throughout the world. This was the manhood and the vigorous maturity of the empire. From the time of Caesar Augustus down to our own age [i.e., Marcus Aurelius Antoninus] there has been a period of not much less than two hundred years during which the Roman people, as a result of the inactivity of the emperors, has grown old and, as it were, lost its potency. (*Intro.*I)

Florus' commingling of the fable of Aesop with the notion of Four Ages, probably originated by Seneca the Elder, was to have great consequences. It was a canard with far-reaching implications: like the human body, the "life span" of a nation must follow discernible stages; its progress from birth to death was irrevocable; cultural factors were equatable with biological traits; and history was guided by a form of organic determinism. To the English classicist, the secondary implications were no less important; the age of Caesar Augustus was followed by cultural decline, thus any nation attaining an "Augustan Age" would soon afterward fall into inevitable decay and collapse. When Waller, Dryden, and Rymer were trumpeting the "Augustan" title, they did not anticipate the frightful echoes that would grow until they confounded Swift and his circle.

As young classicists at Oxford, Cambridge, and Trinity Dublin worked at getting up their Latin and Greek by reading Polybius, Livy, and Florus, they were constantly faced with historiographical warnings that sank deeply into their minds. Said Polybius:

> That all existing things are subject to decay (phthora) and change (metabole) is a truth that scarcely needs proof; for the course of nature is sufficient to force the conviction on us. There being two agencies by which every kind of state is liable to decay, the one external and other the growth of the state itself; we can lay down no rule about the first, but the latter is a regular process. . . . When a state has weathered many great perils and subsequently attains to supremacy and uncontested sovereignty, it is evident that under the influence of long established prosperity, life will become more extravagant and the citizens more fierce in their rivalry regarding office and other objects than they ought to be. As these defects go on increasing, the beginning of the change for the worse will be due to love of office and the disgrace entailed by obscurity, as well as to extravagance and purse-proud display. . . . (vi.57)

Dionysius of Halicarnassus compiled a host of charges of corruption and decline in men "of our own day" [*i.e.*, Augustan Rome]: religion was sunk into impiety and atheism (ii.6), factionalism was rampant (ii.11), the triumph had become a lavish,

expensive display (ii.34), common thieves and prostitutes had
risen to positions of public eminence (iv.24), and everywhere
was evidence that the Augustan Age was ushering in evil times
for Rome.[27]

Nor was Livy more optimistic. He began his history with a
shudder at the "present age" and stated his preference for the
past, full of glory and virtue as it supposedly was. In Book
xxxix, he launched a wholesale attack on the manifold corruptions of the Augustan Age. Diodorus reluctantly commented on the social and political faults of the time and sor-
rowfully concluded: "Indeed there is no noble thing among
men, I suppose, which is of such a nature that the long passage
of time works it no damage or destruction" (x.7-10). The dole-
ful refrain was sung in chorus thereafter: by Appian (i, ii),
Justin (vi.9), Plutarch (*Pompey* l-lv), and Dio Cassius (xli).

And its chords continued to sound in historians of England,
who modeled their works on the "classical" authors. Polydore
Vergil, after he had worked his way from Noah to the Saxon
kings, wrote:

> . . . and so bie writinge, I am comme to the destruction of
> the Brittishe kingdom, founded on litell principels, yeat
> afterward, when it was growne to great perfection and
> maiestie, and established with artilirie, lawse, relligion, and
> councell, at the lengthe it came to ruine, even as in auncient
> times the mightie dominions of the Assirians, Medes,
> Persians, Macedonians, and Romans, camme to desolation;
> suche is the fickel nature, and propensitee to deathe, bothe
> of menne and humaine affayres.[28]

Polydore's treatment of the "dominion of the Englishemen"
suggested that the Norman Conquest inaugurated a new cycle
of cultural rise and growth to replace the fallen Saxon kingdom, however; see the *English History*, Book iv. Holinshed believed "There is a certeine period of kingdomes, of 430 years,
in which commonlie they suffer some notable alteration";
moreover, he thought the Norman Conquest began a downward trend in culture and morals, and he compared events

in English history to those in Roman, without, however, drawing extensive parallels.[29] Daniel's *History of England* (1611), terminated his account of Edward III's reign in this fashion:

> Thus farre have I brought this Collection of our History, and now come to the highest exaltation of this Kingdome, to a State full built, to a Government reared up with all those Complements of Forme and order, as have held it together ever since: notwithstanding those dilapidations made by our civill discord, by the Nonage or negligence of Princes, by the alterations of Religion, by all those corruptions which Time hath brought forth to fret and canker-eate the same.[30]

Tudor–Stuart historians were not entirely of one mind as to the cultural apex of English history: Holinshed placed it in the time of Henry VIII; Speed located it in the Elizabethan Age; Daniel placed it generally toward the end of the sixteenth century. The "Glorianist" historians naturally praised the Elizabethan as the age of greatest splendor, and the effect of their judgment continued well into the Restoration period and after. Clarendon held up the ages of Elizabeth and James I as the political apogee; Defoe concurred; Swift and Bolingbroke gave evidence that they subscribed to the same view.

But if the classicist accepted the idea of the Elizabethan Age as the culmination of English history, and if he also believed that a nation followed a "life" cycle like that of Rome, he was forced to some disturbing conclusions. From the "high instances of power and sovereignty," the "happy times," and the *imperium et libertas* of the Age of Elizabeth, said Clarendon in his *History of the Rebellion*, there was no way for England to go but downward into strife and corruption. Like Polybius, Clarendon assumed that the national glory following the defeat of a major enemy would tarnish with the indulgences of prosperity and power. Holinshed and others had compared the English fleet with the Roman just before it destroyed Carthage. Obviously, then, the Elizabethan period was synonymous with the Roman Republic of the second century B.C.; and if he applied the hypothetical periods of Florus or Holinshed to subsequent events, Clarendon had to see his own age as the final one before the advent of some Caesar or Augustus. He stopped short of that logical end, though many of his contemporaries did not. Laurence Eacherd's *History of England,* for instance, took its premises as far as they could go.

As the poets kept on eulogizing the English kings as "Augustus," other men of letters worriedly kept inspecting the historical condition of the nation. Temple saw a definite political and cultural decline from the time of Elizabeth to the 1670s: the nobility had degenerated; literature had declined; and morality was at an all-time low. In the reign of William and Mary, Defoe traced in *The Poor Man's Plea* the cyclic rise and fall of public morality in England: Edward VI and Elizabeth had managed to produce "such a degree of Humanity and Sobriety of Conversation, as we have reason to doubt will hardly be seen again in our Age." Luxury got a footing in the court of James I; prophanity spread under Charles I; and under Charles II, "Lewdness, and all manner of Debauchery arriv'd to its Meridian." In *An Essay upon Publick Spirit,* John Dennis praised the hardy Englishmen of Henry VII's and Henry VIII's day, trotted out the body politic analogy in full strength, castigated the introduction of French fashion in Charles II's day, and concluded sonorously: "There is not a greater difference between what London was in Harry the Eighth's Time and what it is at present, than there is between the Manners of our Ancestors and our own. This overgrown Town may be said to be a visible, palpable Proof of the Growth of the *British* Luxury."

It may be possible to dismiss the apprehensions of Clarendon and Temple as the qualms of old men, eclipsed statesmen, and to smile at those of Dennis and Defoe as the commercial quaverings of second-rate minds. It is not so easy to explain away the very real, intense fears of men like Swift, Pope, Arbuthnot, Gay, and Bolingbroke. Dr. Johnson's contemptuous remark that the letters of these men indicate a belief that all the virtue of the age was concentrated in them has obscured the real issue: the absolute sincerity of their apprehensions. In recent years, the Tories have been allowed the legitimacy of their gloom, but its basis is still incompletely understood.

The truth would appear to be that they took quite literally the paradigm of rise and fall contained in ancient historiography, and their genuine apprehensions about political and social affairs in the period from 1710 to 1740 were based on their conviction that the "Augustan Age" of the Georges would lead to a succession of absolute, tyrannical Tiberiuses and Caligulas. Such fears may look absurd to us today, but they were understandable to men like Goldsmith and Boswell, both of whom saw the ministry of Walpole as a harrowing threat to letters and liberty; it was understandable to Junius and Burke and the Pitts. To American colonials of the late eighteenth century, George III was a tyrant as odious as Tiberius, certainly. And even to modern historians, there appear grounds for many of the apprehensions held by the Augustan Tories; see Wolfgang Michael's *England Under George I: The Beginnings of the Hanoverian Dynasty*.

The historiographical foundation of Augustan gloom is revealed mostly in fragmentary hints, since even the boldest Tory was still subject to the direct displeasure of George I and his minister, as Gay discovered. But the hints are enough. Bolingbroke's *Letters on History* and his Correspondence show the Rome–England analogy in operation: "Our temple of Janus was shut by Henry the Seventh. . . ."; "The Truth is, nations, like men, have their infancy . . . and grow up to manhood. . . ."; ". . . no history can be more fruitful in examples of the danger to which liberty stands exposed from the natural, and therefore constant desire of amplifying and maintaining power, than the Roman history is, from the last of the kings to the first of the emperors"; "we shall find not only the first general proposition, but the others, relative to it, illustrated and confirmed through the whole course of our [English] history." Bolingbroke's *Remarks on the History of England* shows in detail his equation of the Elizabethan Age with the Roman Republic of the third and second centuries, the decline of England into successive stages of degeneration, and the probability of an absolute monarchy being established. And his political tract, *On Luxury*, once again traces moral decline in England, repeatedly citing ancient historians as authorities for general premises.

The same view is developed in the writings of Dr. John Arbuthnot, where the standard opinions are often cited humorously but with a basic conviction. In *An Account of the State of Learning in the Empire of Lilliput*, Arbuthnot took Swift's account of the religious controversy over egg-breaking in Lilliput and used its historical allegory of decline from the Elizabethan Age to the present. The *Critical Remarks on Gulliver's Travels* contained the opinion that "From the Time of *Augustus Caesar*, Rome was evidently declining," and so forth, an analogy with England being implicit. *The Freeholder's Political Catechism* is a collection of historiographical wisdom: the Roman history shows how "Faction, Corruption, and Standing Armies" lead to decline; "All Nations sink and rise in proportion as this Virtue (patriotism) prevails"; the present state of decay in England is due to loss of respect for virtue and religion; and the essence of the theme is contained in a question and answer—"What is become of the Scipio's and Cato's of Rome? They sing now on the English Stage." Arbuthnot's *Political History of John Bull* shows the same structural analogy between Rome and England that his lesser works employ.

The same kind of examination of the writings of Pope and Gay indicate the source of their satiric estimates of contemporary affairs was the Roman paradigm of decline and fall. Pope's letters to Swift, his steady use of the Augustan analogy, the terminal despondency of his short, eschatological poem, *1740*—all these show that Pope, too, shared Bolingbroke's and Arbuthnot's theories of historical determinism. Gay, likewise, in the *Fables, The Beggar's Opera, Polly*, and the shorter poems, drew many of his satiric references from the historical analogy prevalent in his circle.

But it is in the writings of Swift that the effects of historiographical premises are most striking.[31] From his earliest

published work in 1701 to the last bitter and trivial literary
exercises of his old age, Swift saw English society through a
glass of Roman grinding. His increasing pessimism through
the years may have stemmed from personal disappointment,
but it was channeled and swollen by the tributary notions
derived from ancient history. One has but to look at typical
comments by Swift in a chronological sequence to see the historiographical elements of eighteenth century classicism.

In *Contests and Dissentions in Athens and Rome* (1701),
Swift began his publishing career with a defense of Lord
Somers that appealed to ancient historians for authority, drew
extensive comparisons between Rome and England, and set
up a comparative time schedule: the period from Romulus to
Julius Caesar was "not many Years longer than from the
Norman conquest to our Age." The *Sentiments of a Church
of England Man* (1708), showed how the arts depended upon
political freedom and how they had declined in Rome shortly
after the introduction of the empire; a similar suppression of
freedom and art must be guarded against in England. *A
Project for the Advancement of Religion* (1709), not only
advocated the establishment of a censorship and sumptuary
laws; it declared, ". . . the Ruin of a State is generally preceded by an universal Degeneracy of Manners, and Contempt of Religion; which is entirely our Case at present." In
the November 30, 1710 issue of *The Examiner*, Swift
searched ancient historians in vain for the proper character
of a minister in England, but all parallels were detrimental
to "Roman memory." In the December 21 issue, Caesar's
grasp of power and suppression of liberty were viewed as
alarmingly close to current political trends. Then in the May
24, 1711 issue, the failure of the English to praise God for their
victories in battle was contrasted with the Roman custom of
building a temple after a victory; the dreadful condition of
English culture was due to advanced factionalism. Modern
politicians were violating all the maxims that had permitted
England to flourish "so many hundred Years."

In 1712, in *A Proposal for Correcting the English Tongue,*

The Role of Historiography

Swift traced the changes in England from the time of William the Conqueror to his day and compared them with changes in Latin from Romulus to Caesar. English received its greatest improvement in the reign of Elizabeth, and it had been increasingly corrupted ever since, especially in the Restoration era. Latin was similarly corrupted from its pristine beauties down to its debased form in Tacitus and other writers "even before the Goths invaded Italy." In *The Public Spirit of the Whigs* (1714), Swift remarked that Virgil "lived but a little after the ruin of the Roman republic, where seditions often happened, and the force of oratory was great among the people," an oratory like that presently used by the Whigs. Again in 1714, in the *Memoirs of the Change in the Queen's Ministry in 1710*, he declared that his conversance with Greek and Roman authors had inclined him to Whig principles in politics. In his marginal notes during the years between 1714 and 1730, Swift kept to his view of England as declining in the style of Rome. In the margins of Clarendon's history, when Clarendon said liberty continued to exist in Rome after the establishment of the empire, *Imperium et Libertas*, Swift underlined *libertas* and scrawled *Nego*. In *The Freeholder* of June 15, 1716, "Cautions to be observed in the reading of ancient Greek and Roman Historians," Addison said the Whigs followed the political principles of Greece and Rome, and Swift marginally noted, "yet, this we see is liable to be wholly corrupted." In 1717, in his sermon "On Brotherly Love," he said, "whoever reads the Characters of the *English* in former Ages, will hardly believe their present Posterity to be of the same Nation or Climate."

The *Drapier Letters* (1724) saw George I a despotic Caesar, deliberately destroying the remnants of personal freedom. *Gulliver's Travels* (1726) launched its vehement attack on Augustus and the venery of his court, the luxury that had produced decline in Rome and was producing it in England, and the degeneration of sturdy English yeomen into effete, dissipated political opportunists. In 1732-33 Swift hoped the Earl of Orrery might help salvage "a most corrupt, stupid, and ignorant age and nation." In 1734-35 he told William Pulteney in a letter:

> I will do an unmannerly thing, which is, to bequeath you an epitaph for forty years hence, in two words, *Ultimus Britannorum* . . . it is altogether impossible for any nation to preserve its liberty long under a tenth part of the present luxury, infidelity, and a million of corruptions. We see the Gothic system of limited monarchy is extinguished in all the nations of Europe. It is utterly extirpated in this wretched kingdom [Ireland], and yours [England] must be the next. Such has ever been human nature, that a single man . . . is able to attack twenty millions, and drag them voluntarily at his chariot-wheels.

Again to Pulteney in 1735:

> If my health were not so bad, although my years be many, I fear I might outlive liberty in England. It has continued longer than in any other monarchy, and must end as all others have done. . . . As to the lust of absolute power, I despair it can ever be cooled, unless Princes had capacity to read the history of the Roman Emperors. . . .

To John Barber in 1735:

> I take my age with less mortification, because, if I were younger, I should probably outlive the liberty of England, which, without some unexpected assistance from Heaven, many thousand now alive will see governed by an absolute monarch.

To Thomas Sheridan in 1736:

> I have seen since the death of the late Queen . . . so great a contempt of religion, morality, liberty, learning, and common sense, among us in this kingdom; a hundred degrees beyond what I ever met with in any writer ancient or modern.

To Charles Ford in 1736:

The Role of Historiography

I am heartily sick of the worst times and people, and oppressions that history can show in either kingdom.

And to the Earl of Oxford in 1737:

I am grown altogether weary of the world by my years and infirmities, and hourly fretted to the heart by the course of public proceedings in both kingdoms, which cannot be matched by the greatest corruptions in Rome or Greece.

The despair of Swift and his circle did not entirely dissipate during the last half of the eighteenth century. Johnson, the Great Cham of later classicism, as a high Tory in principles naturally did not share Swift's historical pessimism. But Burke, Goldsmith, and Boswell of the Johnsonian inner circle found historical analogies distressingly apt on occasion; Goldsmith in particular clung to the analogies between Rome and England. Sir Joshua Reynolds repeated the old maxims about artistic decline and liberty, both in Rome and England. And Gibbon's history of Rome owed much of its acclaim to classicists who read it in order to profit from Roman example and thus forestall English decline and fall. It was, finally, in the paradigm of Consequences that ancient historiography had the most lasting effect on classical thought between 1660 and 1800.

In any understanding of Neo-Classicism, certainly as much emphasis should be placed on its historiographical antecedents as on its literary sources. The Augustan Age of Rome was famous for its historians as well as its poets; the English classicist revered Livy, Dionysius, Diodorus, Trogus, and Cornelius Nepos equally with Virgil, Horace, Ovid, and Tibullus. English politicians practiced a statecraft formalized by Polybius; English scholars relied on Justin and Varro for their information on ethnology, art, geography; English historians patterned themselves on Tacitus, Plutarch, and Thucydides; English schoolmasters used Florus and Quintus Curtius to indoctrinate their pupils; and English gentlemen saw their nation as a new Greece or Rome and themselves as versions of Epaminondas, Scipio, or Maecenas.

Formation of English Neo-Classical Thought

Despite its significance for the intellectual leaders of the country, classicism did not make England into another Attica or Latium. Nor did it convert Lord Somers into Themistocles, Bolingbroke into Alcibiades, or Warren Hastings into Verres. It never intended to. There was nothing of sham about the purview of classicism; it was neither an intellectual charade or an elaborate self-deception. Classicists of the late seventeenth and eighteenth centuries used ancient literature to throw their own age into perspective, to light its outstanding qualities so they could be objectively examined. They used that literature to get at the inner meaning of daily affairs, a meaning that would otherwise be revealed only by time. They used it as a standard of achievement, a model and warning the more effective for being remote, whole, and exhaustive. Classicism was not a monolithic penchant for literary imitation but a rationale of life. The catalytic role of classical historiography in forming this rationale cannot be stressed too much.

3 · Greece

In critical histories of English literature composed from about 1850 to 1930, Greece was almost invariably the property of nineteenth century writers. Byron, Shelley, and Keats were given the credit for discovering it literarily and Arnold was honored for divining its essence. The term "Hellenism" changed its meaning from "a Greek idiom" to "the cultural ideal typified by ancient Greece." Although earlier writers had used the terms "Hellene" and "Hellenic" to denote certain characteristics of antique Greek culture, it was the Victorian commentators—Arnold, Pater, Swinburne—who endowed "Hellenism" with mythic, archetypal attributes. As it was applied to such works as Shelley's *Hellas*, Keats' *Endymion*, Byron's *Childe Harold's Pilgrimage*, Tennyson's *Ulysses*, or Swinburne's *Atalanta in Calydon*, "Hellenism" came to mean a subjectively oriented enthusiasm for certain artistic and philosophical aspects of Greek culture. Though interest in Homeric literature and legend was strong in nineteenth century England, literary Hellenism was primarily Periclean in nature, patterning its attitudes toward Homeric Greece on those of Periclean Athens and largely ignoring the Alexandrian Hellenism of later date. In any event, "Hellenism" came to be considered a Romantic and post-Romantic trait of mind and literary historians treated it as such.

The claim of nineteenth century England on ancient Greece was strengthened by activities not entirely literary. Advances in Greek scholarship by such brilliant classicists as Richard Porson and Benjamin Jowett, the archeological pursuits of Sir Arthur Evans, the treasure hunts of Lord Elgin all confirmed the idea of a Greek revival. Byron's championing of the Greeks in their revolts against the Turks and improved travelling conditions that permitted thousands of tourists to invade the Aegean territory also led to the notion of a greater Hellenism among the English. The conjunction of these factors conspired to warp the perspective of literary historians and make them improve their case for nineteenth century Hellenism by emphasizing the Roman "Augustanism" of the eighteenth century. They conveniently forgot that Lady Mary Wortley Montagu went to Greece long before Byron, that Richard Bentley had smoothed the way for Porson and Jowett, and that Pope had been dazzled by Homeric translation some time before Keats read Chapman.

The belief that writers of the Restoration and eighteenth century knew little and understood less about Greece has been gradually, painstakingly chipped at by scholars during the last thirty or forty years. But it was a canard that emerged from several centuries of small literary anecdotes that made it inevitable. As early as the sixteenth century, the notion existed that England was indifferent to Greek studies. Skelton deplored the way Greek was taught in English universities, and Ben Jonson's aphorism about Shakespeare's deficiencies in the language loomed larger than the realization that the Bard had, after all, written *Timon of Athens* and *A Midsummer Night's Dream*. The Puritan's attack on Greek philosophy and the Royal Society's attack on Aristotle were better remembered than the wild enthusiasm for Homer and Aesop during those decades. The Phalaris controversy besmirched the Hellenic learning of Temple and Boyle, among others. Dryden's adaptation of Sophocles seemed ample indication that the classicist was ignorant of the classic. Pope's struggles with Homer were recorded and anecdotes conceived to show his ignorance of Greek. When Boswell defended posthumously Johnson's Greek learning, it had the effect of damning with faint praise. So to the nineteenth century poet or critic, it was easy to find himself the first Englishman ever to thrill to the glory that was Greece and to thrust willingly the grandeur that was Rome on the previous century.

This is just what Victorian critics did. Gosse declared the "classical" literature of the past age to be entirely Latinate and deliberately imitative of Virgil and Horace before all others. Saintsbury used the "Augustan" epithet with a bludgeoning lack of discrimination, ignoring any Hellenic elements in eighteenth century classicism. Even Elton, the most perceptive commentator on the "Augustan Age," wrote:

> The truth is that classicism became so perfect on its own lines that it instinctively reached out to something higher [i.e., Greek literature and thought]. But the check of the operation of the Hellenic spirit is seen in what may be strictly called the conceit of classicism, its pride in its own perfections. . . . Still, in the main, classicism, in its relation with the antique, does mean Latinism. . . . But our greatest writers, like Dryden and Swift, are ever ill at ease in the confines of Latinism. . . .

Elton's teeter-totter appraisal shows the conflict in the nineteenth century critical mind anxious to define the difference between the literature of Dryden, Swift, and Johnson and that of Keats, Byron, and Tennyson in terms of an "Augustan"–"Hellenist" disjunction. In subsequent decades, the disjunction, false as it was in those terms, was readily accepted and other terms—"Pre-Romantic" is a particularly unhappy instance—were superadded. Even today, in spite of the efforts of Spencer, Stern, and others, literary historians still ignore the existence of an Hellenic influence in English literature before 1800, and even the iconoclasts draw the line of Hellenism in England somewhere excluding the decades 1660 to 1740.

Certainly there is sufficient evidence to show that Greek literature was well known and admired by English men of letters long before the Dilettanti organized and the Graveyard poets began frequenting necropolis. There is also evidence that it strongly affected their outlook and literary productions. The Restoration era witnessed an outpouring of texts and translations unprecedented in England, even during the Renaissance epoch of scholarship. Before 1660 the classicist had been able to acquire the majority of Greek authors in editions with parallel Greek–Latin texts, though the Greek texts were often corrupted to the point of being nonsense. It is these parallel texts that literary critics have used to demonstrate the ignorance of Neo-Classicists in Greek. The reasoning runs thus:

the texts were in Greek and Latin, therefore the classicist read the Latin because it was the easier and more commonly taught language. This non sequitur vanishes when one realizes that the parallel texts were the only ones available; that the student needed such texts to be able to construe Greek in an age before Liddell and Scott; and that even today Greek scholars find uses for the parallel English–Greek texts of the Loeb Classical Library. No doubt, some classicists read the Latin translations of Greek writers—Congreve obviously did, and so did Pope—but to generalize about others when there is evidence to the contrary is fallacious.

Publication records of the era between 1660 and 1750 are strong evidence that Greek studies reached a level of interest and importance seldom attained in England. Before the earlier date, some Greek lexicons, dictionaries, and grammars had been available; the Greek–Latin dictionary of Robert Constantin and the 1581 *Lexicon Graecolatinum* of Jean Crespin were the chief philological works on Greek. The survey of Greek study in Harris Fletcher's *The Intellectual Development of John Milton* indicates the meager quantity of grammars and lexicons in England before 1625. But in 1657 William Burton published his history of the Greek language, the *Graecae Linguae Historiae*; in 1661, Joseph Caryl's English–Greek lexicon appeared; and others followed in rapid succession.[1] The flurry of grammars and dictionaries was doubtless due to a need for aids in reading the new Greek editions of Hellenic masters. The older 15th and 16th century editions were doubled in number by the new editions of the period after 1660.[2] Moreover, the post-Restoration decades saw new translations of Greek classics into English, some of them for the first time.[3] After the turn of the century, Greek drama began appearing in translation in greater numbers. In 1703 Rowe published his *Ajax* with scholarly examinations of the Greek cruces. In 1714 Lewis Theobald produced the *Electra* in English and, in 1715, the *Oedipus*. Also in 1715, Theobald translated Aristophanes' *Clouds*, and Ozell printed his translation of Racine's version of *The Wasps*. George Adams, in 1729,

Greek source. The *Cleomenes* (1692) was extricated from Plutarch's life of the Spartan, which was duly translated by Thomas Creech and published with the printed version of the play. Dryden himself had written a life of Plutarch to accompany the edition of 1683; and ten years later, he produced a life of Polybius for a new translation of the *History*. His knowledge of the Greek language was evident in his translations: of Theocritus, Agathias, and Homer, most notably. And the Greek influence on Dryden's writing may also be seen in his use of the animal fable in *The Hind and the Panther*. Dryden's interest in Greek literature was a very real one.

Similarly, Matthew Prior, a literary and political link between Dryden and his successors, was pervasively affected by his study of Greek. A highly proficient Latin scholar and writer, Prior nevertheless found the Greek idiom and attitude a constant stimulation. Certain of his early poems—the epistle "Written in the Year 1696"—depicted his delight in the lyrics of Anacreon and Sappho; others, "To the Honourable Charles Montague, Esq.," for example, used Greek allusions. His later, more serious Greek studies included a critical examination of the *Iliad* in "Observations on Homer. A Letter" (1715), an epilogue to the drama *Phaedra and Hippolytus* by Eugene Smith in 1707, translations of the First and Second Hymns of Callimachus, translations and imitations of Anacreon, and various scholarly examinations of Greek texts. Prior's light verse domesticated the myths of Jove and Alcmaena (the Amphitryon legend), Narcissus, Oedipus and the Sphinx, Protogenes and Apelles, and others. And though his touch was typically Prioresque and light, he displayed in "Democritus and Heraclitus" (1718) his grasp of the recesses of Greek philosophy.

Swift was a student of Greek all his life though the literary effects of his interest are most pronounced in the years 1697 to 1714.[4] His earliest writings show a detailed knowledge of Herodotus, whom Swift often cited on Persian history, the Scythian race, or ancient views of climatic influence. *The Battle of the Books* and *A Tale of a Tub* reveal his close reading of Xenophon (both the *Hellenica* and *Memorabilia*),

Plutarch, Aristotle, Pausanius, Homer, and Hippocrates. The majority of heroic Ancients in the *Battle* are Greeks, with Pindar assuming a special importance. *Of Contests and Dissentions* (1701) traces the development of Greek politics in a succinct and accurate fashion, citing Thucydides, Xenophon, Herodotus, Polybius, and Dionysius of Halicarnassus. In fact, the most brilliant, satirical pieces of Swift's first fifteen years of writing and publication are more thickly saturated with Greek references than Latin ones. The Greek deities appear constantly; and Greek heroes are lauded time and again in Swift's memos and notes, as well as in the poems, political tracts, and letters. In his youth Swift even tried his hand at imitating Pindar in the "Ode to the Athenian Society"; but his efforts were more poor Cowley than good Pindar. His extensive poetical productions are generally devoid of Hellenic influences. Such Greek legends as those of Midas or Apollo and Daphne came from Roman sources, and Swift chose to imitate Horace and Catullus or write his idiosyncratic verse rather than model himself on the ancient Hellenes. The truth seems to be that he read Greek prose adequately and thus was vitally affected by Greek history; but unlike Dryden and Prior, he could not grasp Greek metrics and prosody, so classical poetry and drama left him largely unmoved.

Joseph Addison, on the other hand, had a perceptive understanding of Greek poetry and wrote much illuminating criticism about it in the *Tatler* and *Spectator*. Addison's role as the leader of eighteenth century Augustanism has been so overemphasized that his part in popularizing Greek studies has been lost sight of. That Addison was an excellent Greek scholar we have Tickell's word for, as well as the internal evidence of his works. While still at Oxford, he undertook a translation of Herodotus for Tonson. His library included the major Greek classics and many of the minor ones as well. When he began writing for the *Tatler*, he was conservatively Latin in interests, though he showed an acquaintance with the Greek historians, in addition to Diogenes Laertius, Pythagoras, Archimedes, Musaeus, and Phalaris. With the passing of time, however, his interest in the range of Greek literature became more apparent. *Tatler* No. 81 dealt with Greek history and literature in general. No. 90 restated the Platonic love allegory from the *Symposium*. No. 97 was an allegory of Love and Pleasure from Xenophon told in the myth of Hercules. No. 122 recounted the issues of the theater and morality with a story about Socrates and Euripides and the playing of *Hippolytus*. No. 123 initiated the long series of papers on Homer, which were to become a comprehensive classicist purview of Homeric literature.[5] From his early, sly spoofs of Greek pedantry in the *Tatler* (Nos. 158, 226), and the *Spectator* (Nos. 2, 31, and 59), he went on to serious Greek scholarship. He examined the nature and uses of allegory by Aesop, Homer, Plato, and Xenophon (*Spectator*, 35, 183, 391), discussed the Aristotelian theory of tragedy and its English application (Nos. 39-42), translated and evaluated the lyrics of Pindar (No. 160) and Sappho (No. 223), criticized the wit and form of Greek epigrams (Nos. 58, 59, 62), rescued fragments of Apollodorus (No. 203), Simonides (Nos. 209, 211), and various proverbs (Nos. 124, 189) from oblivion, and lucidly discussed the nature of the Greek language (No. 285). The first Greek quotation in *The Spectator* (No. 26), a line from Homer, soon multiplied into epigraphs from Pythagoras, Hesiod, Simonides, Theocritus, Menander, Theognis, Euripides, and long quotations from Homer. Addison noted with delight that his female readers were enchanted with his Greek and the "natural love of Latin among our common people" was becoming broadened by a love of Greek among the fashionable world. Finally, Addison's periodical papers developed a number of Greek models of behavior, notably Socrates (Nos. 23, 86, 183, 207 ff.), and so stimulated his own Hellenic enthusiasm that he planned, as Tickell tells in the Preface to the 1721 edition, a tragedy based on the trial and death of Socrates, written in true Attic style.

It is not necessary to present similar catalogs for other writers of the period from 1700 to 1750 demonstrating their Hellenic concerns. Many of them—Gray, Collins, the Wartons, Dyer,

Thomson, Akenside—are acknowledged to have felt a strong attachment to Hellas and Greek studies. Others—Gay, Bolingbroke—had tenuous attachments, if we are to judge by their literary remains, though Gay wrote crypto-Greek masques and the musical play, *Achilles,* and Bolingbroke showed a surprisingly thorough knowledge of the history of the Greek language in his letter to Pope of February 18, 1723/24. Incidentally, poor, maligned Pope, who struggled with Homer and misquoted Dionysius of Halicarnassus, apparently knew Pindar quite well (Letter of Oxford, Dec. 26, 1727). Anthony Ashley Cooper, the Third Earl of Shaftesbury, condescended to set up a program of Greek studies for the young University student with whom he corresponded in 1707-10, remarking that Greek was a "Foundation of Learning" and a "Foundation of those Lights we have" in Morality and Divinity. Chesterfield declared Greek "necessary for everybody." Goldsmith's essay "On the Study of Belles Lettres" showed a wide-ranging acquaintance with Greek language and literature with examples of poetry, drama, and oratory. Finally, it may be pointed out that Dr. Johnson, the arch-Latinist, constantly read Greek works, according to Sir John Hawkins. He even planned to enter the lists of classical scholarship by translating Aristotle, Plutarch, and several Greek historians and grammarians, and by compiling a collection of Greek apothegms as well.[6]

If we turn from individual authors to literary genres popular between 1660 and 1750, similar Greek forces are visibly operative. Foremost among these are the double influences of the Greek historiographers. On the one hand, they perpetuated a number of premises about the course of human events which became the fiber of Neo-Classical historical theory. It was the Greeks who evolved the utilitarian theory of history and it was their historiography that spread the views of climate, luxury, and the body politic already discussed in the last chapter. On the other hand, Greek historians founded the three chief schools of historiographical technique: the ecumenical (Herodotus), the politico-military (Thucydides), and the anecdotal-biographical (Xenophon). Greek historians therefore influenced both the world-view of the classicist and the kind of historical writing he undertook.[7]

The historical pessimism of Swift and his circle was one result of the former influence. Swift's essay on Herodotus shows plainly the esteem in which "the father of historians" was held; constant citations of him by Swift, Thomas Hearne, and others show that veneration for him had not yet been lessened by the disdain of later, more sophisticated historians. The Herodotan premises of time, climate, luxury, and decline were readily embraced: by Temple, Clarendon, Dennis, and many others, who cited him directly as authority. Likewise, the prestige of Thucydides and Xenophon made them ultimate mentors in political affairs and civic morality; classicists relied on their wisdom with unreserved confidence. Polybius, closely akin to them in spirit and political theme, was accepted as the third Greek authority on government and, even more than Plato, was used as a model for political theory in the years after 1660. Dryden's praise of Polybius is a typical expression of the classicist's opinion of him. Thus, Herodotus, Thucydides, Xenophon, and Polybius were in large measure the classical historians who most directly determined the basic political and cultural assumptions of the Neo-Classicists.

Neo-Classical historiography also showed Greek influence. *The History of the Rebellion*, by Edward Hyde, Lord Clarendon, was Thucydidean in its delineation of the single state in the throes of military upheaval and political machinations. The *History of My Own Time*, by Gilbert Burnet, was like Xenophon with its personal biases determining the presentation of a limited perspective on social and political change. The Plutarchan model is evident in a number of historical biographies: Aubrey's *Brief Lives*, Walton's *Lives*, the life of Henry Hastings, and so on. It was only the ecumenical or "universal" history that was not imitated by Neo-Classicists until late in the eighteenth century, though the Restoration era brought the apogee of chronological, "universal" histories that outdid Herodotus; Stillingfleet, Sir Isaac Newton, Thomas Burnet, and a host of others wrote these Christianized versions of ecumenical history.

Greek history had other effects, besides its shaping of Neo-Classical cultural perspective and historiographical form. It stirred the imaginations of poets and playwrights, who culled from its pages suitable subjects for their literary exercises. Some of the lyrics of Dryden and Prior deal with themes from Hellenic history. Thomas Sprat's versification of the account of the Plague in Thucydides, *The Plague of Athens* (1659), ran through a half dozen editions before 1700. People and events from Greek history were the stuff of which many popular plays were made.[8] And, of course, there were the hordes of allusions to Greek history in pamphlets, such potboilers as Goldsmith's *History of Greece*, and a number of operas dealing with Alexander and Thaïs.

Greek poetry left its mark on English literature from 1660 to 1750 as surely as Greek history did on English thought. Homer challenged several would-be epic poets, such as Blackmore; he was translated partially by Dryden and Tickell and more fully by Pope; and the mock epic tradition of the pseudo-Homeric *Battle of the Frogs and Mice* provided a stimulus for Parnell, Pope, and Fielding. The Aesopian fable was adapted or imitated by Dryden, Rochester, Swift, Gay, and Bernard Mandeville. Anacreon was imitated by Cowley, Parnell, and Prior; Callimachus by Prior; Theocritus by Dryden and Gay. Pindar became the ideal of a host of imitators.[9] Whatever evaluation the critic may place on Anglo-Hellenic poetry of the period, he must admit there was an ample supply of it.

There was also much interest in the Greek tragedians following the new editions of the 1660s and 1690s. Some of the fascination that Greek tragedy exerted for English writers may have been due in part to the continental revival of interest generated by Racine and spread to England by St. Evremond among others. In any case, playwrights hastened to adapt the ancient tragedies, and audiences thronged to see them. Dryden's *Oedipus*, for example, was on the boards virtually without interruption from 1701 to 1730 and it was often revived after that. Other versions of Aeschylus, Sophocles, and Euripides appeared and reappeared.[10] In addition to the direct imitations and translations of Greek tragedians, there were many plays loosely based on Hellenic history and legend. The Persian wars and the legends of Troy were particular darlings of English play-makers.[11] Librettists for the fashionable operas of the period lost little time in filling their works with admixtures of Greek history and legend. Purcell, for instance, set Dryden's *Oedipus* and "Alexander's Feast" to music.[12] At least a dozen popular operas between 1700 and 1745 capitalized on the Hellenic vogue.[13] There were also masques, interludes, pantomimes, and divertissements.[14]

The extent of the English playgoer's delight in things Greek may be judged by a list of the productions available to him in a single month—November 1736. Beside such standard dramatic fare as *The Spanish Fryar, The Double Dealer, Cato, The London Merchant, The Beggar's Opera, The Beaux' Stratagem,* and *Jane Shore,* the theatergoer could choose from an exotic variety of Hellenically inspired entertainments: Dryden's *Oedipus, Timon of Athens, Apollo and Daphne, Atalanta, Amphitryon, The Rape of Proserpine, The Fall of Phaeton, The Rival Queens,* or *Perseus and Andromeda.* Or he might choose an entertainment with an *intracte* dance by Cyclopes or Furies and a choral presentation of "The Passion of Sappho" and "Alexander's Feast."[15]

Among the literary products of neo-Hellenic bent around 1700 must be mentioned the *Athenian Mercury,* or *The Athenian Gazette;* its derivative, *The Athenian Oracle;* and *The Athenian News.* Along with *The British Apollo,* which was a clearinghouse for some poets and many poetasters, these periodicals tried to capitalize on the current vogue and admiration for things Greek. The Athenian Society, a group of "curious" thinkers in more ways than one, organized in 1690 to explore such fascinating topics as whether Adam was a giant, why equine excrement was quadrilateral, and whether Negroes would be resurrected with black or white skins. In *The His-*

tory of The Athenian Society, Charles Gildon explained the
origin of the society's title: Athens was the home of every
Greek writer, thinker, and politician of note (including Homer
and Herodotus) ; it was a "place of Study . . . from thence was
all Europe civiliz'd." Gildon gave a chatty résumé of Greek
thought and literature and declared that the glorious tradition
of Greek inquiry was now removed to England. Motteux, in
a dedicatory poem, stated that the Society had removed the
intellectual climate of Athens to the north. And Swift's Pin-
daric ode clinched the case. The wisdom of the Society was
published in the *Mercury* from 1690 to 1697; the collected
Mercuries were published under the title of *Gazette*; and the
excerpted *Mercuries* were reprinted as *The Athenian Oracle.*
In 1710 John Dunton began the ill-fated *Athenian News,* in
competition with the *Tatler*; but the old formula of the
Mercury was amended and the *News* failed, despite its dedication to satisfying the reader's "Athenian Itch" (intellectual
curiosity) .

Certainly, if sheer bulk is a basis for generalizing, one may
say that popular culture in England between 1660 and 1750
was directly affected by Greek historiography, poetry, and
drama; and quantitative criteria also indicate the importance
of Greek geography, medicine, and criticism. Extensive catalogs of minutiae—references, allusions, quotations of Greek
sources—can be made to demonstrate that English geographers
relied on Strabo and Pausanias, that English physicians drew
from Hippocrates and Galen. And the vital influence of Aristotelian and Longinian literary principles in molding Neo-
Classical opinion and literature is now well known through
the scholarship of Ker, Atkins, and others.

Possibly the most penetrating effects of Hellenism on Neo-
Classical beliefs were those constituents of Greek philosophy
that were absorbed into English thought following the Restoration. Evanescent though such philosophical influences may
be, a number of critical studies have successfully indicated
the importance of various schools of Greek philosophy in forming the rationales of leading thinkers of the seventeenth cen-

81

tury. The concepts of the Cambridge Platonists, the ethical tenets of the Stoics, Pyrrhonistic scepticism—all have been shown to have significance within the configuration of Neo-Classical thought after 1660. It may be unnecessary to point out that English classicists derived many of their posits directly from the Greek founders of philosophical systems (Plato, Aristotle) or from the Greek followers of those systems (Epictetus *et al.*) .

Of the various Hellenic philosophies, the one that left the most distinctive yet varied imprint on English Neo-Classicism is the one that has received the least specific attention by scholars: Epicureanism. Though the teachings of Epicurus are known to have been widely disseminated after 1660, and though Swift and others have attested to the spread of Epicureanism in the times of Charles II, literary critics have been inclined to assume that it was a courtly, dilettantish hedonism and to let it go at that. In point of fact, Epicurean physics, epistemology, and ethics not only thematically impressed Neo-Classical thought but directly led to the development of several types of literary investigation.

The extensive writings of Epicurus, now largely lost, were substantially the same in the seventeenth century as they are today.[16] There were two main sources of Epicurus' teaching, both re-edited and reprinted from Byzantine and Renaissance manuscripts; these were Diogenes Laertius' *Lives of the Philosophers* and Lucretius' *De Rerum Natura*. Additionally, Pierre Gassendi's *On the Life and Death of Epicurus* was printed in London by the mid-seventeenth century; and St. Evremond's essays supplemented it with the Gallicized Epicureanism that Gassendi propounded and that Charles II absorbed during his French exile. It is the degenerate version of Epicurean hedonism—"Eat, drink, and be merry . . ."—with which Charles and his circle are associated that commentators have emphasized to the exclusion of more important components of Epicurean thought.

To attempt to summarize Epicurean philosophy here is neither feasible nor necessary. Modern readers may find the collected remains of Epicurus' works in several well edited versions, the reading of which takes only an hour or two.[17] Or if he prefers, he can find most of the chief premises of Epicurus' system in a few seventeenth century works: Hobbes' *Leviathan* (Part I, 1-16); Dryden's verse translations of Lucretius; and Temple's "Upon the Gardens of Epicurus." W. J. Oates' brief précis of Epicurean tenets may serve for guideposts to the short examination of Epicureanism and Neo-Classicism possible below. Oates writes:

> . . . what Epicurus sought primarily to do was to rid men of certain besetting fears which tainted their lives, namely the fear of the gods which led to superstitious enormities, and fear of death with all its concomitants. Once rid of these fears by an increasing consciousness of what is implied in the view that everything consists of atoms and void, man is able to achieve peace of mind—inner calm and security—which is his final desideratum, the best of pleasures. Epicurus also urges a careful discrimination among the several pleasures and categorically rejects such pleasures as may be momentarily intense but which are followed by attendant pain. Hence he argues for the principles of the mean, or moderation, the joys that accrue from friendship, and the advantages of living a simple life, even a withdrawal from active participation in life, as is summed up in the famous maxim, λάθε βιώσας, "Live unknown." Only by a rigorous development and discipline of the will can these precepts be followed.[18]

To implement his basic ethical concepts, Epicurus developed the materialistic physics of Democritus, borrowed the pleasure-pain principles of Cyrenaic hedonism, and fused them into a system provable by sensory perception and the exercise of reason. Though often condemned as an atheist, Epicurus was not an atheist in any sense. He postulated a "perfect" thus noninterventionist god, and his materialistic conception of the soul as an arrangement of atoms that dissipate at death precluded any notion of personal immortality. But there was nothing in Epicurus' theology that would offend Christians of a liberal mind; Saint Paul's epistles are asserted to have drawn heavily upon Epicurean doctrines, in fact.[19]

In Restoration literature, the assumptions of Epicurean physics may be seen in Hobbes' *De Corpore* as well as the *Leviathan*; in Dryden's "Song for Saint Cecilia's Day" most obviously and in submerged metaphors elsewhere (though Dryden made a show, in the Preface to *Sylvae*, of repudiating Lucretian–Epicurean physics); and scattered throughout the publications of the Royal Society. It was Epicurean assumptions that Swift assaulted in "The Mechanical Operation of the Spirit" and Johnson outreasoned in the concluding chapters of *Rasselas*. Epicurean epistemology is present not only in the *Leviathan* but is vital in Locke's *Treatise Concerning Human Understanding* and Shaftesbury's *Characteristics*, and Hume's *Inquiry* (xi) employs Epicurus as a spokesman.

The ethical ideals of Epicureanism, most totally espoused in Temple's essays, became fragmented and so affected many Neo-Classical works. Ironically enough, though Swift consciously disputed Epicurean philosophy, he made the practices of his Houyhnhnms conform to Epicurus' ideas of proper attitudes toward death, sexual intercourse, justice, society, and goodness. Addison's Sir Roger de Coverley represented a practical English version of the Epicurean gentleman; and the ideal of behavior incessantly emphasized by Shaftesbury, Chesterfield, and other "ethical" writers reverberated with Epicurus' maxims. Practicing Epicureans of the period between 1660 and 1800 included not only Charles II and Temple, but Clarendon, Pope, Gray, Gibbon, and Horace Walpole, not to mention the Cyrenaic hedonists: Rochester, Bolingbroke, Wilkes, Churchill, and the rest.

Many of the leitmotifs of Neo-Classical literature are traceable to the Epicurean source. The preoccupation with "reasoning" away the fear of death, the insistence on prudence and moderation, the deprecation of sexual love and the praise of friendship, and the stress on practical experience—these were indebted to Epicurean emphases. Moreover, the sequence of

84

tracts that traced the development of religion or the evolution
of language or the concept of law often arose from Epicurean
matrices.[20] The ramifications of Epicurus' teachings are ubiquitous in literature between 1660 and 1800, often consciously
put there by the writer, more often probably not. Of the leading Neo-Classicists, only Dr. Johnson appears to have consistently dispelled the tenets of the insidious philosophy,
though some of his practices—notably the gastronomic—
approached the borders of Cyrenaic hedonism.

Even from the limited amount of evidence presented above,
it seems clear that the English classicist of the Restoration and
early Georgian periods considered his world truly attuned to
the harmony of the Attic scale. From the interest in new
editions of Greek authors to literary translations and adapta-
tions to such quasi-intellectual entertainments as the masques
and the *Mercury* to the revival of Epicureanism, all signs
point to the conclusion that the Neo-Classicists considered their
classical interest as much Greek as Roman. They believed
themselves as genuine Hellenophiles as later generations declared themselves to be, and their interest in Greek literature
and thought determined a noteworthy part of their own.

But the question asserts itself: how "true," how "genuine"
was English literary Hellenism of this period? Did the Neo-
Classicists really empathize with Greek culture or did they
see it from their provincial English vantage point and wrench
from it, only to distort, those elements superficially appealing
to them. Most nineteenth and twentieth century critics have
been inclined to consider them pseudo-Hellenes or Hellenophiles at best who failed to understand the Greek mind for
what it was. Certainly, the early eighteenth century concept
of ancient Greece was not precisely that of the English Romantics, the Victorians, or the scholarly classicists of twentieth
century America and England.[21] Nor can the question be an-
swered by computing quantities. To enumerate the various
works from 1660 to 1750 that contained Greek references or
imitated Greek forms and attitudes may reveal the range or
breadth of Hellenic influence, but it cannot indicate the depth

of that influence. Impressive lists of Hellenic influences in contemporary America could be drawn up—from best-selling novels about Theseus and Socrates to television presentations of *Medea* and motion pictures based on Homer and Apollonius of Rhodes—but it would prove little about the intrinsic Hellenism of American culture. The presence of the *Iliad* on college reading lists, the Greek Revival post-office, and the Polybian elements of the Constitution of the United States hardly prove that contemporary American culture is "Hellenic" in the imitative, classical sense of the word.

One must begin to assess the Hellenism of the Neo-Classicists by realizing its eclecticism. Quite obviously no dynamic nation can straiten itself by the self-imposition of the laws, mores, and taste of a dead culture and by blindly imitating artistic and social modes. At the same time, historical continuity, intellectual influence through literature, and basic human nature make it impossible for a dynamic nation to subsist entirely within its private historical tradition. The configuration of events, ideas, and people that was eventually designated as "Greek" was actually two thousand years of the history of disparate societies and unlike individuals, grouping and regrouping in compliance with circumstance and will. Just as there really was no "Greece" or "Greek" literature—just the interactions of the polyglot peoples in the geographical region they themselves called "Hellas" and their records of those interactions—so there was no essential "Greek" attitude or spirit for the Humanist or Neo-Classicist or Romantic to divine. Out of the varied riches and poverty of a literature definable solely by the common dialect it was composed in, successive generations took what was of use to them and ignored the rest. Thus the English humanists of the Renaissance took Greek nationalism (chauvinism), ideals of personal heroism, the conception of a cyclic pattern in human and national affairs, and a refined appreciation for the bucolic. This was their Hellenism. To the English Romantic, Hellenism was the Greek's joyfully spontaneous individualism, his passion for physical sensation and emotional expression, his pleasure in the plastic arts, and his primitive simplicity and innocence, expressed in mythology. The Humanist and the Romantic, each in his turn, looked into the depths of Greek literature and, Narcissus-like, saw reflected there his own face.

So did the classicist of the late seventeenth and early eighteenth centuries. He looked into Hellenic letters and they spelled out his own beliefs. In Plato he found a rational, orderly universe, a confidence in man's reasonable faculties, a distrust for the passions. In Homer he saw disapproval of human savagery and superstition and a code of bravery and integrity. Aristotle and Strabo showed the comprehensive methodicity of the man with disinterested judgment and universal concerns. Hippocrates displayed a scientific objectivity about the human body and human society and the factors controlling them. Herodotus and Thucydides propounded a view of historical destiny and political procedure. Pindar described proper civic conduct, and Aesop's moralistic tales provided universal truths about human nature. Greek orators warned of human error, and Greek dramatists showed the ill consequences of it. Everywhere in Hellenic literature, the English classicist found *language* the agency for discovering an intelligible world, his own world.

This was the spinal cord of Neo-Classical Hellenism—a preoccupation with Greek philology. It moved Dryden, Prior, and Pope to labor over translations, anxiously collating texts and appealing to experts for information. It was the nerve of the Phalaris controversy, as all the principal combatants knew, though the general public did not. It stimulated the lexicography of the Restoration era and the translations of the Queen Anne decade. It animated Dryden's prefaces on translation, Swift's linguistic parodies, Gray's *Correspondence*. Unlike the Hellenists of other periods, those between 1660 and 1750 saw knowledge of the Greek language as the most important constituent of their Hellenism.

As a consequence, most of the Neo-Classicist's energy went not into rhapsodizing over broken columns and the lost vales of Arcady or spurning the Turks in ottava rima but in poring over Greek texts and reconstructing syntax. Plenty of Greek syntax needed it. The polymaths of the fifteenth, sixteenth, and seventeenth centuries had amassed an imposing array of Greek works in various collections. They had added their notes and comments. But they did not eliminate the errors of generations of tired copyists and bored anthologers, so the job of correcting fell to the Greek scholars of the late seventeenth and eighteenth centuries.

Undoubtedly foremost among these was Richard Bentley. Protégé of John Evelyn, friend of Locke and Boyle, and colleague of Newton, Bentley was the last of the great classical scholars of the Renaissance and the first great textual critic of the modern era. In 1690, in his youth, he published a prefatory letter to Mill's edition of the Byzantine chronologer, John Malelas, that revolutionized Greek dramatic scholarship. Bentley clarified the canon and texts of Aeschylus and Euripides in particular; and a little later he worked on the Greek poetic texts with reconstructions that one critic has called little short of miraculous. Homeric scholarship was radically changed when Bentley, with brilliant imagination, rediscovered the digamma and restored it to the Homeric text. He helped Barnes with his edition of Euripides, gave assistance to the German Latinist, George John Graevius, with an edition of Callimachus, and furthered Rudolph Küster's edition of Suidas. He planned an edition of Greek lexicons to promote Greek learning: those of Hesychius, Suidas, and a composite volume of Julius Pollux, Erotian, and Phrynicus. His scholarly rejoinders to Boyle's Phalaris pamphlets, ill-tempered though they were, contained masterfully scholarly analyses of Greek syntax and discussions of Greek philological development that demonstrated stupendous classical knowledge. Swift and Pope, confronted with Bentley's linguistic superiority, were reduced to attacking his personality and "pedantry." The philological nucleus of the Phalaris literature—by Temple, Boyle, Bentley, Swift, Arbuthnot, and Pope—is readily perceivable.

Greece

There were other groups of eighteenth century compositions that grew from a Greek crux. Pope's efforts at translating Homer led to his encounter with the commentary of Bishop Eustathius, whose Greek completely stymied the frail Hellenist. He therefore petitioned first Thomas Parnell and William Broome, then John Jortin, to aid him in translating Eustathius, and another complex of Greek–English scholarship developed. Parnell, "an accomplished Grecian," not only helped Pope translate Eustathius; he wrote a life of Homer to preface Pope's *Iliad* [Pope had to rewrite it several times for style] and he composed his *Life of Zoilus* to satirize Dennis, Bentley, and other critics. *The Battle of the Frogs and Mice* was a byproduct of Parnell's Homeric studies for Pope; and various other poems—Parnell's "To Mr. Pope" and Gay's "To Mr. Pope on His Return from Greece"—were the direct products of the publication of the *Iliad*. Venal though they were, John Jortin's labors with Homeric and Eustathian syntax located some errors in Pope's scholarship that were corrected in subsequent editions; and Jortin published under his own name in 1731 *Miscellaneous Reflections*, a collection of scholarly parsings and constructions of numerous Greek and Latin texts.

The scholarly concerns of Thomas Gray and his circle with Greek language and literature also effected a number of literary productions. Gray's Greek scholarship was penetrating and exact, as his *Correspondence* amply shows: he made an elaborate chart of Greek writers in chronological order, dated by Olympiads; he translated Greek epigrams for Richard West and criticized his now lost tragedy, *Pausanias*; he wrote critiques of Herodotus, Lysias, Strabo, and Aeschylus. His *Odes* were the best of all the imitations of Pindar written after 1700 in England, and they may be the best in English. In any event, Gray's Pindarics, like Cowley's, derived from a close scrutiny of the Greek text; and if Gray surpassed Cowley, it was due to his superior Greek scholarship and the advances made in Greek learning after 1660. Gilbert West's translations of Pindar were good enough to win the respect of Dr. Johnson (where

Gray's *Odes* did not), and some of the credit must go to Gray for stimulating West's interests. He also encouraged William Mason's preoccupation with Greek literature: Mason's *Sappho* and *Pigmalion* carried the writing of Hellenistic musicales into the 1770s. Gray further exchanged copies of Greek authors with Thomas Warton and made suggestions for Warton's *History of English Poetry*, which stressed heavily the role of Greek literature and learning in England, as did Lord Monboddo's *Of the Origin and Progress of Language* (1773-92).

The conclusion is inescapable. The intellectual atmosphere of England was fanned by Attic winds and Alexandrian gusts long before the mid-eighteenth century. It need hardly be pointed out that Hellenism was an attitude held by only a few hundred educated Englishmen or that serious Greek scholarship was the property of a few dozen. Yet, these were the men who wrote the books of the day and helped formulate political and literary creeds. Their importance as spokesmen of the times cannot be ignored, nor can the Hellenic direction of their literary interest. If that interest was more scholarly than emotional, more syntactic than aesthetic, it was nonetheless a vital and productive interest.

4 · Rome

Although in many ways the Neo-Classicist's obsession with historical authority and his enthusiasm for things Greek complemented each other, in one important way—the formulation of personal codes of conduct—they did not permit a very satisfactory reconciliation. It was partially because of this failure that the Neo-Classical emphasis after 1700 came to be put more strongly on Roman culture than Greek so that eighteenth century England was led to call itself "Augustan" rather than "Periclean" or "Alexandrian."

For a time during the Restoration decades, it seemed that an Hellenic epithet might well outweigh the poets' choice of "Augustan." Charles' accession to the throne may have initially seemed analogous to the era of Roman history when Octavius assumed command of the destiny of the Empire; certainly the military and political past encouraged the classically oriented writer to stress the cultural or national similarities. But historiography taught that history held a double value for its reader: it provided a cultural perspective through its factual blueprints of the rise and fall of nations, and it presented models of behavior in the famous men of the past. The classicist was implicitly induced to search for patterns of conduct among historical figures in order to fuse in his own life a cultural outlook with a utilitarian ethical code. Presumably the most useful code of behavior would be illustrated by some outstanding figure of the past in an era historically parallel to the present.

In casting the Restoration era as another Augustan Age, the English classicist assumed a logical obligation which he frequently did not acknowledge. If his era was "Augustan," then proper models of conduct most reasonably could be found in the Augustan Age of Rome. And for a while, English writers did hold up Augustus Caesar as a model for Charles and Horace or Virgil as models for themselves. The practice was inconsistent, however, as Dryden's "Astraea Redux" demonstrates with its heterogeneous "examples" of heroic conduct drawn from Hebrew, Greek, and Roman mythology and history.[1] In positing some historical model of conduct to serve as a guide for his own age, the Restoration writer often forgot or ignored his Augustan cultural analogy to develop a Greek hero as a personal archetype.

The Greeks chosen were of a sort to appeal to the most influential consumers of the writer's wares, namely Charles II and his aristocratic circle. The concern of Dryden, Otway, and other Restoration authors in prescribing a code for the non-aristocrat to follow was very slight indeed, at least before 1688. They aimed to please the nobility and to set up historical models of gallantry and bravado to pique them.[2] There were several Hellenic figures who might have filled this function—for instance, Epaminondas, Leonidas, Alcibiades, or Pericles—and most had minor vogues.[3] The most popular Greek hero in Restoration England, however, was Alexander the Great.

That English monarchists took pleasure in contemplating the career of the god-like Alexander was quite natural. The exploits of the great man could be found in the many editions of Arrian's *Expeditions* and Quintus Curtius's *Actions of Alexander the Great*, as well as in Plutarch and Cornelius Nepos. In France, Racine's Greek plays helped to encourage a French admiration for Alexander and his barbarian opponents, an admiration that was not discouraged by Louis XIV's fondness for seeing similarities between himself and the Hellenic conqueror of the world. Saint Evremond's essays served to spread enthusiasm for *le grand* Alexander in England; and the spate of poems, plays, and operas about Alexander and various regal adversaries was one consequence of the fad. Inevitably, the Alexandrian vogue ended with the Glorious Revolution. The imprudence of exalting an absolute monarch become obvious to literary men in light of political trends of the time, and classicists began to reassess their ideas of which men in history constituted the most efficacious models of conduct.

Rome

Other Greek archetypes of behavior, while less monarchist and absolute, still retained aristocratic connotations even as they strove to appeal to wider audiences. On the one hand, such men as Socrates and Epicurus provided examples of non-political behavior. On the other, Epaminondas and Miltiades showed the glories—and distresses—of men involved in the public business of their country. Lord Clarendon and General Monck may have found solace in their contemplation of the Greek generals and their fates, but the public at large could find little in the way of principles of conduct in those examples. Sir William Temple could extol the life of withdrawal counselled by Epicurus, but it was scarcely feasible for everyone among the aristocracy or anyone of the laboring classes. Political detachment might have been possible under William and Mary, but in the days of Anne, no devoted classicist could have praised withdrawal from the "world" of political involvement and still felt himself using the classics wisely.

After 1700, then, Greek history and biography were still consulted for their wisdom, but the roster of Greek heroes and citizens failed to provide an attractive, workable model of conduct for the newly enlarged groups of Whigs, city-dwellers, and merchants. The search for historical archetypes consequently turned English eyes more squarely on Rome, and the resuscitation of the "Augustan" political analogy encouraged English classicists to look with special interest at the noble Romans of the first century B.C. The ensuing interest produced a body of attitudes that contained the most important neo-Roman elements of eighteenth century English classicism.

If the Neo-Classicist came to be discriminating in his selection of Hellenic values, he was just as carefully selective in his use of Roman civilization for a model. The rise and fall of Rome was a cultural archetype, but the English classicist was by no means the fawning admirer of all affairs Roman that some critics have made him out to be. Though he was intimately acquainted with the details of Roman history, he made constant value judgments of men and events; and in appropriating Roman practices or principles for use in contemporary English life, political and personal, he strenuously rejected many "Roman" values and procedures.

English admiration for Rome as a culture was based on several characteristics stated by British historians from Eacherd to Gibbon. Roman civilization was admired for its stability, its durability, its material prosperity and achievement, and its "strength." These general characteristics were attributed to various specific procedures or social and political structures. Thus, to the classicist, Roman stability was due to tripartite balanced government and a carefully codified legal system. Its durability was the result of a sensible and scrupulously observed constitution and carefully inculcated political values. Roman prosperity was caused by solidly established agricultural practices and the regulation of monetary policy by the Senate. Its art and artifacts were the product of a national spirit or "genius" in part the result of climate. And Roman "strength" was synonymous with "public spirit" or "patriotism."[4]

Simultaneously, English classicists dismissed those elements in Roman culture they disapproved of, even though many of these contributed mightily to the very stability, durability, prosperity, and strength the classicist extolled. The importance of the military dictatorship in Rome was ignored, and the standing armies that made Rome "strong" were anathema to the Briton. Roman "prosperity" was often the companion of usury and plutocracy, but the classicist's eyes were shut to that fact as they were to the system of slavery that underpinned the Roman economy. Furthermore, Roman polytheism and its part in stabilizing Mediterranean civilization were widely ignored by Neo-Classicists of Christian persuasion.

This is not to say that English classicists glossed over the weaknesses of Rome in order to glorify it as the nonpareil of nations. They were well aware of the vicious and bloodthirsty aspects of Roman culture: the bestial hedonism of the "mob," the cynical demagogues, the famines and plagues, the civil wars. But many aspects of Roman culture they thought usefully applied to English culture; and they adopted a theory of cultural causation which permitted them to find some factors relevant and others not. In a final analysis, the classicist believed Rome's greatness to be the consequence of the moral character of its "great men." It was this belief that led the English "Augustan" to search for a Roman prototype, whose "public spirit" accounted for the virtues of the state. If a Roman model could be found and successfully emulated, English civilization might gain an added strength, durability, and prosperity.

Each of the lustrous public names of the Augustan Age of Rome found its English admirers.[5] Yet most of them lacked something or other to make their owners a generally and popularly acclaimed favorite. Atticus was an elegant and sympathetic figure to many English aristocrats, but he was also an Epicurean who chose to remain aloof from the vital struggles of his time.[6] Brutus was the example par excellence of self-sacrificing public spiritedness, but his life did not present a very extensive model for those who sought solutions short of regicide. Pompey presented a noble mien to British eyes, but his military professionalism and his autocratic manner—to say nothing of his conspicuous failures—marred his perfection. Dryden's popular tragedy was a graphic representation of Anthony's limited usefulness as a public model of behavior. Cicero far exceeded most of his fellow Republicans in his qualifications for symbol. He had enjoyed a long-standing popularity as a rhetorical model in England, and his incorporation of both Stoical and Epicurean principles argued for his acceptance by both philosophical sects.[7] Yet, the historical Cicero was not totally free of the taint of opportunism and temporization; and if his ultimate sacrifice and heroism were unquestionable, they lacked a certain dramatic flair. Moreover, Cicero was something of a professional talker and politician, a breed that was not extravagantly admired in the age of Bolingbroke and Wharton.

With the acting of Addison's *Cato* in 1713, the era formalized its symbol in the person of Cato Uticensis, whose death had marked the end of Republican Rome and the birth of the new imperialistic stage of Roman history. Cato's great success as a model for both Whig and Tory circles was due to several factors. The historical Cato was a folk hero to Romans of the Augustan and post-Augustan eras, and he was venerated as a legend in centuries of tradition known to the Neo-Classicists. He was useful as a political model to diverse Englishmen—the layman as well as the politician, the bourgeois as well as the aristocrat. The details of his life were well enough known to make him a practical model for daily life as well as critical situations, for private as well as public behavior. His life presented such a diversity of activities that he could be used as a constantly manipulable symbol with shifting emphases and allusive values. An examination of these factors shows why Cato became a preeminent neo-Roman symbol in English literature for several decades.

First of all, Cato enjoyed a vast bulk of laudatory biography and history, beginning with some composed in his own time. The Cato family was inextricably involved with the great Republican era of Roman history and shared some of the credit for those personal virtues which made Rome the nation so celebrated in Polybius' histories. The first Cato, the Censor, was most famous for the fierce nationalism contained in his cry in the Senate, "Carthago delenda est," at the time of the Punic Wars; but his prototypal patriotism also animated his history of Rome and his tract on agriculture, and the austerity of his private life, celebrated later by Plutarch, was a model for his countrymen.[8] His great-grandson, Cato Uticensis, preserved the personal and public virtues of the clan, opposing the tyranny of Julius Caesar until he was defeated in Africa and died by his own hand in Utica.

For a while, Cato's virtues were somewhat relative to the political position of his commentator. Caesar wrote some virulent pamphlets attacking him, the *Anti-Cato*, which were so extreme that Cicero turned them against their author by privately copying and circulating them. Cicero's own affection for Cato, his political rival, was limited; but his *Letters to*

Atticus praised Cato for his nobility and sacrifice to liberty. Whether he was an admirer of Caesar, Atticus, or Cicero, therefore, the English Neo-Classicist found himself confronted with the figure of Cato.

Roman historians also furnished abundant material for English interest in Cato. Sallust's impartial comparison of Caesar and Cato provided the basis for Richard Steele's discussion of the two in *The Christian Hero* (1701).[9] Augustan historians, working under the patronage of Caesar's nephew, maintained a careful impartiality as well. Livy's opinion of Cato Uticensis was lost with the last books of his history, but he sharply criticized the reactionary policies of Cato the Censor.[10] Tacitus, writing some fifty years later, praised Cato in the *Annals* and *History* without effusion; but Livy's adapter, Florus, waxed warmer in his admiration, and historians after him—Appian, Dio Cassius, Ammianus Marcellinus—readily accepted Cato as an historical example of noble conduct.[11]

The Neo-Classicist educated by reading Roman history also found a flowering Cato cult in Latin satire, epic, philosophy and biography. Persius' satires reported that schoolboys of Rome were obliged to learn Cato's dying speech and repeat it upon sundry occasions; and Martial's epigrams contrasted the sodomitic philosophers of his own day with Cato of "brow austere."[12] Cato's role in epic literature added immeasurably to his fame. Virgil dared, in the face of Augustus, to depict Cato in the *Aeneid* giving out laws in a beatific vision of Roman glory; and Lucan's *Pharsalia*, an epic dealing with the civil wars, virtually succeeded in apotheosizing Cato to the detriment of Caesar and Pompey.[13] Lucan's uncle, Seneca, took Cato as a suitable example to illustrate his Stoic principles of steadfastness, forebearance, and courage.[14] And if Seneca did not succeed in making Cato a model for Nero, the later emperors Hadrian and Marcus Aurelius carefully patterned their actions on the virtuous example of the Noble Republican.[15]

The Ancients' admiration for Cato was summed up most lavishly in Plutarch's *Life of Cato Minor*. Read in conjunction with the rest of Latin poetry, philosophy, and history, it must have exerted a strong effect on young students like Addison and Swift. Of Cato, Plutarch wrote that he "set out to accomplish his purposes with a vigour beyond his years"; he was "imperturbable in virtue," and "masterful toward those who tried to frighten him." He "built up his body by vigorous exercises, accustoming himself to endure both heat and snow with uncovered head, and to journey on foot without a vehicle." In sickness he retired to his room in solitude and would see no one until he felt himself recovered. His "reason, self-control, courage, and sagacity" were equal to those of his great-grandfather, Cato the Censor.

> And, in general, Cato thought he ought to take a course directly opposed to the life and practice of the time, feeling that these were bad and in need of great change.[16]

Nor was Cato's legendary virtue lauded only in ancient and pagan literature. English Neo-Classicists found Cato praised by the Christian fathers from Tertullian to Augustine and Jerome.[17] He was lauded by mediaeval authors, including Chaucer and Dante, who actually made Cato the guardian of Purgatory in the *Divine Comedy*.[18] Catonic wisdom was learned by English schoolboys from 1300 to 1750 in the form of *Catonic Distiches*.[19] Cato's popularity did not fade with the advent of the Renaissance. He may have met distrust on the part of Melanchthon and Bodin, but Montaigne called him "in truth a pattern, which Nature chose out to show to what height Human Virtue and Constancy could arrive."[20] And Cato and his family found honorable depictions in the dramas of Chapman, Jonson, and Shakespeare.[21] New seventeenth century editions of such classics as the *Pharsalia* and the Roman historians and poets revived the earliest encomiums of the last Republican.[22] Wherever he turned in his perusal of the intelligible world of the past, the English Neo-Classicist found ample proof of the greatness of Cato. No other ancient hero had such complete and impeccable credentials as he.

In addition to his ubiquity, Cato had the additional advantage of being a figure that men from many walks of life could identify with themselves. A patrician, Cato nonetheless stood for the causes of justice and individual liberty that the populists championed. He came from an agricultural family background but his extended residence in Rome and his participation in its civic affairs made him urbane as well as rural. He was a private citizen first and a senator and general second. In short, he was a model whose appeal to the segments of the British populace was astonishingly wide-ranging. To such a molder of public opinion as the Whig or Tory propagandist, he therefore combined the sacrosanct values of tradition with broad popular attractiveness.

It was this combination that made him a natural subject for Addison, the writer who desired to teach men what to think and to make virtue fashionable. Cato had always been an interesting figure to Addison, even during the young classicist's residence at Oxford. It is probable that Addison composed as much as four acts of his drama while still an undergraduate there; and it is certain that as a youth during the Restoration era he was combining the present enthusiasm for Greek heroes with an anticipatory interest in Cato.[23] The *Tatler* and *Spectator* papers made desultory compliments about Cato to suit Addison's "political," "literary," or "fashionable" maxims. So when in the latter days of Queen Anne, political unrest became pronounced, upon the urging of his friends Addison exhumed his play, saw that Cato might serve as a useful example, and finished the "tragedy" for immediate production.

Pope also saw the immediacy of Cato's example. He wrote to Caryll in February 1712/13:

I have had lately the entertainment of reading Mr. Addison's tragedy of *Cato*. The scene is in Utica, and the time, the last night of his life. It drew tears from me in several parts of the fourth and fifth acts, where the beauty of virtue appears so charming that I believe (if it comes upon the theatre) we shall enjoy that which Plato thought the greatest pleasure an exalted soul could be capable of, a view of virtue itself great in person, colour, and action. The emotion which the mind will feel from this character and the sentiments of humanity which the distress of such a person as Cato will stir in us, must necessarily fill an audience with so glorious a disposition, and so warm a love of virtue, that I question if any play had ever conduced so immediately to morals as this.

Pope's certainty that a large and heterogeneous theater audience would be "stirred" by sentiment and the spectacle of virtue shows that he too acknowledged the universality of Cato as a symbol.

The acting of *Cato* and its subsequent history demonstrated the accuracy of Addison's and Pope's prediction of Cato's wide appeal. Both Whigs and Tories so identified themselves and their cause with Cato that, alas, morality was inundated by partisanship. Common to all of the periodical attacks and counterattacks, however, was the conviction of every participant that *his* view was Cato's and *his* cause the cause of "liberty." Ministers and Oxford students, Grub Streeters and country rectors, squires and royal physicians, deans and printers—everyone saw something of himself in Cato and a great deal of Cato in himself.[24]

English Augustans other than Addison shared the practice of using Cato in order to attract a wide and sympathetic audience for their views. Swift cited the example of Cato to instruct Anglicans in proper sentiments, to teach Stella principles of logic, to advise a Whig lord, and to improve his congregations at Saint Patrick's.[25] Nicholas Rowe's translation of Lucan's *Pharsalia* captured as subscribers virtually everybody from Doctors Blackmore and Garth to Lady Mary Wortley Montagu to those notorious citizens of the stage, Colley Cibber and Mrs. Oldfield.[26] Cibber's play, *Caesar in Aegypt,* was an open bid for the favor of George II and a large, generous theatergoing group.[27] And Bolingbroke, who contemned Cato in private, was quite happy to employ the conditioned reflexes accompanying mention of him in *The Craftsman.*[28] Cato's

universal appeal as a public symbol for Englishmen of the first
half of the century was best summed up by Pope's Prologue
to Addison's drama:

> While Cato gives his little senate laws,
> What bosom beats not in his country's cause?
> Who sees him act, but envies ev'ry deed?
> Who hears him groan, and does not wish to bleed?

Furthermore, thanks to Plutarch and other biographers, the
English admirers of Cato could pattern themselves on him in
their private behavior as well as their public actions. No doubt
there was more lip service paid to the austere ideal of conduct
seen in Cato than there was actual emulation of it; but a number of dedicated and intelligent men seriously proposed Cato
as a constant guide for life. Of these, the most interesting is
Jonathan Swift, whose identification with the Roman was
lifelong.

The genuineness of Swift's Catonic fixation is testified by
Remarks on the Life and Writings of Dr. Jonathan Swift, by
John Boyle, Earl of Orrery. Orrery wrote that of the great
heroes of antiquity—Socrates, Epaminondas, and the rest—
Swift venerated Cato above all others and that his admiration
was sincere though that of many other classicists was not.[29] The
greatest proof of Swift's veneration, however, lies in the constant references to Cato in Swift's writing, from his private
journals and scribblings to his public compositions.[30] The attitude he described in the 1720 poem to Stella apparently was
truly his own:

> In Points of Honour to be try'd,
> All Passions must be laid aside:
> Ask no Advice, but think alone,
> Suppose the Question not your own:
> How shall I act? is not the Case,
> How would *Brutus* in my Place?
> In such a Case would *Cato* bleed?
> And how would *Socrates* proceed?

It is probable that Swift, like Addison, developed his enthusiasm for Cato during his student days. His earliest composition, the "Ode to Sancroft" (1692), echoed Lucan in its reference to Cato, and the flip tone that characterized mention of Pompey, Caesar, and other Romans in his youthful writings was never present in his citation of Cato. The pieces composed during Swift's London years abound with allusions to Cato's public behavior; and it is implicitly clear that Swift identified his position with Cato's, even in the proposals for establishing an office of British censor.[31] Privately, Swift's actions, recorded deliberately in the *Journal to Stella*, are so like the mannerisms of Cato as Plutarch subscribed them, one has to suspect Swift of conscious imitation. Swift walked briskly in the snow with uncovered head; he dined frugally on ten-pence worth of gill ale, bad broth, and three chops of mutton; he did without a fire and felt himself in better health as a result; he saved six shillings on clothing; he was sick in bed all day and refused to see anyone until he felt himself recovered.[32] Probably the most convincing evidence of Swift's absorption with Cato is his undue irritation at the criticism leveled at the patriot's conduct by Bolingbroke, and his amazing susceptibility to flattering comparisons between himself and Cato.[33] When Mrs. Laetitia Pilkington, that proto-Becky Sharp, determined to ingratiate herself with the Dean, she wrote a birthday ode comparing him to Cato and was received with alacrity. Adoring young ladies embroidered letters to Swift with coy references to himself as Cato. And when Dr. Sheridan found himself once more in financial straits, he smoothly wrote to Swift of a "dream" about "honest Cato," nobly combatting his enemies. Even Deane Swift hauled out the analogy with Cato to please his uncle.[34]

Swift's belief in the Augustan political analogy between England and Rome and the facts of his own career may have warranted to some extent his confidence in the propriety of using Cato for a private as well as public model. But quasi-classicists who posed as Cato came in for reproofs. Bernard Mandeville castigated several such; and Henry Fielding, a sincere admirer of Cato, humorously spiked the neo-Catoes by writing of those who imitated the Censor by going about "with bare feet and sour faces."[35] Once the Augustan political analogy began to wane in popularity, those who struck the moralistic pose of Cato found themselves the butt of criticism. James Boswell suffered some rude shocks when he appropriated the Cato image. To one of his youthfully prim letters, de Guiffardière wrote in answer: ". . . lessons in virtue (lessons from a Cato! a Cato only twenty years old!) ." The entrancing Zélide turned the poignard savagely:

> I was shocked and saddened to find, in a friend whom I had conceived of as a young and sensible man, the puerile vanity of a fatuous fool, coupled with the arrogant rigidity of an old Cato.

After midcentury, Cato and his avatars were no longer courted, obviously.

The fourth characteristic of the Cato symbol, its manipulability, helped at first to popularize it and at last to destroy its effectiveness. The life of the historic Cato contained such multifarious activities that it could be used as all things to all men. During the Restoration period, Cato was primarily seen as an embodiment of Stoic—or pagan—virtue, and he was praised or attacked accordingly. John Evelyn heard him lauded from the pulpit on occasion, but many agreed with Malebranche that Cato's magnanimity was "abominable before God; whatever the Wisemen of the World may think of it."[36] In the Augustan period, this diversity of views was repeated in Swift's sermons and Steele's *The Christian Hero*, respectively. Once Cato's ambiguity as moral symbol was subjected to partisan quarrels resulting from the staging of Addison's play, confusion grew. The Whigs wished to support Cato as a symbol of "liberty" and "public spiritedness" in order to buttress the Hanover regime; the Tories emphasized the historical fact that Cato was a Republican who died opposing absolutism and tyranny (like that of George II).[37] To compound the confusion, Cato was variously used as a synonym for immortality, morality, vengeance, inhuman behavior, prurience, and cowardly suicide.[38] The inevitable happened. Public interest in Cato perished, victim to the miasma rising from a literary swamp of allusions and prejudices.

Cato's preeminence as the symbol of English neo-Romanism was never without challengers, and it lasted only thirty or forty years, at most, of the 140 years of the Neo-Classical era. During the Restoration period, the Roman Age most respected was the Augustan. In the English "Augustan Age," the Roman Republic (and Cato, the last Republican) commanded the greatest interest. In the last half of the eighteenth century, influenced by Gibbon's history, the age of the Antonines assumed the place of honor. It would be wrong to suppose that Cato was a totem of equal importance in all three periods or that he embodied all of the elements which constituted English neo-Romanisn.

From 1660 to 1800, however, British interest in Rome followed the same determinants, and the Cato literary nexus of the early eighteenth century reveals the most vital constituents of the neo-Roman strains of that phase of classicism. The core assumptions of neo-Romanism may be found in *The Freeholder's Political Catechism*.[39] Starting with a defense of the monarchy, the *Catechism* anticipates the downfall of all political systems in due course and takes up the question of cultural degeneracy: "I have read the *Roman* History, and by what I can judge, it was by Faction, Corruption, and Standing Armies." The historical example of Rome can teach the English right political principles to prevent the decay of government through "extravagance" and "luxury." Only proper national morals, the summation of the morals of the people, are a true safeguard against degeneration. And for the good and virtuous man, the highest principle is "patriotism":

> It is an Instinct as well as a Duty of Nature; the very Soil from which as from a common Mother, Mankind are nourished. . . . All Nations sink and rise in proportion as this Virtue prevails. When I read the *Roman* history I am transported with Joy, and a profound Reverence for those Worthies who sacrificed their Lives, and what was perhaps dearer to them, to the Love of their Country.

Rome

Of those worthies, Cato possessed the most apt qualifications to become a practical guide for the Englishman. He had been the epitome of self-sacrifice and patriotism, yet he was but one man, a single private citizen, in a representative republic. He lacked the ambition and thirst for fame which rendered kings suspect in their actions. He eschewed luxury and extravagance, as well as the other characteristics of the intemperate man. His reason and self-control were Neo-Classical ideals. As a model, however, Cato was not so far removed from the generality of mankind as to be a useless abstraction or an unapproachable ideal. Cato's admirers thought him a working model, a man for practical men to look to and imitate.

Those theorems in the Neo-Classical purview derived from Roman precedents were much less the result of a blind adoration of Rome than a sharp-eyed scrutiny of its history. The extrapolation of certain Roman phenomena into British culture was determined by utilitarian rather than aesthetic criteria.[40] English neo-Romanism, in the main, was more widely disseminated than neo-Hellenism because it was conceived for pragmatic purposes and because its principles were enunciated in such a way as to appeal on nationalistic grounds to as large an audience as possible. Neo-Roman principles were inherently functional, as British unity, strength, and prosperity defined functionalism. Contrary to critical assertion, neo-Romanism did not appeal primarily to smugness and complacency.[41] Though literary commentators stressed the self-congratulatory aspects of the Roman–British analogy—notably the Restoration eulogists, Atterbury, Tickell, and Goldsmith—English historians, social critics, and moralists used the analogy to raise apprehensions and self-doubts. As Cato served for an example and warning to the individual, Rome became a model and threat to England. In his virtue, Cato perished. From its glory, Rome fell. In his tears for Cato, the English classicist expressed grief at the realization of his own fate. And even as he sought to make England as long-lived a polity as Rome, he sadly acknowledged that it, too, must pass away.[42]

5 · Carthage, Alexandria, Nicaea

To the twentieth century observer, it may seem paradoxical, or even contradictory, for the leading Neo-Classicists to have professed their confidence in the lessons of secular history and their admiration for pagan heroes and at the same time to have believed themselves thoroughgoing Christians. It seemed a contradiction to some contemporary observers as well. Steele indignantly inquired, ". . . why is it that the Heathen struts, and the Christian sneaks in our Imagination (?)" Malebranche testily declared, "Saint Paul and the Primitive Christians, had doubtless more vertue than *Cato* and all the Stoicks. . . ." But in spite of such criticism, many leading English clergymen were also champions of the classics and ancient civilization. Of the Ancients, Atterbury could write:

> [They] are Men, whom the universal Applause of so many succeeding Ages has put beyond the reach of our Censure, and whom it will ever be our Happiness to admire and our Glory to imitate.

Swift's sermon, "Upon the Excellency of Christianity," unequivocally stated that "the truth of the gospel" far exceeded the philosophy and virtue of the "Gentile Sages," which were not esteemed in the early Christian era. Yet Swift could write to a young clergyman:

> Before you enter into the common unsufferable Cant, of taking all Occasions to disparage the *Heathen* Philosophers; I hope you will differ from some of your Brethren, by first enquiring what those *Philosophers* can say for themselves.[1]

The same ostensible double vision afflicted many pious laymen; in fact, only four or five of the most prominent names

Athanasius' key tenets, and *The Hind and the Panther* postulates an extensive doctrinal knowledge on the reader's part. Milton's allusions to patristic authority are everywhere, including the preface to *Samson Agonistes*, which cites Saint Paul and Gregory Nazianzen in defense of the theater. Jeremy Collier's attacks on the Restoration stage include more than a dozen citations of the Fathers and their castigations of the drama; Thomas Rymer's counterattacks refute an equal number of patristic critics.[6] Sir William Temple's essay "Upon Ancient and Modern Learning" praises Minucius Felix, Origen, and Tertullian among the Ancients and facilely declares that after Tacitus, Minucius was the best Latin stylist.[7] Swift's *A Tale of a Tub* is a dazzling array of allusions to and parodies of patristic sources.[8] Defoe, Addison, and Mandeville wrote defenses of Christianity, replete with references to Justin Martyr, Irenaeus, Clement, Polycarp, Arnobius, and myriad others.[9] Sterne's *Tristram Shandy* harkens back repeatedly to patristic doctrine for its humor, relying on the reader's knowledge of such abstruse doctrines as baptism *in utero* for pages at a stretch. Dr. Johnson's *Diaries* show that he not only read extensively in patrology but kept a list of the Fathers and their works and checked off those he owned and knew firsthand.[10] Boswell's *Life of Johnson* attests the popularity of theological disputation as a form of post-prandial entertainment in Georgian England, including arguments about patristic authority. Boswell himself whiled away the tedium of his days in Holland by disputing the points of the Athanasian Creed with Rose, his tutor. Gibbon's expertise in patristic thought and his enormous knowledge of primitive Christian literature are constantly in proud evidence in the form of footnotes to *The Decline and Fall of the Roman Empire*. The list could be considerably expanded with reference only to the literateurs of the Neo-Classical period. If ax-grinding clerics and antiquarians were also considered, the list would be infinite.

Commentators have been inclined to assume, often tacitly, that the Neo-Classicist got his knowledge of patrology third or fourthhand, depending on popular encyclopaedias and anthologies or relying on the commentaries of seventeenth century Anglican divines. Certainly one would not wish to argue that William Cave's *Apostolici, or Lives of the Primitive Fathers* (1677) or Edward Stillingfleet's *Origines sacrae* (1662) were unread and lacking popularity; there is too much evidence to the contrary.[11] But if Addison owned *Epistles of the Apostolic Fathers* (1710) and Dr. Johnson owned Cave's collections, it must not be supposed that all their knowledge came from those sources.[12] Neo-Classical libraries were generously equipped with editions of the Fathers themselves, and there is incontrovertible proof that they were read.[13]

The English clergyman or lay scholar of the Neo-Classical period had available extensive and authoritative editions of early Church literature, and records show that he took advantage of every issuance. He owned the *editiones principes* published in Rome in the sixteenth and early seventeenth centuries as a consequence of the Counter-Reformation.[14] He owned the continental *opera omnia* published in France, Switzerland, and Holland, and edited by the great names of Renaissance scholarship.[15] In England, the university presses published a steady procession of individual and collected works; and the rate increased after the Restoration of Charles. Oxford, for instance, published editions of Minucius Felix (1627, 1631, 1636); Cyprian (1682); Clement of Alexandria (1683, 1715); Tatian (1700); and Athenagoras (1706). Cambridge added, among others, Origen (1677), Eusebius (1720), and Justin Martyr (1768). London presses also produced versions of the Fathers, chiefly in translation for vulgar consumption; viz., P. B.'s *Those Two Excellent Monuments of Ancient Piety and Learning, Minucius Felix's Octavius, and Tertullian's Apology for the Primitive Christians, Render'd into English* (London, 1708). Editors of the various editions ranged from the profoundly scholarly Bentley and Thomas Gale, who did an edition of Lactantius (Utrecht, 1692) as well as the Oxford Tatian, to Jeremy Collier, who translated Cyprian, to such Grub Street Ecclesiastics as Deacon Pontius, who wrote an astonishing doggerel translation of Cyprian.

Even Dr. Johnson contemplated "a comparison of philosophical and Christian morality, by sentences collected from the moralists and fathers."[16]

In the hundreds of Neo-Classical references to patristic literature, there are no primitive works then known which are not referred to more or less regularly, even the most arcane, such as Hegesippus and Sulpicius Severus.[17] But some works were more popular than the rest; the preference of certain patrists to others may surprise the scholar. Of the ante-Nicene writers, Tertullian, Minucius Felix, Origen, Clement, Irenaeus, Cyprian, and Lactantius received special attention for a half dozen or so works.[18] Of the Nicaean fathers, Eusebius was the most constantly cited by English writers, both pro and con; Athanasius and Arius came in for much dissenting comment as well. Of the post-Nicaean writers, Gregory Nazianzen, Dio Chrysostom, and Jerome were far more often cited than their counterparts in the Western Empire: Prudentius, Orosius, and Augustine. The influence of Augustine on leading Neo-Classical works and authors is incontestable; but the fact remains that he was sparingly cited and seldom directly quoted as an authority, probably because of Protestant England's identification of him with the cause of Roman Catholicism.[19]

If the polemical and doctrinal treatises of the period are set aside, the literary uses of patristic sources by Neo-Classical writers may be divided into four general categories, one stressing historical and "classical" elements, two concentrating on the reconciliation of Christian and pagan thought, and the last deriving from the moralistic cast of Christian teaching. For the sake of reference, the categories may be termed the Factual, the Synthetic, the Apologetic, and the Didactic.

Of these uses, the Factual is both the most obvious and the most secular. In his exploration of "ancient" literature, the Neo-Classicist was gathering data to serve as the basis of opinion; and he painstakingly sifted as many sources as possible to amass the "facts" he termed "truth." If he wanted to know what the ancients ate or what medicine they took or how they embalmed the dead or built aqueducts, he took his information where he found it. Often he found it in a patrist's works, whereupon he simply listed the Father along with other, pagan sources. The most systematic use of this technique can be found in Neo-Classical histories—Hearne's *Ductor Historicus* is a case in point—but it also appears in many essays on ancient civilization and learning.[20] It is the Neo-Classicist's parodies of the technique that the modern reader probably finds most appealing, however. The ersatz documentation of such specious thinkers as Tindal and Collins is bitingly remarked in Swift's *Mr. Collins's Discourse of Freethinking; Put into Plain English for the Use of the Poor* (1713), where Origen and Minucius Felix are forcibly conjoined with Socrates, Solomon, Epicurus, Cato, and Seneca as examples of "Freethinkers." Arbuthnot's *Critical Remarks on Gulliver's Travels*, a light-hearted and learned variation of the parody, cites Julius Africanus and Clement as proof of the ancient existence of Houyhnhnms, together with multiple pagan authorities. Gay's *Trivia* embellishes its passages on sewers with a discussion of the origin of the goddess Cloacina taken from Minucius and Lactantius.[21] In another mood, Swift, Arbuthnot, and Gay were able to use the patrists quite seriously as documentation for their views. Whether seriously or humorously, the Neo-Classical use of patristic writing as a mine of facts was a necessary adjunct to the classicists' postulations about the usefulness of ancient knowledge.

Less obvious and far more revealing are the uses of patrology made when piety overbalanced antiquarianism and the classicist became submerged in the Christian. The devout classicist, troubled by problems of reconciling his spiritual beliefs with his education or the beliefs of others or the practices of his society, turned to the primitive Christians and found them preoccupied with precisely the same problems. The Englishman who was both classicist and Christian discovered that the writings of the Fathers had an astonishing degree of relevance to the present and that patristic literature was full of solutions to the dilemmas that plagued post-Restoration England. His belief in the universality of human experience was again confirmed.

Like the English gentry, Greco-Roman patricians for centuries were educated by studying the masterworks of the pre-Augustan and Augustan epochs, which of course were pagan. In the Christian era, many of those educated to classical paganism discovered the literature of revelation, Jewish and Christian. They then had to retain the old and dismiss the new, accept the new and reject the old, or fuse the two. Having accepted the teachings of revealed religion, the primitive Fathers differed, even as English Neo-Classicists differed, in their treatments of the heathen culture they were accustomed to revere. Some passionate converts—Tatian, Tertullian, Augustine—were disposed to proclaim their liberation from the errors of pagan superstition by condemning all non-Jewish and non-Christian learning.[22] Others—Origen, Minucius Felix—made plain their distaste for paganism while they argued plausibly for those parts of it which agreed with a Christian mode of life.[23] The rest of the Fathers, who well realized that the best way to convert the heathen was to avoid antagonizing them unduly, attempted a judicious fusion of Christian and pagan thought. (It may be incidentally noted that whatever course he took, the patrist risked the accusation of heresy, and a number of the most stalwart spokesmen for Christianity died excommunicant from the Church, just as some of the most outspoken defenders of Anglicanism lost preferment and honor in eighteenth century England.)[24]

The most persuasive, if not the most sophisticated, of those who used the Synthetic approach were the Fathers of the first three centuries A.D. These included Justin Martyr, Athenagoras, Theophilus of Antioch, and Clement of Alexandria. Trained as patriotic Romans or Greek philosophers, these primitive Christians hopefully composed dialogues appealing to the Antonine emperors or literate contemporaries on the grounds that pagan thought was precursor to Christian belief. Their arguments, strengthened by anagogical interpretations in many instances, attempted to synthesize Greco-Roman literature, phi-

losophy, and history with the Judeo-Christian. Their echoes
can be found in many Neo-Classical works.[25]

With the assimilation of pagan literature and philosophy,
the Fathers managed quite well. The Greek tragedians testified
to the truth of monotheism, as Aeschylus did, or, like Euripides, furnished invaluable clues about the erroneous premises
of pagan religion.[26] The Greek poets—Homer, Hesiod, Menander, *et al.*—furnished evidence of the existence and glory
of God.[27] Greek rhapsodes, political theorists, and philosophers
were trained in Egypt, where they absorbed the ancient wisdom
of the Jews, which was the basis for Hellenic thought.[28] Greek
philosophy was simply a variant of Hebraic, God-given knowledge: Clement asked, "For what is Plato, but Moses speaking
in Attic Greek?"[29] As sharers of the same sources of divine
truth, nominal pagans were in reality true believers; Justin
Martyr wrote:

> . . . those who live reasonably are Christians, even though
> they have been thought atheists; as, among the Greeks,
> Socrates and Heraclitus, and men like them; and among
> the barbarians, Abraham, and Ananias. . . .[30]

In truth, there was little difference between Socrates and Christ,
both teachers of truth, attackers of false theology, and sublime
martyrs.[31] And Cato was entirely a fit model for conduct so long
as Christians awaited on earth for the Second Coming.[32] The
Neo-Classicist found his fondness for pagan poetry and philosophy serenely sanctioned by primitive Christianity.

Profane history was quite another matter, unfortunately.
The ante-Nicene Fathers who tried to synthesize pagan records
with Jewish chronicles found they had grasped a particularly
painful nettle. Their anguished struggles were duplicated, over
and over again until at last the centuries-old controversy ex-
ploded in England during the Restoration and continued to
erupt with vehement regularity throughout the eighteenth century. It was the problem of reconciling sacred and profane
history which commanded the attention of every prominent
Neo-Classicist in England; and wrangles over chronology that

engrossed the attention of Newton, Bolingbroke, Johnson, and Gibbon to an extraordinary degree are among the most striking instances of the importance of patristic literature in the Neo-Classical age.

The history of the chronological controversy is too long to rehearse here, but it can be found elsewhere.[33] Briefly, it began when the conquered Jews, represented by Philo Judaeus and Josephus, began to present themselves to their Roman conquerors as an ancient and honorable people with a history that antedated that of Rome itself. Roman historians, confronted with records that contradicted Greco-Roman history, attempted to compose ecumenical accounts derived from all sources but found insuperable obstacles. Justin, for instance, could not fit the Jewish account of the Flood into his scheme of time, and he failed to see how the Jews could antedate the Scythians, whom everyone knew to be the oldest race on earth.[34] Realizing that the truth of revealed religion depended on justifying Jewish chronology, the Fathers hastened to try their hands at correlating the data of the Pentateuch with the records of the Greeks, Romans, and—in time—the Egyptians, the Persians, the Babylonians, and everyone else.

The patrists of the first two centuries A.D. tried to emphasize Moses the philosopher over Moses the historian, but they were firm in their insistence that he was preeminent over his heathen competition. Justin, Athenagoras, and Theophilus, as usual, employed the most tact; but Tatian and Tertullian proudly and contemptuously asserted Moses' vast superiority as a historian over all pagans, and Tatian worked out a table of dates to prove the priority of the Jewish patriarch.[35] Clement of Alexandria, still later, expanded the tables in his *Stromata*; Julius Africanus combined the records of such ancient national historians as Manetho (Egyptian) and Berosus (Babylonian) with the Jewish; and at last, Eusebius, the great synthetist, wrote his *Chronicon* to settle the matter once and for all. Discrepancies persisted, nonetheless, especially when the Goths appeared on the scene; and later Church writers—Jerome,

Hegesippus, Sulpicius Severus—continued to modify Eusebius' accounts.[36]

The many issues that attached themselves to the chronological tradition were renewed during the Renaissance. The newly discovered peoples of Asia and South America had histories that needed to be correlated with the dates of West European events. The new science questioned old assumptions about geology and the squabbles over the age of the world and the date and manner of the Great Flood were raised once more.[37] The issues became focused in England after the Restoration in part because of the formation of the Royal Society; and the avidity with which the pious consulted patrology was due in great measure to their hope of finding in the Fathers solutions to the doubts raised and often publicly exposed in the pages of *The Athenian Mercury*.

A very large number of Neo-Classical works, today considered of negligible value, were written in consequence of the concern with patristic chronology and its derivatives. The Neo-Classicists themselves considered them of prime interest and importance. Chronology was deemed a vital study by leading thinkers from Hobbes and Locke to Johnson and Burke; and virtually every important Neo-Classical treatise on education ranked it as important a subject as history.[38] Dr. Johnson even maintained chronology to be superior to history on many occasions, and he authored a preface to John Kennedy's astronomical and cosmological chronology.[39] The literature stemming from the Great Flood debates of the Restoration period was chronologically inspired: Burnet's *Sacred Theory of the Earth* and scores of other essays depended upon patristic posits.[40] The Decay-of-Nature literature, based on the Age of the World controversy, cited the computations of patristic chronology by way of proof.[41] The host of pamphlet essays asserting the historiographical excellence of Moses that were composed during the reigns of William III and Anne— by Wotton, Defoe, and others—were manifestations of Neo-Classical involvement with the issues confronted by patristic chronologers.[42] And the relevance of the chronological disputes to the literature of Deism and historiography is apparent in Bolingbroke's *Letters on the Use of History*, which scorned the work of Julius Africanus and Eusebius as "holy romances" and "pious lying." Bolingbroke's repeated references to "that vile fellow Eusebius" were calculated to discredit patristic chronology and thus Scriptural authority; the ensuing blizzard of clerical responses served to extend the fame of the Fathers and their synthetic tables all the more.[43] It would be difficult to exaggerate the importance of the Neo-Classical obsession with patristic chronology.

Though the Fathers did not provide in their chronological syntheses a very helpful weapon for the English defender of Christianity, ringed as he was by jeering Deists and Freethinkers, they did furnish in their defenses of revealed religion some persuasive logic for the pious Neo-Classicist to employ. Some of the arguments presented in the primitive apologies for Christianity were so effectively used in post-Restoration England that exponents of "natural" religion appropriated them. The Apologetic literature of early Christianity thus affected such diverse Neo-Classical writers as Swift and Shaftesbury, Addison, and Bolingbroke.

Patristic writers, themselves ringed by jeering pagans and atheists, formulated a number of arguments proving the existence of God from natural phenomena. Minucius Felix, for example, asserted that pagan religion was based on a fear of "violations" and "suspensions" in celestial order, whereas Christians found proof of God in the observable patterns of the universe:

> . . . things are so coherent, so closely combined and interconnected that, not without careful investigation of the nature of deity, you cannot know that of man. . . . Look at heaven itself, its vast expanse, its rapid revolutions, at night studded with stars, by day illumined by the sun; it brings home to you the wondrous and divine balance maintained by the supreme controller.[44]

116

Theophilus similarly argued that the order of the stars, the moon, the sun, and the revolution of the seasons were demonstrations of God's existence.[45] Athenagoras scrupulously removed connotations of pantheism from the naturalistic argument.[46] And Clement of Alexandria rhapsodized over the harmony of nature, its musical themes, the four elements combining, the insignificance of earthly musicians like Jubal and David in comparison with the melodies of nature tuned by God.[47] Strikingly close parallels to the patrists' arguments appear in such Neo-Classical works as Swift's *Further Thoughts on Religion*, Shaftesbury's *The Moralists*, Addison's *Spectator*, and Dryden's "Song for Saint Cecilia's Day."[48]

The primitive Fathers also developed the biological arguments for Divine Existence and Supreme Wisdom often found in Neo-Classical compositions. Arnobius of Sicca urged that man leave a final knowledge of things to God but that he also observe in the peculiar structure and uses of eyes, the function of hawks and spiders, the distinctive orders of plants a proof of Providential intent and arrangement.[49] Pope's *Essay on Man* (i) at once comes to mind. Tatian argued that the parts of the human body, all organically separate, show Divine control in the beauty, coherence, and organization of their parts into a whole.[50] Addison argues similarly in *The Spectator*, No. 120. Clement's inquiry as to what man could mold the flesh, string the sinews, arrange the nerves, and assemble all into a unity reminds the reader of Steele's parallel argument in *The Christian Hero* and a line of poetical questions culminating in Blake's "The Tiger."[51]

Though analogues between patristic and Neo-Classical reasoning are numerous, perhaps more directly indicative of the influence of the Christian apologists are the rhetorical similarities between some Neo-Classical treatises and the *apologiae* of the Fathers. Such works as Defoe's *The Poor Man's Plea* and *The Shortest Way with the Dissenters*, Steele's *The Christian Hero* and Swift's *The Sentiments of a Church of England Man* are well within the tradition of the patristic defense; they may be illuminated by direct comparison with apologists who trace the decline of non-Christian culture down to the present (Lactantius, Minucius Felix), or who argue for the superior merit of the Christian life (Clement), or who expatiate on doctrine and belief (Athanasius, Gregory of Nyssa). Addison's "Of the Christian Religion," which meant to demonstrate the sanctity of Christ by historical evidence and which Tickell said hoped "to add the *Jewish* to the Heathen Testimonies, for the truth of Christian history," is a specimen of the synthetic apology composed by Justin and Athenagoras. Mandeville's "Free Thoughts on Religion" is a version of the wide-ranging survey of Christian and anti-Christian thought that Cyprian and Orosius wrote. And even the kind of ironic "apology" made famous by Tertullian finds a Neo-Classical counterpart in Swift's "Argument Against Abolishing Christianity." Like their patristic antecedents, English defenders employed a range of attitudes in tones scaled from the mildly exhortatory to the astringently scornful.[52]

Finally, the moral vantage point from which the Christian Fathers wrote was the sort of lofty height well suited to the Neo-Classical commentator on society. Whether he wished to shame his fellows or laugh them into self-improvement, the English classicist was dedicated to reforming his society. In this desire, he was again allied with the primitive writers, who felt compelled to criticize the shortcomings of non-Christian behavior and suggest methods for its betterment.

The reader is nowhere more struck by the patrists' resemblance to the Neo-Classicists than in those didactic portions of their writings which point out social wrongs and suggest remedies. Not only could the criticism of the pagan theaters by Tertullian and other Fathers be excised bodily and applied to the Restoration stage, as indeed it was.[53] The Fathers were much concerned with luxurious, ostentatiously expensive clothing and its moral effect. They deplored the display of jewelry and wealth and bemoaned the surcease of ancient thrift. The venality and corruption of servants received considerable notice. And the behavior of women in general and wives in particular was much discussed. Clement's *Stromata* asserted that women who can "attain perfection as readily as men" must be educated in a proper manner; and he described in detail the proper qualities of a good wife (duty, modesty, thrift, et cetera). Personal cleanliness and exercise were desirable for everybody.[54] And sluggards could look to the sober, industrious honeybee for models of praiseworthy activity, as well as examples of God-given engineering and political skills.[55]

These concerns and these metaphors were not confined to the patrists alone; they appeared in classical pagan literature and Renaissance thought as well. But English Neo-Classicists who extolled the bee and hymnodized about it found reassurance in having the precedent of Clement, Origen, and Gregory Nazianzen.[56] In proposing seriously that women be educated with the same care as men, Defoe, Swift, Addison, and Hannah More were supported by Clement and Minucius Felix in thus flouting seventeenth century Puritan prejudice.[57] The similarities between a number of Neo-Classical works and patristic sources vary from the nearly identical to the casual. Swift's "Letter to a Young Wife," for example, is startlingly close to Chapter II of Clement's *Stromata*, where there can also be found the idea of passion rising from the body to the brain like vapors from the ground and so creating mental images and fantasies, a conceit basic to the "Digression on Madness" in *A Tale of a Tub*.[58] The resemblance between the didactic techniques and devices of the Neo-Classicists and the Fathers does not need belaboring. It is sufficient to note that, as Christian reformers, both patrists and classicists faced the same eternal human frailties; they assailed these in the same way, drawing on a common literary heritage and the traditional attitudes of their religion.

Of the theological and doctrinal elements in patristic literature and their effects on Restoration and eighteenth century secular literature, it is impossible to say much here. Their influence may be seen in many Neo-Classical works, fictive as well as factual. Fielding's Parson Adams and Sterne's Mr. Shandy are concerned in their own ways with the doctrinal problems that are to be found in Dryden's poems of faith, Swift's allegories, Addison's lay sermons in essay form, Johnson's table talk, and Boswell's *Journal*. The close tie between theological disputes and the literary productions of Restoration and eighteenth century writers may be observed in many episodes, but perhaps one instance will illustrate the interrelationship adequately.

Walter Moyle, the classicist, Whig, and sometime protégé of Dryden, became interested in Christian miracles and their authenticity in the course of his classical and ecclesiastical reading; and in a series of letters to Edward King, he documented his doubts regarding the Miracle of the Thundering Legion, originally recounted by Eusebius. After Moyle's death, Edmund Curll included these letters in *The Works of Mr. Moyle* (London, 1726-27). Moyle's questioning of miracles, one of the crucial proofs of the truth of Christianity, horrified a number of staid clergymen—including William Whiston and Thomas Woolston—who wrote replies. Thomas Hearne, as an eminent historian and pious Christian, penned a criticism of Moyle's argument which quoted the Fathers in support of miracles; and Hearne in turn was assaulted by Edmund Curll, whose truculent comments on patristic authority were plainly anti-Catholic.[59] Conyers Middleton, attempting to breech this unfortunate clash between classicism and Christianity, wrote a series of pamphlets "Concerning the Miraculous Powers Which Are Supposed to have Subsisted in the Christian Church from the Earliest Ages" (London, 1747, 1749, 1751). Middleton's compromise, which asserted that miracles ceased to happen after the apostolic era, was read by Edward Gibbon as a young man and started the sceptical reasoning recorded in Gibbon's *Autobiography* and immortalized in the account of Christianity and its miracles contained in his *History of the Decline and Fall*.[60]

This skein of influences connecting patristic literature with Neo-Classical thought may appear to be a singular entanglement but it is actually one of many threads that interwove Christian ideology with the fabric of Neo-Classicism. Even those like Shaftesbury, Bolingbroke, and Gibbon, who thought Christian beliefs an inferior stuff, were forced by their education and intellectual milieu to include it in their patterns of thought. For men like Dryden, Swift, Pope, and Addison, the whole cloth of the mind was the weaving of a Christian warp with the woof of classical knowledge.

If he would understand the organic whole of Neo-Classical thought, the modern reader must begin by acknowledging the inseparability of its Greco-Roman and its Judeo-Christian elements. He may well take a hint from Sir John Hawkins as to how the Neo-Classical perspective was formed and how it finally operated. Hawkins' account specifically describes Dr. Johnson, but it can aptly be applied to almost every other leading thinker and writer of the era.

> . . . the sentiments of piety which he had imbibed in his youth, directed him to those studies, which . . . he thought of the greatest importance to his future happiness. In conformity to this motive, he applied himself to the study of the Holy Scriptures, and the evidences of religion, to the writings of the fathers and of the Greek moralists, to ecclesiastical and civil history, and to classical literature and philology.

After his studies were completed, he had a "thorough conviction of the truth of the Christian religion."[61] It was the same result to be found in Neo-Classical thought as a whole. The Neo-Classicist's ability to combine widely disparate systems of thought into a synthesis confirming his faith in Christianity, and his use of all ancient literature to arrive at a "thorough conviction" in its truth, separate his species of classicism from the other forms developed in England: the secular anthropocentrism of Humanism, the agnostic Hellenism of the Romantics, the Hebraic-Hellenist disjunction of the Victorian. The function of patristic literature in producing this distinctive synthesis demands a greater recognition than it has so far received.

6 · Byzantium

In modern surveys of intellectual and literary history, there recurs a most persuasive metaphor. Originated by a few Enlightenment historians and philosophers as a form of self-praise, it has been popularized by historiographers and borrowed by literary critics.[1] A visual image, it depicts the urbane classicist of the eighteenth century standing on a lofty cultural summit, gazing sympathetically back at the summit of Roman culture across the empty, dark abyss of time. Impressive as this metaphor may be, it is quite misleading in a number of ways, as preceding chapters of this study have suggested. Its most serious shortcoming, however, is the assertion that Neo-Classicists were ignorant of all mediaeval culture or that they unanimously disdained it.

Of the Neo-Classical conception of the Latinate, Catholic culture of Western Europe during the Middle Ages, it is probably not necessary to go into detail to point out the limitations of the simplified trope. Certainly there was no ignorance of mediaeval chronology and theology in Restoration and Georgian England. Early writers from Bede and Sprott to Twysden were known and used by would-be writers of British history: Milton, Swift, Bolingbroke, Goldsmith, and others. The political theorists made much of the "Gothic" system of government; and literary Gothicism in England, present throughout the eighteenth century, found a full expression during the reign of George III. Anglo-Saxon and Middle English literature was praised, studied, and anthologized by Temple, Addison, Warburton, Bishop Percy, and many more. Chaucer was admired and translated by Dryden, imitated and plagiarized by Pope and Steele. Pinkerton and other cultural historians extolled mediaeval civilization. Certainly the Neo-Classicist preferred ancient culture to mediaeval European culture, but he was far from disdaining the latter.[2]

It is even less true that English Neo-Classicism was a state of mind that rested firmly on a total ignorance of the Eastern,

or Byzantine, culture of the Middle Ages, though the superficial evidence indicates otherwise. On the one hand, Neo-
Classical literature, aside from travel books and journals, looks
bare of cultural influences derived from Constantinople and
its satraps. There are a few scattered, quasi-historical dramas:
Nathaniel Lee and Philip Francis wrote plays about Constantine the Great in 1684 and 1754 respectively; and both
Charles Goring and Samuel Johnson (in 1709 and 1736) re-
vised the story of Irene, the fair Greek, who bartered her
Byzantine loyalty for the favor of the Moslem conquerors of
Constantinople. Another Byzantine Greek lady, the brilliant
and lovely Hypatia, had her lamentable tale recounted by
Goldsmith in *The Bee*, No. 3. Occasionally, the name of
Byzantium was vaguely employed to further English taste for
the Orientally exotic: Addison did this in *The Spectator*, and
Goldsmith averred his "Story of Alcander and Septimius" was
"Taken from a Byzantine Historian."[3] Finally, there is the
Byzantine documentation of such historians as Hearne, Pin-
kerton, and Gibbon.[4]

To counterbalance this sparse, positive evidence, there are
some resounding negative statements by the Neo-Classicists
themselves. These are the basis for the assertion that eighteenth century England despised the crude mediaevalism of
the Byzantines. Shaftesbury wrote to the University student:

> If the *Antients*, in their Purity, are as yet out of your Reach,
> search the *Moderns*, that are nearest to them. If you cannot
> converse with the most Antient, use the most Modern. For
> the Authors of the middle Age, and all that sort of Philos-
> ophy, as well as Divinity, will be of little Advantage to you.

Pope's consignment of mediaeval Greek learning to perdition
in *The Dunciad* appeared unqualified:

> For Attic Phrase in Plato let them seek,
> I poach in Suidas for unlicensed Greek.
> In ancient Sense if any needs will deal,
> Be sure I give them Fragments, not a Meal;

What Gellius or Stobaeus hashed before,
Or chewed by blind old Scholiasts o'er and o'er.

Goldsmith's *An Enquiry into the Present State of Polite Learning* (1759) wrote off the intellectual products of "the obscure ages, which succeeded the decline of the Roman empire" in this fashion:

> But their writings were mere speculative amusements, and all their researches exhausted upon trifles. Unskilled in the arts of adorning their knowledge, or adapting it to common sense, their voluminous productions rest peacefully in our libraries, or, at best, are enquired after from motives of curiosity, not by the scholar, but the virtuoso.

And Gibbon's disparagement of the "moderate" Greeks and the "complex machinery" of Byzantine civilization, everywhere apparent in his *History*, seemingly gave the last judgment of the Neo-Classicists on the significance of the Eastern Empire and its intellectual legacy.[5]

Despite this very operative prejudice, mediaeval Greek studies were quite important in England between 1660 and 1800; and Byzantine literature and thought left a decided imprint on English Neo-Classicism though in subtle and well concealed ways. Negative as they are, the castigations of Pope and Gibbon indicate the widespread nature of the scholarly concern with mediaeval Greek studies in the Neo-Classical era; and Goldsmith's glib summary was simply inaccurate. Even as he penned it, Gibbon, Pinkerton, and Richard Porson were pursuing Byzantine studies with an interest far more scholarly than virtuoso, and Dr. Johnson was considering editorial tasks involving the lexicography of the mediaeval compilers.

Strange as it seems, the interest in Byzantine letters manifested in England during the Neo-Classical period was among the keenest displayed by scholars and editors prior to the twentieth century, and it attracted an unprecedented amount of public attention and comment by nonscholarly literature. The transmission of Byzantine literature to Western Europe, both before and after the collapse of Constantinople, has been well documented, by Gibbon among others.[6] Histories of classical scholarship indicate that Renaissance scholars were so taken with the ancient works preserved by Byzantine scholarship that, while editing much of it, they neglected mediaeval literature itself to further their studies of classical texts. Homer, Pindar, and Aesop were far more pressing interests than Eustathius, Tzetzes, and Planudes, who preserved and commented on them. By the seventeenth century, however, scholarly attention began to shift toward mediaeval studies, and in England a number of Byzantine authors found editors and translators.[7] Literary disputes around 1700 emphasized the relevance of Byzantine studies to classical expertise. When the authenticity of Aesop or Phalaris considerably depended on the authority of mediaeval Greek scholars, one had to consult those scholars.[8]

It was the deep interest in Byzantine letters by leading scholars of the post-Restoration era that produced such literary by-products as Parnell's *Life of Zoilus* and Pope's smacks at the pedantry of Regius Professors. Meric Casaubon, who inherited from his father Isaac the Humanist's concern with manuscripts, propagated an interest in Synesius and other Byzantines in his essays. Isaac Vossius was similarly interested in Byzantine manuscripts, and at his death, John Evelyn and others tried vigorously to secure his vast collection to aid English scholarship, but the collection returned to the continent. Thomas Gale, himself a collector and Regius Professor at Cambridge, owned the manuscript of Photius' *Lexicon*, from which he excerpted the writings of Ctesias to append to his edition of Herodotus (1679). John Mill's edition of John Malelas (Oxford, 1690) was a notable piece of Byzantine scholarship. And to this edition, Richard Bentley's prefatory letter to Mill added some highly significant Greek scholarship that helped establish Bentley's reputation. Not only was Bentley's Homeric scholarship dependent on Eustathius, Tzetzes, and other Byzantine commentators; he helped Rudolf Küster prepare an edition of Suidas (Cambridge, 1705), and he planned a three-part lexicon based on Hesychius, Julius Pollux, and other mediaeval anthologers.[9] It was Bentley's Byzantinism that Pope sneered at, in the *Dunciad* and elsewhere; but Pope could not deny the necessity of Byzantine scholia to classical learning.[10] Similarly, Goldsmith's garbled scholarship could not deny the importance of Richard Porson's Byzantine studies. Porson edited Suidas (1790) and transcribed Photius from Gale's manuscripts twice, the first time in 1796. And it was Porson who read through all of Byzantine history to see whether Gibbon was guilty of misquoting. Beneath the Neo-Classical satires on pedantry, there flowed a steady stream of serious Byzantine scholarship.

Whichever introit the English classicist chose to the world of the past, he was likely to find that his way took him through a Byzantine arch. If he was concerned with historiography, he could not fail to see the importance of Byzantine historians: Ammianus, Eutropius, Zosimus, and Procopius.[11] If he was exploring ancient Greek language and literature, he had to confront the Byzantine scholars: Michael Syncellus, Psellus, Tzetzes, Eustathius, Planudes, Moschopolos, and their transmitters, Gaza and Chrysoloras.[12] English neo-Romans found themselves dependent on Byzantine abstracts for otherwise vanished accounts or on Byzantine biographers for the lives of their Roman heroes. Xiphilinus's preservation of Dio Cassius was duly appreciated by classicists; and Julian's *Lives* of the Caesars was used to supplement the earlier biographies. Those engaged in chronological argument had constant recourse to the Byzantines. The chronological art was exquisitely refined through eight centuries of industrious speculation by Byzantine writers; and the first crude synthesis made by Eusebius in the outskirts of Constantinople was extended and modified by a score of chronologers—John Malelas, the Paschal Chronicler, George Syncellus, Nicephoras, Theophanes, Constantine VII, John Scylitzes, Georgius Cedrenus, John Zonares, and Michael Glycas being the most prominent.[13] Finally, English Neo-Classicists, who loved eclectic information and who adored to quote, found the compilations of Synesius, John

may not prevent a tentative examination of some probable Byzantine influences on English Neo-Classicism. J. E. Sandys, whose authority *is* impeccable, has asserted that Renaissance Humanism was evolved from Byzantine thought and was inseparably connected with it.[18] A generalized discussion of the intellectual background of Neo-Classicism may, then, begin with the assumption that "Byzantinism," as a largely transmuted phenomenon, was not a "pure" influence but nevertheless exerted some forces worth identifying. As for the second obstacle, even a rudimentary knowledge of Byzantine and Humanist literature, conjoined with the prima facie evidence in Neo-Classical literature, gives the reader a glimmering of some new light on English classical thought. Having already presumed to curse the darkness, the current investigation must venture to try to light one small, tentative candle.

Of the probable Byzantine influences on Neo-Classicism, the lexicographical are among the most demonstrable. Bentley's interests in the Byzantine lexicographers (notably Hesychius, Julius Pollux, and Suidas) are affirmed not only by his biographers but by the evidence in his various essays. Bentley's opponents—especially Atterbury, Boyle, and King—made attempts to argue with him on etymological and syntactic grounds, appealing to various Greek synopticists. Pope's embroilments with the etymologies of Eustathius led to lexicographical labors by Parnell and Jortin, as we know. In the complex of literature involving the Phalaris controversy and the ensuing satires on Bentley, one can find regular citations of Byzantine lexicographers, including Photius. John Jortin's *Miscellaneous Observations* (1731) includes in its parsings of classic words references to the chief Byzantine authorities prominent in the Phalaris disputes and is itself a fair sample of the sort of etymological imitations of Suidas being written before 1750.[19] Among other examples of linguistic Byzantinism may be mentioned Addison's etymological excursions in the *Spectator*, Gray's word hunts recorded in the *Correspondence*, and Swift's linguistic parodies, composed when he was most interested in Photius's writings, not to mention the etymological parodies in Gulliver's explanation of the derivation of "Laputa" and his account of the Houyhnhnms' language.[20]

Suidas and Photius, in particular, not only affected the specialized etymological investigations of the Neo-Classical period; they also provided the pattern for English dictionaries and encyclopaedias. The Suidas lexicon, originally of the period between A.D. 950 and 976, was an anthology of selections from earlier lexicons (many lost), scholia on classical authors, histories, biographies, and miscellaneous topics. Renaissance editors picked and chose from Suidas material suited to special interests. The *Suidae Historica*, for example, edited by Jerome Wolf (Basle, 1581), was cast in the form of alphabetical entries, ranging from "Adam" to "psychomachontes" and containing citations from Greek and Roman pagans, the Fathers, and earlier Byzantines.[21] It was, in brief, the modification of the Suidas material into the encyclopaedic forms implicit in the Greek original. Similarly, Robert Constantin, the author of the most famous Renaissance Greek lexicon, borrowed much of his material directly from Suidas, giving word meanings in Latin and citing Greek authors (Suidas itself, Gregory Nazianzen, the classics) to illustrate the usage of the term defined.[22] Photius' *Lexicon*, preserved in the C. 1200 Codex Galeanus (Gale's Collection), was used similarly by continental editors. Later encyclopaedists and lexicographers, introduced to Suidas and Photius through the intermediation of Constantin, Wolf, Joachim Camerarius, and other editors, consulted the originals and modeled their own works on it. Pierre Bayle's *Historical and Critical Dictionary*, 2nd ed. (London, 1734) depended exclusively on Suidas and Photius for its Byzantine sources and its format; otherwise Bayle's knowledge of the Byzantines was limited.[23] The *Encyclopaedia Britannica*, first published in 1768, owed its format and its encyclopaedic techniques to Bayle and other precursors deriving originally from the Byzantines. Similarly, Johnson's *Dictionary*, adhering to tradition—and shaped by a lexicographer who read extensively in Byzantine literature and correlated the various editions of Photius—borrowed the technique of giving root meanings, definitions, and then quoting authorities to show accepted usage.[24] Just as today, the history of dictionaries, encyclopaedias, and lexicons in English is traced back to the eighteenth century, so the Neo-Classicist saw them derived from Byzantine authors of the ninth and tenth centuries.[25]

In a similar way, Neo-Classical literary criticism was affected by Byzantine innovations. It was, to be sure, the "classic" examples of criticism that English writers acknowledged as their mentors: Aristotle, Horace, Longinus. But the virtual disruption in the development of literary criticism that took place in Western Europe was not repeated in Byzantium. Not only did the Byzantines preserve portions of ancient critical writings that otherwise would have perished; they also rung some notable variations on their predecessors and produced a version of applied criticism that came to a flowering in Neo-Classical England.

The preservation of ancient critical texts by mediaeval scholars has already been thoroughly examined and does not need repeating.[26] A further note on Byzantine literary criticism itself may not be amiss, however. As it was adopted by Humanist commentators and passed on to the Neo-Classicists, Byzantine critical techniques were significant in two forms. First there was the theoretical criticism, which followed Aristotle in establishing categories of literature. The most important Byzantine practitioner was John Tzetzes, whose classifications of dramatic, epic, and lyric poetry with their subdivisions were the basis of much of J. C. Scaliger's *Poetics* and were simply repeated by G. J. Vossius, from whom they were copied by Neo-Classical critics. Tzetzes' categorical insights also illuminated much of the specific criticism he made of such lyricists as Lycophron.[27] The other important kind of criticism was the sort of paraphrasing and *explication de texte* to be found most notably in the *Myriobiblon* and *Epistolae* of Photius.[28] The former, an anthology of book summaries and evaluations, was the preservative source for many of the lost works beloved by Neo-Classicists—Ctesias, Manetho, Theopompus, Diodorus Siculus, Julius Africanus—and Photius' extractive techniques were duplicated by Swift and Johnson, in principle if not the letter. Swift's period of interest in Photius was also the time he was busily abstracting the books he read; and Johnson's knowledge of Photius may well have stimulated the kind of critical evaluation and summary contained in *The Lives of the Poets*.[29] These conjectures, while unprovable, are supported by the evidence that exists.

There is stronger evidence that the critical techniques applied to Homer by the Byzantines affected the rash of Homeric criticism printed during the early eighteenth century. The imprint of Eustathius (*pace* Leo Allatius and John Spondanus) is to be found on Pope's prose discourses concerning his translation, as well as in Prior's examination of Homer (1715) and Addison's *Spectator* papers on Homer.[30] Parnell's *Life of Zoilus*, composed after Parnell had been working his way through Byzantine *scholia*, implicitly supports the belief that Neo-Classicists traced the history of literary criticism from the ancients through the mediaeval Greeks to the Renaissance polymaths and so to Bentley and his fellows.[31] A similar lineage appears in Swift's *Battle of the Books* and *Tale of a Tub*. The kind of evolution of literary criticism described by Vossius and accepted by eighteenth century critics thus finds a confirmation in Neo-Classical parody, as well as exegetic and biographical criticism. Neo-Classical literary criticism, practical and theoretical, may not have set out to imitate Photius, Tzetzes, Eustathius, and the rest; but it would not have been the same if the Byzantine influence had been totally absent.

Diffused as it was through Humanist thought, Byzantine ideology cannot be asserted to have had immediate effects on the outlook of Neo-Classicism. Most of the themes treated by the mediaeval Greeks had their sources in ancient literature, pagan and Christian; they were an organic part of the Renaissance thought that melded ancient and Byzantine data; and the Neo-Classicist may have gotten his premise from any one source in the intellectual tradition or he may simply have inherited the evolutionary end product. There are some entertaining analogues to be seen between the Byzantine and

Neo-Classical treatments of giants, evil spirits, climatic influence, women, servants, beggars, and other things; but a causal relationship would be impossible to establish in most cases.[32]

In one instance, however—the Neo-Classicist's rejection of the idea of the Divine Right of Kings—the tie with Byzantine thought is apparent. The eighteenth century works that dealt with the subject often explicitly referred to certain of the Byzantine chronologers—Malelas, Cedrenus—who had prepared the way for dismissing Scriptural authority as supportive of Divine Right; or they used data and logic unmistakably connected with the chronological tradition.

The conception of Divine Right, as it was operative within Christian belief, was originally the product of some close patristic reasoning. The pagans had deified their emperors or watched approvingly while the emperors declared themselves gods.[33] In their condemnation of heathen customs, some of the primitive Fathers singled out the errors of supposing that a pagan emperor was anything but a mortal, often criminal man.[34] For the Nicene patrists, the problem was a good deal more difficult. After all, it was the gracious patronage of Constantine that ended the persecutions of the Christian sect; and the sanctity of Constantine's pious mother, Helena, was indisputably a factor in Constantine's conversion and subsequent sanctioning of Christian practice.[35] After scrutinizing the Scriptures, Eusebius concluded that God indeed appointed rulers, as He had Saul and David, and that Constantine ruled by Providential dispensation. This happy solution opened the way for a cult of emperor worship in Byzantium under the auspices of the Christian church.[36]

The secular imperiousness of later emperors often tried the patience of religious plenipotentiaries, however. Athanasius found himself in the difficult position of dealing with an erratic succession of rulers pietistic, apostate, submissive, and dictatorial. To justify a Constantius, a Julian, a Valens and Valentinian all with the same doctrine of Divine Right took an agile mind.[37] Later churchmen found themselves forced to

warn the emperor that Divine Right was subject to reinterpretation, depending on the ruler's abilities. The *De Regno*
of Synesius, the Bishop of Ptolemais, pointed out to the
Emperor Arcadius that kings could make errors, that their
virtues alone could lead to God's blessing of prosperity, and
that God's hierarchy demanded some self-conscious and proper
demeanor in kings. Similarly, Synesius' *De Providentia, An
Egyptian Tale* contrasted two royal brothers as examples of
the wise, prudent ruler and the debased, amorally selfish one.[38]

This willingness to find fault with the Divinely supported
king also appeared in the Byzantine chronologers, who busily
continued to scan Holy Writ. Eusebius had decided that Adam
was the first divinely sanctioned ruler, given sway over all
creation by God, and thus established the primordial principle
of Divine Right. Later chronologers, however, were puzzled
by the way men degenerated under this Divinely given system.
Malelas tried to explain the crimes of Cain and Lamech by
resorting to the sort of numerical allegory Irenaeus and Basil
had taken pains to refute; and he also introduced a jarring
note by saying that a giant, Nembrodus, was responsible for
the impious construction of the Tower of Babel.[39] The
Paschal Chronicle asserted that Adam was the "head" of all
men, just as Christ was head of the Church, a rather significant
mutation of the Divine Right idea. The *Chronicle* also decided that Seth's progeny (angels) and Cain's (men) had co-
habited to produce the giants mentioned in the Pentateuch,
and that the giant Nembrodus was Ninus, King of Assyria,
otherwise known as Nimrod. He first taught the Assyrians to
worship fire, and he was the first king created by them *after*
the Flood.[40] Georgius Cedrenus said that man had a *sensus ab
omni malicia puros* before the Fall but was altered afterwards,
at which time Monarchy arose. Michael Glycas quoted Cyril
to prove that Arbylus of Assyria was the first ruler to declare
himself divine and that Ninus, founder of Assyria, was his
son.[41]

When Joseph Scaliger composed his *De Emendatione Temporum*, he borrowed extensively from the Byzantine chronol-

ogers, including their conjectures about the historical moment of the establishment of monarchy.[42] Other sixteenth century chronologers, including Melanchthon and Bodin, saw the relevance of the problem to the issues involving the monarchy that came with the Reformation and Counter-Reformation. Was the right of kingship given by God or was it seized by ambitious, powerful men? If it was God-given, when was it bestowed? If Adam was the first to rule by Providential sanction, how did affairs degenerate to the point that God punished men with the Flood? If the monarchy was given after the Flood, why did the Scripture not say so? And how could the deplorable behavior of Nimrod–Ninus–Nembrodus, the first Scripturally mentioned monarch, be justified as God's will?

These questions perturbed Englishmen considerably after the Restoration of Charles II. Charles I had lost his head over the matter; and both Monarchists and Puritans had wrestled with the problem of defining royal prerogatives within a democratized government. Milton's *Eikonoklastes* supported the antimonarchist position by identifying Nimrod as the first monarch and denying the sanctioning of his rule.[43] After the Restoration, Tory apologists labored under the burden of supporting the monarch either with or without Scriptural authority. To do so, they found themselves turning again and again to chronological reasoning.

Lord Clarendon, for example, defended the principle of Providential sanction most ingeniously in his *A Brief View and Survey of the Dangerous and Pernicious Errors to Church and State, In Mr. Hobbes' Book, Leviathan* (London, 1676). Clarendon argued that God gave Adam the right of rule, which in turn was passed on to Seth. Lifespans being what they were in the old days, Seth lived long enough to transmit the principle to Noah, who carried it safely through the Flood and passed it to Shem and Japhet in opposition to the Nimrod line of pretenders and upstarts.[44] Dryden managed to avoid the issue by identifying Charles II with David, whose right to the throne nobody could question, whatever position he took in regard to the broader principle of Divine Right.[45] Laurence

134

Eacherd's updating of Sir Walter Raleigh's *History of the World* (1700) provided a compendium of rational solutions to the various corollaries of the Divine Right issue.

> What the Government before the Flood was more than Paternal, is uncertain; or from what better kind of publick Government the Tyranny of that Age did grow. After the Flood, three sorts of Governments are found approved.

These were the three forms described by Plato: the monarchy (degenerating into tyranny), the aristocracy (into oligarchy), and democracy (into ochlocracy). Nimrod was the Saturn mentioned by Julius Africanus; and as for the giants, Josephus and Lactantius supported the idea of angels begetting them on mortals but Augustine and Chrysostom did not. Raleigh himself thought the "giants" to be metaphorical ones; they were physically and mentally superior men whom fable immortalized and exaggerated into titans.[46] Raleigh's assimilation of patristic and Byzantine authorities into a common sense attitude served as a guide for later writers and the virulence of the controversy over Divine Right lessened somewhat in the chronological arguments of the eighteenth century.

There were still traces, nevertheless, of the Byzantine-inspired logic. They can be found in Swift's speculations on religion:

> The Scripture-system of man's creation, is what Christians are bound to believe, and seems most agreeable of all others to probability and reason. Adam was formed from a piece of clay, and Eve from one of his ribs. The text mentioneth nothing of his Maker's intending him for, except to rule over the beasts of the field and birds of the air. As to Eve, it doth not appear that her husband was her monarch, only she was to be his helpmeet, and placed in some degree of subjection. However, before his fall, the beasts were his most obedient subjects, whom he governed by absolute power. After his eating the forbidden fruit, the course of nature was changed, the animals began to reject his government. . . . The

135

Scripture mentioneth no particular acts of royalty in Adam over his posterity, who were contemporary with him, or of any monarch until after the flood; whereof the first was Nimrod, the mighty hunter, who, as Milton expresseth it, made men, not beasts, his prey.

These sentiments are very close to those of Cedrenus, Scaliger, and other chronologers Swift studied.[47] Likewise, Bolingbroke, whose interest in chronology was oriented oppositely to Swift's, used chronological data to support his treatises on kingship in *The Craftsman*; and *The Idea of a Patriot King* devoted its opening pages to establishing the sources of royal prerogative vis-à-vis Divine sanction.[48] Political theoreticians of the latter century continued to ponder the matter of Providential ordination and monarchic rights as they were Scripturally and chronologically expounded; Burke, for example, made many statements relating the king's powers to chronological precedents. Burke's theories are almost directly opposite to those of Eusebius, but the line of inquiry connecting them was unbroken from the age of Constantine to that of George III.

Since much of the foregoing discussion has been based on a limited number of Byzantine primary sources, it is not feasible to attempt here to summarize the overall relationship between English Neo-Classicism and Byzantine literature, nor is it necessary. This investigation can try only to suggest connections for which evidence exists in eighteenth century references, allusions, and reading lists. The full study of the evolution of Humanist thought from mediaeval Byzantine ideology which Sandys called for some years ago has yet to be written, and any extensive study of Neo-Classical thought and Byzantine antecedents must await its appearance or include its writing.

Yet it may be asserted with some measure of confidence that despite the antagonism that several leading English classicists expressed toward Byzantium and its wisdom, Byzantine learning was appreciated by others and its formal techniques were adapted by them to their own uses. The legacy of Byzantium to the Renaissance was shared by English classicists of the

Restoration and eighteenth century; and if none of them ever glorified Constantinople above Athens or Rome or yearned to sail to the "holy city" of Byzantium to find a home for the spirit, they profited from its heritage nonetheless. Byzantinism only occasionally produced some surface rills on the face of Neo-Classical literature, but mixed with the currents of Humanist thought, it flowed beneath the surface, enriching the intellectual soil from which Restoration and eighteenth century literature grew.

7 · Holland

As the temporal successor to sixteenth and seventeenth century Humanism, English Neo-Classicism has always been assumed to be patently related to the earlier form of classicism. Intellectual historians, however, have often encountered considerable difficulties in trying to relate the later phase of classicism to the Humanist variety. If the antecedents of Neo-Classical thought are sought in the posits of Ben Jonson and his school, one must confront the finite nature of both Jonson's premises and his cultural influence, even in his own day. Furthermore, the obvious break in the intellectual continuum effected by the Interregnum, and the insistence of literary scholars that Milton was the *last* great English Renaissance writer have tended to suggest an estrangement, if not a divorce, between the forms of English classicism present in the first decades and the final decades of the seventeenth century. If Neo-Classicism is traced, on the other hand, to continental sources—that is, France and Italy —it must be admitted, as several critics have done, that English Neo-Classicism bears remarkably little resemblance to French Neo-Classicism in an ultimate analysis and that Italian Humanism seems to have affected Neo-Classicism relatively slightly and primarily in the area of literary criticism by way of Sidney, Jonson, and Milton.[1] The obvious conclusion would appear to be that English Neo-Classicism was essentially an insular, self-contained phenomenon that originated from the Humanist interest in reviving Greco-Latin literature but that evolved *sui generis* to meet the literary demands of English society and politics in the post-Restoration era. At least this is the conclusion that underlies many critical studies of Neo-Classical literature.

There is impressive evidence, however, that the themes, perspectives, and attitudes of English classicism after 1660 *were* a part of a continuous tradition growing out of Renaissance Humanism, that this influence was in fact continental, and that it was a direct and constant source of Neo-Classical lit-

erature. The embryos of Restoration and eighteenth century
attitudes were perhaps sown less by Castelvetro, Malherbe, and
Jonson, than by Scaliger, Vossius, and Casaubon. And they
were nurtured less by the atmosphere of Italy and France than
by the chill air of the Lowlands. It was in the close political
and intellectual ties between England and Holland in the
seventeenth and eighteenth centuries that Neo-Classicism discovered its tightest literary bonds with the ancient, mediaeval,
and recent past.

The political interaction of England and Holland before
1660, together with its economic and military side effects, has
of course been treated by many historians and has left its imprint upon such works of English literature as *The Faerie
Queene*.[2] After 1660 the entanglements caused by commercial
rivalry and military alliances, wars and treaties, not only involved in Dutch affairs some leading Englishmen of letters;
they also were preserved in many Restoration compositions.
Pepys' *Diary* is perhaps the most factual account of Anglo-
Dutch affairs during the period, but Temple's *Essays* on the
government and history of Holland supplement it. Dryden's
plays, essays, and topical poems are narrated against the back-
drop of contemporary events involving the Dutch, just as some
of the lyrics of Dorset, Sedley, and Rochester are voiced during
encounters with the Dutch fleet. The enthronement of William
of Orange in 1688 intensified the English preoccupation with
Holland and its culture. And subsequent dealings between
England and Holland are reflected in the periodical essays of
Steele, Addison, and Swift; in *Gulliver's Travels*; in Arbuthnot's *The Political History of John Bull*, and other works.[3]

As the refuge of homeless intellectuals during the continental wars and religious controversies of the sixteenth and
seventeenth centuries, and as the site of several great universities—in Leyden, Amsterdam, and Utrecht—as well as the
largest printing presses of the Renaissance era, Holland inevitably became a citadel of Humanist scholarship and thought.
Many of the greatest names of Renaissance letters belonged to
native Dutchmen: Erasmus, Grotius, G. J. Vossius, Justus Lip-

sius, Johannes Meursius, Erycius Puteanus, Daniel Heinsius. And Batavia became the home of other eminent peripatetics, the Scaligers, Casaubon, Salmasius, Comenius, Boxhorn, Graevius, and Gronovius among them.[4] Not even the London of King James, the Stockholm of Queen Christina, the Paris of Louis XIV, or the Rome of Pope Urban VIII could compete with this array of scholarly geniuses. Holland was esteemed the Athens of the North long before Charles Gildon belatedly (and jealously) claimed the title for England.[5]

Inevitably, the commerce between England and Holland included the intellectual as well as other kinds; from the time of Henry VIII to that of George III there were steady interchanges between English men of letters and the Dutch polymaths.[6] Erasmus' friendship with Sir Thomas More, the prebendary granted to Isaac Casaubon by James I, the visits of Comenius to England, and Milton's pamphlet engagement with Salmasius, whom Charles II had hired to write pro-monarchist tracts—these and many other links between the intellectual spheres of Holland and England before the Restoration are common knowledge. After 1660 the Anglo-Dutch intellectual community continued its disputes, its collaborations, and its exchange of manuscripts. Charles II gave Isaac Vossius, the son of Gerard Johan, a prebend at Windsor, and he was befriended by John Evelyn and Richard Bentley, who sought to buy his library after his death in 1689. Meric Casaubon, the son of the great Isaac Casaubon, lived out his life in England, a constant tie with continental Humanist tradition until his death in 1671. Temple, Prior, and Chesterfield conversely represented English letters as well as government in Holland and were much admired in The Hague and the Dutch centers of literature. Bentley collaborated with Graevius (Johann Georg Greffe), a Professor of Eloquence at Utrecht, on an edition of Callimachus; Graevius called him the *novum sed splendidissimum Britanniae lumen.* Jakob Gronovius, on the contrary, a Professor of Greek at Leyden for thirty-seven years, edited the Byzantine collections of Manetho and ran afoul of Bentley, with whom he engaged in the sort of acrimonious dispute typical of Renaissance pedantry. Bernard Mandeville's migration from Holland to England and subsequent entry into literary affairs is evidence of still another sort of Anglo-Dutch relationship. And in the last part of the century, the continuing significance of the intellectual relationship between Englishmen and Lowland scholars may be seen in Sir David Dalrymple's injunctions to young Boswell to look up Abraham Gronovius and ask him about manuscripts of Anacreon at Leyden, and in Edward Gibbon's pedantic correspondence with J. M. Gesner.[7]

As the intellectual center of Europe between 1550 and 1650 —geographically as well as institutionally—Holland radiated its influence to the perimeter nations: England, Sweden, Germany, Italy, and France. Not even Switzerland, with its own universities and the Stephen presses, was so vital a center of Humanist scholarship. The significance of the Dutch polymaths to France and England as sources and guides may be seen in two Neo-Classical works, one a French essay translated into English and the other, a later composition written by an Englishman in French. Jean Le Clerc's *Parrhasiana* (1700) declared:

> 'Tis certain we have not seen, for a long time, in any part of *Europe*, any Men, who equal the illustrious Criticks, who lived in the last Century, and the beginning of this. For Example, We see no Body, who equals in Learning, Application of Mind, and Bulk as well as Number of Books, *Joseph Scaliger, Justus Lipsius*, Isaac Casaubon, Claudius Salmasius, Hugo Grotius, John Meursius, John Selden, and a great many others, whom I need not name, because they are known to every Body. I have a due Esteem for many learned Men of my Acquaintance; but I am persuaded that none of them will complain, if I say that I know none who equals those great Men in Learning. We have seen nothing for a long time, that can be compared with their Works.

Later in the century, the youthful Gibbon smoothly agreed with Le Clerc that modern letters had declined from that high pinnacle. In the *Essay on the Study of Literature,* he classified himself as often the defender of the polymaths but never their zealot and went on to comment:

> If we direct our attention now to those who devoted them-selves exclusively, or almost so, to literary work, true con-noisseurs will always be able to distinguish and appreciate the broad and delicate mind of Erasmus, the accuracy of Casaubon and of Gerard Vossius, the vivacity of Lipsius, . . . the resources and fecundity of Isaac Vossius, the bold penetration of Bentley, . . . the profound philosophical mind of Le Clerc. . . . They will not confound these great men with mere compilers, such as . . . a Saumaise . . . and hosts of others who are useful indeed through their labors but who never win our admiration, rarely appeal to our taste, and merely exact our esteem.[8]

Though Le Clerc and Gibbon may have disagreed in their estimates of Salmasius, their essays demonstrate the acknowl-edged leadership of the Renaissance polymaths in literary matters in France and England and show the direct tie be-tween them and such Neo-Classicists as Le Clerc, Bentley, and Gibbon himself.[9] Certain elements of the Italian Renaissance may have terminated in England with Milton, but the core assumptions of Humanism as they were propagated via Hol-land were instrumental in English Neo-Classicism at least until the time of Gibbon and his contemporaries.

So numerous, so extensive were the effects of international Latin scholarship on Neo-Classical thought that only a full length study could begin to treat them all. Some of the "great Men" of the Dutch Renaissance have already been studied and their influence in England indicated, notably Erasmus, Grotius, and Comenius. Others—Lipsius, Puteanus, Casaubon—have been the subjects of specialized investiga-tions.[10] Still others, Daniel Heinsius, the Vossii, Meursius, are today largely unread and forgotten except in footnotes. Yet these were the authorities venerated in England between 1660 and 1800, the men whose works were studied and scrutinized as the sources of contemporary thought. Neo-Classical scholarship derived from them; Neo-Classical literature borrowed from them; and though Neo-Classical thought rejected some of its Humanist heritage and laughed at some, it absorbed and used much more.

Renaissance scholars were influential in Neo-Classical letters in three or four chief ways, as English classicists cheerfully acknowledged, often in the form of parody. Initially Humanist concern with the Greek and Latin languages started the etymological investigations that continued through the seventeenth and eighteenth centuries in much the same way. Such linguists and lexicographers as Henri Estienne (Henricus Stephanus), Robert Constantin, Guillaume Budé (Gulielmus Budaeus), and Friedrich Sylburg (Sylburgius) stimulated the interests of later English classicists—e.g., Gale, Bentley, Barnes, Gray, Gibbon—and sent them back to the classical and mediaeval sources for the principles of lexicography. Such linguistic theorists as Christopher Helwig (Christophorus Helvicus) and Jan Amos Komenský (Johan Amos Comenius) determined the teaching methods used to instruct the young Sam Johnson, among others.[11] When Boswell harkened back to the example of Robert Stephen's Latin thesaurus, he was typifying the Neo-Classicists' reliance on Renaissance linguistic techniques, just as Swift's linguistic parodies cited Sylburgius or Stephanus as mock authorities for his etymological flights.

Secondly, the preeminent editions of ancient writers were those of the polymaths. From Erasmus to Graevius, Dutch editors labored to collect the scattered texts of Seneca, Justin, or Aristotle and collate them, together with comments and notes, into authoritative editions. Frequently, Humanist editors resorted to wild guesses to supplement their Herculean labors of restoration, so editions of, say, Virgil varied widely.[12] This led, among Neo-Classicists, to editorial partisanship, as Addison's *Tatler* No. 158 humorously shows. Disputes over the superiority of Stephanus' edition to Heinsius' may have been exaggerated at times into absurdity, but they all attested to the ubiquitousness of the Humanist influence on Neo-Classical concerns.

Then, the polymaths were the great compilers, the great anthologers of data on such subjects as Roman military behavior, ancient games, or patristic chronology. Their compendia, complete with interpretations and built-in arguments, were the reference works for post-Restoration classicists. If the Neo-Classical scholar wished to explore the history of the phalanx or the Praetorian Guard, he naturally began by reading Justus Lipsius' *De Militaria Romana*. If he wanted all available information about the Sybilline oracles, he consulted Isaac Vossius. On ornithology or dendrology, he went to Ulysses Aldrovandus or Samuel Bochartus.[13] In such eighteenth century compendia as Goldsmith's *History of the World* may be found a serious imitation of polymathic techniques of synthesis, while *Tristram Shandy* and *The Memoirs of Martinus Scriblerus* are superb parodies of the inherent absurdities of the polymath's assumptions and approach. It has been demonstrated that the Scriblerists had an intimate knowledge of some sixteen Renaissance scholars and their work.[14]

Finally, the Dutch titans were the subject of much gossip among their English admirers, who discussed the peccadillos of their mentors in much the same way students everywhere speculate about their teachers or critical biographers ruminate about Swift's relationship with Stella. Bayle's *Dictionary* shared the penchant for tale-telling typical of the biographical compositions of the sixteenth and seventeenth centuries, e.g., Aubrey's *Brief Lives* or the later *Anecdotes* of Joseph Spence, and he exploited to the fullest such coterie talk as J. C. Scaliger's nasty assaults on Erasmus or the way Peter Scriverius seduced the mistress of Gaspar Barthius.[15] The polymaths themselves supplied much of the gossip, with their malicious exchanges about each other preserved in *Epistolae* or such compositions as J. J. Scaliger's *Confutatio Fabulae Burdonum* (1608), which insisted his family certainly were descended from the aristocratic La Scala family.[16] If English Neo-Classicists thought of Cato and Atticus as their living contemporaries, the Dutch Humanists were no less real presences in eighteenth century England. John Jortin's partisan comment was typical:

> The pride of Joseph Scaliger, which was almost equal to his great abilities, and his censorious humor, cost him many an uneasy hour, and raised him up enemies. . . . What is the reason why Nicholas Heinsius was universally respected, and Salmasius, like Esau, had every man's hand against him? The reason is, that Heinsius wrote like a gentleman, and that Salmasius, who had a prodigious deal of learning, and a surprising memory, had as great talents in railing.[17]

Bentley and Gibbon overtly identified themselves with J. J. Scaliger; Dr. Johnson identified himself with Hugo Grotius; and the appropriateness of the comparisons was generally admitted by the Neo-Classicists themselves. Of Bentley's errors in construing Horace, Johnson wrote: "Mallem cum Scaligero errare quam cum Clavio recte sapere."[18]

Considering the abundant proof in Neo-Classical writing of the esteem in which the continental Humanists were held, it hardly comes as a surprise to the researcher in Renaissance scholarship to discover the antecedents of a great deal of Neo-Classical thought and practice. Precedents for the Neo-Classical theories of history and tragedy may be found in J. C. Scaliger and G. J. Vossius. Such prominent Neo-Classical genres as the ode with its emphasis on the universal and its dependence on the personified abstraction are directly anticipated in Scaliger's *Poemata*; and all the elements of the Addisonian informal essay are to be found in the *Suada Attica* of Erycius Puteanus, who discoursed on such subjects as the usefulness of books, the facility of the Greek language, education of the young, and Roman coins. Such ubiquitous Neo-Classical symbols as the ass—found in the works of Rochester, Swift, Gay, and a host of others—may have departed from Aesop and Apuleius but the ass was also treated in Daniel Heinsius' *Laus Asini* in terms very like those of the later English satirists.[19]

The close relationship between the rationales, the generic experiments, the thematic concerns, and the metaphoric instruments of continental Humanism and English Neo-Classicism is indicated everywhere in the two literatures. The main influences, however, may be seen in the works of four polymaths, many of whose productions remain untranslated from the Latin or whose English compositions have not been critically stressed. These forebears of Neo-Classicism are Joseph Just Scaliger, Gerard John Voss, Johan Amos Komenský, and Meric Casaubon.

With the exceptions of Erasmus and Grotius, Scaliger was the most venerated of the Humanists in post-Restoration England. The son of the vile-tempered Julius Caesar Scaliger, Joseph Just (1540-1609) was an outstanding Latinist whose efforts at teaching himself Greek were a model to English admirers.[20] He became interested in editing during his youth and engaged in negotiations about manuscripts with English scholars; he obtained a copy of Photius' *Lexicon* from Richard Thomson of Clare College, for instance. His editions of the Latin poets, e.g., Tibullus, Catullus, made him famous as a textual critic; his professorship at Leyden, as the successor of Justus Lipsius, added to his academic renown; and his eminence as the foremost of the modern chronological synthetists added to his fame. His works, studied in the Latin, were excerpted for wider circulation in *Scaligeriana Sive Excerpta Ex Ore Josephi Scaligeri* (Leyden, 1668), a Latin and French version. To Neo-Classicists he was truly a "great Man." Addison studied and quoted him at Oxford and cited him in the "Remarks on Italy." Prior composed a poem on a passage from *Scaligeriana*. Pope deferred to his Homeric scholarship. Gay cited him in the preface to *The Mohocks* and elsewhere. And Johnson, who admired Scaliger even in error, praised him second only to Grotius.

Of Scaliger's works, the *De Emendatione Temporum* (Leyden, 1583), was undoubtedly the most important to later generations; the bulk of *Scaligeriana* was taken from it.[21] An undertaking basically historiographical in nature, *De Emen-*

datione was a survey and correlation of previous histories and chronologies founded on the assumptions which Le Clerc later summarized and which underlay the Neo-Classical viewpoint. Scaliger posited the vitality of ancient literature and its relevance to the present. He asserted the necessity of correlation and arrangement as the basis of comprehension. *All* of ancient literature was his province: Babylonian, Greek, Hebrew, and Latin. He attempted to assimilate patristic data with secular, examining carefully the writings of the Fathers but subjecting them to the same objective assessment as nonreligious sources. He operated within the Byzantine tradition of chronological synthesis, drawing upon writers from Eusebius and the Paschal Chronicler to Cedrenus and Scylitzes; and he was among the first of the Humanists to fuse the literary heritages of the Eastern and Western Empires. Something of a sceptic, he doubted the trustworthiness of such *ipse dixit* authorities as Eusebius and he appraised Roman history coolly and without either adoration or cynicism.[22] All these attitudes in time were absorbed into Neo-Classical thought.

The specific subject matter of *De Emendatione Temporum*, while entertaining, is not likely to impress the modern reader as much more than another Renaissance conglomeration of facts, myths, and esoterica. Scaliger sifts authorities and sources to settle on exact dates. He establishes historical landmarks as the guideposts of history and makes the birth of Christ the focal moment in history. He speculates about Sabbatical years as a means of Divine discipline; divides the hour into 1,080 parts; differentiates chronology from history; muses over the legality of the line of Roman kings; and deplores the "penuria bonorum scriptorum . . . quae hodie est apud nos."[23] But as Giambattista Vico was to do in other areas, Scaliger set up precedents that determined the nature of a later school of thought.

Scaliger's emphasis on the *totality* of knowledge, his vivid awareness of the continuity of thought and tradition, and his insistence that through reason men could reconcile disparities to form cogent and coherent systems of thought—all became key concepts of Neo-Classicism. At the same time, his refusal to countenance obvious error or biased judgments and his criteria of applicability and functionalism provided other standards for the Neo-Classicists. Universality and practicality —these were the tests for Scaliger and his followers. The assumptions of *De Emendatione Temporum* may be found stated over and over in such works as Prior's *Solomon*, Pope's *Essay on Man*, and, tangentially, Reynolds' *Discourses* and Hume's *Essays*.

Unlike Scaliger, Gerard John Voss seems to have exerted the greatest influence through his encyclopaedic collections of information that provided convenient references for Neo-Classical scholars. The father of three brilliant sons, Gerard John (1577-1649) spent most of his life in various distinguished professorships at Leyden and Amsterdam, though he was offered a position by Cambridge, at last accepted a prebend at Canterbury without residence, and was given an LL.D. by Oxford. His son, Isaac, spent most of his life in England, on the contrary. Gerard John was admired by Addison and Bentley; Swift even presented him kindly in *The Battle of the Books*; and Johnson loaned his works to Queeney Thrale to read for the improvement of her mind.[24]

Vossius' works were collected in an edition published in Amsterdam between 1695 and 1701: the *Opera in Sex Tomos Divisa*. They have not been re-edited or published since, and translations are lacking. Yet they are obviously the source of much Neo-Classical ideology as even a short summary shows.

Volume I, the *Etymologicon Linguae Latinae*, is a prototype of the sort of Renaissance dictionary that provided models for Neo-Classicists who had linguistic concerns. It gives derivations, meanings, and cites authoritative usage, following the pattern of Suidas and Constantin; Voss's chief authorities are J. C. Scaliger, Salmasius, and other sixteenth century polymaths. The *Etymologicon* thus provides a supplement to the classical references given by Suidas and the other Byzantine lexicographers.

Volume II is a Grammar, dedicated to Charles I of England.

There is also a glossary of Latinisms-Barbarisms. Voss apparently intended this to be an addendum to other grammatical works rather than a preemptive one. It is an interesting collection but its significance to any aspect of Neo-Classicism except that of linguistic preoccupation is limited.

Volume III of Voss's *Opera* contains discussions of Rhetoric, Poetics, Arts, and Sciences; and it is of the utmost interest to literary historians and students of Neo-Classicism. The *Poetics* in fact contains explicit statements of the rationale inherent in such major Neo-Classical treatises as Dryden's *Essay of Dramatic Poesy* and Johnson's *Lives of the Poets* as well as Pope's *Essay on Criticism* and the lesser prose criticism of the era. One is disposed to wonder whether Voss was not a more important influence on the Neo-Classical theories of literature than Scaliger's *Poetics*.

Voss's discussion is basically Aristotelian but it incorporates many of the assumptions of Byzantine criticism as well, citing many critics by name, e.g., Suidas, Photius, Zonares, Stobaeus, Planudes, and Psellus. It also assimilates certain dicta formulated by Voss's contemporaries, notably Barthius, Scaliger, and Casaubon; and it harkens back to Minturno as well.[25] The *Poetics* is far from a mere aggregation, however; it is an orderly and directive exposition of literary theory which draws upon most previous theory. It is so complete a statement of the later views of Neo-Classicism that it may account for the lack of a similarly complete discourse in English.

Voss begins with the assertion that poetry concerns human action and therefore is about people. Since people are good and bad, weak and strong, poetry must deal with all kinds of actions. The characters in poetry are epitomized so human nature will be heightened. The *fabulae* (i.e., themes or subjects) of poetry are necessary or "natural." The poet sometimes chooses his fabula from necessity, sometimes to illustrate his point. Voss's discussion of the manipulation of the subject is very close to Aristotle, whose theses of *peripeteia* and so on are illustrated with examples from Sophocles. Voss's section, *De Sententia*, however, is his own and is impressively close to the Neo-Classical theory. The *sententia* (wisdom or message) of poetry is directly connected with *dianoia* (reason or intelligence). Thus the very form and order of poetry must be "reasonable" and "orderly" and sententious in the Neo-Classical sense of the terms. The cardinal virtues of poetry are *ratione* (proportion), *magnitudinis*, and *ordinis*, which lead to *peripeteia* (perception). Voss's subsequent discussion of tragedy, derived from Aristotle, takes on specific Neo-Classical connotations when seen within the didactic framework of poetic theory contained in the *De Sententia* and is reflected in dozens of Prologues to Restoration and eighteenth century dramas.[26]

Voss's survey of Greek poets is interesting for several reasons. It is an anthology of references to Byzantine criticism. It contains material about lyric verse that possibly affected the practice of Gray and Collins. And it begins the Phalaris controversy. Scaliger had speculated about the date and circumstances of composition of the Phalaris letters earlier; and Voss disagrees with him, in *De Poetis Graecis*, in the section entitled "De Temporibus Poetarum." This altercation over the Phalaris letters was, of course, taken up by Temple, Boyle, Bentley, and others; and the dispute between Vossius and Scaliger, also recorded in Bayle's *Dictionary*, is significantly used not only in the Phalaris essays but *The Battle of the Books*, where Scaliger's reproof of Bentley and Voss's alliance with Temple are to be fully meaningful only if the earlier dispute is remembered.

Volume IV of the *Opera* contains essays on the Art of History, the History of Greece, a History of Rome, and an Epitome of Universal History. These discourses are antecedent to the Neo-Classical concerns treated in former chapters of the present investigation; the dependence of historiographical theory in eighteenth century England on Voss's ideas is unmistakable. The *Ars Historica* gives derivations of terms, defines the areas of history as natural (floods, earthquakes) and human, and subdivides the human into *res gestae, automata, causae,* and so on. History is an art, not a science. It is a necessary art for man must *retain*: "There is no one who has a *memory* of all Roman affairs." Voss repeats the ancient maxim that Bolingbroke was to propagate: "Historiam justam nihil' esse alius, quam philosophiam exemplis constantem." The end of all historical study and writing is to inculcate prudence in the reader.

The most important feature of Voss's writing on history is his opening of the way to separate history and theogony. Scaliger had questioned the reliability of ecclesiastical historians but his *De Emendatione* remained primarily a synthesis. Voss placed the "divine" and the "human" in separate categories, and his treatment of specific historians confirmed the division. Manetho and Sanchoniathon, for instance, should not be used as sources for "divine" history; Voss cited Minucius Felix and Arnobius in confirmation. He also attempted to separate the species of writing now termed "ecumenical" or "international" from other forms: "animal" history (naturalist or zoological studies), nationalist history, et cetera. Voss may have been largely responsible for the secularization of historiography in the eighteenth century; certainly his ideas are echoed strongly in the essays of Manwaring, Whalley, and other precursors of modern thought. Voss's emphatic theories of biography also prepared the way for Johnson and Boswell, among others. Chapter xvii of the *Ars Historica* declared, formalizing the views of Plutarch, that the writer of biography must depict the private behavior of his subject as well as the public, for a man's character was best to be shown in his personal actions.

The remaining volumes of Voss's *Opera* may be briefly mentioned since their influence on Neo-Classical opinion, though pronounced, came in areas primarily ecclesiastical and theological. Volume v, *The Origin and Progress of Idolatry*, is a fascinating survey of primitive mythology, its national mutations and subsequent reinterpretation by the Fathers. Voss's survey is the culmination of centuries of speculation by Christian writers, and his views are paralleled in *Paradise Lost* as well as the accounts of idolatry composed by Pope, Mandeville, Shaftesbury, Hume, *et al.* Volume vi is Voss's contribution to chronology. Asserting that he disagreed with that *summus Vir*, J. J. Scaliger, Voss summarized his opinions about the time of Creation, the Flood, the Japhetic genealogy, and so forth. Though Neo-Classical chronologers often cited him, Voss never attained much repute as a titan of chronological thought. The theological writings that make up the last half of Volume VI, however, were in constant use by such men as Addison and Johnson. Voss wrote on the genealogy of Christ, His birth, the Sacraments, Baptism, Christian symbolism, the Pelagian Heresy, and so forth. It was the essay on Baptism that Johnson lent Queeney Thrale; and in general the English Christian who rejected Lipsius' theological position readily countenanced that of Voss. The Neo-Classical reconciliation of classicism and Christianity discussed earlier finds its precedents in Voss as well as Scaliger.

If the impact of Scaliger and Voss upon English thought has gone largely unheeded, that of Comenius has not. Jan Amos Komenský (1592-1670), as a Moravian and a pioneer educational theorist, has received a great amount of critical attention from fervent Czech nationalists and professional educators. His works have been translated into English; the details of his life have been repeatedly recorded; and his role in the development of educational theory and practice has been painstakingly traced. There are, however, some phases of his writing that have been slighted, and these relate directly to the formulation of Neo-Classical creeds.[27]

The constant interaction between Comenius and English men of letters is well documented. He spent a period of exile in England before settling finally in Holland; and he wrote a portion of the *Via Lucis* there in 1641 when he travelled to London to urge the Parliament to create a pansophic college. Comenius' role in stimulating the establishment of the Royal Society has been debated; but his dedication to the Society, as well as the adoption of his educational theories in British schools after 1660—even at Harvard College in the Colonies— and Milton's educational tracts attest to the prominence of the polymath in English affairs.

Comenius' educational theories were a primitive form of

Deweyan pragmatism: learn by doing and seeing. Comenius borrowed from other theorists—Christopher Helwig in particular—but his illustrated language texts were his own idea. Comenius expounded on his theories in several works, all of them widely read in England: *The Great Didactic, The Analytical Didactic,* and *The School of Infancy.* The improving maxims contained in these works were partially extracted and made available to the public by the Most Reverend Dr. Edward Synge in *Some Rules for the Conduct of Life, Chiefly done from the Latin of J. A. Comenius* (London, 1736). His textbooks—the *Orbis Pictus, Janua Linguarum,* and *Porta Linguarum Trilinguis Reservata et Aperta*—were used in England as early as 1631 in translation; Charles Hoole translated the *Visible World* in 1685; and the principle of teaching by enticing "tender Wits" to think learning Latin a "sport and merry pastime" gained currency.[28] From that time on, Comenius' cardinal rule of education was to creep into Neo-Classical educational treatises: "The whole Art of Teaching all Things to all Men . . . Quickly, Pleasantly, & Thoroughly."

Comenius' principles affected Neo-Classical thought and literature in several ways. In its insistence on pleasure as an element of learning, the *Didactic* discarded the traditional notion of education for children as grimly moral. Comenius' own child-oriented books—*A Bed of Violets, The Fruit-Tree Nursery* —encouraged the rise of amusing literature for children and permitted Matthew Prior to venture into writing verse for Peggy Harley and Namby-Pamby Phillips to compose his poems for children. The rapid growth of entertaining literature for the young in eighteenth century England, though not strictly a Neo-Classical phenomenon, was inspired by the Comenian school. And the Neo-Classical emphasis on education for women *was* directly stimulated by Comenius' arguments that women were God's creatures, too, and not inferior to men in their faculties; they should, therefore, be educated like men to prevent the shameful waste of God-given talents. Both the *Didactic* and the *Way of Light* employed similar Christian logic to open schools to the female sex.

Comenius' *The Angel of Peace*, composed in 1667 to celebrate the close of the Anglo-Dutch wars, is another sample of the fusion of classical and Christian scholarship to effect practical social ends. Its combination of precedents drawn from ancient and patristic literature, its topicality, and its focus on synthesis and functionality make it a forerunner of one kind of Neo-Classical essay. *Public Counsel on the Reform of Human Affairs*, which departs from Rabelais, Montaigne, and Bacon, is another composition that anticipates the Neo-Classical projects to reform human behavior. But the most interesting of Comenius' works from the standpoint of its prototypal Neo-Classical characteristics is the *Labyrinth of the World*.

The *Labyrinth*, a long satirical poem, obviously depends on the example of the mediaeval morality and the Humanist allegory for many of its devices; it is a narrative of man's search for truth with Searchall (or Impudence) as a guide in a world ruled by the queen, Vanity. In some ways, the *Labyrinth* seems quite close to Bunyan and the didactic allegorists of the seventeenth century. In its entirety, however, the *Labyrinth of the World* is clearly the kind of systematic examination of the modes of life to be found in Neo-Classical works from *Gulliver's Travels* to *Rasselas*. From its opening chapter to its last, the *Labyrinth* resounds with the tones of Swift, Prior, Johnson, and other eighteenth century moralists, and in its structure and details, it is strikingly close to *Solomon* and *Rasselas*.

The *Labyrinth* begins with a Prioresque statement that ultimately traces back to *Ecclesiastes*:

When I had attained that age at which the difference between good and bad begins to appear to the human understanding . . . it seemed most necessary to me to consider what group of men I should join, and with what matters I should occupy my life. [I wanted] that fashion of life which contained least of cares and violence, and most comfort, peace, and cheerfulness. . . . Thus yearning and turning the matter in solitude in my mind, I came to this decision that I should first behold all earthly things that are under the sun, and then only, having wisely compared one thing with another, choose a course of life. . . .[29]

Having thus remarked his kinship with Prior's Solomon and Johnson's Rasselas in his search to make a "choice of life," the narrator enters the World, a naive stranger in a city laid out in six streets: Marriage and Domesticity, Trade and Commerce, Scholars, Clergy, Magistrates and Rulers, Knights and Warriors. The way of life in each is examined in turn.

The city is described in Swiftian terms. Like the Brobdingnagians, the inhabitants are physically ugly, being deformed in various ways, pimpled, mangy, or leprous. Yahoo-like, the people are naked, dirty, and noisy; they fight and jabber among themselves, pick up and hide trash, or steal things from each other and conceal them. A few, like the Lilliputians, walk on stilts or pattens to exalt themselves.[30] There is an aggregation of alchemists, who live in dark, reeking cellars amid trash and filth, where they conduct their experiments, that always fail or are ridiculously visionary. The "scientists" rationalize their failures as due to the stars or too little money; some die of smoke fumes or the victims of their own experiments. They are impressively like the members of the Academy of Lagado in many ways.[31] There are other "learned" men in the street of Scholars: Partridge-like astrologers make up predictions and sell them to the gullible; fustian critics spout pedantese; and the foolish mathematicians include J. J. Scaliger and Johannes Clavius.[32]

Many of the sentiments of the *Labyrinth* are strongly Johnsonian. The discussion of the pros and cons of marriage is very like that in *Rasselas*, with the same points made regarding love, early and late marriage, and children: of marriage versus celibacy, "Then there is indeed but little pleasure; and whether it is worth such fetters, I know not." The remarks on competition between children and parents, child discipline or lack of it, and the misery of the childless concludes: "Thus, then, did I understand that both to have and not to have offspring is misery." The section of the *Labyrinth* that shows the fears and trials of the mighty is also very like *Rasselas*. Plots, envy, exiles, banishment are the rewards of authority. Comenius anticipates Johnson in his conclusion that the most thorough search into the ways of life leaves little to be concluded save that all is vanity. And in the section of Solomon's wooing of Queen Vanity and his fall into idolatry, Comenius duplicates closely still another of the episodes of Prior's poem.[33]

If Comenius seems twice removed from English Neo-Classicism, despite the similarities between his theories and didactic or satiric compositions and those of the later group, Meric Casaubon does not. In many ways, Casaubon, like Isaac Vossius, was an embodiment of the relationship between Neo-Classicism and continental Humanism; as a contemporary of Milton, Dryden, and Temple, he was the immediate precursor of fully developed Neo-Classical thought. Several of his essays are the earliest, full-fledged expressions of assumptions basic to English Neo-Classicism; that his role in forming the Neo-Classical school has been so generally ignored is quite unaccountable.

Without doubt, the fame of Meric the son has been eclipsed by the glories of his father, Isaac Casaubon, who together with J. J. Scaliger and Justus Lipsius composed the great triad of Renaissance scholarship. Certainly, Isaac's involvement with the chief religious and political issues of his day was notable, and his place in the Court of James I was a vital one. His labors as an editor produced some of the most outstandingly brilliant texts of the classics—Polybius, Polyaenus, Athenaeus. And his patristic scholarship not only engendered significant ecclesiastical quarrels but vitally affected the course of Anglicanism in the seventeenth century with its emphasis on returning to the forms of primitive Christianity. In all these activities, Isaac Casaubon left an important legacy to English thought.[34]

Yet as the direct link between seventeenth century Humanist thought and eighteenth century Neo-Classicism, Meric Casaubon is more of a key thinker. Born in 1599, he spent his early childhood on the continent with his father who was struggling for his intellectual and religious freedom with the strongest figures of his day. After Isaac's removal to England and subsequent naturalization as an English citizen, Meric entered Eton, where he received a degree and then passed on to Oxford. Sponsored by James I and Charles I, he nevertheless survived the regime of Cromwell, though at one time he was imprisoned. Cromwell requested that he write a history of the recent wars; though Casaubon refused, Cromwell granted him a large sum of money in recognition of his talents. Upon the Restoration, Casaubon regained all his preferments, including his post at Oxford. He died in 1671.[35] Thus, his entire life was involved with the political and intellectual events of seventeenth century England which helped to structure the Neo-Classical outlook; and in adapting the Humanist premises of his father and other scholars to the immediate realities of current events, Meric Casaubon became one of the architects of English Neo-Classicism.

Casaubon was never regarded very highly for his efforts at editing the classics. Though his versions of Marcus Aurelius, Epictetus, Cebes, and others were adequate enough and encouraged the contemporary interest in Stoicism, he did not achieve the editorial renown of Gale, Bentley, or Porson.[36] Even today, his activities as classicist are of little significance. His pamphlets and tracts, however, though equally unknown, are significant historically and instrumental intellectually in the Neo-Classical tradition. A survey of some six or eight of Casaubon essays covering the span of six decades shows the evolution of Neo-Classical ideology.

The Vindication or Defence of Isaac Casaubon (London, 1624) was undertaken at the insistence of King James I; in Meric Casaubon's canon it is interesting for its parallels to J. J. Scaliger's *Confutatio* and its extension of Isaac's synthetic techniques to defend the postulates of primitive Christianity. Meric's hits at the Papists and the anti-Papist Reformers, who "superciliously contemne the ancient and holy Fathers" in order to abrogate laws, not only defends Isaac's patristic scholarship; it also sets up the middle-of-the road position of the later Anglican apologists, building the via media between Catholicism and Reform Protestantism on the grounds of classical scholarship and patristic authority. The later *A Treatise of Use and Custom* (London, 1638), argues the defense of the status quo on the grounds of tradition, ancient wisdom and authority, classical scholarship, and synthetic but functional knowledge tested by common sense. The *Treatise* is an exegesis of the social arguments subsequently advanced by Neo-Classicists from Dryden to Burke.

The Original Cause of Temporall Evils (London, 1645) takes up the doctrine beloved by Puritans and Calvinists but again succeeds in giving it a characteristic Neo-Classical focus. Casaubon accepts, as Swift and Johnson did, the idea of the Fall. But he explores, as they were to do, the problem of human happiness within the largest possible context. Asserting the fact of man's tendency to unhappiness and acknowledging the presence of evil in life, Meric Casaubon calls upon the ancient Hebrews and pagans (Solomon, Cicero, Pliny) for relevant opinion, surveys the beliefs of Clement of Alexandria and other Fathers concerning evil spirits and demons, and at last draws upon contemporary Humanist thought to conclude at last with the Neo-Classical paradox: for man the greatest happiness is not to be born and the second greatest is to die. Neo-Classical pessimism, as it is to be found in Temple, Mandeville, and Goldsmith, as well as the major writers, is fully anticipated in Casaubon's pamphlet.

A Discourse Concerning Christ and His Incarnation and Exinanition (London, 1646), ostensibly a Christian tract, prepares the way for Burnet, Middleton, Warburton, and other Christian classicists, who "proved" theological points by resorting to pagan wisdom. Casaubon's "logic" is typical. He takes up where Grotius' *On the Truth of the Christian Religion* left off, refuting the heresies of the Turks and Anabaptists, quoting Scripture in one sentence and appealing to Origen and Marcus Aurelius in the next. Casaubon's early effort at "rationalizing" faith in this essay found a fuller expression in later works.

A True & Faithful Relation of what Passed for many Yeers Between Mr. John Dee and Some Spirits (London, 1659) introduced several posits that were repeated throughout the late seventeenth and eighteenth centuries. Dr. Dee was a mathematician and mystic who was mentioned by Camden. He engaged in ectoplasmic exchanges for many years, recording his experiences in a manuscript that found its way into Sir Robert Cotton's famous library. Casaubon discovered and edited it, together with a summary of ancient and modern opinion about ghosts and spirits. Casaubon insists in his preface that spirits are a refutation of atheists, since ghostly appearances "prove" the existence of the soul. He cites myriad authorities (Camerarius, Tristemegisthus, Paracelsus, Aldrovandus, Mirandola, Casaubon, Vossius, Scaliger) to support his argument, and solemnly avows the spiritual world to exist as proved by Dee's confessions. Obviously, Defoe's *Apparition of Mrs. Veal* is a lineal descendant of this sort of reasoning and literature; and the eighteenth century school of ghost literature and Graveyard poetry called upon the Casaubonian thesis of spirits as refutation of rationalist atheism. It must be remembered that even Dr. Johnson believed in ghosts, and Neo-Classical literature often showed its "Christian" base by countenancing the spirit world.

With the 1660s and the publication of *A Treatise Concerning Enthusiasme* (London, 1665), Casaubon's prototypal Neo-Classicism is fully revealed. Stimulated by the classicist's dislike of autonomous "inspiration" and the patriot's apprehension of recurrent zealous strife, *A Treatise* is a sourcebook of Neo-Classical opinion. It begins with a survey of ancient leaders who claimed divinity in order to impose their wills on the people, deplores ancient religious frenzies, and cites Tertullian and Augustine on the disgusting nature of the religious orgy. The meanings of "enthusiasm" are given with a nod to the etymological authority of Henricus Stephanus: the basic denotation is "replenished with wind." Says Casaubon: "By natural *Enthusiasme*, I understand an extraordinary, Transcendent, but natural fervency, or pregnancy of the soul, spirits, or brain, producing strange effects, apt to be mistaken for supernatural." Enthusiasm can be divided into categories (as Grotius had categorized Stobaeus on death, or Burton had anatomized melancholy) : Contemplative, Philosophical, Rhetorical, Poetical, Supplicatory, Martial, Musical, Erotical (or Amatory) , Mechanical, and Divinatory.

To summarize all the points of *A Treatise* is impossible; hopefully, it will become available to a wider audience through a reprinting. A few of Casaubon's comments under the various categories, however, may serve to indicate his importance to Dryden, Swift, Gay, and other writers on enthusiasm. According to Casaubon, much religious enthusiasm is "organic": it is feminine hysteria, melancholia, maniaca, or ecstasy; "Nobody doubts of that." On religious hermits: nobody but madmen seek out caves and solitude for contemplation. As for women who experience transports and visions, Casaubon has only ironic scorn. Indeed, a book about a French girl who had such seizures had stimulated Casaubon to compose his *Treatise*. Ancient parallels, such as Tertullian's account of a *soror* who had visions, are treated with exquisite Gibbonian irony: after all, Tertullian fell into the Montanist heresy so his word was perhaps of doubtful value, though the *soror* may well have had such seizures, especially if she was "an ancient maid," or *virgo vetula*, as Thuanus said. Casaubon disposes of visionaries as epileptics or opportunists, and comments: ". . . true divine knowledge comes from the use of reason, as well as careful study and preparation." As for Rhetorical Enthusiasme, Casaubon includes under it demagoguery and rant and deplores it with the vigor of Swift; while the section of Poetical Enthusiasme castigates J. C. Scaliger for his inaccuracies and lack of documentation and questions his preeminence as the authority for poetic theory.

If *A Treatise Concerning Enthusiasme* is an exhaustive study of some cardinal Neo-Classical beliefs, *A Letter to Peter du*

*Moulin, D.D. . . . Concerning Natural experimental Philoso-
phie, and some books lately set out about it* (Cambridge, 1669)
is a full exposition of the Neo-Classicist's view of the natural
sciences, experimental knowledge, and the ancients versus the
moderns controversy. Du Moulin had given Casaubon a work
by a member of the Royal Society which professed the greatness of modern scientific knowledge. Smarting, as later classicists including Temple were to do, Casaubon defended the
ancients by attacking the moderns. After avowing that the
veneration his subjects owed the monarch did not extend to all
the productions of the Royal Society, Casaubon went on to
defend the teaching of classical languages as the instruments
to wisdom, incidentally assailing Comenius for wanting "to
make every man wise" through his simplified *Janua*, which
would destroy all classical learning and make men's lives empty
without ancient myth, history, and literature. Casaubon then
presented his main pro-Ancient arguments, all smacking of
Temple, Boyle, and Swift. The moderns were inferior to the
ancients not only in history and literature but sculpture,
surgery, and the other "natural" sciences. Classical learning,
moreover, was the means to Christian belief; one must know
Greek to read many of the primitive Fathers. Experimental
philosophy would lead to atheism. Only the ancient philosophers, e.g., Aristotle, were to be trusted; and Casaubon countered the moderns' attack on the *Ethics*. Finally, Casaubon
employed *un mythe animal* to symbolize the vituperation of
the Moderns. He recounted the anecdote of Peireskius, who
learned to rule his passions by watching a louse and a fly fight
under a microscope. The fury of these trivial insects, and the
violence of the louse, which became so angry the blood rushed
into its tail, was typical of the character of the Ancient–Modern
controversy. Certainly, Casaubon's louse and fly must take
their rightful place as antecedents of Swift's spider and bee as
Neo-Classical satiric symbols used to defend the Ancients.

Finally, *Of Credulity and Incredulity: In things Divine and
Spiritual* (London, 1670), which epitomizes Casaubon's ultimate fusion of Christian faith with classical authority, pro-

vided the kind of fundamental rationale that permitted later Neo-Classicists to adopt fideistic or deistic postulations in support of Christian doctrines of faith. *Of Credulity* emphasizes the possibility of using reason as the basis of Christianity. Though divine grace is ultimately necessary for "infused Faith," man can logically arrive in a Christian state by starting with reason. By way of illustration, Casaubon examines the matter of resurrection of the dead and declares it far from improbable; in fact, resurrection is quite likely. Aristotle, Marcus Aurelius, and Plutarch all believed in it; and the Fathers, cited everywhere, supported it. Casaubon's prolix documentation, ranging from the ancient Greeks to the patrists to the Byzantines to the earlier Humanists, is the forerunner to later Neo-Classical apologists, e.g., Addison, Mandeville, Middleton, Warburton, and others. Printed just a year before Casaubon's death, *Of Credulity* contained posits and techniques which were to persist throughout the course of Neo-Classicism.

From Joseph Scaliger to Meric Casaubon, the Humanist tradition was slowly altering to form the matrix of Neo-Classical thought. From Scaliger's broad, synthetic approach to Vossius' compilations to Comenius' pragmatic theories, the predications of continental Humanism were changing into the specific attitudes enunciated finally by Meric Casaubon and shaped in accordance with the particular ideological demands of English culture in mid-seventeenth century. Neo-Classicism depended, to be sure, on many other sixteenth century polymaths and their seventeenth century adapters. Lipsius, Salmasius, Puteanus, Erpenius were all important sources for Neo-Classicists; and such latter-day compilers as Le Clerc, Montfaucon, Guichart, and Bayle were other vital links between English Neo-Classicists and their Humanist models.[37] But the four polymaths treated above illustrate sufficiently the nature of the connection between continental Humanism of the sixteenth and seventeenth centuries and the full-blown Neo-Classicism of eighteenth century England.

The role of Holland and Dutch scholarship in forming English Neo-Classicism has been largely forgotten by students of eighteenth century literature, in part because of the effect of British detractors of that country and scholarship. We have perhaps been too inclined to accept at face value Milton's furious condemnations, Temple's complaints of Dutch phlegmatism and dullness, and Goldsmith's writing off of Holland as devoid of real learning.[38] Though the Perizoniuses and Gronoviuses of eighteenth century Holland could not compete with their illustrious predecessors, they nevertheless kept alive the learning of earlier centuries and propagated it, either directly through their universities to English Fieldings and Boswells or through print to the literary Swifts, Johnsons, and Gibbons.[39] English thought and letters were constantly stimulated by Dutch learning until the last years of the eighteenth century.

In a very real sense, the English Renaissance was extended through the Neo-Classical Age because of the effects of Dutch Humanism. The polymaths of Holland served as examples to English writers in many ways, as linguists, editors, critics, satirists, and as men of far-flung interests and talents. The Renaissance ideal of "universal interests" animated the Scaligers and Vossii, who in turn passed it on to the Neo-Classicists. This ideal can be seen in many forms in Restoration and eighteenth century literature: in Dryden's amazing versatility at writing every kind of prose and poetry on a multitude of topics; in Swift's wide-ranging interests and his abilities at compiling and synthesizing; in Addison's and Arbuthnot's knowledge of subjects from numismatics to anatomy; in Johnson's prolific and diverse knowledge and the fantastic array of his literary products; in Gibbon's polymathic mind and works—even in the "virtuoso" minds of Goldsmith and Walpole. The literary *uomo universale* was less an Italian than a Dutch Humanist ideal, and it held sway in England until the close of the eighteenth century.

The end of the Neo-Classical era in England coincided with the decline and cessation of British interest in Dutch Humanism. When English writers stopped viewing the polymaths as Great Men and authorities and ceased deferring to them and using them as sources, the intellectual tides of the literary Renaissance ebbed at last. When Addison visited Italy, he quoted Scaliger. When Gibbon went to Rome, he prepared by reading Lipsius. But when Shelley or Byron or Browning contemplated the beauties of the Italian landscape, the charms of the Italian people, or the intricacies of Italian Renaissance history, they responded in cultural rather than historical terms; they saw the specific, the immediate, the living rather than generalized human experience and thought transmitted through intellectual history. So the polymaths, the intellectual historians, were forgotten; and the Dutch inheritors of Italian Renaissance Humanism were dismissed by English poets who, like Wordsworth, believed truth was to be found by sitting on a stone and regarding the landscape—or one's own mind— rather than by grubbing through the Latinate *scholia* of past centuries. Thus the English Romantic lamented the extinction of the Venetian Republic as a vague symbol of classical and Renaissance cultural splendor. But the extinction of the Dutch republic of letters, the real legacy and trust of Humanist learning, drew little interest and no laments in England, even among the later Neo-Classicists, whose ideals were derived from it and whose world-view was to perish with it.

8 · Neo-Classicism and the Tragic Drama

With our survey of its historical surroundings finished and our examination of its ideological sectors completed, we are now at a vantage point to look at the total configuration of English Neo-Classicism and Neo-Classical literature. Like the ancient traveler to Athens or Rome, we have traversed and crisscrossed the interlocked districts of the earthly city of Restoration and eighteenth century literature. Having climbed to the summit and core—the conceptual acropolis—of English Neo-Classical writing, we look back at its urbane structure before confronting its literary monument. And at once we are struck with the absence of the Theater of Dionysos. The orderly arrangement of Neo-Classical assumptions admitted no successful construction of dramatic tragedy. The distinctive character of Neo-Classicism, paradoxically, prevented the writing of that kind of literature which is considered one of the consummate expressions of the classic spirit.

Since only three or four cultural epochs have produced great tragic drama, the lack of it in post-Restoration and Georgian England has been duly noted but regarded as a commonplace state of affairs.[1] The situation appears less ordinary, however, when one can see the vitiation of dramatic tragedy from *All for Love* and *Samson Agonistes* to *Cato* to *Irene* and *Elvira*. Furthermore, this took place in an era when the revival of Greek tragedy was at its peak, both editorially and theatrically, when dozens of playwrights (including the most prominent literary names of the age) were attempting to write tragic plays, and when critical discussion of the elements of dramatic tragedy was more intense and widespread than in any time saving our own.[2] The failure of dramatic tragedy in Neo-Classical England is a phenomenon that resulted from the synthesis of the intellectual traditions traced in previous chapters of this study; an awareness of its nature discloses one of the ordinates of Neo-Classicism.

The Neo-Classicists themselves were aware of the dearth of tragic drama in their age; though they were not quite certain what this signified, they were disturbed by it and they tried anxiously to identify its causes. As classicists and pro-Ancients, they naturally turned to the past for comparisons and standards. Even those who admired Shakespeare—e.g., Dryden, Addison—were disposed to take ancient drama for a model and a criterion of judgment; and by common admission, the greatest ancient tragedy was the Greek. When they judged contemporary English tragedy by Greek standards, the Neo-Classical critics found it severely wanting, and they evolved various hypotheses to explain the deficiences of the present age.

English critics before 1700 in general accepted the premises of French commentators regarding the excellence of Greek tragedy. Thomas Rymer followed the example of Dacier in praising *Oedipus Tyrannos* as one of the greatest tragedies of all time; as for tragedies "of a Modern Cut," said Rymer, "quantum Mutatus!" As to the cause of this disparity, Rymer doubted the ultimate validity of the climatic argument:

> These objectors urge, that there is also another great accident, which is, that *Athens* and *London* have not the same *Meridian.*
>
> Certain it is, that *Nature* is the same, and *Man* is the same, he loves, grieves, hates, envies, has the same *affections* and *passions* in both places, and the same springs that give them *motion.* What mov'd *pity* there, will *here* also produce the same effect.

Though he countered the theory of climatic determination with that of uniformitarianism, Rymer finally was unable to pinpoint precisely the tragic deficiencies of the English, who had as much wit and as apt a language as the Greeks. He contented himself with remarking that had the moderns begun where the Greeks left off, the English tragic drama would have surpassed that of Greece and Rome.[3]

Neo-Classicism and the Tragic Drama

Saint Evremond, resident in England, provided further comments on the relative merits of ancient Greek tragedy and modern efforts. He customarily lauded the excellence of the Greeks and the Greek theory of tragedy as Aristotle had explicated it; and he chided Racine for his inability to enter into the "genius of antiquity." But he also felt Plato correct in desiring to ban tragedy from the stage for moral and social reasons, and thought that *Oedipus*, "the masterpiece of the Ancients," would prove barbarous, depressing, and immoral if put into French.[4] Saint Evremond's critical standard, while dependent upon Greek models, nevertheless seemed to him inapplicable to modern tragedy, which he still considered wanting. In a somewhat similar manner, Dryden approved the superior standards of Greek tragedy, in *An Essay of Dramatic Poesy,* while postulating another applicable standard for modern drama. Saint Evremond found all tragedy, Greek and modern, lacking; Dryden found both with characteristic merits though imperfect in varying degrees. Each critic, however, began with the example of ancient dramatic tragedy as a frame of reference, and each finally estimated modern tragedy in the context of the Greek tradition.[5]

After 1700 English critics relied more directly upon their own knowledge of Greek drama and less upon the views of French Hellenists, but their relative judgments continued to find contemporary tragedy short of Greek standards. A few tried to temper the severity of their judgment. Addison, for example, in *The Spectator* No. 39, expressed the opinion that though English drama in toto fell short of Hellenic excellence, in some ways it was superior: "The modern tragedy excels that of Greece and Rome in the intricacy and disposition of the fable. . . ." Other classicists, however, declared, as George Adams did in his Preface to *The Tragedies of Sophocles,* that the writing of tragedy had been abused in England until there was "not such abominable Stuff, as our English Theatres have been crowded with since [the Greeks'] Times."[6] Bolingbroke complained to Voltaire that the English did not have a single good tragedy but by way of recompense there were "some admirable scenes in plays that are monstrous"; and Voltaire readily agreed.[7] William Guthrie's *Essay upon English Tragedy* flatly asserted that the period between William III and George II held a "mighty blank" in tragedy which not even Addison and Rowe could fill.[8] And though the anonymous author of *The Temple of Tragedy, A Poetical Essay* (London, 1764), took issue with the classicist critics of modern drama, his argument failed by default. His dream allegory showed a lover of drama enter a midnight grove to find a Doric temple ruled by a queen, Tragedy, and populated by Sophocles, Aeschylus, Euripides, Shakespeare, Otway, Milton, Addison, and Rowe. Then one Mr. Mador was welcomed into the group on the basis of his tragedy, *Mona,* and the poetic defense collapsed. Dryden might have been able to argue credibly for the comparative merits of Greek and English tragedy in an age that produced *All for Love, Samson Agonistes,* and *Venice Preserved*; but no critic of stature in eighteenth century England imitated him, though Thomas Gray went so far as to declare that *Cato* was a better model for English tragedy than anything by Shakespeare.[9]

Having diagnosed the condition of English tragedy as anemic by ancient standards, Neo-Classical critics hastened to prescribe various panaceas for the ailing Muse in hope of a complete cure. John Dennis and Edward Manwaring advocated heavier doses of Aristotle.[10] George Lillo wanted to purge the audience by metamorphosing the tragic hero into a *petit bourgeois.*[11] William Guthrie instructed playwrights to forget about "correctness" and to decrease the number of *dramatis personae* who were motivated by the *grand passion.*[12] Other critics declared that the Licensing Act or the size of the theaters or the English language were the viral causes of tragic malaise. Roger Pickering even resorted to the suggestion that the composition and production of English tragedy would be improved simply by cleaning up the private morals of the actors.[13] Some of these contemporary diagnoses are countenanced by twentieth century dramatic historians.[14]

But there were other forces that served to devitalize the

dramatic tragedy, as it was defined by Aristotle and appropriated by Neo-Classical critics. The Neo-Classical attitude toward history and "truth" was introduced into tragic theory and caused aesthetic if not logical contradictions. The selective Hellenism of the English Neo-Classicists chose elements of Greek philosophy that fundamentally denied a tragic ontology and ethic. The pragmatic and Stoical aspects of English Augustanism further served to alter the classical notion of the tragic hero and the function of tragedy; and Christianity, fused with these pagan elements, radically altered the metaphysical conception underlying Greek tragedy. Finally, the categorical and didactic heritages of Byzantine and Humanist criticism, adopted to the social utilitarianism of English Neo-Classical thought, resulted in a view of tragedy as a species of pedagogy. Neo-Classical literary theory could cope singly with the posits of the broader synthetic outlook of Neo-Classicism; but it could not deny their collective force or encourage tragic drama that contradicted a system of thought overwhelmingly antitragic in its fictive expression.

One of the first problems encountered by Neo-Classical dramatic theorists was the reconciliation of the prevalent worship of historicity ("truth") with the essentially fictional nature of tragic drama. The veneration for historiography characteristic of evolving Neo-Classicism in the seventeenth century led to a disparagement of the "fancy" (or "phantasy") implicit in most "poetry" (fictional literature) ; this prejudice was confirmed by the Puritan ethic that persisted in critics like Jeremy Collier.[15] The common distrust of fanciful literature had to be met by writers in every genre—Milton's handling of the epic and his defense of it is a case in point—but in the area of dramatic tragedy the objection was validated by many critics, who proposed that tragic drama concern itself exclusively with historical subjects.

In his discussion of Greek tragedy Corneille had set certain precedents by recognizing the implicit relationship between tragedy and history, though his specific conclusions were based on some dubious generalizations. The *Discourse on Tragedy*

(1660) said the Ancients took very few liberties with history (i.e., recorded facts) and had dealt in their tragedies with a very few families because historically only a limited number of families in Hellas had been involved in the bloody action emphasized by tragedy. Indeed, said Corneille, such action *ought* to be drawn from "history or fable. The enterprises against relations are always so criminal and so contrary to nature that they are not credible unless supported by one or the other. . . ." Ancient history and fable must be allowed equal authority, since the two could not be separated readily, except in such obviously fabulous cases as Oedipus' slaying of his father. Corneille asserted that the accidental slaying of relatives was rare in history. In concluding, he appealed to the authority of Aristotle, saying that the large events in history cannot be altered with impunity by the dramatist, though they might be improved with the addition of "probabilities" and lesser events might be altered.[16]

Saint Evremond was also interested in the relationship between historic truth and tragedy as it animated Greek and modern drama. He often referred to it, but his *Dissertation on the Tragedy of Racine's Entitled Alexander the Great*, revised in 1668, contained most completely his chief beliefs. Saint Evremond thought Racine's tragedy a failure because it was inaccurate in its depiction of the characters of Alexander and his antagonist, Porus. History had left to posterity a true account of Alexander's character and the facts of his career. Though that career may have been full of fabulous elements, it was nonetheless true, and to represent Porus as a greater man was to leave the realm of accuracy and violate all principles of belief. Like Corneille, Saint Evremond thought the external character of an historical personage must correspond exactly to that given by historians, but the dramatist ought to "enter into the interior and draw their most secret motivations from the recesses of these great souls. . . ." In so arguing, Saint Evremond was imputing to tragedy the same raison d'être that theorists of historiography ascribed to the writing of history: the disclosure of the "springs of action" (motivations) of men whose actions were recorded by historiography. Rapin similarly declared that tragedy is "furnished with all the most moving and terrible adventures that history can afford . . ."; and Dacier saw tragic drama as a reflection and introduction to men "of those accidents which happen in their lives . . . in the Grand Theatre of the World."[17]

English critics and writers of tragic drama accepted the idea of tragedy and historicism as inseparable the more readily because it was confirmed by English practice as well as French theory. Shakespeare and other Elizabethan tragedians had drawn their plots and characters from historiography; and if historicism was common to the sacrosanct Greeks and the loved Bard, certainly Dryden for one would not dispute its absolute nature. He may have questioned the aesthetic quality of the handling of historic data in the chronicle plays and called Jonson's *Sejanus* and *Catiline* "oleos," but Dryden had Lisideius forthrightly praise the French for their plotting of tragedies, which led to surprise and recognition: "they are always grounded upon some known history . . ." and thus are superior to the Ancients. Dryden's choice of historical subjects for his own "tragedies" was entirely in keeping with his acceptance of the principle of historical accuracy as the basic requisite of the tragic plot.[18]

Dryden's contemporaries and successors differed somewhat in their individual theories of tragedy and history, but they generally admitted a vital relationship. Rymer's *The Tragedies of the Last Age, Considered and Examined by the Practice of the Ancients* (1678) expressed some not altogether compatible views. On the one hand, he defended the idea of Poetic Justice by positing the Greek tragedians' observation of history, then declared that they did not rely on history for plots, for history can provide only an "index" (frame of reference) for the spectator but its raw material can neither please nor instruct. Later, in *A Short View of Tragedy* (1693), he stressed the idea that tragedy is basically Action, which must be credibly represented and historically topical; Aeschylus' *Xerxes* he found outdated. In their entirety, Rymer's statements indicate that he realized the essentially historical elements in tragedy but tried to deprecate excessive emphasis on historicity and phenomenal "truth."[19]

John Dennis's *The Impartial Critick: or, Some Observations Upon a Late Book Entitled, A Short View of Tragedy* (1693) assayed an estimate of Rymer's views in light of Corneille's dicta concerning tragedy and historical accuracy. Common sense, according to Dennis, shows that "Tragedy is the imitation of a Publick and Visible Action . . ."; and Aristotle's categorization of things as they are, ought to be, or are thought to be should be read "true history, probability, and common opinion." Dennis quotes Corneille as holding that there are three kinds of tragedy: "some follow history; others interpolate history; the third falsify history." Tragedies that are "true history" need not concern themselves with probability. Tragedies that interpolate history must accurately present their historical elements and observe probability in their interpolations. A "poet" (writer of fiction, specifically drama) may take liberties with history but not gross ones that contradict established fact or probability; once something has happened, not God Himself can change it. Dennis concludes his discussion by noting that history is not generous in providing actions that please and instruct but also conform to the unities, all of which dramatic tragedy must do. The dramatist may engage in some factual tinkering so long as the result is pleasing and not exaggeratedly improbable.[20] Of all Neo-Classical critics, Dennis held the most conventional views of the laws of dramatic composition on one hand and the sacredness of history on the other. His compromise of the two reveals the basic dilemma of the theorist anxious not to offend either cardinal principle.

In the eighteenth century, the problem of correlating historical fact with the requirements of dramatic tragedy continued to demand attention. It was reflected in many essays ostensibly about Poetic Justice, Decorum, or Appropriateness (verisimilitude).[21] And it was directly dealt with by those who for whatever reason were dissatisfied with English efforts at high tragedy. George Lillo's Utilitarian argument for the superiority of plebeian tragedy restated the common assumptions about the nobler form and its kinship to historical fact:

> I am far from denying that tragedies founded on any instructive and extraordinary events in history or a well-invented fable where the persons introduced are of the highest rank are without their use, even to the bulk of the audience. . . . The sentiments and example of a Cato may inspire his spectators with a just sense of the value of liberty when they see that honest patriot prefer death to an obligation from a tyrant who would sacrifice the constitution of his country and the liberties of mankind to his ambition or revenge. I have attempted indeed, to enlarge the province of the graver kind of poetry and should be glad to have it carried on by some abler hand.[22]

William Guthrie's *An Essay upon English Tragedy* disagreed entirely. Using *Cato* as a straw man, Guthrie divided writers into "poets" (the lesser breed within the laws of composition) and men of genius (masters beyond all rules). The former were slaves to historical "truth," like Addison:

> The poet's heroes and his princesses all speak his language, that is, the language of poetry without passion. He never touches upon an effect without describing the cause; he never starts a sentiment but instead of considering, how the character, were it real, would express it, he consults how Virgil, Lucan, Seneca, or any great ancient or modern author would turn it out. . . .[23]

Guthrie's *Essay* is fully aware of the result of testing dramatic tragedy by the yardstick of historiographical accuracy.

But the yardstick continued to be applied. The anonymous author of *An Essay on Tragedy* (1749) appended an "examen" of Johnson's *Irene*, which distinguished tragedy from history: history is full of similitudes but poetry is full of rarities that cheer and refresh the soul. The Essayist then allowed that the tragedian might depart from historical fact for the sake of dramatic economy and effectiveness; but the historical account of *Irene* already had these qualities. Therefore Johnson was to be censured for emending and altering recorded events. Johnson himself, as critic if not playwright, took a typical common sense view of the question of tragedy and history. His emphasis on tragedy as the mirror of life tended to diminish the transcendent importance of historiographical authority. And his defense of Shakespeare's portrayal of Roman senators as buffoons and fools on the grounds that such would have been afforded by the Senate was a perfect instance of his reconciliation of historical "accuracy" with the demands of tragic drama. For Johnson, "truth" was never equatable with a picayune historicity.[24]

In spite of the reasonable view of Johnson and other critics, the Neo-Classical veneration for historiography persisted in its effects on dramatic theory. William Hodson's postscript to *Zoraida: A Tragedy* (1780) shows how little dogma changed in 120 years. Hodson asserted once more that historical events were the best subjects for tragedy, especially the events in the national history of the writer. Authors must be careful, however, not to select a subject too remote in time, for the spectator might lose the sense of immediacy and relevance (thus interest). Nor would a contemporary event be much better, since the viewer might know so much about it as to destroy suspense and dimension (thus interest). Like his predecessors, Hodson took for granted the significant relationship between the historic and tragic senses; but he was unable to discern its true nature.[25]

The parade of English "tragedies" from 1660 to 1800 gives unmistakable proof of the importance of the Neo-Classical obsession with history and the consequent critical assumption that tragedy was dramatized history. From Dryden and Otway to Addison and Rowe to Johnson and William Mason, Neo-Classical playwrights combed history for characters and situations. Plots came from histories of Greece, Mexico, China, or Turkey; and a succession of Montezumas, Jane Shores, Sophonisbas, Lucius Junius Brutuses, and Elfridas was the result. Their pallid quality was caused at least partly by the Neo-

Classical belief that the historiographical virtues of "accuracy," "usefulness," and "universality" were also the virtues of dramatic tragedy. Moreover, the notion that tragedy must be derived from history not only restricted the choice of plots. It produced plays that merely represented historical scenes (often statically as in tableaux), or that purported to explain historical actions by contrived sentiments, or that versified the historian's prose, or that depersonalized the human beings of the past and made them nothing but spokesmen for differing points of view on Neo-Classical issues.

More deeply, the Neo-Classical philosophy of the continuity of human experience subverted the two posits of Greek historiographers which invested Greek tragic drama: mutability ("flux") and human inability to probe the unknowns ("mysterion") of existence. English Neo-Classicism was rooted in the belief that the study of historiography revealed the patterns of change; and if this did not result in a static theory of history, it encouraged an emphasis on the sequential nature of the inertia of events and produced a conception of historic movement as a predictable dynamism.[26] The extreme form of this view, of course, was to be found in Enlightenment historical theorists, but a version of it was necessary to conservative Neo-Classicists as well. A further factor was the Neo-Classical departure from the Greek interest in specific historical phenomena ("particulars") in order to cultivate the general and constant truths ("universals") to be determined by a study of the past. At the same time, the Neo-Classicist personified the "universal" or "natural" truth in historical archetypes: Republican Rome *was* Cato; Imperial Rome *was* Augustus; Justinian *was* fifth century Byzantium.[27] The Neo-Classical concern with social functionalism caused speculation "only about what is immanent in this world." Such an historical attitude is described by Karl Jaspers as follows:

> [It] proceeds to assign substance and personality to historic units which actually cannot be verified. It ends by endowing historical patterns with quasi-demonic self-direction.[28]

When this view entered into theory of tragic composition, it resulted in the impeding of dramatic movement by historical fixations, the oversimplification and "freezing" of characterization, and the submergence of the sense of heroic choice and meaningful action in a philosophy of human limitation and determinism.

Neo-Classical tragedy might have surmounted the handicaps imposed by contemporary historical attitudes, but the particular cast of contemporary Hellenism raised other difficulties. Though the English classicist of the Restoration and Georgian eras admired Aeschylus, Sophocles, and Euripides, he also venerated Plato, Epicurus, and Zeno (*pace* Epictetus and others). The ancient Greek was free to believe whichever philosophers and thinkers he liked, even contradictory ones on occasion. He could admire Herodotus, Plato, and Sophocles without being concerned about the disparities in their positions; even Plato, who had to condemn Homer and the tragedians in consequence of his own system, personally enjoyed them. The Neo-Classical Hellenist, however, assuming a consistency within Hellenic culture and working to systematize his own thought, had to choose for emphasis those elements of Greek thought compatible with each other (as he thought) and with his own beliefs and needs. This meant that the Neo-Classicist was constrained to follow somewhat more logical patterns of choice and belief than the ancient sources of those beliefs.

Thus the classicist who admired Aeschylus and Plato at the same time found himself in the unenviable position of having to reconcile antithetical conceptions of justice, filial duty, and piety. Or, if he prided himself on being a true disciple of Epicureanism, he could scarcely empathize with such tragic figures as Oedipus or Agamemnon. In short, the English conception of tragedy, the legacy of centuries of elaboration on the views of Aristotle and other ancients, simply did not correlate easily with the English utilization of Greek systems of philosophy to strengthen Neo-Classical ethics.

Neo-Classicism and the Tragic Drama

Of the three main schools of Greek philosophy prominent in seventeenth century England—Platonism, Epicureanism, and Stoicism—none provided a cosmology and ethic compatible with the tragic sense. All three insisted that man's emotional nature be suppressed and his passions be subordinated to his reason and will. If it is true, as Edith Hamilton has asserted, that the chief element in the character of the Greek tragic hero was his exceptional capacity for "feeling" and reacting emotionally to the events engulfing him, the Hellenic philosophers' rejection of the tragic drama in theory if not practice was essential.[29] Certainly, Plato's castigation of the emotionalism of tragedy is explicit enough. The Epicurean and Stoical insistence on reason and self-control implies a similar disapproval of the postulates of tragic behavior. Furthermore, the Epicurean doctrine of "Live unknown" and the Stoical doctrine of "Eliminate all wants" are the very antipodes to the Aristotelian definition of the tragic hero as a man of fame and outstanding status, possessed of an ambition approaching *hubris*. As for the metaphysics of Greek philosophy, neither Plato's orderly, just, and rational universe nor Epicurus' concourse of atoms nor the Stoics' void filled with fire, air, and stars of stone satisfied the dramatic needs of the Neo-Classicist or his theological hopes. The final scene of *Cato*, with its cosmic speculations, shows the problems the Christian Neo-Classicist was baffled by.

The most debilitating aspect of the Neo-Classical dismissal of the passions was the elimination from contemporary tragedy of legitimate and necessary emotion, both in the dramatic characters and in the audience's response. Neo-Classical critics acknowledged in theory that passions had to be shown to stimulate the Aristotelian emotions of pity and fear. Corneille attributed to the Stagirite the notion that tragic actions must transpire between blood relatives: "The reason for this is clear. The opposition of the feelings of nature to the transports of passion, or to the severity of duty, forms powerful emotions which are received with pleasure by the audience."[30] Dryden's

Neander remarked that tragedy needs "the soul of Poesy, which is imitation of humour and passions."[31] In his odes to Pity and Fear, William Collins gave his highest praise to the Greek dramatists for their ability at creating situations which gave rise to two prime passions. William Guthrie insisted upon the artist's obligation to place himself in the minds of his characters with "all failing and propensity to guilt" that "are the true springs which captivate, engage, move, and animate the passions."[32] By the end of the eighteenth century, the emergent cult of sentimentalism had pervaded this aspect of tragic theory. In *The Tragic Muse: A Poem Addressed to Mrs. Siddons* (1783), William Russell identified the tragic sense with sheer emotionalism:

> Thy piercing eyes, through Passion's maze that roll,
> Mark all the painful feelings of the soul, . . .
> The Glance of Rage, Distraction's frantic stare,
> The pangs of Grief; the working of Despair . . .
> . . . Fury . . . Self Reproach . . . Public Shame . . . Disdain . . .
> Thus far, great Actress! on the stormy main
> Of strong Emotion. . . .

Russell's idea of the audience's response is noteworthy.

> ——O Siddons, cease to strain
> The nerve of Pleasure on the Rack of Pain;
> It thrills already in divine Excess!
> Yet fondly we the fair Tormentor bless,
> And woo her to prolong our exquisite distress.

Russell may have borrowed the phrase "divine excess" from Collins, but he must be given full credit for "exquisite distress." A final example shows the confusion in Neo-Classical criticism between legitimate emotion in a character and histrionic rant on the one hand and on the other the mingling of sentimentalism and Aristotelian catharsis. James Boswell's *An Ode to Tragedy, By a Gentleman of Scotland* (1761) began by invoking the Tragic Muse, "whose power divine/ The yielding passions all obey," then continued:

178

'Tis thine the soul to humanize
By fancied wo;—Goddess! 'tis thine
To bid compassion melt the eyes,
And all the feelings soft refine.
'Tis thine, with great Apollo's skill,
The inmost springs of life to thrill;
'Tis thine to move a breast of stone,
And make a brazen heart to own,
That solemn tragic numbers are of force,
To stop a villain in his bloody course.

In steady antiphony to the emotional rhapsodists, however, were the comments of the critics who spoke most authoritatively for the literary taste of the Neo-Classical era. These judges, some of them open advocates of Epicureanism, Platonism, or Stoicism, were not disposed to deny completely that tragic drama must represent the emotions or that the audience must respond emotionally to tragedy. Even so, these leading dramatic spokesmen placed the major emphasis on the cerebral rather than the visceral, the intellectual rather than the emotional constituents of tragedy. Corneille thought the chief benefit of depicting powerful emotions was to enable the spectator to learn to control his own small feelings.[33] Saint Evremond doubted that *catharsis* operated in the purgative sense for more than six or seven people in a given audience; the rest were schooled to the deplorable emotions of fright and compassion, neither of which was conducive to intelligent living or good citizenship. Saint Evremond agreed with Plato regarding the undesirable emotional effects of ancient tragedy, and he found modern tragedy exploiting suspense and charitableness; but he summed up his opinions by stating that the best tragedy ought to "seek above all things to show a greatness of mind well expressed that excites a tender admiration in us."[34] Dacier similarly felt that tragedy should "refine" the emotions above all; and he quoted Marcus Aurelius' Stoical opinion of the practicality of tragedy residing in its teaching of judgment and control.[35]

English critics in the main agreed. Even those Neo-Classicists who realized the vital place of the emotions in achieving the tragic effect often ended by shifting their emphasis from the aesthetic to the rational and ethical. Rymer wrote:

> Say others, *Poetry* and *Reason,* how come these to be Cater—cousins? *Poetry* is the *Child* of *Fancy* and is never to be school'd and disciplin'd by Reason; Poetry, say they, is blind inspiration, is pure enthusiasm, is *rapture* and *rage* all over.
>
> But *Fancy,* I think, in Poetry is like *Faith* in Religion; it makes far discoveries, and soars above reason, but never clashes, or runs against it. Fancy leaps, and frisks, and away she's gone; whilst reason rattles the chains, and follows after. *Reason* must consent and ratify whatever by *fancy* is attempted in its absence; or else 'tis all null and void in law.[36]

In *The Usefulness of the Stage,* John Dennis initially seemed to champion the cause of the emotions: "Nothing but passion, in effect, can please us, which everyone may know by experience. . . ." Then he went on to argue that no passion can please when Reason opposes and Reason cannot approve in daily life such passions as terror, anger, and so on. Tragic drama, therefore, is a means of providing reasonable passion, with the stress on "reasonable." Dryden's *Heads of An Answer to Rymer* urged that "upon a true definition of tragedy, it will be found that its work extends farther" than merely moving the passions. Tragedy must "reform manners" and lead to the control of the passions that lead to vice and social evil.[37] Both Addison and Steele constantly urged that tragedy was a way to persuade the viewer to a sweet reasonableness in his own life. Lillo, who did not scruple to make the most blatant emotional appeals in his play, declared in his preface that the primary purpose of his tragedies was to "carry conviction to the mind." David Hume's essay, "Of Tragedy," modified the prevalent opinion of tragic response somewhat; but his departure from the sentiments of Du Bos (Tragedy is a way to escape from languor and ennui into a more satisfying emotion) and Fontenelle

Neo-Classicism and the Tragic Drama

(Tragedy provides a "weakened and diminished" form of emotions that would pain in a stronger degree) led to a continued belief in the necessity of the ordered and rational elements in tragedy as a means to reasonable pleasure.[38] Johnson's concern with formal and ethical matters, as well as his horrified aversion to such unbearable emotions as those caused by *King Lear*, served to place him among the Neo-Classicists who basically sought in tragedy the confirmation of reason. William Hodson, for one, saw the result of applying the Neo-Classical separation of reason and emotion to tragic theory. Noting that poets who wrote for the public must appeal to the passions while those writing for a select audience ("the closet") must invoke the judgment, Hodson commented:

> In the one case, it is the heart we address, in the other the head; but the beauties by which the heart and the head are attracted are generally so different that to unite them, and compose a piece equally adapted to the closet and the theatre, has been held, from the example of so many Poets who have failed in one or other of these ends, an almost hopeless attempt for a genius less fertile than Shakespeare's.[39]

Even as they pronounced their judgment that tragedy must be passionate in a rational way, Neo-Classical critics wavered a bit when they came to consider the plays written to comply to this view. The view itself, however, stood unwavering for more than a hundred years, shored up by the Neo-Classical doctrine of a schism between Reason and Passion which was inherited from the dualistic philosophies of Greece.

If the Neo-Classical theories of history and philosophy helped to erode the assumptions underlying the Greek tragedy that English writers hoped to emulate, the adamantine beliefs of Christianity also wore them away. The conflict between Christian faith and pagan tragedy took the form of Puritan attacks on the theater, to be sure; and the Church Fathers were summoned to support this superficial antagonism, as we know.[40] But for every Christian-Classicist who declared that tragedy and Christianity were mutually exclusive codes of be-

181

havior, there were a dozen more who championed tragedy and devised means of reconciling its ostensible contradictions with revealed religion. Many of the most staunch apologists for Christianity also wrote tragic plays, e.g., Milton, Dryden, Addison, Lillo, and Johnson. The narrow Puritan attitude toward dramaturgy in general and tragedy in particular as inimical to Christianity was not operative within the Neo-Classical frame of mind.

The profound antagonism between the Christian and tragic purviews, as they were conceived in Neo-Classical England, was not something to be disregarded, however; it was recognized by leading critics, who dealt with it in ways that were unlike but that all had the effect of diminishing the tragic drama.[41] In "Christianizing" tragic theory, the Neo-Classicist drastically altered the classic tragedian's conception of the agonist and his cosmic background. Milton may have been able to alter successfully the pagan epic form to serve the demands of Christian theology, but a similar effort to alter pagan tragedy proved abortive.

French Neo-Classicists, as usual, anticipated the problem. Corneille attempted in his "tragedy," *Polyeucte,* to synthesize the formal elements of classic drama and the postulates of Christianity with some success.[42] But he concluded that a total assimilation of Christian metaphysics into tragic drama was undesirable though theoretically possible. The *Discourse on Tragedy* mentioned the French scorn of the deus ex machina in classic drama and its imitations because the pagan gods were now dead. Corneille himself thought the modern belief in saints and angels was comparable in its practice but he did not include such products of Christian dogma in his plays because it was not "the fashion" to do so.[43]

Saint Evremond saw the problem more pointedly. As early as 1672 he declared categorically:

> The spirit of our religion is directly opposed to that of tragedy. The humility and patience of our saints are directly contrary to the virtue of that kind of hero that the stage demands. . . .

And though he echoed Corneille's view of Christian *daimon-ology* as unfashionable, Saint Evremond stated it in terms that stressed its opposition to Christian orthodoxy:

> And if, in wishing to imitate the Ancients somehow, an author should introduce angels and saints on the stage, he would scandalize the devout as a profane man and would appear an imbecile in the eyes of the libertines. The preachers would not allow confusion of the pulpit with the theatre, or that one should go to learn from the mouths of actors what is retailed with authority in the churches to the whole population.[44]

To the French critics' postulations about the Christian hero and the paraphernalia of daimonology, English commentators superadded another problem: the reconciliation of the Christian doctrines of Salvation and Damnation with the metaphysics of tragedy. The Greek tragedians for the most part predicated the impossibility of determining the exact nature of justice (*themis*), guilt (*hubris*), and their relationship, though Aristotle saw a direct connection between *hubris* and Nemesis, or Retribution. Though the early Neo-Classical critics never penetrated very deeply into the issue of Christian salvation and sin, they did raise the issue in connection with their speculations about Poetic Justice. According to Rymer's *The Tragedies of the Last Age Consider'd*, it was the ancient Greeks who first established the principle of Poetic Justice in tragedy:

> For, said they, if the World can scarce be satisfied with God Almighty, whose holy will and purposes are not to be *comprehended*; a Poet . . . shall never be pardon'd who . . . is not incomprehensible. . . .

Rymer's comparison of the playwright to an incomprehensible but omnipotent God meant that the creator of the fictional world, like the Divine Maker of the universe, was expected to administer justice to his creatures.[45]

John Dennis argued the problem more fully if not more lucidly in an essay composed for *The Spectator*, No. 40. Addison and Steele had stated their opposition to Poetic Justice in tragedy on aesthetic grounds, and Dennis replied in quasi-theological terms that showed again the schism between Christian and ancient tragic metaphysics, though Dennis meant to close it. He reasoned as follows: man has an immortal future; the wicked in this life will be punished in the hereafter; but the tragic hero is imaginary and has no life after the end of the play; therefore if he is wicked his sins must be punished in the drama itself. Just as God knows and will reward or punish the hidden motives of real men, so the dramatist must judge and reward the hidden motives of his imaginary creations. Dennis's logic was muddled enough, but it at least realized that the Christian playwright, equipped with doctrines of afterlife and Divine Justice, faced a dilemma not known to the Greek tragedians. Fielding's barbs at Dennis's naiveté in assuming the British nation could be at once "Christian and tragical" were meant for Old Appius alone, but they could have hit Addison just as well for arguing that tragedy should "subdue the mind to the dispensations of Providence."[46]

English Neo-Classicists, finding themselves in a theological quandary regarding tragedy that they had satisfactorily avoided in their acceptance of pagan historiography, found one way out by setting their dramas in non-Christian settings. They could thereby avoid the problem of presenting life as tragic within a Providentially benevolent cosmos. Probably the most successful playwrights adopted this method. Dryden's *All for Love* suspended for all practical purposes the Christian metaphysical background in favor of a vaguely polytheistic one; and such plays as *Aureng-Zebe* and *The Indian Emperor, Troilus and Cressida* and *Oedipus* similarly skirted the theological issue. *The Conquest of Granada* was unique in its mixture of the Scourge of God theme with a majestically autonomous and successful hero who embraced conventional Christian belief in the tenth act. Addison's *Cato* uneasily donned a pagan metaphysic and then undermined it in the last act without substituting anything in its place. Other eighteenth century "tragedies," set in Celtic Britain, ancient Persia, or Peru, often found themselves similarly bereft of a meaningful cosmos and therefore a dramatic point when they ignored the Christian tenets and neglected to supply others in their place.

Another solution was adopted by at least one English writer with considerable success. This was the choice of an Old Testament subject as a topic for dramatic tragedy. Saint Evremond considered the pros and cons of such a choice:

> In truth, the stories of the Old Testament are much more useful on our stages. Moses, Samson, and Joshua had quite a different effect there than Polyeucte and Nearque. The amount of the marvelous that they can bring to it has something that is more proper for the [stage than saints' miracles]. But it seems to me that the priests would not fail to cry out against the profanation of these sacred stories with which they fill their ordinary conversations, their books, and their sermons. And, to speak sensibly, the miraculous crossing of the Red Sea, Joshua's stopping the sun in its course by prayer, Samson defeating armies with the jawbone of an ass—all these marvels, I say, would not be believed in a play, because in the Bible one adds faith to them, but soon the Bible would be doubted too because none of this would be believed in a play.[47]

By adopting some conventions of Greek tragedy, Milton's *Samson Agonistes* missed the pitfalls spotted by Saint Evremond, though whether his drama is both "high tragedy" and "Christian" is still debated. But if English Neo-Classicists were willing to exploit Old Testament subjects in epic poems and topical verse, in philosophical couplets or even an opera, they shied away when it came to composing tragic dramas.[48] Aside from *Samson Agonistes*, it is difficult to name a single play based on the *Old Testament* other than *The Tragedy of King Saul*, which was written by Roger Boyle or Joseph Trapp, never acted, and not published until 1703.

A third way chosen by Neo-Classical writers of tragedy to combine tragic and Christian premises was to retain only those classical assumptions that did not refute Christian orthodoxy and to substitute articles of faith for those that did. Pious critics even went so far as to argue that the substitution of Christian doctrines strengthened the weaknesses inherent in pagan tragedy. Nicholas Rowe hinted in his notes to *The Ajax of Sophocles* (1714) that ancient tragedy was actually penalized by its heathen metaphysics:

> It seems unworthy of the Divine Nature, that the Gods should take such part with the perverseness of our passions, as to punish one Man only to gratify the Malice of another. But this is one ill effect of what was very ornamental to their writings, The Machinery of the Ancient Poets, where the Gods are every moment descending and mixing with the affairs of human Life. In *Homer* there is hardly a Stone or a Javelin thrown, or an Arrow shot, that is not either directed or turned aside by some God. What miserable wooden Puppets upon Wires are the Heroes all the while! How much more noble, and suitable to the dignity of those Notions we ought to have of God, is the Christian System of Providence; where tho' there is a constant Care of us that accompanies the whole course of our Lives, yet Man is still left in the dignity of a free Agent.

Rowe's eminently defensible position might have enlarged the stature of the Christian hero; but it avoided confronting the implications of the Christian idea of a benevolent but omnipotent God and the antitragic doctrine of an afterlife.

Samuel Richardson, on the contrary, made his case for a Christian metaphysic at the expense of the tragic agonist. In his apologia to *Clarissa* (1748), his "Christian tragedy" in novel form, Richardson wrote of himself:

> He was resolved, therefore, to attempt something that never yet had been done. He considered that the tragic poets have as seldom made their heroes true objects of pity as the comic theirs laudable ones of imitation, and still more rarely have they made them in their deaths look forward to a future

hope. And thus when they die they seem totally to perish. Death in such instances must appear terrible. It must be considered as the greatest evil. But why is death set in such shocking lights when it is the universal lot?

The author of the History (or rather, Dramatic Narrative) of Clarissa is therefore well justified by the Christian system in deferring to extricate suffering virtue to the time in which it will meet with the completion of its reward.

And who that are in earnest in their profession of Christianity but will rather envy than regret the triumphant death of Clarissa, whose piety from her early childhood, whose humility, whose forgiving spirit, whose meekness and resignation Heaven only could reward?

It did not occur to Richardson, as it had to Saint Evremond, that the tragic poets made death the "greatest evil" for philosophical and aesthetic reasons or that a pitiable agonist full of meekness, resignation, forgiveness, and piety was not the best embodiment of tragic heroism, no matter how exemplary a Christian he might be.

In practice, George Lillo's *The London Merchant* is the most outstanding effort to fuse a Christian hero, the Christian attitude toward death, and the Christian doctrines of Divine Justice, Salvation, and Damnation into a dramatic tragedy. Although Lillo's "hero," George Barnwell, the apprentice to a London merchant, had not the tragic potential of a Polyeucte, a Saint Joan, or a Becket, his trial, fall, and apparent salvation clearly showed the difficulty of making a tragedy "Christian." Like Clarissa, Barnwell had the virtues of meekness, humility, dutifulness, chastity, piety and so on until his seduction by the Satanic Millwood. His "tragic reversal" was to be seen as he sank deeper into the mire of lust until at last he murdered his uncle-benefactor and was sentenced to the gallows for his crime. With the Christian capitalist Thorowgood, the pious Trueman, and the conformist Lucy as Greek chorus, Lillo showed Barnwell mounting the gallows, uttering such sentiments as these:

See, Millwood, see, our journey's at an end. Life, like a tale that's told, is passed away; that short, but dark and unknown passage, death, is all the space 'tween us and endless joys, or woes eternal. . . . Who knows but heaven, in your dying moments, may bestow that grace and mercy which your life despised? . . . To sin's like man, and to forgive like heaven.

Millwood's bleak despair and proud refusal to beg mercy from God strikes a faint reverberation of the tragic defiance of Clytemnestra or Hecuba: "I can't repent, nor ask to be forgiven." But the sledgehammer sentiments of the pious chorus drown out the tragic note:

> Lucy: Heart-breaking sight! O wretched, wretched Millwood!
>
> Trueman: How is she disposed to meet her fate?
>
> Blunt: Who can describe unutterable woe?
>
> Lucy: She goes to death encompassed with horror, loathing life, and yet afraid to die; no tongue can tell her anguish and despair.
>
> Trueman: Heaven be better to her than her fears! May she prove a warning to others, a monument of mercy in herself!

Like Lillo, other eighteenth century dramatists who chose to incorporate Christian doctrines in their plays finally refused to compromise those doctrines to the demands of tragedy. It may be possible to combine Christian faith and the tragic sense, to write a tragic drama about a hero who believes in a benevolent God but who paradoxically lives in "fear and trembling."[49] The eighteenth century taste for paradox did not extend to its religious dogmas, however. There was an either-or disjunction between belief and unbelief, faith and doubt, Christianity and atheism; and if the writer introduced the disjunction into his play, like Lillo he ended by rejecting one of the alternatives.

At least one popular playwright *began* by defining the disjunction and rejecting the tragic alternative. In *The Christian Hero*, Richard Steele systematically set out to destroy the notion of the pagan tragic hero and to put the Heroic Christian Soldier in its place. The tragic agonist acts from "the Changeable Heat of mere Courage and Blood" but the Christian acts "upon the firm Motives of Duty, Valour, and Constancy of Soul." The pagan dies for his own sense of false honor; the Christian dies for others:

> . . . nor is it an Ordinary Struggle between Reason, Sense, and Passion, that can raise Men to a calm and ready Negligence of Life, and animate 'em to Assault without Fear, Pursue without Cruelty, and Stab without Hatred.

Steele took care to prevent the reader from equating these virtues with a simple Stoicism. Why, said he, do we thrill at the mention of actions "done like an old *Roman* . . . when, on the other side, to say 'twas like a Primitive Christian,' chills Ambition and seldom rises to more than the cold approbation of a Duty that perhaps a Man wishes he were not oblig'd to."

> Or, in a word, why is it that the Heathen struts, and the Christian sneaks in our Imagination: If it be as *Machiavil* says, that Religion throws our Minds below noble and hazardous Pursuits, then its Followers are Slaves and Cowards; but if it gives a more hardy and aspiring Genius than the World before knew, then He, and All our fine Observers, who have been pleas'd to give us only Heathen Portraitures, to say no worse, have robb'd their Pens of Characters the most truly Gallant and Heroick that ever appear'd to Mankind.

The Christian Hero then went on to deride the supposed nobility of Caesar, Cato, Cassius, and Brutus; dismiss Ambition as foolish and unworthy; and insist upon man's submission to the loving and just will of God.

As a necessary adjunct to his attack on the ethical posits of pagan tragedy stood Steele's view that dramatic comedy, based on Christian optimism, was the most useful way to work men's minds into the Christian temper that surpasses tragedy. Steele's belief that tragedy is not enough led him to derogate repeatedly tragic pessimism in *The Tatler* and *The Spectator* and to adopt the rationale of literature expressed in the preface to *The Conscious Lovers*. When Addison's *Cato* proved successful, however, without incorporating overtly Christian principles, Steele modified his views to the extent of praising the happy effects of didacticism, Christian or pagan, that improved the spectator as *Cato* did.[50]

In its insistence on a literature that teaches as well as pleases, the Neo-Classical rationale found the last critical thread to bind down the titanism of ancient tragic drama. The Neo-Classical obsession with practical knowledge leading to personal improvement and the betterment of society was confirmed by history, Greek philosophy, and Christian dogma. As they inherited dramatic literary theory from such Humanist critics as Scaliger and Vossius, English Neo-Classicists were able to synthesize all their favorite posits about the usefulness of past knowledge with their assumptions about tragic drama.[51] Vossius' "De Sententia" prepared the way for a critical stress on the "message" of tragedy. And as a rigid Neo-Classical principle, it was summarized by Rapin in the *Reflections on the Poetics of Aristotle*:

> Tragedy, of all parts of poesy, is that which Aristotle has most discussed, and where he appears most exact. He alleges that tragedy is a public lecture, without comparison more instructive than philosophy; because it teaches the mind by the sense, and rectifies the passions by the passions themselves, calming by their emotions, the troubles they excite in the heart. . . . [It] is furnished with all the most moving and terrible adventures that history can afford to stir in the heart those motions it pretends, to the end it may cure of those vain fears that may annoy it, and those childish compassions that may soften it.

English Neo-Classicists from Dryden to Johnson were unanimously agreed as to the didactic nature of tragedy, though in their definitions of the "lessons" to be found, they differed.

Neo-Classicism and the Tragic Drama

Dryden and Dennis thought tragedy served to eliminate social evils arising from uncontrolled passions. Dryden and Rymer felt that English national pride would be served. Addison theorized that tragedy would lead men to a greater piety, and his tragedy was supposed to produce "public Spiritedness." Pope found tragedy the means to refining the morality and sensibility of the man of taste. Lillo was certain that tragedy would make thriftier and more pious Christian burghers, and George Adams hoped it would aid the Church in proselytizing the godless to Christianity. Johnson believed that tragedy disclosed elemental human nature and led to the contemplation of the cosmic order sustaining human life. And all of them supposed that tragedy ought to appeal to as wide an audience as possible and that its moral should be so obvious as to escape the understanding of no one.

The Neo-Classicist's trust in the use of tragedy to teach an ever-enlarging audience meant that Neo-Classical drama grew more and more formulated as it grew less ambiguous. The *mysterion* of ancient tragedy became lost in the process. Shakespeare's ambiguous cosmos was carefully simplified by such "adapters" as Dryden and Tate, or excised by Pope and Warburton, or damned by Johnson. In *All for Love, Venice Preserved*—even *Samson Agonistes*—enough of the Greek and Shakespearean cosmic ambiguity remained to prevent the reduction of the tragedy to an axiomatic lesson. As the didactic premise strengthened in the eighteenth century, more and more "tragedies" became five act illustrations of simple "truths": "Death before dishonor"; "Sinner, repent, the Day of Judgment cometh"; or "Dulce et decorum est pro patria mori" (as with *Cato*). If the Neo-Classical adapters of Shakespeare were never able to reduce *King Lear* to "Honor thy father and thy mother" and *Hamlet* to "Procrastination is the thief of Time," it was not for want of intention.

The dramatic tragedy of the Restoration and eighteenth century suffered from the effects of its combined historicism, repressive ethics, Christian predilections, and didacticism to such an extent that it suffered a period of invalidism. One critic

191

has suggested that it even died.[52] Allowing for the limitations of twentieth century standards, it must be admitted that whatever other form it took, the tragic sense did not animate the dramatic genre to such an extent that tragedy became the transcendent literary expression of the life-view of English Neo-Classicism. Ironically enough, the Neo-Classical drama is of interest to modern readers largely because of its "historical" significance.

To one surveying the symmetrical arrangement of Neo-Classical thought and literature, the hollow tragedies of the period seem akin to the sham facades that dotted eighteenth century landscapes. The English classicist, who admired Greek tragedy and assumed his own Hellenic literary bent, knew that the configuration of Neo-Classical literature demanded the presence of a temple to tragedy, and he accordingly constructed a fake Doric front here and there to complete the aesthetic landscape. Though mere appearances, formal surfaces, the tragedies of the day satisfied the Neo-Classicist, who willingly suspended his disbelief and used his classical education to "fancy" the false fronts real.

The most impressive literary monument of English Neo-Classicism, however, was not to be a shrine to the tragic Melpomene but to another Muse. Slowly, painstakingly, in the latter part of the Neo-Classical era, a single builder was constructing a literary work that arose as a monument to the architectonic ideology of Neo-Classicism. Ostensibly a temple of Clio, Gibbon's *The History of the Decline and Fall of the Roman Empire* is the literary embodiment of the world-view of Neo-Classicism and today it remains the most triumphant expression of that view.

9 · Gibbon

Since the publication of the first volume of *The History of the Decline and Fall of the Roman Empire* in 1776, Edward Gibbon has been the object of speculation and commentary by many critics. Irritated clerics have disputed his depiction of the growth of Christianity. Historians have praised him as one of the founders of modern historiographical technique and have faulted his historical theses. Biographers have searched into the records of his life and puzzled about the rather odd combination of qualities comprising Gibbon's character. Most recently literary critics have begun to assess Gibbon's work thematically and stylistically.[1]

With a few notable exceptions, Gibbon's critics display an uneasiness somewhere or other in their discussions of the great historian. Historiographers are inclined to fidget over Gibbon's apparent refusal to explain precisely *why* Rome fell and often end by discussing his style. Ecclesiastical apologists are both baffled and affronted by the imperturbable coolness of their opponent. Literary men indicate an uncertainty about dealing with an historical work. And biographers, though most are fascinated with Gibbon, often feel constrained to apologize for their subject or to condemn him roundly for his failure to meet their own standards.

In brief, the critical treatment afforded Gibbon resembles that given to such figures as Dryden, Swift, Pope, and Johnson. Critics search for a clue, a key to the minds of these men; but each of the major figures of the Neo-Classical Age displays such diversity of talents and interests and provides such a range of productions that it often proves difficult critically to do more than treat a limited aspect of Swiftian or Johnsonian thought. Furthermore, the major—the "representative"—writers differ so widely from each other in certain opinions and techniques that the common basis of their "Neo-Classicism" is equally difficult to establish. This study has suggested some of the individual ideas and concepts which appear prominently in the thought of the major Neo-Classicists, as well as the minor ones; but in most cases, the writer's assimilation of these has been partial, implicit, and subtle.

With Edward Gibbon, however, the common bases of Neo-Classical thought become so total and explicit as to provide a veritable paradigm of the world-view of English Neo-Classicism. There are two factors in the case of Gibbon that permit him to function as the model of Neo-Classical behavior and thought. Unlike the other leading figures of this age, Gibbon preserved a detailed, firsthand account of his intellectual development: in the *Journals, Letters,* and *Autobiography.* These works provide the most complete possible information about the growth of the mind of an eighteenth century classicist in England, and they furnish insights into the minds of his contemporaries as well as Gibbon's own. Furthermore, unlike his compeers, Gibbon concentrated on writing one great composite work as his life's task instead of gearing his interests and literary productions to the topical demands of the moment. As a consequence, Gibbon's *History* was the most total synthesis of the beliefs and attitudes of his age. A modern historian has said of Gibbon:

> He is the perfect representative of the eighteenth-century spirit in all its strength and weakness; its self-confidence and self-satisfaction, its classicism and formalism, its mature and cosmopolitan civilization. Indeed he is in a sense more eighteenth century than his age, for his classicism and rationalism are still undisturbed by the revolutionary spirit of romanticism that was invading and conquering European society.

And again, the same commentator:

> . . . we no longer read Gibbon in order to understand the causes that led to the decline and fall of the Roman Empire. . . . Nevertheless we do read him for his own sake and his work will remain a classic. . . . For we read history not only for the light it throws on the past but also for the light it throws on the world of the writer. We cannot fully under-

stand an age unless we understand how that age regarded the past, for every age makes it own past. . . . Few historians have possessed in so high a degree as Gibbon the power of transforming the chaos of the past into an intelligible order. . . . It is as it were a translation of the past into the language of eighteenth century culture. But that culture was itself the product of the tradition that inspired his work—the tradition of the classical world transmitted through medieval Christendom and reinforced by the Humanism of the seventeenth and eighteenth centuries; and consequently Gibbon's treatment still had a vital relation to its subject.[2]

An examination of Gibbon's mind and his masterpiece bears out these contentions and demonstrates the synthetic coherence of the "intelligible order" of English Neo-Classicism.[3]

I. THE ROAD TO ROME

If there can be any such thing as an archetypal Neo-Classicist, Edward Gibbon was it. The evidence to be found in his personal writings is confirmed by the accounts of such contemporaries as Reynolds, Walpole, Boswell, and Maria Holroyd to support his Neo-Classical attributes. Even the facts of his life epitomize the careers of most of the literary men of his age.[4] Like the majority of his illustrious cohorts, he was born into a genteel but nonaristocratic family with just enough money to support the claim of good birth. Gibbon was a sickly boy who, like Pope and Shaftesbury, spent a good deal of time reading in libraries and educating himself. At a normally precocious age he entered Oxford, the alma mater of Swift, Addison, Johnson, and others; and Gibbon, too, departed without a degree. He became enamoured of the classical world in his youth and joined Addison, Gray, and Goldsmith by writing an essay extolling its merits. His youthful vacillations in religious matters caused him to change from Anglicanism to Catholicism to a form of skeptical Deism—positions varyingly advocated by Dryden among others. In the manner of Addison, Gray, Boswell, and Walpole, he took the Grand Tour.

And of course he underwent the required flirtation with a young woman whose interest in marriage far exceeded his own, with the result that Gibbon—as did Prior, Swift, Gay, Pope, Gray, Collins, Reynolds, and Walpole—chose the life of bachelorhood. He first entered the literary lists as Swift, Atterbury, and Parnell had done: by attacking a formidable literary giant. Gibbon's prudence made him assail Warburton anonymously, however, to his later regret. In his prime, Gibbon was a member of The Club, together with every literary Londoner of importance. He sat in the Parliament of Sheridan, Walpole, Burke, and Pitt. And like a score of others, he kept a diary, wrote copious letters, went to the theater, played whist and loo with dowager ladies, and finally, weakened by eighteenth century medical practices, died in bed. Gibbon's life was little more than commonplace for a man of his class and interests.

His character was something else again. Gibbon's later biographers have wondered at the admixture of sangfroid, sensuality, gregariousness, aloofness, self-indulgence, self-control, laziness, and prodigious learning in Gibbon's personality. Yet Gibbon's personality holds little mystery despite its qualities. Gibbon was not complex and tortured as Swift or Sterne or Johnson was. He lacked the personableness and inner qualms of Dryden, the warmhearted and impetuous partisanship of Steele, the wry gusto of Fielding, the reticent dedication of Gray, the driving sensuality and hidden terrors of Boswell. Even as a literary bachelor in the age of bachelors he was unusual. He never became a sycophant to his friends, as Gay did, nor did he retire from the world like Gray. Swift, Reynolds, and Walpole may have found solace in the presence of auxiliary ladies in their own, or adjacent, households; but Gibbon was easiest when removed even from the women dearest to him. In some ways, Gibbon was most like Pope and Walpole in his social and emotional independence, but he never developed their accompanying vehemence, self-pity, and waspishness. Gibbon was uniquely himself.

But if he was alone, he was by no means atypical. He was, in fact, the living Neo-Classical ideal of behavior. In an era where literature praised normative behavior and devoted a great amount of space to prescribing its limits, most literary men failed to attain their own norm. Other Neo-Classicists are interesting because of the ways they fell short of their common ideal. Gibbon is interesting because he *was* the ideal. While others theorized about the life of reason and self-control, Gibbon lived it. As others sighed for or castigated Utopia, Gibbon systematically created a series of one-man Utopias in Buriton, Bentinck Street, and Lausanne. As the rest raged for order, Gibbon created order—in his life and his work. He was an emotional Houyhnhnm among the Lilliputians and Brobdingnagians.

The sources of Gibbon's "reasonable" attitude toward life may be looked for vainly in his family background and childhood temperament. The early death of his mother, his childhood illnesses, the lifelong moodiness and tyranny of his father, the religiosity of one aunt and the self-satisfied martyrdom of another—none of these factors indicate that Gibbon had much favoring him, from the standpoint of inheritance or surroundings.

Nor can his character be ascribed to innate disposition or temperament, what Gibbon himself called "genius." Gibbon's idea of what composed "genius" seems to have varied slightly as he grew older, but in general he used the term to denote intelligence in differing degrees, capacity, and predisposition. In his youth Gibbon used "genius" to mean "intelligence"; thus in his *Journal* he spoke of an acquaintance as "proof how well an ordinary genius may go through the world," and he remarked that Erasmus had a "genius which could see thro' the vain subtilties of the school, revive the laws of criticism, treat every subject with eloquence and delicacy, sometimes emulate the ancients, often imitate them, and never copy them." High intelligence, then, possessed the qualities of incisiveness, taste, comprehension, and originality; this faculty, which grasped "first principles," Gibbon believed a "direct gift from heaven." But he further believed that "Brilliant genius allows itself to be dazzled by its own conjectures and sacrifices freedom to hypotheses" so that straitening systems and falsification often were its products. Gibbon's lifelong opinion is summarized in the *Essay on the Study of Literature*:

> It may well be worth while to formulate certain laws capable, not indeed of promoting genius, but of saving it from error; perhaps if men had always balanced these laws carefully, they would not so often have confounded subtlety with delicacy of mind, obscurity with depth, or a turn for paradox with creative genius.[5]

Gibbon was loath to overrate the presence of genius in himself. He was always able to view his talents objectively. In the summer of 1760 he wrote to his father:

> Whatever else I may be ignorant of, I think I know myself, and shall always endeavor to mention my good qualities without vanity, and my defects without repugnance.

And the famous passage from his *Journal* is an instance of his self-candour: ". . . while everyone looks on me as a prodigy of application, I know myself how strong a propensity I have to indolence." He acknowledged his limitations in order to live with those he could not change and to alter those he could. Unlike Johnson or Boswell, who agonized over their "slothfulness" and the "sin" of wasting time, Gibbon matter-of-factly identified his predispositions without self-recrimination. He could therefore say of himself in the *Autobiography*:

> After his oracle Dr. Johnson, my friend Sir Joshua Reynolds denies all original genius, any natural propensity of the mind to one art or science rather than another. Without engaging in a metaphysical or rather verbal dispute, I *know* by experience from my early youth I aspired to the character of an historian.

This was the nature of the "genius" Gibbon ascribed to himself: an innate capacity that had to be cultivated in order to develop, and he thought development came from the inspiration born of learning. When Richard Porson, tempering sweet praise of the *Decline and Fall* "by a reasonable mixture of acid" (the phrase is Gibbon's), gave the history a "high encomium," Gibbon declared: "I am less flattered by Mr. Porson's high encomium on the style and spirit of my work than I am satisfied with his honorable testimony to my attention, diligence, and accuracy. . . ." As he defined his own genius, Gibbon meant his infinite capacity for taking pains.[6]

It is this capacity that permitted Gibbon to become the ideal of English Neo-Classicism, in its social and personal as well as its intellectual manifestations, and it is this capacity that explains the seeming contradictions in his character. In his personal behavior, he carefully trained himself to be the practicing Epicurean that has captivated his biographers. His *Journals* show the youthful Gibbon gambling and drinking to excess and calmly resolving never to exceed moderation again. He never did. His *Correspondence* shows the systematic way he constructed his Epicurean life. The letters constantly proclaim his disavowal of ambition and his limited interest in public and political life. They praise the contemplative life of withdrawal and busy themselves with descriptions of Gibbon's taste in clothes, wallpaper, food, entertainment, and gardens.[7] Yet, trivial as much of his correspondence may appear, Gibbon, unlike Walpole, seldom bent to gossip; and if strong passions and burning issues are absent from his letters, Gibbon's concern with trifles never turns him into a trifler. His ideal of behavior was that of the "universal man," as it had been developed in ancient Greece:

> When one reads these dissertations [on Greek stadia], one admires the active spirit of the Greeks, sensible to every species of entertainment and glory; who could at the same time, and with the same application bring to perfection, dancing and Philosophy, boxing and poetry.[8]

He approached this ideal with his usual determination to take pains; and even as he was perfecting his Epicurean external life, he was internally the most exacting kind of Stoic.

It was his Stoicism that Gibbon systematically developed into the working habits which resulted in his *History.* The letters from Bentinck Street proudly recount the schedule of his days, which carefully included study, exercise, and social intercourse. The records of his life in Lausanne with Georges Deyverdun show a similar pride in his mixture of assiduous scholarship with frivolous conviviality. And the two later stages of his scholarly life are prepared for early in the *Journal* when Gibbon matter-of-factly records an illness that ended in his being blooded while he continued to work on his Greek grammar, practicing tense inflections and the "moods of the Barytone verbs in ω."⁹ Gibbon's "genius" and his scholarly ambition forged in him a Stoical endurance and self-control. Under the velvet suit, within the pampered flesh, there lived an austere and determined mind.

His determination was constantly tested during the early years when he was forced to educate himself and during the twenty year period that he was working on the *History.* In silent privacy, enclosed by the library walls of Buriton, Bentinck Street, and Lausanne, he marched with the patience and self-control of Cato over the desert stretches of the mediaeval chronologers and through the tangles of Renaissance *scholia.* His records give a vivid portrayal of the obstacles encountered by the eighteenth century classicist on the *via sacra* to Rome; and if Gibbon attained his goal where others faltered, it was because he knew his own strength and weakness and could pace himself. Moreover, he had a clear sense of direction, though it was neither that of the pagan or the Christian. His goal was "Truth—naked, unblushing truth" in "more serious history" and the "personal narrative."¹⁰ He achieved it in both.

The way was not easy, however. As a boy, Gibbon lacked the pedagogical guides that could have directed his intellectual energy, partly because his sporadic illnesses kept interrupting his studies, first at his aunt's Westminster school and later at Kingston-upon-Thames, and partly because of a series of narrow or lazy masters. Gibbon fed his "indiscriminate appetite" with Pope's *Homer* and the *Arabian Nights' Entertainments,* "two books which will always please by the moving pictures of human manners and specious miracles; nor was I then capable of discerning that Pope's translation is a portrait endowed with every merit excepting that of likeness to the original. . . . In the death of Hector, and the shipwreck of Ulysses, I tasted the new emotions of pity and terror. . . ." And he was encouraged by the rod to learn rudimentary Latin at Kingston:

> By the common methods of discipline, at the expense of many tears and some blood, I purchased the knowledge of Latin syntax, and not long since was I possessed of the dirty volumes of Phaedrus and Cornelius Nepos, which I painfully construed and darkly understood.[11]

The mature Gibbon approved the choice of Phaedrus and Nepos as "not injudicious" since the animal fables of Phaedrus "convey in familiar images the truths of morality and prudence" and Nepos, "the friend of Atticus and Cicero," not only writes simple, elegant Latin but "exhibits a series of men and manners; and with such illustrations as every pedant is not indeed qualified to give, this *classic* biographer [italics mine] may initiate a young student in the history of Greece and Rome." Though his study was not thorough, in retrospect Gibbon approved the discipline of the grammar school:

> Our seminaries of learning do not exactly correspond with the precept of a Spartan king that "the child should be instructed in the arts which will be useful to the man". . . . But these schools may assume the merit of teaching all that they pretend to teach, the Latin and Greek languages. They deposit in the hands of a disciple the keys of two valuable chests, nor can he complain if they are afterward lost or neglected by his own fault.[12]

He was more excoriating in his condemnation of eighteenth century Oxford, with its smug, inbred, gossipy dons who left gentlemen-scholars to their own intellectual devices. Gibbon had definite ideas, adapted from those of Le Clerc, as to what made a profitable college education:

In the discipline of a well-constituted academy, under the guidance of skillful and vigilant professors, I should gradually have risen from translations to originals, from the Latin to the Greek classics, from dead language to living science.[13]

At Oxford, he did not; but though he castigated Oxford, he never felt himself excused by the deficiencies of his university to approve his own. Samuel Johnson, who also came to Oxford with prodigious knowledge and profound ignorance, only to drop out after a year, provides an interesting contrast to Gibbon. Though neither rationalized his failure, Johnson never condemned Oxford and always basked in the praise of Oxonians; Gibbon scorned Oxonians and their praise. The difference between the two men seems to be that Johnson, a natural "brilliant genius" who formulated rigid systems, was unwilling to blame the University for his failures; Gibbon, the painstaking, self-cultivated genius, was unwilling to credit it with his successes. Johnson felt he had nothing to learn from his teachers; Gibbon knew that he had everything to learn and he at last was forced to teach himself.

Gibbon's continual struggles with Latin and Greek syntax, fully recorded in his *Journal* and *Autobiography*, are a reminder that Neo-Classicism was an intellectual outlook that was attained only by syntactic agony. Even after centuries of editors and commentators, the classical scholar in the mid-eighteenth century had to parse and collate, compare texts and reconstrue, to reach that Intelligible World which could provide a "living science." Even texts used in the grammar schools were corrupt; Gibbon said of the "dirty volume" of Phaedrus that he studied at Kingston:

> The labors of fifty copy editors confess the defects of the copy, as well as the value of the original, and the schoolboy may have been whipped for misapprehending a passage which Bentley could not restore, and which Burman could not explain.[14]

If Latin texts were bad, Greek were worse. In December 1755, at the age of eighteen, Gibbon began to study Greek but its difficulties proved too much for him. In the summaries of his studies for 1756 and 1757 he concluded, "upon the whole, I rather neglected my Greek." By November 2, 1761, however, he decided to enliven his military service by working up Homer and thereafter he systematically read Homer every day, using Pope's translations, Racine's *Grecques*, Guichart's *Mémoires Militaires*, Bayle's *Dictionary*, and Dodwell's *Annals* as aids. His primary editions were those of Küster and Burman (he preferred the former); and he laboriously translated lists of verb roots from Greek to French and back again to improve his vocabulary. On October 28, 1762, he received a copy of Robert Constantin's *Greek Lexicon* (London, 1637) to assist his labors, but he disliked its alphabetical format though he admired its exact definitions and well distinguished word senses. In the *Journal* entry for August 16, 1762, Gibbon justified his reasons for beginning his intensive study of Greek with Homer, in opposition to the advice of Le Clerc: Homer was a cultural historian, a storehouse of classical knowledge, and an excellent testing ground for syntax. Gibbon was well aware of himself as a scholar in the Humanist tradition. He weighed the syntactic conjectures of Bentley, Küster, and Burman and made some conclusions of his own; his critical commentaries on Homer in the *Journal* are in the conscious tradition of Addison, Pope, Parnell, Jortin, and, more remotely, Photius, Psellus, Eustathius, and Spondanus (all of whom Gibbon eventually consulted).[15] His evaluation in the *Autobiography* of his early Greek study drew a conscious parallel.

> As soon as I had given preference to the Greek, the example of Scaliger and my own reason determined me on the choice of Homer, the father of poetry and the Bible of the ancients. But Scaliger ran through the Iliad in one-and-twenty days, and I was not dissatisfied with my own diligence for performing the same labour in an equal number of weeks.[16]

"Diligence," "labor"—Gibbon's estimate of his talents was constant; and his apparent praise of the nimble Scaliger is not without a faint note of disapprobation for still another "brilliant Genius."

If Gibbon was tied to the Classical–Humanist tradition by his interest in ancient literature and syntactic exegesis, he was even more strongly bound to the Patristic–Humanist tradition of chronological speculation. In fact, his boyhood aspiration was more properly stated to be "the character of a chronologer" than that of the historian. Not that there was much difference between history and chronology to the Neo-Classical mind. Dr. Johnson's differentiation between the two in Boswell's famous anecdote is about as advanced as the nonhistorical intellect ever got. Johnson declared there was very little "real authentick history":

> Johnson: That certain Kings reigned, and certain battles were fought, we can depend upon as true; but all the colouring, all the philosophy of history is conjecture.
> Boswell: Then, Sir, you would reduce all history to no better than an almanack, a mere chronological series of remarkable events.

Boswell jeered later at Gibbon for sitting silent during this exchange in 1775, when the *Decline and Fall* was in the making.[17] But Gibbon's silence may very well have been in agreement. It is true that Gibbon had spoken of a "philosophy of history" in his *Essay* in 1759; but if Johnson was attacking the rationalist theory of history as productive of a science of human behavior, as he very possibly was, then Gibbon had no cause to speak. In both the early *Essay* and the late *Autobiography*, Gibbon dismissed this theory, as he did in practice with the *Decline and Fall*. Moreover, in 1775 he was still meditating over the form and style of the *History* and he was as yet unaware of the span of time it would cover. There is evidence that his desire to discover historical "truth" may have been identical with his desire for chronological accuracy.

In any case, when his indiscriminate boyhood appetite "sub-

sided by degrees in the historic line," he began his studies with
a new encyclopaedic work and an old, familiar one.

> . . . I must ascribe this choice to the assiduous perusal of the
> *Universal History*, as the octavo volumes successively ap-
> peared. This unequal work, as a treatise of Hearne, the
> *Ductor Historicus*, referred me to the Greek and Roman
> historians, to as many as were accessible to the English
> reader.[18]

The *Universal History*, which eventually ran to twenty octavo
volumes, began to be published in 1749 under the general
editorship of John Campbell. The forerunner of such series
as the Cambridge and Oxford *Histories*, the *Universal History*
was a sequence of individually written works by contributors
including George Sale, since called the best Orientalist in
Europe in his day; Shelvocke, and George Psalmanazar, whose
fraudulent history of Formosa became something of a scandal
on the order of the *Ossian* and Chatterton affairs. It was truly
an "unequal work," as most such series are; but Gibbon was
led by it to a voracious consumption of English translations of
Greek and Roman history, and descriptions of India, China,
Mexico, and Peru. The summer of 1751 found him devouring
the *Continuation of Eacherd's Roman History* in Mr. Hoare's
Wiltshire library until the dinner bell summoned him to a
more corporal feast. And still later at Bath, he found Howell's
History of the World, which dealt with the Saracens, the
Orient, and other exotic peoples and places.

By this time, the youthful prodigy was suffering from mental
indigestion, and he sought for an antidote. It came as the pre-
scribed double dose of geography and chronology compounded
by the Renaissance chronologers:

> Such vague and multifarious reading could not teach me to
> think, to write, or to act, and the only principle that darted
> a ray of light into the undigested chaos was an early and
> *rational* [my italics] application to the order of time and
> place. The maps of Cellarius and Wells imprinted in my

mind the picture of ancient geography; from Strauchius I imbibed the elements of chronology. The tables of Helvicus and Anderson, the annals of Ussher and Prideaux, distinguished the multitude of names and dates in a clear and indelible series. But in the discussion of the first ages, I overleaped the bounds of modesty and use. In my childish balance I presumed to weigh the systems of Scaliger and Petavius, Marsham and Newton which I could seldom study in the originals; the dynasties of Assyria and Egypt were my top and cricket ball; and my sleep has been disturbed by the difficulty of reconciling the Septuagint with the Hebrew computation.[19]

Gibbon did not identify the part played in his religious alterations by his chronological deliberations; but since chronological study in the seventeenth and eighteenth centuries was never free of religious implication, and since Gibbon confessed himself troubled by "reconciling the Septuagint with the Hebrew computation," we may safely suppose that even before he read Conyers Middleton's disturbing *Inquiry* into miracles, he was theologically unsettled by his studies.

After being proselytized into the Roman Catholic Church and sent down from Oxford, Gibbon, "Unprovided with original learning, unformed in the habits of thinking, unskilled in the arts of composition, . . . resolved—to write a book." It was a chronological study, *The Age of Sesostris,* that tried to place the legendary conqueror in the time of Solomon. Gibbon showed a daring in discarding the dates of Manetho—"falsehood, I will now add, is not incompatible with the sacerdotal character"—but he also disagreed with the computations of the great Isaac Newton, who stood in opposition to Marsham: "I was then enamoured of Sir John Marsham's *Canon Chronicus,* an elaborate work of whose merits and defects I was not yet qualified to judge." When he reached the age of qualification, Gibbon found *The Age of Sesostris* "not devoid of ingenuity" for "a youth of fifteen." But he came to agree with Temple, Swift, Bolingbroke, and Goldsmith about the futility of much chronologizing:

At a riper age I no longer presume to connect the Greek, the Jewish, and the Egyptian antiquities, which are lost in a distant cloud. Nor is this the only instance in which the belief and knowledge of the child are superseded by the more rational ignorance of the man.[20]

If he outgrew his preoccupation for correlating legendary events, he did not lose his chronologer's obsession with dating the events of the historic era. *The Letters of Edward Gibbon* contains some self-conscious attempts of the nineteen-year-old exile in Lausanne to become a latter-day polymath.[21] Written in Latin or French to two of the most eminent continental scholars of the period—Johan Jacob Breitinger, a professor of Greek and Hebrew at Zurich, and Johann Matthias Gessner, a professor of Belles-Lettres at the University of Göttingen, who edited classical texts—they show Gibbon trying hard to be another young Salmasius or, hopefully, a Vossius or Scaliger. The correspondence with Breitinger is concerned with a chronological crux in Justin; Gibbon wants to establish the chronology of the Scythians and he cites, in detail, Justin, Orosius, Augustine, Curtius, Phaedrus (his old school text), Xenophon, Livy, and Diodorus. To the initial letter of October 15, 1756, the august scholar replies with patience but little concurrence. Gibbon's subsequent letters on November 5, 1756, and January 24, 1757, persist in his thesis and trot out his knowledge of Trogus, Cicero, Horace, Livy, Appian, Dio Cassius, and Tertullian. The correspondence with Gessner is more confined (Gessner was less indulgent than Breitinger). In it, Gibbon makes another chronological-textual attempt. He cites Scaliger and Isaac Vossius on the dates of Catullus; parades his awareness of Bentley and Grotius; and refers grandly to a passage of Velleius Paterculus "qui a donné tant de peine aux Savans," i.e., Heinsius and Burman. Naturally, Gibbon has a ready solution.

When at last he came to the writing of the *Essay on the Study of Literature* Gibbon had plainly assimilated the educational and historical views of his age with his personal interest in chronology in such a way as to form the rationale for his future efforts. The great popularity of the *Essay*, particularly in France, was in large measure due to the succinctness with which Gibbon restated accepted critical opinion. The sections on the usefulness of the "classics," the relationship of historiography to poetry (especially dramatic tragedy), the value of chronological computation, the Augustan Age of Rome, and the universal values of history are aphoristically expressed:

> Knowledge of antiquity: this is our true commentary; but what is more necessary still, is a certain temper of mind which results therefrom, a temper of mind which not only enables us to understand the past—but familiarizes us with it, and allows us to see it with the eyes of the ancients.

> On Perrault's strictures of Homer and Boileau's reprimand: A classic taste (I mean in conventional matters) would have enlightened him more than all the lectures of his adversary.

> Aristotle has declared that the poet should present his heroes to us such as history has shown them. . . . When an author desires to venture on such changes, he should reflect whether a delicate or striking beauty will result—a beauty proportioned to the violation of the law. . . . Of how many beauties history would have robbed the poet (Virgil). Encouraged by success, however, he sometimes abandons it where he should have followed it.

> . . . the characters of great men should be sacred, but poets may write their history less as it was than as it should have been.

> What insight the physican may derive from the description of the plague that devastated Athens! I admire with him the majestic force of Thucydides, the art and energy of Lucretius; but he goes farther, he studies in the sufferings of Athens those of his own countrymen.

And concluding a specimen of chronological computation by himself: I have taken pleasure in defending a useful and interesting episode in history, but my chief object has been to show how delicate are these critical discussions in which it is not merely necessary to grasp the demonstration, but to compare the weight of opposing probabilities, and to show how we must be on our guard against the most dazzling of theories, since so few can sustain the ordeal of a free and careful examination.[22]

Though such sentiments are redolent of those expressed by other Neo-Classical writers antecedent to and contemporary with him, Gibbon fuses them into his dominant theory of historiography given in sections XLVI-LV of the *Essay*. From the partial insights of a Swift or Addison, Gibbon goes on to a total view of historical writing:

Among the multitude of historical facts, there are vast numbers which prove nothing beyond their own existence; there are others which may be sighted in partial conclusions, whence the philosopher may judge the motives of an action, or of a trait of character which lights up some link in the chain. Those again which dominate the general scheme, or are closely bound up with it and move its springs are rare; and it is still more rare to find minds which are able to discern these in the vast chaos of events, and to bring them out pure and without admixture.

To those who have more judgment than erudition, it may appear superfluous to state that causes should always be proportioned to effects; that the character of an age should not be built upon the action of one man; that the measure of the strength and riches of a state should not be sought for in a single ruinous and compulsory act; that it is only by weighing acts together that they can be judged, for while a striking deed may dazzle like a lightning flash, it teaches nothing, unless by comparison with others of the same kind.

Pay greater regard to the facts which form themselves into a system than to those which you discover after having conceived your system. Prefer above all little traits of character to startling incidents. It is with an era as with a man.[23]

The rest of Gibbon's discussion is in kind: he examines Tacitus and Livy and appraises them by his criteria; *all* facts must be collected and examined, not selected ones as Fontenelle had said; brilliant hypotheses are suspect and rigid systems even more so; the historian must concern himself with the "study of fixed but general laws" and the examination of "those general events whose slow but sure influence changes the face of the earth without our being able to trace the period of these changes." Unsurprisingly, Gibbon's requirements for the historian are not the same as those for the philosopher who seeks "first causes": "Let us avoid this error; whenever an action appears complicated, let us admit that it results from general causes without rejecting design and chance." For Gibbon, the historian's judgment must depend upon the extent of his learning, and learning is the mastery of all details.

With his knowledge of Greek and Latin perfected, his practice in chronological techniques experienced, and his theory of historiography enunciated, Gibbon had only to choose his subject and start gathering all known data about it. After one or two false starts, he decided on the history of the Roman Empire; the *Autobiography* painstakingly lists the works that he read to prepare for the writing of each successive volume. First he went through Tacitus, Pliny the Younger, Juvenal, "the ocean of the Augustan history," "the original records, both Greek and Latin, from Dion Cassius to Ammianus Marcellinus," inscriptions on medals and coins, the patristic corpus, and a host of Humanist commentators: Tillemont, Muratori, Sigonius, Baronius, and others. For subsequent volumes, he absorbed the writings of the age of Justinian, Procopius, Agathias, the codes, and the "fathers and councils." His pride in mastering so much "testimony" is obvious in the detailed documentations for *The History of the Decline and Fall*; but it is even more explicit in the *Autobiography*, where Gibbon shows his pride in having his scholarship defended by Porson when the Reverend Davis attacked him.[24] And Gibbon's ire was raised at last by the one pamphleteer who dared to impugn his thoroughness and accuracy:

> If I am indeed incapable of understanding what I read, I can no longer claim a place among those writers who merit the esteem and confidence of the public. If I am capable of wilfully perverting what I understand, I no longer deserve to live in the society of those men, who consider a strict and inviolable adherence to truth as the foundation of every thing that is virtuous or honourable in human nature. . . . I cannot profess myself very desirous of Mr. Davis's acquaintance; but if he will take the trouble of calling at my house any afternoon when I am *not* at home, my servant shall shew him my library, which he will find tolerably well furnished with the useful authors, ancient as well as modern, ecclesiastical as well as profane, who have *directly* supplied me with the materials of my History.[25]

Gibbon's library was one of his great prides. His servant, Caplen, drew up a catalog of the volumes at Bentinck Street in 1777; the breakdown of the 3,000 volumes and 1,920 separate titles shows the Neo-Classical interest in history, theology, science, belles lettres, and tracts and its dislike of philosophy, what Gibbon called "contentious metaphysics." Gibbon's collection, subsequently expanded to five or six thousand volumes in Lausanne and since recorded by Geoffrey Keynes, is the *primus inter pares* as the reflection of its owner's mind. Gibbon's books—like Swift's, Congreve's, Hearne's, Addison's, and Johnson's—reveal the extent of the part played by Greek literature, patristic writing, Byzantine scholarship and Humanist learning in creating his world-view. Gibbon's reading *directly* supplied him with the materials of his history, as he testified; and in his reading and writing the direct correspondence between the Neo-Classical intelligence and the shaping tradition is manifest.

Like the other leading thinkers of his century, Gibbon was enthralled by Greek literature. It was Homer who thrilled him as a schoolboy. As a young militiaman, he studied Homer again (this time for syntax), Strabo, Herodotus, Hesiod, and Pindar. He rhapsodized over the *Iliad*, the hymns of Callimachus, and especially the "divine Longinus"; and it was at this period that he conceived his admiration for the Greek ideal of *sophrosyne*. Gibbon's Epicurean and Stoic qualities seem to have been less the result of his study of Greek philosophy than the consequence of his own determination, though he knew such philosophical sources as Diogenes Laertius, Lucretius, Epictetus, Marcus Aurelius, and Seneca. But Gibbon's fascination with dramatic tragedy throughout his life led him to peruse Aeschylus, Sophocles, and Euripides at a crucial point in his thinking; and the presence of the tragic vision in the *History* may be traced to Gibbon's preoccupation with Greek drama at a crucial stage of its composition. More of this later. Gibbon's deep interest in Hellenic culture is obvious everywhere in his writing. That he failed to be interested in journeying to Greece—"Un voyage de la Grèce ne peut pas piquer la curiosité"—does not prove the opposite. That he had no wish to see a degenerate Hellas overrun by barbarous Turks confirms rather than denies his Hellenism. It was bad enough to see Rome in ruins and overrun by barbarous friars.

If Gibbon's attitudes toward Hellenic culture and literature were conventional ones for the English Neo-Classicists as a group, his opinions of early Christian writing were not, though they were far from unique. Gibbon's patristic scholarship may have been superior to that of many traditionalist defenders of Christianity, including Swift, Steele, Addison, Hearne, and Middleton; but it is doubtful that Gibbon was a more knowledgeable scholar than Milton, Collier, Warburton, or Johnson. Nor were Gibbon's attacks on patrology more devastating than Shaftesbury's, Bolingbroke's, or Walter Moyle's. They were simply more extensive and more weighty because of the learning they summoned in their cause.

Gibbon's very superiority as a patristic scholar probably was due to his early disillusionment with Roman Catholicism and his subsequent repudiation of revealed religion. The *Autobiography* shows his contempt for the "monks of Magdalen," those Oxford dons who failed to match the "manufactures" of the single abbey of St.-Germain-des-Prés: "the Benedictine folios," "the editions of the fathers, and the collections of the Middle Ages." Gibbon's account of his proselytization into Catholicism, his exposure to Middleton's *Inquiry into Miracles,* and his recantation, ends with a Swiftian exposure of the accretion of doctrines by the Church, all the results of the "marvelous tales which are so boldly attested by the Basils and Chrysostoms, the Augustines and Jeromes. . . ."[26] To be able to speak as positively as he did, Gibbon was compelled by his own criteria to know more about patrology than its defenders; and *A Vindication of Some Passages in the Fifteenth and Sixteenth Chapters of the History of the Decline and Fall of the Roman Empire*, composed in answer to Davis's criticism of his scholarship, is a graphic instance of the extent and particularity of Gibbon's reliance on patristic writing. Gibbon blithely tosses off facts about editions of Cyprian, identifies sources in Justin Martyr and Jerome, and disputes data cited from Tertullian, Prudentius, and Sulpicius Severus ("a classic of good authority"). The shade of Bentley hovers as Gibbon refers to Chrysostom, Ambrose, Isidore of Pelusium, and Hesychius to justify his use of the term *initiati.* Gibbon explains his use of secondary sources for information from Athanasius, Gregory of Nyssa, and others: London has no public library and private ownership of all sources, even when financially possible, is not always practical for extensive collections:

> The Fathers of the fourth and fifth centuries are far more voluminous than their predecessors; the writings of Jerom, of Augustin, of Chrysostom, &c. cover the walls of our libraries. The smallest part is of the historical kind. . . . It would surely be unreasonable to expect that the historian

should peruse enormous volumes, with the uncertain hope of extracting a few interesting lines, or that he should sacrifice whole days to the momentary amusement of his reader.[27]

So Gibbon has used "the diligence of ecclesiastical critics"—e.g., Mosheim, Tillemont—for initial references and then checked the originals. Many patristic works which he did not have access to when writing the first volume of the *History* he subsequently purchased. The unhistoric character of patrology clearly irritated Gibbon, whose castigations of the Fathers' lack of "truthfulness" were the logical end of Vossius' separation of theogony and history:

> Perhaps, on some future occasion, I may examine the historical character of Eusebius: perhaps I may inquire, how far it appears from his words and actions, that the learned bishop of Caesaria was averse to the use of fraud, when it was employed in the service of religion.[28]

And on Moyle's refutation of Eusebius' reported miracle:

> Mr. Moyle [was] a bold and ingenious critic, who read the Fathers as their judge, and not as their slave, and who has refuted, with the most patient candor, all that learned prejudice could suggest in favor of the silly story of the Thundering Legion.[29]

Gibbon shared Bolingbroke's contempt for "that vile fellow Eusebius" for the same reason: the father of chronology had falsified data. His studies convinced Gibbon that it was a common practice among the Fathers.

Gibbon's aversion to much Byzantine literature was the extension of his dislike of pious humbug; but he assiduously applied himself to the study of mediaeval Greek writing and, like other Neo-Classicists, silently accepted some Byzantine elements. His etymological efforts constantly depended on Hesychius, Suidas, Photius, and Eustathius; the chief Byzantine lexicons and *scholia* appeared prominently in his library, his lesser essays, and his *History*. He admired the pagan writers of the Byzantine Empire and he made extensive use of several of the historians Herodian, Ammianus Marcellinus, Procopius. He expressed his admiration of Xiphilinus for preserving the remains of Dio Cassius and Photius for preserving Memnon, Ctesias, and other lost authors. He constantly praised Synesius, despite Synesius' double burden of Christianity and Byzantinism; and he delighted in the *Secret History* of Procopius.[30]

But although he drew from the Christian historians and chronologers of the Byzantine Empire, Gibbon scorned them. Of John Zonares, he wrote:

> ... little dependence is to be had on the authority of a moderate (i.e., mediaeval) Greek, so grossly ignorant of the history of the third century, that he creates several imaginary emperors, and confounds those who really existed.[31]

Zosimus was guilty of a "strange ignorance of history, or a strange abuse of metaphors" in his comments on the Gordians. John Malelas' etymological deductions were "ridiculously" made, as the Venice and Oxford editions recorded them.[32] Yet as he condemned the pious ignorance of certain Byzantine writers, Gibbon coolly demonstrated his own superior Byzantine scholarship.

> Mr. Davis, who talks so familiarly of the Chronicle of Eusebius, will be surprised to hear that the Greek original no longer exists. Some chronological fragments, which had successively passed through the hands of Africanus and Eusebius, are still extant, in the compilations of Syncellus and Cedrenus. They have been collected, and disposed by the labour and ingenuity of Joseph Scaliger; but that proud critic, always ready to applaud his own success, did not flatter himself that he had restored the hundredth part of the genuine Chronicle of Eusebius.[33]

And again:

> Dr. Chelsum styles Suidas "a *Heathen* writer, who lived about the end of the *tenth* century." I admit the period

which he assigns to Suidas; and which is well ascertained by Dr. Bentley. [See his Reply to Boyle, pp. 22, 23.] We are led to fix this epoch, by the chronology which this *Heathen* writer has deduced from Adam, to the death of the emperor John Zimisces, A.D. 975: and a crowd of passages might be produced, as the unanswerable evidence of his Christianity.[34]

Gibbon's confidence in his knowledge of Byzantine literature led him to deem much of that literature both pious and inaccurate, two weaknesses the true historian could never countenance. Gibbon tidily summarized his estimates of Byzantine letters at the close of Chapter LXVIII of the *Decline and Fall*.

That he thought of himself as one of the polymathic scholars produced by the Renaissance is indubitable. Gibbon constantly measured his intellectual progress against the great names of Humanist scholarship. His *Journal* shows Gibbon preening himself on his erudite correspondence with Breitinger and Gessner, resolving to write a treatise on Roman coins, and comparing his learning with that of the Great Men:

> This finished the Memoires, which gave me a much clearer notion of ancient tactics than I ever had before. Indeed, my own military knowledge was of some service to me. . . . I am a much better judge than Salmasius, Casaubon, or Lipsius; mere scholars, who perhaps had never seen a battalion under arms.[35]

Gibbon likened his progress in Greek to Joseph Scaliger's; he developed the highest admiration for Erasmus, which he expressed in the *Journal* as well as the *Essay*, the *History*, and the *Autobiography*. Gibbon saw Erasmus as the founder of modern culture, the preserver of classical culture in an age when that culture was threatened with extinction.[36]

Gibbon traced extensively the history of thought and letters from the classic past up to his own day, and in two accounts paid close attention to the role of the Humanist men of letters. The *Essay* depicts the rise and fall of literature in cycles from Greece to Rome, from Constantinople to Medicean Italy, from

Elizabethan England to Gibbon's day. Gibbon saw the continuous development of learning from the polymaths (Casaubon, G. J. Vossius, Lipsius, Salmasius) to Le Clerc, Bentley, Descartes, Boileau, Rapin, and other Neo-Classicists; and his relating of himself to the tradition is instrumental in the tone and structure of the *Essay*. In the *History*, it is all but overtly stated. In his survey of the cultural influences of Constantinople on Renaissance Italy and the rise of the Humanist movement in Western Europe, Gibbon summarizes the process by writing:

> In the productions of the mind, as in those of the soil, the gifts of nature are excelled by industry and skill: the Greek authors, forgotten on the banks of the Ilissus, have been illustrated on those of the Elbe and the Thames; and Bessarion or Gaza might have envied the superior science of the barbarians, the accuracy of Budaeus, the taste of Erasmus, the copiousness of Stephens, the erudition of Scaliger, the discernment of Reiske or of Bentley. . . . Genius may anticipate the season of maturity; but in the education of a people, as in that of an individual, memory must be exercised before the powers of reason and fancy can be expanded; nor may the artist hope to equal or surpass, till he has learned to imitate, the works of his predecessors.[37]

Gibbon's self-education was the result of his belief that individual genius must grow by absorbing previous thought. It was a belief shared by his Neo-Classical forerunners in the first half of the century, from whom Gibbon derived it. He also derived other of his operative ideals directly from his immediate predecessors.[38] If George III was brought up in accordance with the views of Locke, Bolingbroke, and other political theorists, Gibbon's mind was shaped by the intellectual and literary ideals of Swift, Addison, Pope, and other Neo-Classicists. Gibbon's works record his opinions of antecedent and contemporary thinkers. He constantly refers to the essays of Addison and Arbuthnot, the Hellenic dramas of Rowe, the cosmic theories of Burnet, the opinions of Bolingbroke. Among his contemporaries, he draws upon Goldsmith, Johnson, Pinkerton, Warburton, Stukeley, Hume, and Reynolds. It was from the combined and common assumptions of other Neo-Classicists that Gibbon took the principles that molded his personal behavior and animated his work. He shared the prevalent view of the relationship of man to history: the belief that the attainable ideal of human behavior was to be found in the annals of history and, once found, could be translated into one's life.

The ideal that Gibbon found and extolled in his own historical works was that of the Neo-Classical era—the Man of Reason. Whether he was Cato, Hadrian, Tacitus, Diocletian, or Julian, the Man of Reason was essentially the same: detached, intellectual, appraising, humane, educated in classic modes of thought, unimpeded by a straitening system of philosophy. One of Gibbon's modern critics has stated the ideal in this way:

> . . . the true hero of Gibbon's thinking is a man occupied with affairs of this world and with his responsibilities to his fellow creatures. He seeks private and public happiness and is willing to exert himself for the achievement of both. His education is liberal, in the classical sense of that term. He is a man in whom the raw material of human nature has been refined and developed according to the precepts of the best pagan thinkers. His understanding has been enlarged by a study of letters; his virtue founded in the golden mean of the Greeks; and in his life he approaches the Aristotelian concept of the magnanimous man. His religion consists of humility before the author of all things, whom he cannot presume to understand. His mind is free from the tyranny of superstition, passion, and the appetites, and he is obedient to the dictates of right reason. He is a man of these virtues, whatever role he must play, be it that of a statesman, general, orator, or poet.[39]

Or historian, Gibbon might add. If Swift forever maintained Cato as his modified version of this ideal, Gibbon always kept in mind the Reasonable Man. His recorded behavior indicates

a large measure of his success in being that man. When Gibbon
Senior grew moody and truculent, Gibbon reasoned and appeased. When Mlle. Curchod appealed to rashness and romance, Gibbon became wary. As Dr. Johnson, red-faced with
challenge, turned noisy and brutal, Gibbon sat self-controlled
and silent. When Horace Walpole's tongue sharpened, Gibbon
blushed and silently revised his estimate of the nobleman of
Orford. When clergymen cried infidel, Gibbon smiled faintly
and kept his peace. He calmly studied in his library, emerged
to dine in gourmet fashion on a terrace overlooking Lake
Lucerne, and made plans for routine among threats of war
and political alarums. He accepted the fact of death with calm
when it came to others and, because he was not the one dead,
returned to the business of living. And when finally his own
turn came, he sent his servant from the room in order to die in
dignity alone.

The final pages of the *Autobiography* are a compelling picture of Gibbon, the personal ideals of Neo-Classicism, and the
success (and limitations) of the man and the ideals. In retrospect, Gibbon is not displeased with his life. His health has
been generally good. His "nerves are not tremblingly alive."[40]
He has not a wife and children, but he has friends to supply
him with companionship. His literary fame has been all that
any reasonable man could wish, and if it has not bestowed immortality nothing can. The desire to be immortal is mere
vanity, in any case. "The present is a fleeting moment; the past
is no more; and our prospect of futurity is dark and doubtful."
But Gibbon is content. Time will pass and death will come, so
come it shall. "This reasoning may seem metaphysical, but on
a trial it will be found satisfactory and just."[41]

The examined life that proves "satisfactory and just": this
was the personal goal of Neo-Classical thought. In the case
of Gibbon, the goal was reached. He judged his life and found
it good. The judgment of his mind, however, as that mind was
"embalmed" in the pages of his *History*, he left to his readers.
It is to the *History* that we accordingly turn for a final understanding of Gibbon and his age.

Formation of English Neo-Classical Thought

Though Gibbon may have aspired to be a writer of history from his earliest youth, a suitable subject for his attention did not occur to him until he was a mature man. Commentators have cataloged repeatedly the subjects he considered and rejected, taking their materials from his *Journal*, especially the entry of July 26, 1762; the list need not be recorded again. But it should be noted that as early as his first stock-taking, Gibbon was thinking of an investigation into the rise and decline of states: he contemplated Florence as his subject, with two stages in its development traced in detail, the latter "a republic rich and corrupt, which by degrees loses its independency and sinks into the arms of a master. Both lessons equally useful." He rejected Florentine history, while noting that the period 1420 to 1569 was "worthy the pen of Vertot." The Abbé de Vertot had written on the latter phase of the Roman Republic, and Dr. Conyers Middleton had translated his speculations on Rome and the Republicans into English. The direction Gibbon's mind was taking is apparent in 1762.

That he was temporarily sidetracked from his future decision is not surprising. His affection for Switzerland led him to begin his *History of the Swiss Republic* but his good sense—and the candid criticism of some acquaintances—soon led him to drop it. What *is* surprising is that in an age when everybody from Milton to Johnson was noting the general paucity of English histories and the plethora of Roman histories, Gibbon should have elected to write a history of Rome. He may have been intimidated by the prominence of Hume, whose *History of England* was widely acclaimed—more so than it merited. And he may have felt that the competition of Oliver Goldsmith, whose *Roman History* was published in 1769, and Adam Ferguson, whose *History of the Progress and Termination of the Roman Republic* (1782) was written more or less contemporaneously with the *Decline and Fall*, was negligible. In any event, Gibbon at last chose a subject that Goldsmith described in this way:

There are some subjects on which a writer must decline all attempts to acquire fame, satisfied with being obscurely useful. After such a number of Roman Histories, in all languages, ancient and modern, it would be but imposture to pretend new discoveries, or to expect to offer any thing in a work of this kind, which has not been often anticipated by others. The facts which it relates, have been an hundred times repeated, and every occurrence has been so variously considered, that learning can scarce find a new anecdote, or genius give novelty to the old.[42]

One could hardly dispute the fact that histories of Rome crowded English bookstalls and libraries. Initially, there were the scores of ancient accounts in Greek and Latin, treating different epochs with varying degrees of thoroughness. From Polybius to Ammianus Marcellinus, historians of Rome had preserved their interpretations of the past, together with its events; and every English and French schoolboy had the popularizers drummed incessantly into his head: L. Annaeus Florus, Trogus Pompeius, Eutropius, Justin, Cornelius Nepos. Moreover, the Italian Renaissance had produced two accounts that were still standard histories in the first half of the eighteenth century—Favio Biondo's *Historiarum ab inclinatione Romanorum imperii decades* and Carlo Sigonio's *History of the Western Empire from Diocletian to the Death of Justinian.* These works, plus Sigonio's *History of Italy from 565 to 1286,* were widely known to French and English Neo-Classicists.

The High Renaissance augmented Roman historiography in several forms. The completeness of accounts of Rome made the civilization pivotal in the "universal history" (chronology) ; J. J. Scaliger's *De Emendatione Temporum* hinged on the sequence of events in Roman history, as did the later, imitative chronologies of Petavius, Strauchius, Helvicus, and Ussher. The eschatological histories that were an offshoot from chronological studies, e.g., Sleidan's *The Four Monarchies,* naturally stressed the course of Roman history to demonstrate their pious thesis of decline and Providential punishment. The ecumenical histories (e.g., Walter Raleigh's *History of the World*) inevitably emphasized the growth and decline of Rome. The nationalist historians derived the origins of Britain, France, or Spain from the waning Empire. Finally, such Romanophilism as that of Justus Lipsius produced specialized studies of Roman civilization like the treatises on Roman military affairs and money systems.

In the seventeenth and early eighteenth centuries, a number of histories of Rome, written in the French or English vernacular, preceded Gibbon's. The French were noteworthy for their exhaustiveness. Catrou's and Rouille's history filled six volumes; the English translation by Bundy was written off by Goldsmith: ". . . entirely unsuited to the time and expence mankind usually chuse to bestow upon this subject." Charles Rollin's history, combined with the labors of his "continuator Crevier," took up thirty octavo volumes.[43] The history of de Pouilly was both more concise and more engaging; but Gibbon, in the *Essay*, called him "a brilliant but superficial scholar." And de Beaufort, who suffered from the "historic Pyrrhonism" that Gibbon attributed to French historians of Rome, also used materials inaccurately.[44] There were the works of de Vertot, of course, to add to Roman annals. And Montesquieu's *Sur le Grandeur et Décadence des Romains*, with its philosophy of historic causes and effects, proved provocative to Gibbon, who cited it often in his own history. The French historians also wrote specialized studies of Rome in imitation of Lipsius and Vossius: Gibbon's reliance on Guichart's *Mémoires Militaires sur les Grecs et sur les Romains* and Montfaucon's *Antiquité Expliquée* is well attested.

In England the spate of new editions and translations of Roman history encouraged the writing of English histories of Rome, usually translations of Livy and Tacitus spliced together or a potpourri of close paraphrases from the originals. The Restoration decades saw William Wotton's *History of Rome* published, together with the more popular *Roman History* of Laurence Eacherd, which ran through several eighteenth century editions. Goldsmith characterized it in this way:

. . . so poorly written, the facts so crowded, the narration so
spiritless, and the characters so indistinctly marked, that the
most ardent curiosity must cool in the perusal, and the noblest transactions that ever warmed the human heart, as described by him, must cease to interest.[45]

Hearne's *Ductor Historicus* (1714) presented in its second
volume a veritable skeleton of Gibbon's *Decline and Fall*, out-
lining the collapse of the Western Empire from the time of
Augustus to the fall of Rome and the establishment of the
Byzantine Empire. Hearne wrote:

I hope this Volume will recommend itself sufficiently, in that
it treats of the Roman Monarchy from its Height to its utter
Decay and by it may be perceived, that as the Romans sub-
dued the World, and vanquished in Battle more than double
their Number of Enemies, equal, if not superior to them in
Courage, under the Banners of a severe and regular Discipline; so when they became negligent, they found a strange
Alteration, and that that State is not safe where Discipline is
not cherished, tho' Vice and Luxury had got such a sure footing amongst them, that they could not recover their former
Glory, and so at last the most honourable Republick in the
World became the Object of Scorn and Contempt.[46]

Against the background of English politics in the first half of
the century, this kind of rationale savors of the anti-Augustanism of the Tories. Hearne's dedications to Oxford, like Middleton's later dedication to Hervey in his translation of de
Vertot's *Characters of Augustus, Horace, and Agrippa*, point
up the partisan features of Roman history in the English Augustan Age: it implied the analogy between Augustan Rome
and Georgian England, and increasingly identified the reign
of Augustus with the turning point downward in Roman history.[47] Whether the historian overtly compared England and
Rome or not, his reader was conditioned to; such works as
Walter Moyle's *Essay on the Constitution of the Roman
Government* (ca. 1726) and Hooke's three volume history of

the Republic alone, together with the relevant volumes of the *Universal History*, were read with eye for their immediate applicability.

The general historical attitudes in the works of Gibbon's predecessors are so close to those in *The History of the Decline and Fall* that a précis is useful. Goldsmith may stand for all. *The Roman History, From the Foundation of the City of Rome, To the Destruction of the Western Empire* begins by saying the author's "only aim was to supply a concise, plain, and unaffected narrative of the rise and decline of a well-known empire. . . ." Its materials are directly taken from Polybius and Paterculus, who are mentioned by name, and from Livy; the second volume, Augustus to Constantine, is immediately drawn from the *Lives of the Twelve Caesars* by Suetonius, the *Scriptores Historiae Augustae*, and others, none mentioned by name. Goldsmith has no apparent philosophy of history. Though he professes an interest in the "springs of action," his metaphor of the machine is not very instrumental. The narrative recounts political and military history rather than cultural: the struggles between the people, the Senate, and the ruler (whether tribune, consul, king, or dictator) show no preference for one above the other. In typical eighteenth century fashion, Goldsmith distrusts the "mob," who are moved by passion to destroy, but human nature is the same in all three elements that compose the Polybian tripartite balance: the senators are avaricious and selfish, and the rulers are proud and power-hungry. Ambition and Luxury, the standard bugbears, appear constantly; Goldsmith makes it obvious that the System is the regulator of human nature, which is essentially uncontrolled and unreasonable. Goldsmith's heroes are those of his age: Numa, Camillus, Fabius, Cincinnatus, and especially Cicero. Cato Uticensis is estimable but no longer a demigod; and a few figures traditionally viewed as questionable are favorably shown, e.g., the Gracchi, the Emperor Tiberius. The remaining substance of *The Roman History* is given in a few quotations:

From Pompey's death, therefore, we may date the total extinction of the republic. From this period the senate was dispossessed of all its power, and Rome, from henceforward, was never without a master. (i, 487)

Of Constantine's proclamation establishing Christianity: Thus the new religion was seen at once to prevail over the whole Roman empire; and, as that enormous fabric had been built upon pagan principles, it lost a great deal of its strength and coherence, when those principles were thus at once subverted. (ii, 483)

As Maximin died by a very extraordinary kind of madness, the Christians, of whom he was the declared enemy, did not fail to ascribe his end to a judgment from heaven; but this was the age in which false judgments and false miracles, made up the bulk of their uninstructive history. (ii, 484)

On the removal of the capitol to Constantinople: After this, the empire never resumed its former splendor, but, like a flower transplanted into a foreign clime, languished by degrees, and at length sunk into nothing. (ii, 488)

[Before Constantine] the rise or decline of Rome . . . depended on the virtues and vices, the wisdom or indolence of those who governed it. But from this dreary period its recovery was become desperate; no wisdom could obviate its decadence, no courage oppose the evils that surrounded it on every side. (ii, 492)

Julian, surnamed the Apostate, upon account of his relapsing into paganism, was, notwithstanding, a very good and very valiant prince. He, by his wisdom, conduct, and economy, chased the barbarians . . . out of their new settlements . . . . (ii, 494)

At last, "corrupted by vice and enervated by luxury," attacked by Gothic chiefs "more virtuous" and their tribes, "more courageous people" than the Romans, Rome "sunk" under combined barbarian assaults, not the single thrust of an Alaric or Totila.

When *The History of the Decline and Fall* at last appeared, nothing in its opinions or evaluations could have been startling to the fairly well-read Neo-Classicist. Gibbon followed well-hewn ways in pursuing the "cause" and "springs of action" for the events he recounted. Ambition, Luxury, and Climate— all of them came in for the customary blame for cultural change. The metaphor of the "vast fabric" of Rome "sinking" under its own weight was almost trite. The character portraits— Cato, Hadrian, Constantine—had already become near-stereotypes. The negative attitude toward Augustus and the Roman Age to which he had given his name was the common one; and the apparently strange admiration for Julian the Apostate, which Gibbon held, was in fact shared by Goldsmith, Hearne, and even Bishop Warburton, who printed an examination of Julian in 1751. Furthermore, the Gibbonian version of agnostic Deism was neither new nor shocking. Gibbon's use of the "higher criticism" had been anticipated by Pope's *Essay on Man*, Mandeville's and Addison's essays, Bolingbroke's compositions, and most recently Hume's *Essay on Natural Religion*; and the satire on Roman Catholicism was scarcely new to readers of *A Tale of a Tub, Tristram Shandy*, and other earlier ironic masterpieces. Superficially, Gibbon's *History* was like its forerunners in everything but compendiousness and documentation.

Gibbon's contemporaries immediately saw the difference, however, though they did not clearly define it. The *Annual Register* declared: "We do not remember any work published in our time which has met with a more general approbation than Mr. Gibbon's history," which showed "great industry, deep learning, and sound judgment," plus "the rare talent of rendering the transactions of obscure times and forgotten persons, engaging and delightful." The *European Magazine* added:

Gibbon

Adorned with every grace of composition, every beauty of style; with an acuteness of perception that seizes intuitively the motive of every act; with a patient diligence that traces every consequence to its cause; rich in all the stores of learning, ancient and modern, sacred and profane; the author . . . brings to his undertaking such an assemblage of historic requisites as arrests our wonder while it insures his success.

Sheridan's Parliamentary tribute to "the luminous page of Gibbon" may have been the most eloquent, but surely Hayley's was the most purple:

> England, exult! and view not now
> With jealous glance each nation's brow,
> Where History's palm has spread!
> In every path of liberal art,
> Thy sons to prime distinction start,
> And no superior dread.
>
> Science for thee a Newton raised;
> For thy renown a Shakespeare blazed,
> Lord of the drama's sphere!
> In different fields to equal praise
> See History now thy Gibbon raise
> To shine without a peer!

And Horace Walpole's tribute—"a truly classic work"—has proved to be the most appropriate estimate of all.[48]

Very well, the work is a classic, but why is it so? What qualities in the *Decline and Fall of the Roman Empire* make historians like Christopher Dawson praise it though it has been superseded? What qualities have immortalized Gibbon the historian while Hearne and Ferguson are forgotten? Probably those qualities are four in number. *Decline and Fall* is a "classic" by definition because it is a superbly, self-consciously "literary" production; it preserves more completely than any other single work in English (*Paradise Lost* excepted) the animus of a cultural epoch; it contains insights into forever-re-

227

peated human behavior; and its view of human destiny touches, as all great literature touches, the raw nerve of tragedy.

The fact that his contemporaries, like Gibbon himself, looked upon the *History* as a literary production may be seen in Hayley's panegyric, which categorized history as a liberal art, and by the *Register* and *European* reviews, which eulogized its grace of composition, beauty of style, and delightful, engaging rendering of past events. Gibbon himself, in the *Essay on the Study of Literature,* included both scientific writing and history under the heading of belles lettres, or literature, a classification prevalent in the eighteenth century. A few Neo-Classical historiographical theorists—Peter Whalley, for example—distinguished between the genres, "poetry" and "history"; but no one seriously separated historical writing from the broad humanist classification of "letters," and would-be historians like Swift felt their literary talents a prime requisite for becoming a historian. "Proper words in proper places" was a rule to guide the writer of history even more, perhaps, than the writer of Pindarics or mock heroic verse. Miss C. V. Wedgwood, in her *Edward Gibbon,* sums up the situation in this way:

> *The Decline and Fall of the Roman Empire* is an outstanding work of English scholarship and one of the great monuments of English eighteenth-century literature. This double achievement has had a profound influence on the whole tradition of English historical writing. The increasing complexity of techniques of historical research, and the ever more exacting standards of scholarly accuracy which began to prevail in the later nineteenth century, thanks to the massive and precise scholarship of the Germans, inevitably divorced history from literature. But in England this divorce never became complete and the re-union of history and literature in this country in our time, may be traced in part to the influence of Gibbon. . . . The union of erudition and style which he achieved is still the ideal of the English tradition.[49]

228

Gibbon

Gibbon himself consciously worked to make his history a truly literary composition; to him the *presentation* of his materials was quite as important as the accuracy of the materials themselves, and he seems to have been more concerned with style than an ultimate theory of history. His painful writing and rewriting of the first chapters of the work while he sought for an appropriate style are well known. When Horace Walpole in a fit of ennui and malice railed at the second volumes of the *History* and Gibbon, discomfited, began to blurt out that the materials had never been brought together before *so well*, his near-slip was most revealing. Gibbon was quite right in thinking that his achievement was first and foremost the fusion of literary style and historical subject matter. Goldsmith had criticized Hooke and Eacherd for lacking the former, since style alone could justify the recounting of material known to "everybody." Goldsmith failed to make the fusion but Gibbon succeeded. It was a singular achievement.

Gibbon as the conscious literary artist is apparent everywhere in the *Decline and Fall*, repeatedly reminding the reader that his purpose is the venerable one of all eighteenth century writers: to amuse and instruct.[50] He includes an episode because it is "entertaining as well as useful"; he omits information—e.g., anecdotes about the emperors' privates lives—because it is "impertinent." His syntax is virtually flawless, displaying all the antithesis, parallelism, and verbal dazzle of Pope or Swift, while it reads aloud with the oracularity of Johnson or the urbanity of Addison. It is small wonder that historians feel compelled to treat Gibbon's style and his use of *le mot juste*. That style, as Bond's *The Literary Art of Edward Gibbon* demonstrates, is the introit to Gibbon's mind and the world he creates with such scrupulous word choice. Historiography *is* literature, Gibbon believed, and he made it so.

The second characteristic that makes the *History* a classic is its embodiment of the prevalent ideals of English Neo-Classicism. Gibbon's admiration for history, his judgments of Roman events and heroes, and his predication of the ideal Man of Reason were all typical of his class and period. Gibbon was *not* an original thinker, as he was quick to admit; and when he departed from well established beliefs and practices, he often regretted it. What seemed to be the chief innovation of the *Decline and Fall*—starting the decline with the Antonines rather than the establishment of the monarchy—Gibbon later decided was a mistake:

> Should I not have deduced the decline of the Empire from the Civil Wars that ensued after the Fall of Nero, and even from the tyranny which succeeded the reign of Augustus? Alas, I should: but of what avail is this tardy knowledge? Where error is irreparable, repentance is useless.

In most instances, Gibbon adhered to the habitual beliefs of his age, with the result that one learns more about Neo-Classical English thought from the *History* than about the Roman state of mind. Gibbon tended to identify the two, of course.

The treatment of the Praetorian Guard is a case in point. Gibbon's first chapters describe a Rome that was apparently prosperous and happy, though he underlines the loss of political freedom, the cultural stagnation, and the abuse of wealth and luxury that had prepared the way for decline. He states his purpose in the chapters to come: to describe the prosperity "and afterwards . . . to deduce the most important circumstances of its decline and fall. . . ." Whereupon he commences an account of the military machine, graphically showing its alteration from a citizen's army into a standing army filled with mercenaries. Gibbon makes plain his dislike and distrust of standing armies and mercenaries, even though he admires military discipline and order. Chapter iii describes "the dangers inherent to a military government" and shows the Praetorian Guard as the instrument of a tyrant's repression of representative government and the people. At last, in his account of the death of Commodus and the accession of Septimius Severus, he declares, "The licentious fury of the Praetorian Guard . . . was the first symptom and cause of the decline of the Roman Empire. . . ." Thereafter, he states again and again the evils of an ensconced military, the dangers of the ruler having a personal army or guard, and the eternal threat of a mercenary standing army.[51] Decades of tracts—*The Examiner, The Craftsman,* the *Junius Letters*—expressed exactly the same views; Gibbon's deep-seated distrust of standing armies and mercenaries was shared by practically every literary man of his century.

His beliefs about political parties and "factions" were also typical. The most extended and striking instance of his views comes in the account of the warfare between the Blues and the Greens in Constantinople during the reign of Justinian. This section of the *History* (Chap. XL) has thematic reverberations of a dozen compositions of the English Augustan Age. The absurd rallying beneath two colored banners by contending factions calls Swift and Arbuthnot to mind. The description of women, who Gibbon says ought to have been acting as wives and mothers at home instead of attending public entertainments and disputing their partisanship, evokes Addison's *Spectator* papers. Gay's Mohock and Hawkubite compositions color Gibbon's accounts of the muggings and vicious clashes by night between gangs of Constantinopolitan youths. The Neo-Classical historian has no use whatsoever for such vulgar political zeal and factionalism. He distrusts the mob with the sincerity of Dryden (or Burke) ; and his distaste for collective zeal is that of the classicist who is a reasonable man.

The religious zealot comes off even worse. Gibbon's deprecation of the fanatic Christian martyrs, the wild-eyed Mohammedan invaders of Asia Minor, and the wind-filled Enthusiast deserves to stand beside Meric Casaubon's *Treatise,* Swift's *Tale of a Tub,* and Smollett's *Humphrey Clinker.* Citing Athenagoras, Justin Martyr, and Tertullian as his authorities, Gibbon describes the "inspiration" of the early Christians, prototypes of the Dissenters and Covenanters:

> . . . they were transported out of their senses, and delivered in ecstasy that was inspired, being mere organs of the Holy Spirit, just as a pipe or flute is of him who blows into it.[52]

Gibbon's lengthy description of the accusations of incest and paidophagy against the early Christians and the replies of Tertullian to them stands as a footnote to Swift's *A Modest Proposal*. Furthermore, Gibbon had no hesitation in stating the connection between religious zeal and sexuality that was also clear to others before the advent of Sigmund Freud. From the critics of Bishop Burnet (who attributed his wide conversions among fashionable ladies to his shapely calves) to Swift's Aeolists and Robert Burns' Holy Willie, eighteenth century writers often satirized hypocritical religion for its appropriation of the sexual drives. Gibbon's amusement at the virgins who encountered a new species of martyrdom by sharing the couches of the celibate clergy was a part of the widespread Neo-Classical amusement at the sexuality of Man, God's noblest creature. Contrary to the accusation that he lived his sex life in his footnotes, Gibbon's literary comments on sex are far from prurient. They are ribald and frank but so was his age; and if Gibbon found sex funny and religion often a disguise for sexuality, he was one among many other satirists. His remark on Claudius as the only one of the first twelve Caesars "whose tastes in love were entirely correct" is not salaciousness but irony that cuts at least three ways.

The common attitude toward woman as the frailer vessel appeared often in the *History*, though Gibbon was hardly antifeminist. He thought that female virtues were mainly those of chastity, obedience, and domesticity, the possessions of the ladies dearest to him: his aunt, stepmother and Lady Sheffield. He extolled these virtues in his description of the German woman in Chapter IX of *Decline and Fall*. The virtue of the German wife was "secured by poverty, solitude, and the painful cares of a domestic life" and as he recounted it, Gibbon was moved to a digressive comparison with the ladies of his nation and time. *They* were the victims of an absurdly unreasonable practice: the "gross appetite of love" was "disguised by sentimental passion." No one who had read *The Rape of the Lock* or seen Sheridan's *The Rivals* would have found Gibbon's reproof of Belinda and Lydia the least bit unusual. At the same time, however, Gibbon was moved by the spectacle of a noble gentlewoman suffering. He spelled out his sympathy for Valeria, the hapless daughter of Diocletian, for several pages and noted that her life would make a very affecting subject for a dramatic tragedy.

Other standard Neo-Classical tenets are threaded in and out of the *History*, though Gibbon's real belief in them and his unique style keep them from a standard expression. He cannot escape the idea that culture is determined by climate, though he wants to avoid the deterministic implications of the theory. He thinks that geography and climatic factors affect intelligence and body size; Alexander Severus and Elagabalus both "contracted a tincture of weakness and effeminacy from the soft climate of Syria" and the German physique was undoubtedly due in part to climate though the degree of influence is "difficult to ascertain and easy to exaggerate." But when he states the old view that the inhabitants of Pannonia were climatically afforded "great bodies and slow minds," he cheerfully queries in a footnote: "Will the modern Austrians allow the influence?" Probably his final opinion is expressed in a highly quotable footnote to his discussion of the Germans:

> It may be remarked, that man is the only animal which can live and multiply in every country from the equator to the poles. The hog seems to approach the nearest to our species in that privilege.[53]

Gibbon's simultaneous flirtation with and rejection of the climatic hypothesis was repeated by classicists from Temple to Boswell.

In some thematic concerns Gibbon is very close to the English Augustans. He is unfailingly censorious of the *castrati*; he says of Diocletian's introduction of eunuchs into the court, it "was the most infallible symptom of the progress of despotism." And Constantius weakened the empire by entrusting imperial administration to the eunuchs. Like Swift, Pope, Addison, and the Tory satirists, Gibbon thought homosexuality and castration symptoms of decadence and moral collapse; and if the later writer lived in an age when Italian opera singers and "Mollies" were less remarkable, the prejudice against them was hardly less strong than it had been fifty years before. Gibbon's gibes at astrological hoaxes also seem more Augustan than contemporary; but his contempt for the myth of the Noble Savage is shared by Swift and Johnson; his castigation of the hermit smacks of the era as a whole; and his defense of luxury as economically necessary rings of Goldsmith, Johnson, Mandeville and Pope. Gibbon says that the economic inequality that bears "the odious name of luxury" has the merit of providing work for the "diligent mechanic and the skilful artist."

> . . . in the present imperfect condition of society, luxury, though it may proceed from vice or folly, seems to be the only means that can correct the unequal distribution of property.[54]

Apart from the considerations of money and pride of authorship, Gibbon apparently composed his *History* for two main reasons: to record the truth about human beings and their behavior, and to provide the reader with the wherewithal to achieve insight into himself and his world. Within the confines of Neo-Classical dogma, the former became the motive of preserving the data of universal human nature, the constant verities of human thought and action. Pope had issued the ukase: "The proper study of Mankind of Man." Gibbon appended a couple of significant footnotes:

> Images of the first order, the picture of man, his greatness, his littleness, his passions, his vicissitudes, are those which most surely lead a writer to immortality. . . . The heart recognizes itself in their true and artless pictures and finds pleasure in the recognition.

> He who writes for all mankind should draw his imagery only from sources common to all, from the human heart and the spectacle of nature. Vanity alone can induce him to overstep these limits.[55]

Gibbon

The Gibbonian version of Johnson's (and the era's) belief that only "just representations of general nature" made lasting art is interesting for two reasons: it again demonstrates the lack of distinction between "history" and "literature"; and it explains Gibbon's practice in the *History* of seeing within the behavior of the Romans the unchanging psychological constitution of human nature. In his examination of the effects of Philip's murder of his royal predecessor, Gibbon remarks that a reasonable conjecture can be made though facts are lacking. When the historian has contradictory or imperfect data to go on and he is still short of knowledge after collating and refining, he yet has recourse to

... the knowledge of human nature, and of the sure operation of its fierce and unrestrained passions, [and thus] might, on some occasions, supply the want of historical materials.[56]

Again, in anticipatory contradiction of Wordsworth, Gibbon writes that it is necessary "to suspend our belief of every tale that deviates from the laws of nature and the character of man."

This uniformitarian position caused the historian to postulate certain emotional "causes" and to depict again and again the situations that seemed to illustrate these causes. The reasoning may have been circular—to deduce from a proposition that the particular served to illustrate; but Gibbon's use of intellectual données was confirmed by his "heart" and "the spectacle of nature": i.e., intuition and empiric observation. Just as earlier writers—Addison, Fielding, Goldsmith—created fictional contemporaries to illustrate the general truth of human behavior, and Pope hid contemporary identities under classical pseudonymics, Gibbon imparted his knowledge of real contemporaries to the historical figures of the past.

The recurrent relationships and situations explored in the *Decline and Fall* are personal as well as public but the private and public often merge though the emphasis of the history is necessarily on the latter. For instance, Gibbon explains several occasions of a bad emperor succeeding a good one by cause of a "natural" paternal prejudice. The amiable and virtuous Marcus Aurelius is thus understandable for ignoring the obvious deficiencies of Commodus, who is his son; and Septimius Severus likewise shows a type of constant behavior by paternally preferring the vile Caracalla to an illustrious colleague as a successor. Gibbon also stresses the pathos of the eclipsed old ruler no longer able to protect his child from the jealousy of his successor in the persons of Diocletian and Valeria; and the picture of Maximian and his son, Maxentius, is a "classic" story of the strong, overriding father and the weak son.

Gibbon's variant portraits of husbands and wives stand somewhere between Johnson's marriage sketches in *The Rambler* and Jane Austen's novels. The bachelor historian was no more an enemy to the wedded life than the spinster-novelist, though they both viewed marriage with a certain amused detachment. Gibbon wrote to John Holroyd on the occasion of Sheffield's marriage:

> I am convinced that if celibacy is exposed to fewer miseries; marriage can alone promise real happiness since domestick enjoyments are the sources of every other good.[57]

The marriages described in the *Decline and Fall* tend to be the troubled ones; but Gibbon shows all kinds of uxorial arrangement from the virago wife and patient husband (Faustina and Marcus) to the touchily deferential, arranged marriage (Julian and Helena, Constantius and Theodora) to the erotic union turned respectable (Justinian and Theodora). However, Gibbon does not fail to show a number of driving women, acting as individuals rather than wives. In addition to the flamboyant Theodora, there are Julia Maesia and her sister, Julia Domnia, who bought armies and manipulated their emperor-sons; the magnificent Zenobia of Palmyra, probably the only real heroine of the *History*; the Empress Placidia, mother of Valentinian III; the beguiled and pious Helena, mother of Con-

stantine. Gibbon's gallery of female portraits is no less extensive or detailed than of men.

The *Decline and Fall* throngs with men and women who
were immediately understandable types to the English reader
of Gibbon's day. There is the too-wealthy businessman, Didius
Julianus, who buys the prestige of the imperial throne and
then, abandoned by his bought Guard, foolishly, pitifully finds
himself unequipped to rule. There is the effete, neurotically
perverted Elagabalus, a study in psychopathia sexualis. Julian,
the intellectual turned ambitious, plans and rationalizes his
way to supreme power only to meet an early, violent death by
an assassin. Athanasius, the politically wise churchman, out-
maneuvers a series of rulers while maintaining his appearance
of sanctity and other-worldliness. The clever minister, Rufinus,
manipulates his way through the court of Theodosius while
carefully encouraging the somnolent disposition of his master.
Gibbon's characters, or their equivalents, live in all ages.

The example of characterization in the *History* that was the
most obviously appealing to the Neo-Classical era and typical
of its outlook is the extended generalized portrait of the Roman
aristocrat in Chapter xxxi. The ironic representation of eighteenth century London and its society in crypto-Roman terms
had appeared in the *Moral Epistles* of Pope and Johnson's
Juvenalian satire, *London*, as well as many other works. When
Gibbon stopped his narrative of the invasion of Italy by Alaric
to describe the condition of the threatened Romans, he knew
very well that his adaptation of the account of Ammianus
would be taken personally by contemporary London.

The judicious reader will not always approve the asperity
of censure, the choice of circumstances, or the style of expression; he will perhaps detect the latent prejudices and
personal resentments which soured the temper of Ammianus
himself; but he will surely observe, with philosophic curiosity, the interesting and original picture of the manners
of Rome.

Having disarmed the reader's likelihood of rationalizing away parallels and insisted upon the "interest" (i.e., value and empathetic circumstances) of the passage, Gibbon smoothly comments in a footnote:

> I have developed some observations which were insinuated rather than expressed. With these allowances my version will be found, not literal indeed, but faithful and exact.

Faithful and exact in its depiction of contemporary England, that is to say. And Gibbon proceeds to "translate" Ammianus in all too familiar Neo-Classical terms.

> The greatness of Rome (such is the language of the historian) was founded on the rare and almost incredible alliance of virtue and fortune. The long period of her infancy was employed in a laborious struggle against . . . the neighbors and enemies of the rising city. In the strength and ardour of youth, she sustained the storms of war, carried her victorious arms beyond the seas and the mountains, and brought home triumphal laurels from every country of the globe. At length, verging toward old age, and sometimes conquering by the terror of her name only, she sought the blessings of ease and tranquillity.

At this point, the Neo-Classicist reader, alerted by the metaphor of the body-state familiar to every schoolboy who had read Florus, would automatically begin to read more intently for the "lesson" present in the archetypal nation.

> But this native splendor (continues Ammianus) is degraded and sullied by the conduct of some nobles, who, unmindful of their own dignity and of that of their country, assume an unbounded licence of vice and folly.

For six pages, then, Ammianus–Gibbon levels an assault on a frivolous society in well known fashion. The "Roman" nobles contended for empty titles and surnames, constructed vain marble or bronze monuments to themselves, extracted estate taxes from their groaning tenants, and vied for exotic foods, clothes, and ostentatious chariots. Attended by retinues of servants, they made progresses through the streets or grandly entered the baths to the bending knees of inferiors and the salutations of their peers. For amusement, they hunted on their estates or played at being soldiers. They alternated their conduct toward strangers by being gracious one day and coolly snobbish the next. Their dinners and other entertainments never included "the modest, the sober, and the learned" but haughty nobles surrounded themselves with followers and other social climbers, who talked of nothing but the dinner or gossiped eternally. They played cards, never read in their inherited libraries, received while affecting illness in bed, courted the childless men of wealth in hopes of inheritance, or debated endlessly the legal terms of marriage contracts. They bilked tradesmen and patronized soothsayers. They were profane skeptics who impiously doubted or denied the existence of a celestial power while they practiced the most vain kind of credulity before astrologers. Thus spoke Ammianus, and no eighteenth century reader could fail to get Gibbon's point.

Gibbon wanted to make certain however. His constant references to the "interest" of the modern reader and "instruction" by Roman events may have gone unnoticed to some obtuse few. So in Chapter xxxviii, which traced the impact of the collapse of Rome on Britain and set up a correlative pattern of Roman and British cultural cycles, Gibbon appended his "General Observations on the Fall of the Roman Empire in the West." Beginning with a dismissal of Fortune as the maker of destiny—elsewhere he called Fortune a "popular name" used to disguise ignorance—he recapitulated the austere political and military glories of the Republic, traced its expansion and growing complexity, and declared that Rome's immoderate greatness caused her decline:

> Prosperity ripened the principle of decay; the causes of destruction multiplied with the extent of conquest; and as soon as time or accident had removed the artificial supports, the stupendous fabric yielded to the pressure of its own weight.

The explanation and the trope were conventional. They have not satisfied later historiographers as historic explanation, but they were incontestable truth to the Neo-Classicists. Said Gibbon: "This awful revolution may be usefully applied to the instruction of the present age."

But how? Gibbon's deliberations appear to have demonstrated the inapplicability of a Roman analogy. Using all of modern Europe as the equivalent of the Roman Empire, he noted the improvements that time and human ingenuity had made, said that "no people, unless the face of nature is changed, will relapse into their original barbarism," and concluded that the overrunning of the civilized world by obscure barbarian nations was not likely to occur again. The cheerful optimism of the "General Reflections" has a Panglossian shine: "Everything is for the eventual best in this improving world." Had the *History* ended with Chapter xxxviii, the burden of its message would have been light indeed; the *History* would have denied a fundamental reason for its existence. It did not, however. Gibbon was too much the realist and classicist to avoid a confrontation with his final vision of reality. His world-view demanded an acknowledgment of the infinite darkness that lay beyond the slight areas lit by human reason; and Gibbon found that he could not stop until he had shown the blackness surrounding the small globe of light.

Once the *Decline and Fall* was finished, the historian began to fill his suddenly empty hours by contemplating his own lifespan instead of that of the Romans. The resulting *Autobiography* indicates some fascinating interplay between Gibbon's reading, the confirmation of his private philosophy, and the final cast and tone of the *History*. Of the genesis of the work he wrote:

No sooner was I settled in my house and library [at Bentinck Street] than I undertook the composition of the first volume of my *History*. At the outset all was dark and doubtful, even the title of the work, the true era of the decline and fall of the empire, the limits of the introduction, the division of the chapters, and the order of the narrative, and I was often tempted to cast away the labor of seven years.[58]

The struggle to find a proper style that would "hit the middle tone between a dull chronicle and rhetorical declamation," the writing and rewriting of the materials on the rise of Christianity are then told. The success of the first volume was entirely reassuring to the hopeful author, so that he undertook the next volume with zest. But two years elapsed before the appearance of that portion of the *History* which traced the decline through the reign of Constantine and his successors. Gibbon had to commit "to the flames above fifty sheets" of the first draft before he was satisfied. Then the second and third volumes were less jubilantly received by the public. Disgruntled clerics manned an attack on the historian, "nor could a whisper escape my ear that in the judgment of many readers, my continuation was much inferior to the original attempts." For a time, Gibbon seriously questioned whether he ought to go beyond his finished labors, thus ending the *History* with the collapse of the Western Empire and the optimistic appraisal of the third volume as the historian's final word on his own era.

So flexible is the title of my *History* that the final era might be fixed at my own choice; and I long hesitated whether I should be content with the three volumes, the fall of the Western empire, which fulfilled my first engagement with the public. In this interval of suspense, nearly a twelvemonth, I returned by a natural impulse to the Greek authors of antiquity. In my library in Bentinck Street, at my summer lodgings at Brighthelmstone, at a country house which I hired at Hampton Court, I read with new pleasure the *Iliad* and the *Odyssey*, the histories of Herodotus, Thucydides, and Xenophon, a large portion of the tragic and comic theater of Athens, and many interesting dialogues of the Socratic school.[59]

During this year of continued exposure to ancient Greek thought, Gibbon realized his "design" and promptly "dropped without reluctance from the age of Plato to that of Justinian." Except for the last chapter, the fourth volume was finished before Gibbon returned to the "retreat on the banks of Leman Lake," where he was to complete the design.

The effect of his submersion in Greek literature on Gibbon's ultimate historiographical practice and philosophical purview is inestimable; but there are a good many clues to show that it was vast. The triad of historians, venerated by eighteenth century historiographers, emphasized the cyclic concept together with psychological determinism and the notion of *Tuche*. It was the *Iliad* and *Odyssey* that had first raised in Gibbon the child "the new emotions of terror and pity," the Aristotelian tests of tragedy, whereas the *Aeneid* had merely impressed Gibbon the young man as "truly pathetic." The Socratic dialogues confirmed Gibbon's ideal of "rational ignorance." And the imprint of the Greek drama on the English historian may well have made the *Decline and Fall of the Roman Empire* one of the most complete fusions of the Neo-Classical and tragic world views.

Like most of his fellow classicists of the eighteenth century, Gibbon found himself caught up in the great force of Greek tragedy so that he venerated it without quite knowing why. He appears to have approached it originally through the drama of the French classicists. In 1762, when his knowledge of Greek was still largely confined to Homer, he praised Voltaire for the "fine narrations in his tragedies" *Ismene* and *Merope* while noting the lack of causal narration in his histories. The comments on Phaedra and Hippolytus in Section LXXIII of the *Essay* were more applicable to Racine than Euripides, though Gibbon was purportedly discussing the theology of the "primitive peoples." The *Letters* and *Journal* provide scant evidence for Gibbon's reading of classical tragedy before 1776, though the latter rhapsodizes over the *Peri Hupsous* of Longinus and the sublimity of its insights. And the *Essay* calls Aristotle "the father of criticism" because he "drew his critical laws from the nature of things and from his knowledge of the human heart."

But by the time he was writing the *History*, Gibbon was unstinting in his enthusiasm for Greek tragedy, especially the plays of Euripides. The historian's account of the Chersonesus Taurica praised the *Iphigeneia in Tauris* as a combination of a tale of antiquity with "exquisite art"; it was "one of [Euripides'] most affecting tragedies." Gibbon sneered at Tertullian's philistinism: "This severe reformer shows no more indulgence to a tragedy of Euripides than to a combat of gladiators." And he could find nothing better to say of Roman drama than that it "seldom aspired beyond the imitation of Attic genius."[60]

His admiration for Greek tragedy led Gibbon to the same trap which had sprung on Dryden, Addison, and others; nor was he able to elude it entirely. How were historicity and suspense, Christianity and doom, reason and violence, detachment and emotion to be morally and aesthetically reconciled? Gibbon found a partial answer to the perplexing dilemma by judging the two artifacts, drama and history, by shifting standards while simultaneously seeing within them both a depiction of reality or "truth."

Gibbon's taste in drama was conventional for his age. He appears to have found melodrama and high tragedy indistinguishable. He thrilled to such spectacles as Voltaire's *Fanime* and *Orphelin de Chine* in his youth; and though he frequented the Garrick productions of *Hamlet* and *Richard III*, and viewed *Cleone*, *All for Love*, and *Jane Shore*, he appears to have preferred comedy to tragedy for his theatergoing. He read tragedy, however, and was familiar with such Neo-Classical imitations of classic drama as Rowe's *Ulysses* and *The Ambitious Step-Mother*; Addison's *Cato*; Phillips' *The Distrest Mother*; and Smith's *Phaedrus and Hippolitus* [sic], to say nothing of Ben Jonson's *Catiline*.

Gibbon's spasmodic effort at literary criticism reflects the limitations of the day even as his comments merge dramatic and historiographical perspectives. The early *Essay* praises Queen Elizabeth for heeding the truth of Herodotus, applying it to contemporary events, so that "issuing triumphant from the struggle (against a new Xerxes), she saw herself celebrated by Æschylus with the Conquerors of Salamis" when she translated the Greek dramatist. To comprehend the value of ancient tragedy, the modern reader must suspend his own standards:

> Knowledge of antiquity: this is our true commentary; but what is more necessary still, is a certain temper of mind which not only enables us to understand the past—but familiarises us with it, and allows us to see it with the eyes of the ancients.

To the problem of the relationship between history and the subject matter for the drama and epic, Gibbon paid particular attention. Noting that Aristotle had insisted on the depiction of heroes in the terms transmitted by history—a literal adherence to "received ideas"—Gibbon asks whether the poet must then be "reduced" to "the role of a frigid chronicler"? Though his answer is a prompt "no," Gibbon goes on to say:

> When an author desires to venture on such changes, he should reflect whether a delicate or striking beauty will result—a beauty proportioned to the violation of the law. It is only at this price that he can atone for his error. . . . Of how many beauties would history have robbed [Virgil]. Encouraged by success, however, he sometimes abandons it where he should have followed it.

The poet may at times alter history for greater pleasure and beauty:

> But let him not overturn a century's annals for an antithesis . . . the characters of great men should be sacred, but poets may write their history less as it was than as it should have been. . . .

This doctrine of poetic license was extended by Gibbon toward many works with an indulgence he would have denied to the historian, whose aim is always factual accuracy. Where history and poetic "beauty" were reconciled, he admired the work unstintingly:

(Lucan) is a poet who has been distinguished, and even censured, for his strict adherence to the truth of history.

Dr. Johnson, in the tragedy of Irene, has happily seized this characteristic circumstance. . . .

When the aesthetic quality of the work is paramount, historical verisimilitude can be dismissed:

The story of Polyeuctes, on which Corneille has founded a very beautiful tragedy, is one of the most celebrated though not, perhaps the most authentic, instances of this excessive zeal [of the early Christians].

Gibbon could even speak of Rowe's portrait of Tamerlane as a man of "amiable moderation" with only mild irony, despite its historical implausibility. In "poetry" (fictional literature), anything "beautiful" or "affecting" was its own excuse for being, whether it pretended to historicity or not.[61]

Gibbon's acceptance of the validity, the "reality," of the aesthetic response was to affect tremendously the writing of the *History*, particularly the latter volumes. His feeling of the incompleteness of his "design" after writing the first volumes, the "natural impulse" that sent him back to Greek history, philosophy, and tragedy, together with his original concern about the tone and style of the work—all these indicate Gibbon's pull away from the "dull chronicle" to the "declamation." Or, to use other terms, his awareness of the truth that transcends factual accuracy, first recognized in his encounter with tragic drama, compelled Gibbon to press beyond the partial truth of the fall of the Western Empire to the complete, terrible truth about the fate of all human culture. Gibbon could not end his historical drama with the third, climactic act; he had to go on to the denouement.

Whether Gibbon consciously thought of historic movements in dramatic terms cannot be known, but of the three predominant metaphors in the *Decline and Fall*, the theatrical is se-

lected to begin and end the work. Bolingbroke and others had
talked of history in terms of "acts," "scenes," Nemesis, and
hubris. Gibbon began his first volume by describing the decline and fall as "a revolution which will ever be remembered,
and is still felt by the nations of the earth," and concluded it
by declaring the fall "the greatest, perhaps, and the most awful
scene in the history of mankind." Interspersed throughout are
dramatic terms, both specific and general: "action," "hero,"
"scenic," "spectacle," "theater of events," "climax," and so on.
These phrases are constant reminders of the submerged metaphor of the drama.

Gibbon's commentators, literary critic and historiographer
alike, seem unable—deliberately unwilling—to avoid literary
terms in appraising the *Decline and Fall*. A few of their insights prove the point:

> But history was in Gibbon's view essentially personal and
> dramatic. (D. M. Low)

> To Gibbon the history of Europe, and indeed of the world,
> from Aurelius to the extinction of the Western Empire in
> A.D. 476, appears in the light of a tragic catastrophe. . . .[*De-
> cline and Fall*] is the essence of a literary masterpiece,
> whether it be an epic, a drama, or a novel. In fact, the effect
> produced by the *Decline and Fall* is comparable only with
> that produced by literary works of the first rank; it stimulates
> not only the intellect, but also the imagination. . . . (J. B.
> Black)

> The idea of the transitoriness of all things exerts a powerful
> influence on Gibbon's conception of history. . . . Nothing
> lasts, all human greatness perishes, happiness means but a
> temporary absence of despair. . . . But Gibbon's pessimism
> has nothing morbid or aggressive about it. He examines the
> tragic fate of mankind without illusions, but also without
> bitterness. (Per Fuglum)

> . . . the cosmic irony of *The Decline and Fall* penetrates to
> the very core of human life and accounts for the tone of

genuine tragedy which lies at the centre of the whole work.
. . . The reader who wishes to find in human life a lasting
significance sees the tremendous drama of man's affairs finally overwhelmed by the iron sleep of death. (H. L. Bond)

This critical consensus attests once more to the unified literary
character of the *History*, even though the critics may not be
able to identify the precise structural parallels between Gibbon's work and a novel, epic, or drama. It is, perhaps, in the
widely recognized tragic quality of the "tone" of the *Decline
and Fall* that its unifying principle is to be found.

There is a good deal of evidence that Gibbon himself,
whether he thought of historic movement as dramatic or not,
did view it as tragic. Since his province was all of human life
within certain geographical, chronological, and political confines, and since, in its totality, human experience is too diffuse
and varied to be accurately termed "tragic" or "comic" or anything else, the tone of the *Decline and Fall* shifts repeatedly.
At times—e.g., the description of the early Christians or the
Roman nobles of the fifth century—it is satiric. At others, it is
awed or impertinent or melancholy or cheerful. And nearly
always, it is ironic, as Gibbon, from the perspective of centuries,
looks back on Roman history with the knowledge of its out-
come and implicitly juxtaposes the past with the present. The
irony which in other Neo-Classical literature aided comedy or
satire darkens at times in the *History*; and when it does, the
tragic note is sounded. By looking at some key passages in the
Decline and Fall we can understand why this work, possibly
more than any other in eighteenth century England, has the
ability to evoke the spirit of tragedy.

First, there is Gibbon's attitude toward his subject matter.
Though the narrational voice changes tone, it at times speaks
forth with a candor that proves the writer's feelings about his
topic are intense and personal.

The rapid and perpetual transitions from the cottage to the
throne and from the throne to the grave, might have amused
an indifferent philosopher; were it possible for a philosopher

to remain indifferent amidst the general calamities of mankind.[62]

Gibbon's personal writings confirm the emotional interaction between the historian and the *History*:

> . . . it was the view of Italy and Rome which determined the choice of subject. . . . I sat musing amid the ruins of the Capitol. . . .[63]

> . . . a sober melancholy was spread over my mind, by the idea that I had taken an everlasting leave of an old and agreeable companion, and that whatsoever might be the future fate of my *History*, the life of the historian must be short and precarious.[64]

The constant awareness of the meaning of time for mortal man, present in his private reflections, mounts in the *Decline and Fall* to a view of human destiny at once stark and hopeless. In the *Essay*, Gibbon wrote:

> The history of empires is that of the misery of man. . . . Uncertainty is the inevitable condition of man.

In the *History* he added:

> . . . how much swifter is the progress of corruption than its cure . . . all that is human must retrograde if it do not advance. . . .[65]

Furthermore, no amount of knowledge or reasoning can enable mankind to prevent the calamitous end of all its efforts:

> [General causes] decide the greatness and fall of empires, . . . they borrow in turn the distinguishing traits of fortune, of prudence, of courage, and of weakness, acting without the concurrence of particular causes and sometimes triumphing over them . . . extensive as such causes are, their effect is nevertheless limited, and shows itself principally in those general events whose slow but sure influence changes the face of the earth without our being able to trace the period of these changes . . . whenever an action appears complicated,

let us admit that it results from general causes without rejecting design and chance.

This "design and chance" is not providential. Gibbon's rejection of Christian determinism in history opens the way to the tragic outlook, for he retains the idea of a divinity while denying the benevolence of that omnipotent being. Tragic preoccupation with the questions of justice and guilt thus becomes an element in history. Of the existence of God, Gibbon variously says:

> The Fiat of Moses impresses us, but reason is unable to follow the workings of a Divinity who sets in motion, without effort and without instruments, myriads of worlds. . . .

> The opinions of the Academics and Epicureans were of a less religious cast; but whilst the modest science of the former induced them to doubt, the positive ignorance of the latter urged them to deny, the providence of a Supreme Ruler.

> But there *is* a Providence (such at least was the opinion of the historian Procopius) that watches over innocence and folly. . . .

> Islam is compounded of an eternal truth and a necessary fiction: THAT THERE IS ONLY ONE GOD, AND MOHAMMED IS THE APOSTLE OF GOD.

> The God of nature has written his existence on all his works, and his law in the heart of man.

In sum, Gibbon's ironic dismissal of the loving, paternal God of Christianity and his substitution of a disinterested, cosmic power, though it may not have owed to his reading in Greek tragedy, nonetheless simulated the theistic assumptions that underlay classical tragic drama. The almost bitterly ironic depiction of the citizens of Constantinople at the moment of Mohammedan invasion of the city, running to the Hagia Sophia in the pathetically innocent belief that an angel with a flaming sword would appear to protect them, is tragedy.

And the simultaneous portrait of Constantine, stripped of delusions and led by desperate reason to confront the invaders and death, completes the effect. Gibbon terminates his account of the events in the fall of the empire with the extinction of a man, a culture, human reason, and Christian hope.

When he finished reading the final volumes of the *Decline and Fall*, the Rt. Rev. George Horne, Gibbon's contemporary and a devout Anglican bishop, wrote in a letter of July 2, 1788, that he was so moved by the tragedies depicted in the last volume that he was almost ready to write an ode to despair. Nor was Bishop Horne's bleak reaction unshared. The inevitability of man's fate—the death of the individual and the extinction of human culture—was so graphically shown in Gibbon's *History* that no piously hopeful Christian, no supremely rational agnostic could deny its terror. The classicist who venerated the glory that was Rome saw his model collapse with the ravages of time and human ferocity. Exponents of cultural progress were confronted with an undeniably vivid spectacle of regression. Gibbon's *History* reminded his self-confident, self-possessed century of an unnerving truth: that culture and chaos are separated by the thin line of man's will and that this will, a frail and feeble thing, is destroyed by time. The end of history is doom, Gibbon told his readers; and this tragic view once again confirmed the divine commonplace of the Neo-Classical Age—that all is vanity.

It is not the presence of the tragic vision solely that distinguishes *The Decline and Fall of the Roman Empire*; all of the greatest Neo-Classical writers knew the exultation of tragic despair. But if others of Gibbon's age saw human life in tragic dimensions, they did not permit themselves to present that view in anything more than partial or tentative terms in their public literature. They deliberately confined their utterances to those views which could be socially and morally applied for "constructive" ends: the correction of self and society. If, like Swift, they despaired of the consequences of their efforts, the Neo-Classicists confided their terrors and tears only to personal journals or the eyes of understanding friends by means of letters.

Gibbon, on the contrary, wrote the most placid of letters and the most cheerful of journals; but he produced in his public masterpiece one of the most devastatingly gloomy prognoses of man's fate ever to be printed.

The singularity of Gibbon's *History* lies in its synthetic comprehensiveness. It utilizes virtually all of the intellectual and literary heritage venerated by English Neo-Classicists. It expounds the basic philosophy underlying the "choice of life" and gives multiple illustrations of lives lived in accordance with those systems. It assumes the literary principles practiced by English Neo-Classicists, from the parodic and satiric to the rhapsodic and Orientally exotic. Gibbon commands the dominant tones of Neo-Classical writing: the didactic, the ironic, the exhortatory, the meditative, the comic, and the tragic. And he fuses all of these sources, subjects, techniques, and modes into a literary expression of a complex but unified philosophy of human life and history.

Of course, Gibbon's mind does not transcend the other leading ones of the Neo-Classical Age in England, nor does *The History of the Decline and Fall* preempt all Neo-Classical literature, thematically or otherwise. Yet, the one is so encompassing and the other so inclusive as to be encyclopaedic guides to English Neo-Classicism in its aspirations and fears, as well as its pride and prejudice. The student of literature, searching still for essential Neo-Classicism, may find Gibbon's *History* the proper place to begin. The critical commentator, having tried to grasp that essence, finds the *History* a proper place to end.

Appendix

ACHILLES TATIUS. De Clitophontis & Leucippes amoribus, lib. VIII. Longi Sophistæ de Daphnidis & Chloes amoribus, lib. IV. Parthenij Nicænsis de amatoribus affectibus lib. Gr. and Lat. 12º. Heidelberg, 1606.

ADDISON, JOSEPH. Works. 4 vols. 4º. Birmingham, 1761.

ADDISON, JOSEPH. De la religion chrétienne. Traduit par G. S. de Correvon. 3 vols. 8º. Geneva, 1771.

ÆSCHYLUS. Tragœdiæ VII. P. Victorii cura. Gr. 4º. Geneva, H. Stephanus, 1557.

AUGUSTIN, A., AND ORSINI, F. De Romanorum gentibus et familiis. 4º. Lyons, 1592.

AMMIANUS, MARCELLINUS. Rerum gestarum libri XVIII quorum postremi IIII nunc primum excusi. fol. Augsburg, 1533.

ANASTASIUS, BIBLIOTHECARIUS. Historia de vitis Romanorum Pontificum. fol. Paris, 1649.

[ARBUTHNOT, JOHN.] Tables of ancient coins, weights, and measures. 4º. London, 1727.

ARISTOTLE. Opera omnia quæ extant, græcè & latinè. Accessit commentarius authore G. Du Val. 2 vols. fol. Paris, 1619.

ARISTOTLE. Ethicorum siue de moribus ad Nicomachum, libri decem, opera P. Victorij emendati. Gr. 4º. Frankfort, 1577.

ARISTOTLE. Artis rhetoricæ libri III. Rhetoricis ad Alexandrum lib. I. De arte poetica liber I. Gr. 4º. Frankfort, 1584.

ARNOBIUS. Adversus gentes libri VII. 4º. Leyden, 1651.

ARTEMIDORUS. Artemidori & Achmeti Oneirocritica. Gr. and Lat. 8º. Paris, 1603.

ASTRONOMICI VETERES. fol. Reggio d'Emilia, 1503.

---

* The materials in this Appendix are adapted from Geoffrey Keynes' *The Library of Edward Gibbon*, published by Jonathan Cape Limited, to whom I am indebted for their generous cooperation.

Appendix

ATHENAGORAS. Legatio pro Christianis. De resurrectione mortuorum. Gr. and Lat. 8°. Oxford, 1706.

AUGUSTAN HISTORY. Historiæ scriptores sex. C. Salmasius recensuit. fol. Paris, 1620.

AUGUSTINE, SAINT. De civitate dei. fol. Venice, 1732.

BAYLE, P. Dictionnaire historique et critique. 4 vols. fol. Amsterdam, 1740.

BEDFORD, ARTHUR. Animadversions upon Sir Isaac Newton's book intitled The Chronology of ancient kingdoms amended. 8°. London, 1728.

BEDFORD, ARTHUR. The Scripture chronology demonstrated by astronomical calculations. fol. London, 1730.

BENTLEY, RICHARD. A Dissertation upon the Epistles of Phalaris. With an answer to the objections of C. Boyle. 8°. London, 1699.

BEROSUS. Antiquitatum Italiæ ac totius orbis libri quinque. 8°. Antwerp, 1552.

BIBLE. [Greek.] Ἡ Καινὴ Διαθήκη.

BIBLE. [Greek.] Novum Testamentum Græcum, studio J. Millii. Recensuit L. Kusterus. fol. Leipzig, 1723.

BIBLE. [Greek.] Testamentum Vetus ex versione Septuaginta. Edidit J. J. Breitingerius. 4 vols. 4°. Zurich, 1730-32.

BLONDEL, D. Des Sibylles celebrées tant par l'antiquité que par les saincts Peres. 4°. Charenton, 1649.

BOCHART, S. Opera. 3 vols. fol. Leyden, 1712.

BONEFIDIUS, E. Iuris orientalis libri III ab E. Bonefidio digesti. Gr. and Lat. 2 vols. 8°. (Geneva), H. Stephanus, 1573.

BOSSUET, J. B. An Universal history. vols. 1-4. fol. London, 1736.

BOYLE, CHARLES, EARL OF ORRERY. Dr. Bentley's Dissertations on the Epistles of Phalaris and the Fables of Æsop, examin'd. 8°. London, 1745.

BRUMOY, P. Le Théâtre des Grecs. 3 vols. 4°. Paris, 1730.

BRUNCK, R. F. P. Analecta veterum poetarum Græcorum. 3 vols. 8°. Strasburg, 1772-76.

BUDÉ, G. Commentarii linguæ Græcæ. fol. Paris, R. Stephanus, 1548.

BURGH, WILLIAM. An Inquiry into the belief of the Christians of the first 3 centuries respecting the one Godhead of the Father, Son, and Holy Ghost. 8º. York, 1778.

BURNET, GILBERT. History of his own Time. 4 vols. 8º. London, 1753.

BURNET, JAMES, LORD MONBODDO. Of the origin and progress of language. vols. 1-3. 8º. Edinburgh, 1773-76.

BURNET, THOMAS. The Sacred theory of the earth. 2 vols. 8º. London, 1759.

BURTON, JOHN. Πενταλόγια sive tragediarum Græcarum delectus. 2 pts. 8º. Oxford, 1778-79.

BYZANTINE HISTORY. Corpus Byzantinæ. Editio secunda. Gr. Paris, 1645-1702.

BYZANTINE HISTORY. Corpus Byzantinæ. Editio secunda. Gr. and Lat. 23 vols. Venice, 1729-33.

CAESAR, C. J. Omnia quæ extant. 8º. Leyden, Plantin, 1593.

CALVIN, JEAN. Institutio christianæ religionis. fol. Geneva, R. Stephanus, 1559.

CAPELLA, M. M. F. Satyricon. (Edited by H. Grotius.) 8º. Leyden, 1599.

CASAUBON, M. Of the necessity of reformation. 4º. London, 1664.

CASSIODORUS, M. A. Opera. fol. Paris, 1589.

CATO, DIONYSIUS. Disticha de moribus ad filium. Gr. and Lat. 8º. Amsterdam, 1759.

CATO, DIONYSIUS. Historia critica Catoniana, cum castigationibus Josephi Scaligeri. 8º. Amsterdam, 1759.

CAVE, WILLIAM. Primitive Christianity. 2 vols. 8º. London, 1673.

CAVE, WILLIAM. Scriptorum ecclesiasticorum historia literaria. fol. Geneva, 1720.

CEBES. Tabula. Gr. and Lat. 8º. Amsterdam, 1689.

CHAUCER, GEOFFREY. Works, (edited) by J. Urry. fol. London, 1721.

CHILLINGWORTH, WILLIAM. Works. fol. London, 1674.

CHILLINGWORTH, WILLIAM. The Religion of Protestants a safe way to Salvation. fol. London, 1674.

Appendix

[CHODERLOS DE LACLOS, P. A. F.] Les Liaisons dangereuses. 8°. Neuchatel, 1782.

CLEMENS, ALEXANDRINUS. Opera. Gr. and Lat. 2 vols. fol. Oxford, 1715.

CLEYNAERTS, N. Grammatica græca. 8°. Leyden, 1734.

CONSTANTINUS, R. Lexicon Græco-Latinum. fol. Leyden, 1637.

COTELERIUS, J. B. SS. Patrum qui temporibus apostolicis floruerunt opera. Gr. and Lat. fol. Amsterdam, 1724.

CYPRIAN, SAINT. Opera. fol. Cologne, 1617.

CYPRIAN, SAINT. Opera. fol. Amsterdam, 1700.

DAMM, C. T. Novum lexicon Græcum. 4°. Berlin, 1774.

DANTE, ALIGHIERI. Opere. 5 vols. 8°. Venice, 1772.

DEMOSTHENES. Opera. Gr. fol. Paris, 1570.

DEMOSTHENES. Demosthenis et Æschinis opera. Gr. and Lat. 2 vols. 4°. London, 1771.

DEMOSTHENES. All the orations, translated by T. Leland. 4°. London, 1771.

DERHAM, WILLIAM. Astro-theology. 8°. London, 1767.

DES VIGNOLES, A. Chronologie de l'histoire sainte. 2 vols. 4°. Berlin, 1738.

DICTYS, OF CRETE. Dictys Cretensis et Dares Phrygius de bello et excidio Trojæ. 4°. Amsterdam, 1702.

DIODORUS, SICULUS. Bibliothecæ historicæ libri XV. fol. Basle, 1559.

DION, CHRYSOSTOM. Orationes LXXX. Gr. and Lat. fol. Paris, 1604.

DODWELL, HENRY. De veteribus Græcorum Romanorumque cyclis. 4°. Oxford, 1701-02.

DU CANGE, C. DU FRESNE, SEIGNEUR. Glossarium ad scriptores mediæ et infimæ Græcitatis. 2 vols. fol. Leyden, 1688.

EPICTETUS. Epicteti quæ supersunt Dissertationes, nec non Enchiridion et Fragmenta.

'EPISTOLÆ GRÆCANICÆMUTUÆ (?).' Gr. and Lat. fol. 1606.

ERASMUS, D. Opera. 10 vols. fol. Leyden, 1703-06.

ERASMUS, D. The Apophthegms of the ancients. 2 vols. 8°. London, 1753.

ERASMUS, D. Colloquia. 8°. Leyden, 1729.

ERASMUS, D. Epistolarum d. Erasmi libri XXXI et P. Melancthonis libri IV. Quibus adjiciuntur T. Mori et L. Vivis epistolæ. fol. London, 1642.

ESTIENNE, HENRI. Comicorum græcorum sententiæ. Gr. and Lat. 16°. (Paris), 1569.

ESTIENNE, HENRI. De criticis vet. Gr. et Latinis. 4°. Paris, 1587.

ESTIENNE, HENRI. Glossaria duo e situ vetustatis eruta, ad vtriusque linguæ cognitionem perutilia. fol. (Geneva), H. Stephanus, 1573.

ESTIENNE, HENRI. Poetæ Græci principes heroici carminis et alii nonnulli. Gr. fol. (Paris), H. Stephanus, 1566.

ESTIENNE, HENRI. Thesaurus græcæ linguæ. 5 vols. fol. (Geneva), H. Stephanus, 1572.

ESTIENNE, ROBERT. Thesaurus linguæ latinæ. 4 vols. fol. London, 1734-35.

EUNAPIUS. De vitis philosophorum et sophistarum. Gr. and Lat. 8°. Antwerp, 1568.

EURIPIDES. Euripides quæ extant omnia. Opera et studio J. Barnes, fol. Cambridge, 1694.

EURIPIDES. Quæ extant omnia. Gr. and Lat. 4 vols. 4°. Oxford, 1778.

EUSEBIUS, PAMPHILI. Thesaurus temporum. Eusebii Chronicorum canonum omnimodæ historiæ libri duo. Opera. J. J. Scaligeri. fol. Amsterdam, 1658.

EUSEBIUS PAMPHILI. Eusebii Pamphili, Socratis Scholastici, Hermiae Sozomeni, Theodoriti et Evagrii, quæ extant historiæ ecclesiasticæ. Illustravit Gul. Reading. Gr. and Lat. 3 vols. fol. Cambridge, 1720.

EUSEBIUS, PAMPHILI. Histoire de l'Englise, traduite par M. Cousin. 12°. Paris, 1686.

EUSEBIUS, PAMPHILI. Praeparatio evangelica. 2 vols. fol. Cologne, 1688.

EUSTATHIUS. Commentarii in Homeri Iliadem. 3 vols. fol. Florence, 1730-35.

Eustathius, Παρεκβολαι. 4 vols. fol. Rome, 1542-51.

Appendix

EUTROPIUS, F. Breviarium historiae Romanae. 8°. Leyden, 1729.

FERGUSON, ADAM. The History of the Progress and termination of the Roman Republic. 3 vols. 4°. London, 1783.

FESTUS, S. POMPEIUS. S. Pompeii Festi et M. Verrii Flacci De verborum significatione lib. XX. 4°. Amsterdam, 1699.

FISCHER, J. F. Libellus animadversionum, quibus J. Velleri Grammatica graeca emendatur, suppletur, illustratur. 3 pt. 8°. Leipzig, 1750-52.

FRÉRET, N. Défense de la chronologie, fondée sur les monumens de l'histoire ancienne, contre le système de M. Newton. 4°. Paris, 1758.

FROISSART, J. Le premier (—quart) volume de l'histoire et chronique. 4 vols. in 1. fol. Lyons, F. de Tournes, 1559-61.

GALE, THOMAS. Historiæ poeticæ scriptores antiqui græci et latini. 8°. Paris, 1675.

GALE, THOMAS. Opuscula mythologica physica et ethica (ex recensione T. Gale). Gr. and Lat. 8°. Amsterdam, 1688.

GAZA, THEODORUS. Introductionis grammaticæ libri quatuor. Gr. 8°. Basle, 1529.

GOLDSMITH, OLIVER. A History of the earth, and animated nature. 8 vols. 8°. London, 1774.

GREEK ANTHOLOGY. Florilegium diuersorum epigrammatum veterum. Gr. 8°. (Paris), H. Stephanus, 1566.

GREEK ANTHOLOGY. Epigrammatum graecorum, annotationibus J. Brodaei necnon V. Obsopaei illustratorum, libri VII. fol. Frankfort, 1600.

GREGORY, OF NAZIANZUS, SAINT. Discours contre Julien. 4°. Lyons, 1735.

GRONOVIUS, J. F. De sestertiis. 4°. Leyden, 1671.

HARLES, T. C. Introductio in historiam linguae Graecae. 8°. Altenburg, 1778.

HEATH, BENJAMIN. Notae sive lectiones ad tragicorum graecorum veterum Æschyli, Sophoclis, Euripidis quae supersunt dramata. 4°. Oxford, 1762.

HELIODORUS. Æthiopicorum libri X. Gr. and Lat. 8º. Paris, 1619.

HERMANT, G. La Vie de Saint Ambroise. 4º. Paris, 1678.

[HERMANT, G.] La Vie de Saint Jean Chrysostome. 2 vols. 8º. Lyons, 1683.

HESIOD. Hesiodi quae extant, opera. D. Heinsii. 4º. Leyden, 1603.

HODY, HUMPHREY. De Graecis illustribus linguae Graecae literarumque humaniorum instauratoribus. 8º. London, 1742.

HOLSTENIUS, L. Notae et castigationes posthumae in Stephani Byzantinii editae a T. Ryckio. fol. Leyden, 1684.

HOMER. Homeri quae extant omnia, cum Latina versione. fol. Geneva, 1606.

HOMER. 'Οδύσσεια, etc. 2 vols. 8º. Strasburg, 1525.

HOMER. Index vocabulorum in Homeri Iliade atque Odissae, caeterisque poematis. Studio M. W. Seberi Saleni. 8º. Oxford, 1780.

HUME, DAVID. Dialogues concerning natural religion. 8º. (London), 1779.

JENYNS, SOAME. A View of the internal evidence of the Christian religion. 12º. London, 1776.

JOHN STOBAEUS. Sententiae ex thesauris Graecorum delectae. fol. Basle, 1549.

JOHN STOBAEUS. Sententiae ex thesauris Graecorum delectae. fol. Geneva, 1609.

JOHNSON, SAMUEL. A Dictionary of the English Language. 2 vols. fol. London, 1755.

JOHNSON, SAMUEL. The Prince of Abissinia. 2 vols. in 1. 8º. London, 1759.

JORTIN, JOHN. The Life of Erasmus. 2 vols. 4º. London, 1758-60.

JORTIN, JOHN. Tracts. 2 vols. 8º. London, 1790.

JULIAN, THE APOSTATE. Opera. Gr. and Lat. 3 vols. fol. Leipzig, 1696.

KEILL, JOHN. An Introduction to the true astronomy. 8º. London, 1721.

KEILL, JOHN. An Introduction to natural philosophy. 8°. London, 1720.

LABBÉ, C. Cyrilli Philoxeni, aliorumque veterum glossaria latino-graeca et graeco-latina a Labbaeo collecta. fol. Paris, 1679.

LACTANTIUS, L.C.F. Opera, studio S. Gallaei. 8°. Leyden, 1660.

LA MOTHE LE VAYER, F. DE. Œuvres. 14 vols. 8°. Dresden, 1756-59.

LANCELOT, C. Nouvelle méthode pour apprendre facilement la langue greque. [The Grammar of Port-Royal.] 8°. Paris, 1754.

LARDNER, NATHANIEL. The Credibility of the Gospel history. 17 vols. 8°. London, 1741-62.

LE CLERC, J. Ars critica. 2 vols. 8°. Amsterdam, 1697.

LE CLERC, J. Bibliothèque ancienne et moderne. 29 vols. 12°. The Hague, 1726-30.

LE CLERC, J. Historia ecclesiastica duorum primorum a Christo nato saeculorum. 4°. Amsterdam, 1716.

[LE CLERC, J.] Parrhasiana, ou pensées diverses. 2 vols. 8°. Amsterdam, 1699-1701.

LECTIUS, J. Poetae graeci veteres tragici, comici, lyrici, epi-grammatici. Gr. and Lat. fol. Geneva, 1614.

LE FEVRE, TANNEGUI. Méthode pour commencer les humanites grecques et latines. 8°. Paris, 1731.

LENGLET DU FRESNOY, N. Tablettes chronologiques de l'his-toire universelle. 2 vols. 8°. The Hague, 1745.

LEUNCLAVIUS, J. Historiae Musulmanae Turcorum libri XVIII. fol. Frankfort, 1591.

LIPSIUS, JUSTUS. Opera. 4 vols. fol. Antwerp, Plantin, 1637.

LUCANUS, M. A. Pharsalia. 4°. Leyden, 1728.

MACROBIUS, A.A.T. Opera. 8°. Leyden, 1670.

MACROBIUS, A.A.T. Opera. 8°. London, 1694.

MAGNUS, JOHANNES. Gothorum Sueonumque historia. 8°. Basel, 1558.

MAITTAIRE, M. Graecae linguae dialecti. 8°. The Hague, 1738.

MAITTAIRE, M. Stephanorum historia, vitas ipsorum ac libros complectens. 2 vols. 8°. London, 1709.

MALALAS, JOANNES. Historia chronica. 8°. Oxford, 1691.

MANETHO. Apotelesmaticorum libri sex. 4°. Leyden, 1698.

MANILIUS, M. Astronomicon libri quinque. J. Scaliger recensuit. 2 vols. 8°. Paris, 1579.

MARSHAM, SIR JOHN. Canon chronicus aegyptiacus, ebraicus, graecus, et disquisitiones. fol. London, 1672.

MARSHAM, SIR JOHN. Canon chronicus aegyptiacus, ebraicus, graecus, et disquisitiones. 4°. Frankfort, 1696.

MEURSIUS, J. Opera omnia. 12 vols. fol. Florence, 1741-63.

MEURSIUS, J. Ceramicus geminus. 4°. Utrecht, 1663.

MEURSIUS, J. Creta, Cyprus, Rhodus. 4°. Amsterdam, 1675.

MEURSIUS, J. Graecia ludibunda, siue du ludis Graecorum liber. 8°. Leyden, 1625.

MEURSIUS, J. Miscellanea laconica. 4°. Amsterdam, 1661.

MEURSIUS, J. Regnum atticum. 4°. Amsterdam, 1633.

MIDDLETON, CONYERS. Miscellaneous works. 4 vols. 4°. London, 1752.

MIDDLETON, CONYERS. The History of the life of M. T. Cicero. 3 vols. 8°. London, 1741.

MISCELLANEA Graecorum aliquot scriptorum carmina. Gr. and Lat. 4°. London, 1722.

MOERIS ATTICISTA. Lexicon atticum. 8°. Leyden, 1759.

MONTAGU, E. W. Reflections on the rise and fall of the Antient republicks. 8°. London, 1759.

MONTESQUIEU, C. L. de Secondat, baron de. Œuvres. 3 vols. 4°. Amsterdam and Leipzig, 1758.

MONTFAUCON, B. DE. L'Antiquité expliquée et représentée. 10 vols. fol. Paris, 1719, 24.

MOYLE, WALTER. Works. 3 vols. 8°. London, 1726, 27.

MUSGRAVE, SAMUEL. Two dissertations. I. On the Graecian mythology. II. An examination of Sir I. Newton's objections to the chronology of the Olympiads. 8°. London, 1782.

NEMESIUS. De natura hominis. Gr. and Lat. 8°. Oxford, 1671.

NEWTON, SIR ISAAC. The Chronology of ancient kingdoms amended. 4°. London, 1728.

Nonnus. Dionysiaca. Gr. and Lat. 4°. Antwerp, 1569.

Optatus, Saint. De schismate Donatistarum. fol. Paris, 1700.

Origen. Contra Celsum. Philocalia. G. Spencerus recognovit. Gr. and Lat. 4°. Cambridge, 1677.

Orosius, P. Adversus paganos historiarum libri septem. 4°. Leyden, 1738.

Pagi, A. Critica historico-chronologica in universos annales ecclesiasticos Baronii. 4 vols. fol. Antwerp, 1727.

Pagi, F. Breviarium historico-chronologico-criticum illustriora pontificum Romanorum gesta, conciliorum generalium acta complectens. 3 vols. 4°. Antwerp, 1717, 18.

Pearson, John. Opera posthuma chronologica, viz. de serie et successione primorum Romae episcoporum dissertationes duae. 3 pts. 4°. London, 1687, 88.

Perizonius, J. Origines Babylonicae et Ægyptiacae. 2 vols. 8°. Utrecht, 1736.

Petau, D. De doctrina temporum. 3 vols. fol. Antwerp, 1703.

[Pezron, P. Y.] L'Antiquité des tems, rétablie et defendue contre les Juifs et les nouveaux chronologistes. 4°. Paris, 1687.

Pezron, P. Y. Défense de l'Antiquité des tems. 4°. Paris, 1704.

Photius. Epistolae. fol. London, 1651.

Photius. Myriobiblon. Edidit D. Hoeschelius. Gr. and Lat. fol. Rouen, 1653.

Photius. Nomocanon. Gr. and Lat. 4°. Paris, 1615.

Photius. Librorum quos legit Photius patriarcha excerpta et censurae. D. Hoeschelius primus edidit. fol. Augsburg, 1601.

Pighius, E. W. Annales Romanorum. 3 vols. fol. Antwerp, 1615.

Pindar. Carmina. Gr. and Lat. 2 vols. in 1. 8°. Göttingen, 1773, 74.

Pindar. Olympia, Nemea, Pythia, Isthmia. Gr. and Lat. fol. Oxford, 1697.

Pindar. Odes, translated by Gilbert West. 2 vols. 8°. London, 1753.

Selected Titles from Gibbon's Library

PINKERTON, JOHN. A Dissertation on the origin and progress of the Scythians or Goths. 8º. London, 1787.

PINKERTON, JOHN. An Essay on medals. 2 vols. 8º. London, 1789.

PLATO. Opera. Gr. and Lat. 3 vols. fol. Geneva, H. Stephanus, 1578.

PLUTARCH. Πλουτάρχου τὰ σωζόμενα συγράμματα. 13 vols. 8º. (Geneva), H. Stephanus, 1572.

PLUTARCH. Opera. Gr. and Lat. 2 vols. fol. Frankfort, 1599.

PLUTARCH. Les Œuvres morales & meslées. Translatées par I. Amyot. 7 vols. 8º. Paris, 1574.

PLUTARCH. Apophthegmata graeca regum et ducum, philosophorum item, ex Plutarcho et Diogene Laertio. Gr. and Lat. 12º. (Geneva), H. Stephanus, 1568.

POLLUX, JULIUS. Onomasticon. Gr. and Lat. 2 vols. fol. Amsterdam, 1706.

POLYAENUS. Strategematum libri octo. Gr. and Lat. 8º. Leyden, 1690.

POLYBIUS. Polybii, Diodori Siculi, Nicolai Damasceni, Dionysii Halicar., Appiani Alexand., Dionis et Joannis Antiocheni, excerpta. H. Valesius edidit. Gr. and Lat. 4º. Paris, 1634.

POLYBIUS. Historiarum libri qui supersunt. J. Gronovius emendavit. Gr. and Lat. 3 vols. 8º. Amsterdam, 1670.

PORTIUS, SIMON. Lexicon latinum, graeco-barbarum, et literale. 4º. Paris, 1635.

PORTUS, G. Dictionarium doricum graecolatinum. 3 vols. 8º. Frankfort, 1603-06.

PRIDEAUX, HUMPHREY. The Old and New Testament connected in the history of the Jews. 4 vols. 8º. London, 1749.

PRIDEAUX, HUMPHREY. The Old and New Testament connected in the history of the Jews. fol. London, 1718.

PRIESTLEY, JOSEPH. An History of the corruptions of Christianity. 2 vols. 8º. Birmingham, 1782.

PROCOPIUS. Historiarum libri VIII, opera D. Hoeschelii. Gr. fol. Augsburg, 1607.

Appendix

PROCOPIUS, OF CAESAREA. Arcana historia. Gr. and Lat. fol.
Leyden, 1623.

PRUDENTIUS CLEMENS, A. Quae extant. 12°. Amsterdam, 1667.

PUTSCHIUS, H. Grammaticae latinae auctores antiqui. 4°.
Hanover, 1605.

RALEIGH, SIR WALTER. The History of the world. 2 vols. fol.
London, 1736.

RICHARDSON, SAMUEL. Clarissa. 8 vols. 12°. London, 1768.

RICHARDSON, SAMUEL. The History of Sir Charles Grandison.
7 vols. 12°. London, 1781.

SAINT-EVREMOND, C. Margotelle, sieur de. Œuvres. 10 vols.
12°. Paris, 1740.

SALLUSTIUS CRISPUS, C. C. Crispus Sallustius et L. Annaeus
Florus. 4°. Birmingham, 1773.

SANCHONIATHON. Phoenician history, translated from the first
book of Eusebius De praeparatione evangelica, by R. Cumberland. 8°. London, 1720.

SCALIGER, J. J. Opus de emendatione temporum. fol. Geneva, 1629.

SCALIGER, J. J. Scaligerana. 12°. Cologne, 1695.

SCHOTT, A. Adagia siue prouerbia Graecorum ex Zenobio seu
Zenodoto, Diogeniano, et Suidae collectaneis. Gr. and Lat.
4°. Antwerp, 1612.

SCOTT, DANIEL. Appendix ad thesaurum graecae linguae ab
H. Stephano constructum. 2 vols. fol. London, 1745.

SENECA, L. A. Opera quae exstant omnia a J. Lipsio emendata.
fol. Antwerp, 1632.

SENECA, L. A. Opera omnia, ex ult. J. Lipsii et J. F. Gronovii
emendat., et M. Annaei Senecae rhetoris quae extant. 3 vols.
12°. Leyden, 1649.

SEVERUS, SULPICIUS. Opera. 8°. Leyden, 1647.

SIDONIUS APOLLINARIS. Opera, cum castigatione et commentario
J. Sauaronis. 4°. Paris, 1652.

SIGONIO, C. Opera. 6 vols. fol. Milan, 1732-37.

SOLINUS, C. J. Cl. Salmasii Plinianae exercitationes in C. Julii
Solini Polyhistora. Item C. J. Solini Polyhistor emendatus.
2 vols. fol. Utrecht, 1688, 89.

SOLINUS, C. J. Polyhistor. 8º. Leipzig, 1777.

SOPHOCLES. Tragoediae septem. Gr. and Lat. 4º. Geneva, H. Stephanus, 1568.

SOPHOCLES. Tragoediae VII. Opera G. Canteri. 12º. Leyden, 1593.

SPANHEIM, E. Dissertationes de praestantia et usu numismatum antiquorum. 2 vols. fol. London, Amsterdam, 1717.

SPEED, JOHN. The History of Great Britaine. fol. London, 1627.

STEELE, SIR RICHARD. The Guardian. 2 vols. 12º. London, 1751.

STEELE, SIR RICHARD. The Tatler. 4 vols. 12º. London, 1774.

STEPHANUS, BYZANTINUS. Gentilia per epitomen, antehac de urbibus inscripta. Gr. and Lat. fol. Leyden, 1694.

STEPHANUS, BYZANTINUS. Fragmentum de Dodone. Gr. and Lat. 4º. Leyden, 1681.

STRAUCH, G. Breviarium chronologicum: or, a treatise describing the terms used in chronology. Done into English by R. Sault. 8º. London, 1722.

SUIDAS. Lexicon. Gr. and Lat. 3 vols. fol. Cambridge, 1705.

SWIFT, JONATHAN. Works, with notes by J. Hawkesworth. 22 vols. 8º. London, 1768.

SYNESIUS. Opera quae extant omnia. Gr. and Lat. fol. Paris, 1612.

TACITUS, C. C. Opera quae exstant. J. Lipsius recensuit. Accessit C. Velleius Paterculus. fol. Antwerp, 1627.

TEMPLE, SIR WILLIAM. Works. 2 vols. fol. London, 1721.

TERENTIUS, P. Opera quae supersunt. 8º. Geneva, 1581.

TERTULLIANUS, Q.S.F. Opera. fol. Paris, 1689.

TERTULLIANUS, Q.S.F. Apologeticus. 8º. Leyden, 1718.

THEOCRITUS. Theocriti, Moschi, Bionis, Simmii quae extant, studio et opera D. Heinsii. Gr. and Lat. 4º. Heidelberg, 1604.

THOU, J. A. DE. Histoire universelle. 14 vols. 4º. London, 1734.

TRAGEDIES. 'A Collection of tragedies by various authors in 6 vols.' 12°. (A made-up set as below.)

   I. Phillips, E.: The Distrest Mother
       Rowe, N.: Jane Shore
              The Fair Penitent
              Ulysses
       Fenton, E.: Marianne

  II. Otway, T.: The Orphan
              Venice Preserved
      Hughes, J.: The Siege of Damascus
      Lillo, G.: The Fatal Curiosity

 III. Young, E.: The Revenge
      Rowe, N.: Tamerlane
      Dryden, J.: The Indian Emperor
             Don Sebastian, King of Portugal

 IV. Addison, J.: Cato
      Hill, A.: Zara
      Rowe, N.: The Royal Convert
             Lady Jane Gray

  V. (Titles omitted)

 VI. Hill, A.: Abzira
      Smith, E.: Phaedrus and Hippolitus
      Jonson, Ben: Cataline's Conspiracy
      Rowe, N.: The Ambitious Step-Mother

ULUGH BEG. Epochae celebriores astronomis, historicis, chronologis Chataiorum, Syro-Graecorum, Arabum, Persarum, Chorasmiorum usitatae: ex traditione Ulug Beigi. Eas publicavit J. Gravius. Pers. and Lat. 4°. London, 1650.

USHER, JAMES. Annales veteris et novi Testamenti. fol. Geneva, 1722.

[VALOIS] Dissertations on the following subjects, viz. the Mosaick account of the creation and fall of man. . . . By Philalethes. 8°. London, 1750.

VITRUVIUS POLLIO, M. De architectura. fol. Amsterdam, 1649.

Voss, G. J. Opera. 6 vols. fol. Amsterdam, 1701.

Voss, G. J. De historicis graecis. 4°. Leyden, 1651.

Voss, G. J. De historicis latinis. 4°. Leyden, 1651.

Voss, G. J. Etymologicon linguae latinae. fol. Leyden, 1664.

Voss, G. J. De studiorum ratione opuscula. 8°. Utrecht, 1651.

Voss, ISAAC. De Septuaginta interpretibus. 4°. The Hague, 1661, 63.

Voss, ISAAC. Variarum observationum liber. 4°. London, 1685.

WARBURTON, WILLIAM. The Divine legation of Moses demonstrated. 5 vols. 8°. London, 1765.

WARBURTON, WILLIAM. Julian. 8°. London, 1751.

WARBURTON, WILLIAM. Tracts. 8°. London, 1789.

WOTTON, WILLIAM. The History of Rome from the death of Antoninus Pius to the death of Severus Alexander. 8°. London, 1701.

WOTTON, WILLIAM. Reflections upon ancient and modern learning. 8°. London, 1694.

WOTTON, WILLIAM. Reflections upon ancient and modern learning. With a dissertation upon the epistles of Phalaris. By Dr. Bentley. 8°. London, 1697.

ZONARAS, J. Compendium historiarum. Gr. and Lat. fol. Basle, 1557.

ZONARAS, J. Historia, tradotta dal Greco per M. Emilio. 4°. Venice, 1560.

ZOSIMUS. Historiae novae libri sex. Gr. and Lat. 8°. Oxford, 1679.

ZOSIMUS. Historiae. Gr. and Lat. 8°. Leipzig, 1784.

Notes

The following notes do not contain specific paginations for all the primary and secondary sources referred to in the text. To have made such citations exhaustive would have produced a prohibitively bulky addendum that could add but little to the present work. When the text cites an author of a single work that is easily available, the reference is generally included in the text itself (*e.g.*, Polybius, VI.6), provided the location might otherwise prove difficult to find. When the citation is of a fairly short work (*e.g.*, Thomas Rymer's *A Short View of Tragedy*), the page references are not given unless the work is a rare one or otherwise not liable to easy verification. As a rule, extended quotations, close paraphrases, or references to supplementary materials are documented below. When listing supplementary works would duplicate standard bibliographies—the MLA Annual Bibliography, the yearly bibliography in *Philological Quarterly*, the *C.B.E.L.*, *A Literary History of England*—the Notes ordinarily mention the relevant bibliography.

CHAPTER 1. SOME TERMS AND THEIR USES

This survey of terms does not include all possible examples, obviously, nor even all the readily ascertainable ones. *The Oxford English Dictionary* provides additional usages for the variations of "classic" and "classical" though it is of little help with "Neo-Classicism," "Augustan," and their variants. The various usages discussed in the text are illustrative of the literary bias and do not necessarily reflect the use of the same terms by nonliterary critics. Henry Hawley's *Neo-Classicism, Style and Motif* (New York, 1964) provides an interesting example of how art critics employ many of the phrases also common in literary criticism.

1. For discussions of the elements in eighteenth century English culture best characterized by "the Age of Elegance," see the intellectual and social surveys by Basil Willey, G. M. Trevelyan, and A. S. Turberville. George Sherburn's bibliographies in *A Literary History of England* remain the best general introduction to secondary sources about the period under discussion.

2. Isaiah Berlin, Crane Brinton, and Will Durant are modern writers who have investigated the intellectual components of the eras called "the Age of Reason" and "the Age of Enlightenment." See Berlin's preface to *The Age of Enlightenment* (New York, 1952); Brinton's *Men and Ideas* and *The Shaping of the Western Mind*; and the pertinent volumes in Durant's *The Story of Philosophy*.

3. Cf. *A Literary History of England*, pp. 699-700.

4. The *Oxford English Dictionary*, while circumscribed by its etymological intentions, is the most extensive historical survey of several of the terms mentioned. My discussion is indebted to it for the periodical references to variants of "classical" and "classicism" in the nineteenth century.

Notes

The historical data of the O.E.D. is slightly supplemented by articles in the *Oxford Classical Dictionary* and *The Oxford Companion to English Literature*. A recent essay on "classicism" is among the best of the succinct discussions of historical and modern uses: see Wolfgang B. Fleischmann, "Classicism," in *Encyclopedia of Poetry and Poetics* (Princeton, 1965), pp. 136-41. The short bibliography accompanying the article is a fine one. Additional references are given by Sherburn, *A Literary History*, p. 833.

5. See Sherburn, pp. 710 ff., 823 ff., and 696 ff.

CHAPTER 2. THE ROLE OF HISTORIOGRAPHY

Published comments on the state of historical theory and writing in the eighteenth century are largely those of historians and historiographers. General surveys of historical writing that make evaluations of Neo-Classical theory and practice (*e.g.*, Burnet, Clarendon, Bolingbroke) include Eduard Fueter's *Geschichte der Neueren Historiographie* (Berlin, 1911); J. W. Thompson's *A History of Historical Writing* (New York, 1942); Robin G. Collingwood's *The Idea of History* (Oxford, Clarendon Press, 1948). With the exception of Bolingbroke, none of the essayists mentioned in this chapter are given even a passing glance by historians.

There are two articles that deal directly with the state of historiographical theory in England in the sixty years before the era of Gibbon. R. N. Stromberg's "History in the Eighteenth Century," *JHI*, XII (1951), 295-304, is derogatory to the point of contempt. George Nadel's "Philosophy of History Before Historicism," *History and Theory*, No. 3 (1964), 291-315, is judicious but still disparaging of Neo-Classical theory. The state of historiography and historiographical theory in the mid and later century is described usefully in Thomas P. Peardon's *The Transition in English Historical Writing, 1760-1830* (New York, 1933). J. B. Black's examination of Voltaire, Hume, Robertson, and Gibbon in his *The Art of History: A Study of Four Great Historians of the Eighteenth Century* (New York, 1926) is a succinct statement of twentieth century historians' opinion of eighteenth century historiography.

George Sherburn's "Patterns in Historical Writing" discusses the Restoration antecedents of the theorists and historians taken up in the text. See *A Literary History of England*, pp. 780-92.

1. Jean Bodin, *Method for the Easy Comprehension of History*, p. 9.

2. Bolingbroke, *Works*, II, 177-78.

3. Hannah More, *Works*, IV, 45.

4. Jean Le Clerc, *Parrhasiana*, III, 97-165 *passim*.

5. Thomas Hearne, *Ductor Historicus*, I, 2; I, 97-102 *passim*.

6. Charles Rollin, *The Method of Teaching and Studying the Belles Lettres*, III, 1-3, 184.

7. Bolingbroke, II, 176-77, 186.

8. Edward Manwaring, *An Historical and Critical Account*, pp. iii-iv, 358-59.

9. Peter Whalley, *An Essay on the Manner of Writing History*, pp. B, 9-11, 23.

10. Cf. Irvin Ehrenpreis, "Swift's History of England," *JEGP*, LI (1952), 177-85.

Notes

11. Cf. Temple, *Works*, III, 453, 461, 488-89.
12. Eduard Fueter, *Geschichte der Neueren Historiographie*, p. 166.
13. Swift, *Works*, XI, 184.
14. In all of the libraries mentioned, certain basic historians were to be found, often in triplicate or quadruplicate. Herodotus, Thucydides, Xenophon, Justin, Livy, Paterculus, Cornelius Nepos, and Dio Cassius were owned by all the collectors. Congreve had copies of Herodotus in Latin, English, and French, but not in Greek; similarly, his copy of Thucydides was a French translation. Addison, Swift, and Johnson owned the Greek historians in the original, however; and Swift had several copies of each. Addison had five copies of Justin's History in various editions and with different sets of notes. Sallust, Quintus Curtius, Caesar, Diodorus, and Florus were present in the libraries of all three as well as those of Hearne and Rawlinson. Everyone owned Lucan's *Pharsalia* or Rowe's translation of it; Swift had a copy inscribed to him by the translator himself. Johnson and Swift had extensive collections of the Byzantine Greek historians, as did Hearne. All of the men owned a goodly number of modern historians, Johnson perhaps having the fewest and Rawlinson the most; Rawlinson's collection of fifteenth and sixteenth century authors was truly formidable. Extensive correlations between the collections are perhaps unnecessary, since the relevant issue is simply the extent to which men of classicist inclination relied upon Greek and Roman history for their views. Obviously, their exposure to historiographical opinion was extensive.
15. Herodotus, I.5; Thucydides, I.1; Xenophon, *Memorabilia*, I.1.
16. Polybius, I.35.
17. Diodorus Siculus, I.1.
18. Cf. J. W. Thompson, *A History of Historical Writing*, I, 124-59.
19. See *The Freeholder*, No. 51; Swift, *Works*, I, 241-42.
20. Cf. Manwaring, p. 360.
21. See Francis Haber, *The Age of the World: Moses to Darwin* (Baltimore, 1959) for a readable account.
22. The generalization is liable to severe qualification, of course, but typical references to time as a function of matter may be found in Herodotus, I.5; Diodorus, I.6, X.10; and Dionysius, V.77, VIII.60.
23. Cf. Herodotus, I.172; II.35, 77; IV.107, 172-76, 197.
24. This subject is more completely taken up in J. W. Johnson, "Of Differing Ages and Climes," *JHI*, XXI, No. 4 (1960), 465-80.
25. See Polydore Vergil, pp. 126, 222-23; Holinshed, I, 290, 344-45; Daniel, p. 25. Speed, Stow, and Camden interspersed their histories with similar statements.
26. See Zera S. Fink, *The Classical Republicans* (Evanston, Illinois, 1945).
27. Swift's indebtedness to Dionysius for themes and actual phrases is abundantly clear in the early works.
28. Polydore Vergil, p. 126. Polydore's full statement of the body-state analogy appears on pp. 222-23.
29. Holinshed, I, 49.
30. Daniel, pp. 1-2, 43, 246. See, also, Stow, p. 3ff; Speed, pp. 922-24.

Notes

31. Other aspects of the topic are dealt with in J. W. Johnson, "Swift's Historical Outlook," *Journal of British Studies*, IV, No. 2 (May 1965), 52-77.

CHAPTER 3. GREECE

Certain aspects of Hellenism in England between 1660 and 1800 have been well documented by earlier commentators. In general, critical studies of Hellenic influences on English culture and literature have concentrated on three areas: the accounts of travelers to Greece and the Levant; accounts of English art and art collections in the eighteenth century; and studies of "romantic" Hellenism, which have pushed back the beginnings of the Romantic interest in Greece to 1730. There have also been scattered studies of the place of Greek studies in English universities in the eighteenth century and the cultural effects of modern Greeks in England. My own data should be considered in the light of other studies attesting to the Hellenism of the period between 1660 and 1800. I have tried to show that Hellenism was both literary and widely felt, and that not only travel books and art catalogs manifested it.

The reader is urged to take into account the evidence presented in these studies especially as he assesses the Hellenic elements of Neo-Classicism:

Lionel Cust, *History of the Society of the Dilettanti* (1914)
Theodore E. Dowling and Edwin Fletcher, *Hellenism in England* (1915)
Harry Levin, *The Broken Column* (1931)
Warner Rice, "Early English Travelers to Greece and the Levant" (1933)
B. H. Stern, *The Rise of Romantic Hellenism in English Literature, 1732-1786* (1940)
M. L. Clarke, *Greek Studies in England, 1700-1830* (1945)
D. M. Foerster, *Homer in English Criticism. The Historical Approach in the Eighteenth Century* (1947)
Terence Spencer, *Fair Greece Sad Relic* (1954)
James M. Osborn, "Travel Literature and the Rise of Neo-Hellenism in England" (1963)

Complete references may be found in the Bibliography.

The catalog of Greek works edited, reissued, or translated after 1660 is most certainly incomplete; but it is perhaps extensive enough to demonstrate the point being made. It corresponds to the cataloged works contained in the Houghton and Folger Libraries; I have not checked other library catalogs for titles. My list of translations can be readily checked against that in the *Cambridge Bibliography of English Literature*, II, 758-64, for additions and omissions. Works named in my chapter are those I have actually examined.

Readable accounts of Richard Bentley's place in Greek studies are given in the biography included in the *Dictionary of National Biography* and in the articles of W. S. Maguiness, D. R. Shackleton Bailey, and J. A. Davison, "The Bentley Commemorative Lectures," *Proceedings of the Leeds Philosophical and Literary Society* (February 1963).

Notes

Further accounts of the various dramatic productions utilizing Hellenic themes or sources are to be found in the volumes of *The London Stage* (1660-1776), edited by Avery, A. H. Scouten, *et al.*

The effect of Greek literary criticism on English critics is documented in many places, perhaps most succinctly in the prefaces to the writings of the Neo-Classicists collected by J. E. Spingarn, J. W. H. Atkins, W. P. Ker, and H. H. Adams, and Baxter Hathaway.

1. Benjamin Hederich's Latin–Greek lexicon, Ewaldus Gallus's *Paidologiai* (1666), Francis Gregory's *Onomastikon brachy* (1668), Johan Amos Comenius' *Janua linguarum trilinguis* (1670), R. Sutton's *General Examination of the common Greek grammar* (1689), and reprints of William Camden's Greek grammar (1711).

2. Aeschylus came out in 1664, Sophocles in 1665 and again in 1669, and Josuah Barnes' edition of Euripides appeared in 1694. Anacreon was published in 1684 and 1695; a version of Sappho, with notes by Vossius, was printed in 1695; Pindar in 1697; and Aesop first in the L'Estrange version in 1691 and then in Anthony Alsop's quadrilingual edition in 1698. Herodotus came out in a new Greek edition in 1679, and Thucydides in 1696. There were other Greek editions, to be sure; those listed are ones I have examined personally.

3. Xenophon's *Hellenica* appeared in 1685. Thomas Hobbes' 1628 translation of Thucydides was reprinted in 1676. The ever-enthralling Plutarch's *Lives* came out in translation in 1667, 1683, 1693, and 1700. Herodian appeared in a new translation in 1698. Anacreon came out in 1683. John Ogilby's *Aesopicks* was printed in 1673. Aelian, praised as a model of Attic style, was put into English in 1666. Hobbes' Homer was widely read in the versions of 1677 and 1686.

4. At the time of his death, Swift owned copies of the complete works of Homer, Plato, Aristotle, Xenophon, and Plutarch. Other items in his library included works by Demosthenes, Aeschines, Strabo, Ptolemy, Aristophanes, Pausanius, Pindar, Diogenes Laertius, Aeschylus, Pythagoras, the Poetae Minores Graeci, the Scaliger edition of the New Testament, the Auctores Graeci Historiarum, Procopius, Thucydides, Isocrates, Sylburgius' *Greek Etymology and Grammar*, and the Greek writers of Roman history. The showpiece of his collection was Jacob Gronovius' *Thesaurus Antiquitatum Graecarum* (1697-1702), given to him by the expansive Bolingbroke.

5. Cf. the *Spectator*, Nos. 160, 191, 253, 267, 273, and 391.

6. Johnson's library not only contained the same core collection of Greek literature as Swift's and Addison's, but he further owned four copies each of the major tragedians, Epictetus, Hippocrates, Hesychius, Hierocles, Anacreon, Apollonius, Galen, Theocritus, Dionysius the Areopagite, and more than a half dozen Greek lexicons. For Johnson's Greek scholarship, see Hawkins, *The Life of Samuel Johnson, LL.D. passim.*

7. Cf. Peter Whalley, *An Essay on . . . History*, p. 6. Whalley quotes Lucian in support of the opinion that Herodotus, Thucydides, and Xenophon are "unrivalled Heroes in the Art" of writing history.

Notes

8. For example, Otway's *Alcibiades* (1675), Lee's *The Rival Queens, or The Death of Alexander the Great* (1677), Dryden's *Cleomenes* (1692), Mary Pix's *The Double Distress* (1701), Jane Wiseman's *Antiochus the Great* (1701), *Darius* (1723), and Samuel Madden's *Themistocles* (1729). Cf. Avery *et al.*, *The London Stage, 1660-1800*.

9. Among writers of Pindarics, some of them the best in English: Cowley, Dryden, Congreve, Mrs. Behn, Samuel Cobb, Robert Fleming, Prior, Swift, Gray, and Collins.

10. Charles Gildon's *Phaeton* (1698) was based on Euripides' *Medea*; John Dennis' *Iphigenia* (1700) departed from the *Iphigenia in Tauris*. In 1707 an adaptation of Euripides, the *Phaedra*, was staged with an epilogue by Prior; and Ambrose Phillips' *The Distracted Mother* (1712) was an adaptation of Euripides' *Andromache* which Gay parodied in *The What D'Ye Call It?* In 1714 Mr. Low's Scholars staged a production of Sophocles' *Oedipus Tyrannos* in Greek at Mile End Green; unfortunately, there is no way of knowing how well it was attended. Richard West produced his *Hecuba* in 1726. Charles Johnson's *Medea* in 1731 was not very kindly received. And in 1738 James Thomson saw his adaptation of the *Agamemnon* acted. Cf. *The London Stage*.

11. In 1676 Charles Davenant's *Circe* appeared with a prologue by Dryden. Elkanah Settle's *The Virgin Prophetess* [*i.e.*, Cassandra] and Congreve's *The Judgment of Paris* exploited popular interest in the Troy story. Vanbrugh's *Aesop* was a loose comedy adaptation of the fabulist's life, derived from a French source. Rowe's *The Ambitious Stepmother* (1700) used the Persian background once again, and his *Ulysses* (1705) reverted to the Homeric myths. Dryden's *Amphitryon*, originally produced in 1690, was revived in the first decades of the eighteenth century and had several long runs. In 1708 Charles Goring's *Irene; or, The Fair Greek* was still another forerunner of Johnson's later *Irene*, which was based on a Byzantine Greek story. In 1714 Charles Johnson's *The Victim* paraded Achilles, Agamemnon, and Ulysses once more in a Homeric-Aeschylean farrago. And Gay's musical drama, *Achilles*, written during the 1720s, was staged in 1737 after his death.

12. Handel, Giocomo Rossi, John Galliard, Giovanni Bononcini, Christopher Pepusch, Francesco Manchini, and Peter Motteux also hastened to create words and music that extolled Greek myths. Cf. *The London Stage*.

13. Cf. *Psyche* (1704), *Thomyris* (1707), *Pyrrhus and Demetrius* (1709), *Hercules* (1712), *Calypso and Telemachus* (1712), *Theseus* (1713), *Croesus* (1714), *The Siege of Troy* (1715), *Astyanax* (1727), *Penelope* (1741), *Alexander in Persia* (1741), and *Roxana* (1743).

14. Among their subjects: Acis and Galatea (by Gay with music by Handel), Apollo and Daphne, Jupiter and Europa, Peleus and Thetis, Neptune and Amphitrite, Proteus, Bellerophon, Pan and Syrinx, Perseus and Andromeda, Atalanta, Semele, and Xerxes.

15. Cf. *The London Stage*, III.

16. The two most useful modern editions are Whitney J. Oates, *The Stoic and Epicurean Philosophers, The Complete Extant Writings* (New York, 1940), and George K. Strodach, *The Philosophy of Epicurus* (Evanston, Illinois, 1963). Both editions contain the Vatican Collection of Apho-

Notes

risms, discovered in the nineteenth century; Strodach's edition also has an explanatory introduction and detailed notes but lacks the full text of some secondary materials; Oates gives all of the essential material with little apparatus.

17. Exegeses of Epicureanism and other philosophies prevalent in classical (and Neo-Classical) times appear in Eduard Zeller, *Stoics, Epicureans, and Sceptics,* revised and translated by Oswald J. Reichel (New York, 1962); R. D. Hicks, *Stoic and Epicurean* (New York, 1962); and Cyril Bailey, *The Greek Atomists and Epicurus* (Oxford, 1928). Zeller's notes are invaluable for those interested in classical and mediaeval preservers of Epicurus' thought (Stobaeus, Suidas, *et al.*). English Neo-Classicists were also exposed to Epicureanism through these sources as well as Diogenes Laertius and Lucretius. H. D. Sedgwick, *The Art of Happiness* (Indianapolis, 1933) is a popularized treatment of Epicurus' philosophy.

The continued interest of the French in Epicureanism may be seen in two modern studies: A. J. Festugière, *Épicure et ses Dieux* (Paris, 1946), which is one of the fullest studies of Epicurus' theology; and Jean Brun, *L'Épicurisme* (Paris, 1959).

18. Oates, pp. vii-viii.

19. Cf. Norman W. De Witt, *St. Paul and Epicurus* (Minneapolis, 1954).

20. Cf. the discussion of "natural" religion and priestcraft in Epicurus' "Letter to Herodotus" and elsewhere and the theories of Pope, Mandeville, Bolingbroke, Hume, and Gibbon. Sherburn has already noted the importance of Temple's Epicurean enthusiasm for gardens and its effect on later writers (*A Literary History,* p. 809). Epicurus' rational dismissal of astronomical portents (comets, thunder, and so on) is echoed in the writings of Swift and the Bickerstaff group and the Rationalist cosmologers (Burnet, Whiston). His discussion of language as a cultural phenomenon rather than a divine gift left traces to be seen from Wotton and Addison to Johnson and Monboddo. The Epicurean theory of justice and law, bodily appropriated by Hobbes' *Leviathan,* runs through Neo-Classical thought from Dryden to Burke.

21. See the various works of Werner Jaeger, Edith Hamilton, C. M. Bowra, Moses Hadas, Richmond Lattimore, Gilbert Highet, *et al.* for versions of contemporary Hellenism.

CHAPTER 4. ROME

The number of critical works that touch on the place of Rome in eighteenth century English thought and literature is so large that it is impossible to name them here. Sherburn's bibliography, as well as the *C.B.E.L.* and *PMLA* bibliographies are the best guides to these studies.

The best supplementary study of the aspects of Roman culture discussed in this chapter is E. K. Rand's *The Building of Eternal Rome* (Cambridge, Massachusetts, 1943), which gives a history of the elements of the myth of Roman greatness from their contemporary origins through their various mutations with special emphasis on the role of Virgil as publicist.

Notes

The Cato material in this chapter has been collected entirely from primary sources. I do not know of any other work which has dealt with either the classical or Neo-Classical significance of Cato to any extent. Rand's treatment of Cato and other Republicans may be found in the work cited, page 57 following. An interesting, but by no means complete, discussion of Addison's *Cato* appears in the entry on Addison in the *Dictionary of National Biography*.

1. Dryden's use of the Augustan political analogy, and his confused application of it to the personal code of the monarch and his subjects, may be found in the "Epistle to Sir Robert Howard," "Annus Mirabilis," "Threnodia Augustalis," and many other poems than "Astraea Redux." The ambiguities of Dryden's attitude toward the Augustan analogy, first seen in the poems of 1660, were maintained until the Revolution of 1688 ended, or at least silenced, them.

2. The consequences of this intention in the plays of the period have been extensively developed by Nichol Smith, Allardyce Nicoll, Dobree, and Fujimura.

3. Otway's *Alcibiades* (1675) was dedicated to the Earl of Dorset, whose career presumably justified the implicit complimentary analogy. The fascination with Alcibiades lasted into the eighteenth century, as may be seen in the half-complimentary, half-critical comparisons of Boling-broke to Alcibiades. Epaminondas was probably the most widely admired Greek after Alexander, thanks to the lives of him given by Plutarch and Nepos. Temple and Milton praised him, as did Swift (strongly and repeatedly); and he was favorably looked upon by James Thomson and William Cowper, who referred to him in the *Seasons* and *The Task*. Epaminondas' virtues were, interestingly enough, the same as those of Cato Uticensis if less dramatically revealed by his career and death. In the mid-eighteenth century, a latter-day vogue for Themistocles developed, in part because of Samuel Madden's play (1729). Themistocles and Epaminondas were often conjoined in long Neo-Classical poems composed in Miltonic blank verse.

4. Gibbon's first three chapters in *The History of the Decline and Fall of the Roman Empire* are a compendium of the Neo-Classical criteria for respecting Rome. See also, Laurence Eacherd's, Thomas Hearne's, and Oliver Goldsmith's introductory chapters summarizing the reasons for admiring Rome's accomplishment. Walter Moyle's *An Essay upon the Constitution of the Roman Government*, from which Gibbon drew, is an extended discussion of the points mentioned in the text. See *Works* (London, 1726), I, 3-60.

5. Cf. Conyers Middleton's *History of the Life of Marcus Tullius Cicero* (London, 1741). Middleton thus justifies his personal preference for Cicero: (I, p. xvii)

> But whatever prejudices may be suspected to adhere to the writer, it is certain, that in a work of this nature, he will have many more to combat in the reader. The scene of it is laid in a place and age, which are familiar to us from our childhood: we learn the names of all the chief actors at school, and chuse our several favorites according to our

276

Notes

tempers or fancies; and when we are least able to judge of the merit of them, form distinct characters of each, which we frequently retain through life. Thus Marius, Sylla, Caesar, Pompey, Cato, Cicero, Brutus, Anthony, have all their several Advocates, zealous for their fame, and ready even to quarrel for the superiority of their virtue.

6. Middleton's comparison of Atticus (Epicurean), Cato (Stoic), and Cicero (Academic) is an interesting and instructive example of how the Neo-Classicist chose then gilded his icon. See the *Life of Cicero*, II, 564-67.

7. Cf. Middleton, I, 17; II, 501-49. The midcentury state of the cults of Augustus and Horace is indicated in George Turnbull's *Three Dissertations; One on the Characters of Augustus, Horace, and Agrippa by the Abbe de Vertot* (London, 1740). In a footnote, Turnbull remarks (p. 21): However fashionable it is now to speak of the Age of *Alexander* the Great, and the *Augustan* Age, that was not the ancient Style. Philosophy and the Arts are said by the Ancients to have been at their Height in *Greece, circa Socratis tempora*; and in *Rome, circa tempora Ciceronis.* Turnbull's comment is furthermore a clue to the succession of Alexandrian and Augustan models and the increasing disillusionment with literary, as well as political, Augustanism in the time of George II.

8. Cato's *Origines* was lost, though Dionysius of Halicarnassus and Livy both drew from it. The *De Agri Cultura* was known to the Neo-Classicists and was used to support their insistence on rural, abstemious morality.

9. Cf. Lewis Theobald, *The Life and Character of Marcus Portius Cato Uticensis: Collected from the Best Ancient Greek and Latin Authors: And Design'd for the Readers of Cato, A Tragedy* (London, 1713). Conceived by Bernard Lintot as a way to capitalize on the success of Addison's play, Theobald's anthology of excerpts from ancient history underscored Steele's dependence on Sallust and thus emphasized the disparity between Sir Richard's published opinions of Cato in 1701 and 1713. Steele directly reversed his views in *The Christian Hero* and *The Englishman*, No. 25 (Nov. 26, 1713), and No. 34 (Dec. 19, 1713). Cf. Sallust, *Wars Against Catiline*, LII-LIV.

10. Livy's attitude toward the Catoes was ambiguous at best. See Livy, XXXII.17; XXXIV.15; XXXVIII.53; and XXXIX *in toto*.

11. Appian, II.14.99; Dio Cassius, XVIII, XXXVII; Ammianus Marcellinus, XXVIII.1.39, 4.21.

12. Persius, *Satires*, III; Martial, *Epigrams*, IX, X, XI.

13. Vergil, *Aeneid*, VIII; Lucan, *Pharsalia*, IX *et passim*.

14. See especially, Seneca's *Essays* on Benefits, Providence, and Firmness.

15. Cf. Suetonius, *Lives* of the Deified Julius, Augustus; "Hadrian," in *Scriptores Historiae Augustae*; and Marcus Aurelius, *Meditations*, I.14; IV.33.

16. Plutarch, "Cato Minor," V-VI.

17. See Tertullian, "Apology," XI; Lactantius, *Divine Institutes*, III; Prudentius, *Oration Against Symmachus*, 545; Augustine, *Epistle*, No. 24; Jerome, *Letters*, 125.

18. See Dante, "Purgatorio," Canto I.

19. The Catonic *Distiches*, a collection of Latin aphorisms, were supposed to have been written by some member of the Cato family, though

which is not certain. They were extensively read during the latter days of the Roman Empire, and were in limited use as a Latin textbook in mediaeval English universities. Caxton printed in English some excerpts and titled them the *Parvus Cato*. Joseph Scaliger edited and translated the *Catonis Disticha* into Greek, and Erasmus also edited the Latin text and supplemented it with his notes. The Erasmus edition was used in England in the sixteenth century; there is evidence that Drayton and Jonson knew it. Several new English translations appeared in the 16th and 17th centuries. In 1555 T. Taverner's *Cato's Disticks* was published; a less traceable translation came out in 1624; and in 1636 Sir Richard Baker's translation appeared, stating that to Baker's knowledge the 1624 edition was the first in English. Baker quoted Scaliger's opinion that the author of the *Distiches* was a Cato who lived in the time of Commodus and was a Stoic of the school of Marcus Aurelius. The seventeenth century editions were present in many Neo-Classical libraries, together with Logan's *Cato Major* and John Denham's *Cato Major* (1669). The *Catonic Distiches* were known, in one edition or another, to Swift, Thomas Hearne, Richard Rawlinson, David Garrick, Samuel Johnson, and Edward Gibbon (see Appendix).

Whether Dryden or Pope knew firsthand of the Distiches is unverifiable; but the reader of Baker's couplet translations is struck with the similitude between the form, and sentiments, of the neo-Stoic Catonic couplets and many of the aphorisms of the Neo-Classical masters of the couplet, *viz.*:

> Sleepe is both Prodigals, and Misers Crime:
> It hoords yet wasts, the Chieftest Treasure, Time.

> Speake not at all, or else speake wisely, least
> It shew thee, First a Man, and then a Beast.

> If lives of men, be lookt into and sought:
> Some more, some lesse; but None, without his fault.

> Some physicke is to cure: some to prevent:
> But Fasting serves, both this and that intent.

Other couplets presage Pope's heroic couplets in their deft handling of caesura, chiasmus, antithesis, parallelism, zeugma, and other technical devices. Certainly, Ruth Wallerstein's survey of the heroic couplet before Dryden can be profitably supplemented by a study of the *Catonic Distiches*.

20. Melanchthon said Cato was motivated solely by love of praise, and Bodin remarked that he had blue-gray eyes, ever the sign of a cruel disposition.

21. Cf. Chapman's *Caesar and Pompey*, Jonson's *Catiline*, and Shakespeare's *Julius Caesar*.

22. Seven Latin editions of the *Pharsalia* came out between 1502 and 1651; and English translations were printed in 1614, 1627, 1631, 1635, and 1650. Nicholas Rowe's translation (1721) was the most prestigious, but by no means the only, English version in the eighteenth century.

Notes

23. See Addison, *A Discourse on Ancient and Modern Learning* (London, 1739), p. 25. A full account of the history of Addison's *Cato* has yet to be published; see Thomas Tickell's Preface to the 1721 edition of Addison's works for evidence about the date of composition.

24. Among those who jostled for the honor of being identified with Addison's *Cato* were Harley, Bolingbroke, Queen Anne, the Duke and Duchess of Marlborough, Swift, Pope, Arbuthnot, Gay, Dennis, Theobald, Curll, Mandeville, Cibber, George Sewell, Thomas Gordon, John Trenchard, and Voltaire.

25. Swift, *Works*, II, 2; VI, 133-34; IX, 249.

26. Those interested in charting the development of Catonic sentiment from 1713 to 1725 will find the prefatory materials to the various editions of Rowe's *Pharsalia* helpful.

27. See Colley Cibber, *Caesar in Ægypt, A Tragedy* (London, 1725). Cibber's *The Character and Conduct of Cicero, Considered, From the History of his Life, by the Reverend Dr. Middleton* (London, 1747) is a distillation of ideological placeboes including a lengthy refutation of Cicero's accusations against Cato and a statement of Cibber's infatuation with the Censor. See pp. 96-97.

28. Cf. Swift, *Correspondence*, III, 91-92, 110; Bolingbroke, *The Craftsman*, No. 624 (June 24, 1738). Bolingbroke's Roman favorite was Cicero.

29. Orrery, *Remarks*, 165-68. Lord Orrery's favorites were Alexander the Great and Julius Caesar. (Cf. pp. 158, 162-64.) Orrery's sophistical praise of Caesar led Thomas Babington Macaulay to note marginally that the book made him ashamed to be a human being.

30. Swift's essay for *The Tatler*, No. 81 (Oct. 15, 1709) is a convenient summary of the way he arrived at his admiration for Cato above other ancient heroes. This allegory, based on the House of Fame, depicts Alexander, Caesar, Socrates, Cicero, Hannibal, Cato, and Augustus being assigned places in the Palace of Immortality on the basis of arguments presented by various historians. Swift follows Lucan in allowing Cato highest honors.

31. See the references in Note 25 above; also Swift, *Works*, II, 49 ff.; III, 83-85; XI, 179-80. Swift's list "Of Mean and Great Figures," not published until 1772, included Alexander, Socrates, Epaminondas, Cato, and his other favorites.

32. Swift, *Journal*, I, 34, 46, 73, 89, 105, 107, 154, 171, 177 ff.

33. Cf. the Swift–Bolingbroke correspondence of December and January 1721-22.

34. Laetitia Pilkington, *Memoirs of Mrs. Laetitia Pilkington, Written by Herself* (London, 1748), I, 51-52. Cf. the letters to Swift by Miss Kelly (July 8, 1733) and Sheridan (March 27, 1736).

35. Mandeville, *Fable of the Bees* (London, 1714), pp. 137-38; cf. F. B. Kaye's account in his edition of the *Fable* (Oxford, 1924), I, 386-401. See Fielding, *Miscellanies* (London, 1743), I, 37.

36. See Evelyn's *Diary* for April 1694; Malebranche, *Treatise Concerning the Search after Truth* (London, 1694). Perhaps the most farfetched use of Cato was made in the French *The Amours of Solon, Socrates, Julius Caesar, Cato of Utica, D'Andelot, and Bussy D'Amboyse*, translated into

Notes

English in 1673. The ancient heroes were metamorphosed into Restoration libertines, with masquerades, closet concealments, assignations, and sexual escapades occupying their time. Despite the inclusion of Cato in the provocative title, no "amours" were imputed to him in the book itself. The place of Cato in the Stoic controversy of the late Restoration era is described by Henry W. Sams, "Anti-Stoicism in Seventeenth and Early Eighteenth-Century England," *SP*, XLI (1944), 65-79.

37. See Addison Ward, "The Tory View of Roman History," *SEL*, IV (1964), 413-56.

38. F. B. Kaye makes some good comments on these matters in the place cited in Note 35 above. See *The London Journal* and *Mist's Journal* for 1721 and 1722. Also "Cato," *Serious and Cleanly Meditations Upon a House of Office* (London, 1723).

39. Arbuthnot, *Miscellaneous Works* (Glasgow, 1751), II, 6-13.

40. It may be noted that in time England adopted the suggestion of Swift, Dennis, and others regarding the establishment of a British Censor in imitation of the Romans. During the reign of George III, the Lord Chamberlain was given powers of censorship which he still exercises in the reign of Elizabeth II. In this and other ways, Cato's example is far from extinct in modern Britain.

41. Cf. Saintsbury, *The Peace of the Augustans* (London, 1916).

42. See the discussion of Gibbon's *Decline and Fall* in Chapter 9 below for an elaboration of this point.

CHAPTER 5. CARTHAGE, ALEXANDRIA, NICAEA

The Christian bias of Neo-Classical literature, taken for granted by Victorian commentators, has come in for a good deal of excited notice by American critics during the last twenty or thirty years. The rather exaggerated controversy over the theological allegory of *Gulliver's Travels* is an obvious instance of religiously oriented criticism; but there are other sounder and more illuminating commentaries to be had, for example, Louis Landa's study of Swift and the Anglican Church and his introduction to the sermons (Swift, *Works*, IX); Philip Harth's investigation of Swift and Anglican rationalism; Maynard Mack's notes in the Twickenham Pope; a number of essays by R. S. Crane, and others. Apart from a few specific allusions, however, none of the modern studies of Neo-Classical ecclesiasticism deals to any extent with the patrists.

The fullest study treating matters discussed in this chapter is Charles Cochrane's *Christianity and Classical Culture* (Oxford, 1944). Cochrane's analysis of the mutations of pagan into Christian thought provides a very helpful background for any investigation of the Neo-Classical attitudes toward the two literatures and their relationships.

1. See Steele, *The Christian Hero* (1701); Malebranche, *Treatise Concerning the Search after Truth* (London, 1694); Atterbury, "Classical Remarks to Dr. Freind," in *Dean Swift's Literary Correspondence* (London, 1741), p. 307; Swift, *Works*, IX, 73. Compare Clarendon's comments on the ancient Stoics in *Miscellaneous Works* (London, 1751), p. 96:

Notes

"... it were to be wished that many Christians could govern and suppress and regulate, as well as many of those heathen Philosophers used to do."

2. Notably Shaftesbury, Bolingbroke, Gibbon, and Walpole, all Deists of sorts. Cf. Leslie Stephen, *History of English Thought in the Eighteenth Century* (London, 1881), I, 86-87. Shaftesbury's statement of the dilemma is pithily expressed *in Several Letters Written by a Noble Lord to a Young Man at the University* (London, 1726), p. 31: "We may be as well *Pagan, Heathen, Turk,* or any thing else; if . . . we refuse to look on *Christian* Authors, or hear their sober Apologists, as being contrary to the History imposed on us, with an utter Destruction and Cancelling of all other History and Philosophy whatsoever." Shaftesbury's *Letters* were greatly disliked by Dr. Johnson because they pretended to favor Christianity but drew "invidious comparisons . . . between the philosophers Plato, Epictetus, Seneca, and others, and the fathers, and his many contemptuous sneers at the writers on the side of Christianity." Sir John Hawkins, *The Life of Samuel Johnson, LL.D.* (London, 1961), p. 108.

3. See, for instance, the treatments of patristic literature in the classical investigations of Charles Rollin, Edward Manwaring, and John Jortin. Cf. Le Clerc, *Parrhasiana*, pp. 190-91. The modern ambiguity may be seen in *The Oxford Companion to Classical Literature*, edited by Sir Paul Harvey (Oxford, 1962), where "classic" is quite narrowly defined in Greco-Roman pagan terms but where patrists and their writings are included, albeit erratically.

4. Cf. Swift, *Works*, IX, 73-74.

5. R. F. Jones has shown the place of Cyprian and Esdras in the Ancients vs. Moderns quarrels; Maynard Mack has drawn parallels between Pope's ideas in *An Essay on Man* and the thought of Augustine; Louis Landa has placed Swift in the tradition of the Apologists. Other suggestions of patristic influence have appeared in the studies of Dryden by H. T. Swedenberg and Bernard Schilling, Maximillian Novak's examinations of Defoe, and Robert Quinlan's study of Johnson's religion.

6. Rymer's *A Short View of Tragedy* (London, 1693) disposes of the cavils of Cyril, Tertullian, Cyprian, Basil, Clement of Alexandria, Dio Chrysostom, Augustine, Lactantius, and Jerome. Collier's *Short View* (1698), *Defence of the Short View* (1699), and *Second Defence* (1700) cites additionally the *Annals* of the Councils of Illiberis and Chaalon, Theophilus of Antioch, Minucius Felix, Athenagoras, and Athanasius. It must be admitted that Collier's patristic scholarship is much superior to Rymer's.

7. Temple, *Works*, III, 464, 494.

8. Swift has been maligned by his critical defenders, who assert that he had a very superficial knowledge of Church literature before the Council of Trent. Even Harold Williams, anxious to justify the small number of ecclesiastical works in Swift's library, has strained to reach the excuse that Swift doubtless borrowed such works from other clerics. (See Williams, *Dean Swift's Library*, pp. 38-39.) In fact, Swift's collection of church writing, including the patrists, was far from contemptible, especially when it is remembered that predatory clergymen were carrying off his books at a great rate during Swift's final incapacitation. Internal evidence in his works leaves no doubt that the Dean, a man both pious

and intellectually honest, never stooped to claim a knowledge of works he had not read.

9. See Defoe, *A True Collection of the Writings of the Author of the True-Born English-man* (London, 1703); Addison, "Of the Christian Religion," *Miscellaneous Works* (London, 1914), II, 407-45; Mandeville, *Free Thoughts on Religion* (London, 1720). Addison uses the works of more than a dozen Fathers, including Arnobius, Polycarp, Tatian, and Hegesippus. Mandeville ranges from Origen to Baronius, Melanchthon, and Calvin; but he concentrates in particular on the Nicaean and post-Nicaean writers (Athanasius, Basil, Jerome, Ambrose), and he is one of the Neo-Classicists who does not shrink from mention of Augustine.

10. See Johnson, *Diaries, Prayers, and Annals*, edited by E. L. McAdam, Jr. *et al.* (New Haven, 1958), for the lists. Johnson was reading Cave just before his death. Boswell's *Life* records the gift of a copy of Lord Hailes' edition of Book V of Lactantius sent by Boswell to Johnson in 1777; see *Life*, II, 101.

11. For Cave, see McAdam as cited. Swift's *Correspondence*, III, 110, reveals some interesting byplay. Bolingbroke reproaches "You churchmen" for practicing "one of those pious frauds, so frequently practiced in the days of primitive simplicity," namely placing Seneca in the category of Christian saints because of some spurious letters Seneca supposedly wrote to Saint Paul. Lightfoot's *Dissertations* accepted this evidence for the canonization of Seneca.

12. See *A Catalogue of the Valuable Library, of the Late Celebrated Right Hon. Joseph Addison* (London, 1799); A. E. Newton, *Sale Catalogue of Dr. Johnson's Library* (New York, 1925).

13. Library catalogues for Swift, Hearne, Rawlinson, and the Harleian Collection supply additional evidence. For Gibbon's patristic titles, see the Appendix Tickell attested to Addison's knowledge, as Orrery did Swift's, and Hawkins, Johnson's. The works of the men themselves contain adequate proof.

14. The *editio princeps* of Arnobius of Sicca, for instance, was published in Rome in 1542; it was subsequently issued in twenty-eight separate editions, printed in Leyden, Basel, and Paris, and edited by Salmasius (Claude de Saumais) and Meursius (Jan de Meurs) among others.

15. Among the continental *opera omnia* were the writings of Cyprian, Cyril of Alexandria, Eusebius, Tertullian, and Lactantius.

16. Cyprian, Eusebius, Minucius Felix, and Tertullian were all partially translated into English before 1700. Tertullian was a favorite with Puritans; cf. *A true Christian subject under an heathen prince* (London, 1642-43). See Hawkins, p. 73.

17. Cf. Addison's "Of the Christian Religion." Hegesippus and Severus graced Swift's and other libraries.

18. These were Tertullian's *Apology* and *On Spectacles*; Felix's *Octavius*; Origen's *Against Celsus*; Clement's *Stromata*; Irenaeus' *Against Heresies*; Cyprian's *Discourse to Donatus*, and Lactantius' *Divine Institutes*. Less often cited but of equal importance were the *Apologies* of Justin Martyr, the *Embassy* of Athenagoras, Tatian's *Address to the Greeks*, Theophilus'

Notes

To Autolychus, Arnobius' *Against the Pagans*, and Athanasius' *Contra Gentes*.

19. Hawkins said the "perusal of St. Augustine and other of the fathers prompted Johnson to the employment of composing meditations and devotional exercises." *Life*, p. 70. Cf. Mack's notes to Pope's *Essay on Man*.

20. See Addison on coins; Arbuthnot on coins, mathematics, and medicine; Warburton on Moses; Bolingbroke on politics; John Pinkerton on the Goths; and Gibbon on Warburton.

21. Since the practice of ransacking the ancients to supply data on such subjects as Greek games was a Renaissance habit, the Neo-Classical parody often was directed at polymathic pedantry and those who aped it. *The Memoirs of Martinus Scriblerus* is a *locus classicus* of this kind of parody—as is *Tristram Shandy*—and it is no accident that both these works draw on the factual authority of patristic writers. Cf. Charles Kerby-Miller, *The Memoirs*, p. 222 ff. Pierre Bayle's *Historical and Critical Dictionary* (London, 1710) provided a useful reference for those seeking specific data from patristic authors. Though Bayle did not include entries on the Fathers, he quoted them as authorities on many subjects.

22. Tatian in *The Ante-Nicene Library*, II, 31-43; Tertullian, *Apology*, XVI-XIX; Augustine, *Confessions*, I-IV. Cf. Orosius, *Seven Books of History Against the Pagans*, 32 ff. The comparable position in England was taken by the Dissenters, John Wesley, and William Law. Cf. Law's *A Serious Call* and its attitudes toward classical learning, as well as his "Short but Sufficient Confutation" of Warburton. The state of the less dogmatic Christian is reflected in Conyers Middleton's letter to Lord Hervey (July 31, 1733): "It is my Misfortune to have had so early a Taste of Pagan Sense as to make me very squeamish in my Christian studyes."

23. Origen in *The Ante-Nicene Library*, I, 413-17; Minucius Felix, *Octavius*, XXV, XXXVI.

24. Tatian, Clement, Tertullian, Irenaeus, and Origen all died under a cloud. Athanasius spent half his time in shadow, the other in sunshine depending on who occupied the Byzantine throne. Compare the ecclesiastical careers of Swift, Sacheverell, Atterbury, King, and Butler.

25. Justin appealed to Antoninus Pius and Marcus Aurelius, Athenagoras to Aurelius and Commodus. English religious synthetists resembling them include Thomas Burnet, Conyers Middleton, and William Warburton, to say nothing of such lesser lights as William Stukeley and John Jackson.

26. Justin Martyr, "The Sole Government of God," in *The Ante-Nicene Library*, II, 329-35 *et passim*; Clement of Alexandria, "Exhortation to the Heathen," in *The Ante-Nicene Library*, IV, 18; IV, 48. For a similar use of Euripides, see Gibbon, *Decline and Fall*, I, 227.

27. Justin, in *op.cit.*, II, 301-305; Athenagoras, "Embassy," in *The Ante-Nicene Library*, II, 409-13; Theophilus of Antioch, "To Autolychus," in *The Ante-Nicene Library*, III, 73, 104-106; Clement in *op.cit.*, IV, 68-74.

28. Justin Martyr in *op.cit.*, II, 301. The Cumean Sybil, chief prophetess of Rome, was actually the daughter of Berosus, a Babylonian seer, who migrated to Italy, taking priceless Hebrew wisdom with her. Cf. Justin, II, 326-27.

Notes

29. Clement in *op.cit.*, IV, 449.

30. Justin in *op.cit.*, II, 46.

31. *Ibid.*, II, 10-12, 79-80.

32. See Chapter 4, Note 17.

33. J. W. Thompson's *A History of Historical Writing* (New York, 1942), I, 122-40, gives a survey of the development of chronological writing from Tatian to Sulpicius Severus. A more specialized examination of the chronology as the background of Neo-Classical thought may be found in J. W. Johnson, "Chronological Writing: Its Concepts and Development," *History and Theory*, II (1962), 124-45.

34. Justin, XXXVI, 2.

35. Justin Martyr in *op.cit.*, II, 57-58; Athenagoras in *op.cit.*, II, 395 ff.; Theophilus in *op.cit.*, III, 120-33; Tatian in *op.cit.*, III, 35-43; Tertullian, *Apology*, XIX. Tatian's chronology is now lost, but it was incarnated in the chronologies of Clement, Eusebius, and others.

36. Clement, "Stromata," in *op.cit.*, IV, 421-47; Eusebius, in J. P. Migne, *Patrologia Latini*, XXVII, 14 ff.; Eusebius in Josef Karst, *Die Griechischen Christlichen Schriftsteller der Ersten Drei Jahrhunderte*, V, 1-182. Africanus is lost; see Thompson.

37. See Don Cameron Allen, *The Legend of Noah* (Urbana, Illinois, 1949) for the full background of the Restoration issues in Ernest Tuveson's *Millenium and Utopia* (Los Angeles, 1949).

38. Locke, "Some Thoughts Concerning Reading and Study for a Gentleman," in *Philosophical Works* (London, 1901), II, 502; William Wotton, *Reflections upon Ancient and Modern Learning* (London, 1694); Daniel Defoe, *An Essay on Projects* (London, 1697) and *An Essay on Literature* (London, 1703); Lord Chesterfield, *Letters* (New York, 1925), I, 2, 76; Hannah More, "Hints toward the Education of a Young Princess," in *Works* (London, 1853), IV, 19. Clarendon, Temple, Bolingbroke, Goldsmith, and Gibbon finally eschewed the practice and study of chronology. Cf. Temple, *Works*, III, 483; Bolingbroke, *Works*, II, 175-76, 201-14; Goldsmith, *Letters from a Citizen of the World*, XV.

39. Boswell's *Life* repeatedly declares Johnson's belief that history is but empty tales without the skeleton of chronology. See Chapter 9 below for an incident involving Gibbon. Kennedy's chronology was published in 1763 in answer to John Jackson's *Chronological Antiquities* (1752), which Kennedy had criticized in *An Examination of . . . Mr. Jackson's . . . Errors and Defects* (1753). Anyone interested in eighteenth century chronology can get a sampling in the two specimens by Jackson and Kennedy. Paul Hazard's *La Crise de la Conscience Européenne* (Paris, 1935), contains an amusing and informative survey of chronological opinion between 1680 and 1715; cf. pp. 40 ff.

40. Tuveson and Heinrich Meyer have written on this subject exhaustively.

41. See R. F. Jones' *Ancients and Moderns* and Victor Harris' *All Coherence Gone*.

42. See Note 38 above. Also see Swift, *Works*, IX, 264. The ultimate defense of Moses was Warburton's *The Divine Legation of Moses Demon-*

Notes

strated, which surveyed all ancient literature and which Law scorned. See Warburton, *Works* (London, 1811), I-VI.

43. See Samuel Pye, *Moses and Bolingbroke, A Dialogue* (London, 1765) and *The Mosaic Theory of the Solar, or Planetary, System* (London, 1766); Robert Clayton, *A Vindication of the Histories of the Old and New Testament. In Answer To the Objections of the late Lord Bolingbroke* (London, 1753).

44. Minucius Felix, *Octavius,* XVII. Inevitably the Christian had to scoff at such "violations" of natural order as comets and their use as portents. See Cyprian, in *The Ante-Nicene Library,* I, 97, 130. Orosius, on the other hand, rather liked earthquakes and lightning as God's omens; cf. *Seven Books,* pp. 58-59, 106-15. The flurry over Halley's Comet in the Neo-Classical era produced another odd parallel between patristic and English writers. The deprecation of astronomical portents by Defoe, Steele, Addison, and Swift was based on the same Christian assumptions as those of the Fathers.

45. Theophilus in *op.cit.,* III, 57.

46. Athenagoras in *op.cit.,* II, 319-92. Compare Athanasius, "Contra Gentes" in *The Nicene and Post-Nicene Fathers* (New York, 1892).

47. Clement in *op.cit.,* IV, 20.

48. Cf. Shaftesbury, *The Moralists, A Philosophical Rhapsody* (London, 1709), pp. 157-59; Addison, *The Spectator,* No. 519.

49. Arnobius of Sicca, *The Case Against the Pagans* (Westminster, Maryland, 1949), pp. 150-55.

50. Tatian in *op.cit.,* III, 17.

51. Clement in *op.cit.,* IV, 90-91.

52. Similarities between Swift and Tertullian have been the most noted. See T. R. Glover's introduction to the Loeb Tertullian (London, 1931), p. xix. See also J. W. Johnson, "Tertullian and *A Modest Proposal,*" *MLN,* LXXIII (1958), 561-63.

53. Tertullian, *De Spectaculis,* I-XVI. Gibbon comments on Tertullian's castigations in *Decline and Fall,* I, 396. To the list of Fathers cited by Collier and Rymer (see Note 6 above), Tatian may be added. Tatian, "Address to the Greeks," in *op.cit.,* III, 28.

54. Clement in *op.cit.,* IV, 255-315; Tertullian, *Apology,* VI.

55. Clement in *op.cit.,* IV, 21, 355, 371; Origen, "Against Celsus," in *The Ante-Nicene Library,* II, 246-48; Gregory Nazianzen, "Second Theological Oration," in *The Nicene and Post-Nicene Fathers.*

56. The apotheosis of the bee in Neo-Classical literature, as well as in the hymns of Isaac Watts, is discussed in J. W. Johnson, "That Neo-Classical Bee," *Journal of the History of Ideas,* XXII (1961), 262-66.

57. Clement, "Stromata," IV, 19.

58. *Ibid.,* II, 66.

59. Like Hearne, Moyle also wrote on Roman history and chronology, as well as numismatics and comets. See Moyle, *Works* (1726), II. See, too, Edmund Curll, "An Apology for Mr. Moyle," in *The Altar of Love* (London, 1727), pp. 18 ff.

60. See Chapter 9.

61. Hawkins, p. 70.

Notes

The contemptuous attitude toward Byzantine history and thought cultivated by Enlightenment thinkers has persisted even until the present day. It can be found in commentators on Neo-Classical history in general and Gibbon in particular in a surprisingly virulent form. Among literary critics, a general unawareness of Byzantine literature seems to prevail; to my knowledge no one has discussed its possible ramifications in Neo-Classical thought. There are few aids for the student who wants to extend his knowledge of Byzantine culture but knows no Greek. Stephen Runciman's *Byzantine Civilization* is a useful, general survey; and there are other, more specialized studies in German and French (notably those of Charles Diehl). Hopefully, with the establishment of Byzantine studies at Cambridge and Harvard, as well as Dumbarton Oaks, and the re-editing of Byzantine history and literature by German and American scholars, the paucity of works in English will soon end. J. E. Sandys' *A History of Classical Scholarship* in three volumes (1906) remains indispensable for anyone studying the background of English Neo-Classicism.

1. Cf. Per Fuglum, *Edward Gibbon, His View of Life and Conception of History* (Oslo, 1953), p. 135; Christopher Dawson, "Edward Gibbon," in *Proceedings of the British Academy* (1934), p. 164.

2. There are many specific studies; see, for example, Kenneth Clark's *The Gothic Revival* and Zera Fink's *The Classical Republicans.*

3. Goldsmith, *Works*, II, 349 ff.; Goldsmith, *Essays* (London, 1765), pp. 7 ff.

4. Hearne's recommended reading list of Byzantine historians is given in the *Ductor Historicus*, p. 160. Pinkerton's history of the Goths, or Scythians, cites Theophanes, Stephen of Byzantium, Procopius, Suidas, Photius, the Paschal Chronicle, Eusebius, Jerome, Zosimus, and Ammianus Marcellinus. The selection is typical.

5. Shaftesbury, *Letters* (1726), p. 35; Pope, *The Dunciad*, IV.11.227 ff.; Goldsmith, *Works*, II, 476. Goldsmith does praise the learning and works of Leo the Isaurian, Michael Psellus, and Constantine Porphyrogennetos (whose name he grossly misspells). For Gibbon and the Byzantines, see Chapter 9.

6. Gibbon, *Decline and Fall*, III, 717-26. Cf. Sandys, Vol. I.

7. For example, Synesius (1579), Ammianus Marcellinus (1609), Photius (1651), and Procopius (1653). Post-Restoration editions include: Eutropius (1684, 1694, and the Oxford edition in 1703); Procopius (1674 in English); Zosimus (Oxford Greek edition in 1679, English in 1684); Malelas (Oxford, 1690); and Suidas (Cambridge, 1705). There were also translated excerpts such as the Reverend R. Cumberland's *Sanchoniatho's Phoenician History, Translated from the First Book of Eusebius* (London, 1720).

8. See John Mill, *Joannis Antiocheni Cognomento Malalae Historia Chronica, Cum Interpret. Edm. Chilmeadi . . . Accedit Epistola Richardi Bentleii Ad. Cl. V. Jo. Millium* (Oxford, 1691). The *Epistola ad Joannem Millium* has been edited and reprinted by G. P. Goold (Toronto, 1962) with an introduction that provides an excellent survey of Bentley's scholarship, etymological interests, editorial projects, and concern with Byzan-

tine chronology, pp. 7-24. Bentley's Letter depends on many Byzantine authors for its constructions: Suidas, Malelas, Cedrenus, Hesychius, Photius, Eustathius, as well as their transmitters, Leo Allatius, John Spondanus, and others. See pp. 246 ff., 287, 305, 312, *et passim*. Humphrey Hody's *Prolegomena* to the 1691 edition contains other citations from the Byzantines in addition to the Fathers: Clement, Theophilus, Eusebius, *et al.* See the *Historica Chronica*, pp. 2 ff.

9. See R. C. Jebb's *Bentley* (London, 1882), pp. 9, 124.

10. Pope, Letter to Parnell (May 25, 1714).

11. Both Ammianus and Eutropius wrote in Latin, but their subject matter, as well as their personal involvements with Julian's campaigns and the reigns of his successors, places them in the category of Byzantine historians. Zosimus was a pagan, and he had to be exonerated of the taint found by later Byzantine writers before he could be acceptable to the Restoration reading public. See Leunclavius' apology prefacing *The New History of Count Zosimus, With the Notes of the Oxford Edition* (London, 1684). With the possible exception of Ammianus, Procopius was the most popular Byzantine historian in England between 1660 and 1800. His *History of the Wars* was used by those who argued the "Gothic" system of polity, and the *Secret History* was gleefully read by otherwise abstemious clergymen from Swift to an elderly divine whom Gibbon reported to be fond of quoting Procopius' pornographic libels in the original Greek.

12. See Jebb on Bentley; cf. Gibbon's *Journals, I, II, and III.*

13. Runciman gives a factual survey of Byzantine chronology in his chapter on Byzantine literature and takes up other writers unknown to English classicists, e.g., Anna Comnena.

14. The importance of Synesius' writings in Renaissance England, especially the *De Regno*, is already acknowledged and general information about their publication is available. Publication data about Suidas and Photius are partially included in the text of this book. Stobaeus, a kind of pagan Lord Chesterfield who transcribed for the benefit of his son wisdom culled from ancient authors, was a Renaissance favorite. His "fragments" were often rearranged under separate headings by Renaissance editors to present more or less coherent syntheses about single topics. These *florilegia* were useful for clergymen in the days before *Bartlett's Familiar Quotations*, and Henry Stephen remarked in his edition that Stobaeus' sentiments made instructive reading for small boys. Editions included those of Conrad Gesner and Willem Carter (*Sententiae Ioannis Stobaei*, Basel, 1549), Henry Stephen (*Apophthegmata Graeca Regum & Ducum*, Geneva, 1568), Christopher Plantin (*Eclogarum Libri Duo*, Antwerp, 1575), and Hugo Grotius (*Dicta Poetarum Quae Apud Io. Stobaeum exstabat*, Paris, 1623). Neo-Classical libraries often contained several of these.

15. Swift cites Photius; Prior, Stobaeus; Parnell, Cedrenus; Gibbon, Procopius (and everyone else).

16. Manwaring, *Historical and Classical Account*, pp. 2-8 *passim*, 203 ff.

17. The extent of my acquaintance with Byzantine texts may be gauged by the bibliography to the present work. With the exception of some grammarians, I have read at least one work by each of the writers listed

Notes

on pp. 126-27, but sadly admit the deficiencies of my knowledge of mediaeval Greek literature, most of which must still be consulted in the
original.

18. Cf. Sandys, *History of Classical Scholarship*, I, 435, and elsewhere.

19. Typical of the Phalaris tracts and their use of Byzantine sources
is Charles Boyle's *Dr. Bentley's Dissertations on the Epistles of Phalaris,
and the Fables of Aesop, Examined By the Honourable Charles Boyle,
Esq.* (London, 1699). Boyle's case against Bentley rests on etymological
exegeses taken from Dio Chrysostom, Suidas, Photius' *Epistles*, Tzetzes,
Stobaeus, Eustathius, Hesychius, and Malelas, to mention a few. See pp.
25-42 *passim*, 157 ff. Boyle also refers to modern grammarians, e.g.,
Budaeus, and devotes a good deal of space to discussions of dialects and
literary genres; cf. pp. 29, 42 ff. The Bentley–Küster edition of Suidas in
1705 encouraged a small rash of etymological imitations.

20. Swift's interest in Photius may be roughly correlated with the
writing of *A Tale of a Tub* (ca. 1685 to 1702). His linguistic interests, of
course, lasted much longer.

21. Cf. Suidas, *op.cit.* This is a Latin translation of Suidas, the composite work of Jerome Wolf (Hieronymus Wolfius) and William Xylander
(Vilhelmus Xylander Augustanus). It includes a useful survey of previous
versions of Suidas and appends the additions and emendations of Joachim
Camerarius. Wolf's preface quotes Cicero on the excellence of philosophy
as a guide to life and notes that theology is even better since it is divine,
not human, wisdom. Wolf buttresses his arguments with references to
several patrists and Nemesius.

22. See Robert Constantin, *Lexicon Graecolatinum*, 2nd ed. (Eustathius
Vignon, 1592).

23. Bayle's *Dictionary* was first translated into English and printed in
London in 1710. The first and second editions have the same Byzantine
sources.

24. Cf. Johnson, *Dictionary* (London, 1753). Johnson's library contained
a large number of Byzantine authors, especially chronologers (Nicephoras,
Zonares, *et al.*), and grammarians and anthologers, with multiple copies
of Suidas and Photius. Sir John Hawkins has recorded Johnson's interest
in Greek lexicography as ancillary to his concerns with an English
dictionary.

25. Boswell's *Journal* records his plans for a Scottish dictionary patterned on the Greek lexicon of Henry Stephen, which Boswell admired as
a model of lexicography. (See *Boswell in Holland*, p. 162.) Manwaring
said there had been no good Greek lexicons since those of Constantin and
Stephen. For a survey of encyclopaedias, cf. *Encyclopaedia Britannica*
(1965), Vol. 8, 363 ff.

26. Cf. Sandys on Suidas, Photius, Psellus, Arethas, Tzetzes, and
Eustathius.

27. Gerard Johan Voss, *Opera in Sex Tomes Divisa* (Amsterdam, 1701),
III.II.3-11; Lycophron, *Alexandra, sive Cassandra*, with commentary by
Tzetzes (Basle, 1546).

28. Photius, *Epistolae*, edited with notes by the Rev. Richard Montagu
(London, 1651); Photius' *Myriobiblon, sive Bibliothecam* was edited by

Notes

Dr. A. Schottus, who included a life of Photius. Both editions were selective.

29. See Notes 20 and 24 above.

30. See Pope's letter to Parnell, May 25, 1714; Parnell's *Poems* (London, 1833).

31. Parnell, *Life of Zoilus* (1717).

32. Photius' *Epistolae* contain opinions about most of these topics.

33. Cf. the *Scriptores Historiae Augustae* on the Deified Julius and Augustus; Suetonius on Caligula and Nero; Quintus Curtius on Alexander.

34. Cf. Tertullian, *De Spectaculis*, V; Minucius Felix, *Octavius*, XXV.

35. See Eusebius' *Life of Constantine*. Neo-Classical historians thought Constantine more moved by political than spiritual considerations; compare Goldsmith and Gibbon on the subject.

36. Cf. Charles Cochrane, *Christianity and Classical Culture*, pp. 184-86. Lactantius, later appointed tutor to Constantine's son, also supported Divine Right. Eusebius was a tutor to Constantine's nephews, Gallus and Julian, neither of whom proved a very pious Christian. Cf. Gregory Nazianzen's essay on Julian; also Gibbon's account of the Apostate.

37. See Gibbon on Athanasius and the plight of the post-Nicene Fathers.

38. Synesius was a pupil of the glamorous Hypatia. *The Essays and Hymns of Synesius of Cyrene*, translated by Augustine Fitzgerald (London, 1930), are absorbing reading. The *De Regno* was consulted by political theorists of the Renaissance; the *Dion* was favored by Casaubon; but the modern reader is likely to find *On Dreams*, a pre-Jungian interpretation, of particular piquancy. The *Dion* may have affected Neo-Classical theories of education. Synesius' various works were known to Dryden, Swift, Addison, *et al.* and were referred to by them within diverse contexts; for example, Swift's "Mr. Collins' Discourse."

39. Malelas (London, 1691), pp. 18-19. Cf. Ioannis Malalae, *Chronographia*, Corpus Scriptorum Historiae Byzantinae (Bonn, 1831), XV, 13-17.

40. *Paschal Chronicle*, Corpus Scriptorum Historiae Byzantinae (Bonn, 1832), XVI, 33, 38-39, 50-51.

41. Georgius Cedrenus, *Annales, Sive Historiae Ab Exordio mundi ad Isacium Comnenum usque Compendium* (Basel, 1624), pp. 4-7; Michael Glycas, *Annales*, Corp. Scrip. Hist. Byzan. (Bonn, 1836), XXVII, 255.

42. Cf. J. J. Scaliger, *De Emendatione Temporum* (Leyden, 1583), pp. 206 ff., 434 ff.

43. In France, chronologers taxed their ingenuity to justify the Divine Right of the Bourbons. Bishop Bossuet blithely remarked in his *Discours sur L'Histoire Universelle* (Paris, n.d.), p. 133, that "Ambition" entered the world after the Flood when Nimrod established the first monarchy, but he avoided condemning Nimrod. Chevreau went all out to praise Nimrod: he was mighty because God willed it; furthermore he was a pious ruler who made regular sacrifices to his Maker and was not at all the *voleur insigne* his critics had made him. Chevreau, *Histoire du monde* (Paris, 1701-1707), I, 11-12.

44. Clarendon, *A Brief View*, pp. 67-68. See Clarendon, *Miscellaneous Works*, p. 143.

Notes

45. *N.B.* Dryden's use of David to personify Charles in *Absalom and Achitophel*, where the question of succession and the right to rule is a key one. Dryden began the analogy as early as the "Astraea Redux" (1660).

46. Raleigh, *History* (1700), pp. 23-25, 43-48.

47. Swift, *Works*, Temple Scott, IX, 264. Compare Thomas Hearne's remark on Nimrod in the *Ductor Historicus*, I, 43.

48. See *The Country Journal, or The Craftsman*, Nos. 492, 544, 568; *The Patriot King*, I-II.

CHAPTER 7. HOLLAND

1. Cf. Francis Gallaway, *Reason, Rule, and Revolt in English Classicism*; René Bray, *La Formation de la Doctrine Classique en France*; Walter J. Bate, *Prefaces to Criticism*.

2. See Crane Brinton *et al.*, *A History of Civilization*, I, 577 ff.; *The Works of Edmund Spenser, A Variorum Edition* (Baltimore, 1936), pp. 299 ff.

3. Clarendon, Burnet, and Evelyn throw additional historical light on Anglo-Dutch relations between 1650 and 1700. Dryden's literary exploitation of contemporary events involving Holland is the most extensive; cf. *An Essay on Dramatic Poesy, Annus Mirabilis, Absalom and Achitophel, Amboyna,* etc. But other dramatists—e.g., Mrs. Behn, Settle, Buckingham—also utilized British interest in Holland; Defoe's *The True-Born Englishman*, written to render a Dutch king more palatable to the Britons, contained a stereotypal character sketch of the Lowlanders; and *The Examiner, The Guardian,* and *The Englishman* devoted much space to analyzing Anglo-Dutch relations. The derogatory depiction of the Dutch merchants in *Gulliver* and the caricature of Nicholas Frog in *John Bull* are indicative of the anti-Dutch feeling in the early century. A similar attitude may be seen in the portrait of the Hollander in Goldsmith's *The Traveller*. It was the political hostility expressed in these and similar works that has probably caused critics to overlook the more profound ideological relationships between England and Holland.

4. J. E. Sandys' *A History of Classical Scholarship* contains just and informative discussions of these and other Lowland scholars.

5. See Chapter 3. A number of northern European cities claimed the honor of being a latter-day Athens, Dublin and Edinburgh among them. In Holland itself, there was an interurban dispute over which city was the real Athens. In general, the accolade was given to Leyden; cf. Johannes Meursius' (Jan de Meurs') poem, *Athenae Batavae*, composed to celebrate Leyden's jubilee.

6. The artistic bond between England and Holland may be seen in the presence of Dutch and Flemish painters in the English court in the late sixteenth and seventeenth centuries: e.g., Holbein, Van Dyck, Lely, *et al.*

7. See Sandys, II, 130 ff., 204-10, 322-23 ff.; Jebb, *Bentley*, 200-20 *et passim*; *Boswell in Holland*, pp. 93-94; Gibbon, *Letters*, I, 97-100.

8. Le Clerc, *Parrhasiana*, p. 166; Gibbon, *Miscellaneous Works*, XIII, 3-7.

Notes

9. See Chapter 9.

10. See J. A. Froude, P. S. Allen, J. Huizinga, and M. M. Philips on Erasmus; ter Meulen, W.S.M. Knight, G. N. Clark, and W.J.M. van Eysinger on Grotius; Eduard Beneš, Matthew Spinka, and S. S. Laurie on Comenius. See also: Jason Saunders, *Justus Lipsius, The Philosophy of Renaissance Stoicism*; Thomas Simar, *Étude sur Erycius Puteanus (1574-1646)*; Mark Pattison, *Isaac Casaubon, 1559-1614*; and Charles Nisard, *Le triumvirate littéraire au XVIe siècle: Juste Lipse, Joseph Scaliger, et Isaac Casaubon.*

11. Johnson, *Diary*, pp. 22-23: "we learned Helvicus a long time with very little progress."

12. Cf. Jebb, pp. 210-15; Le Clerc, pp. 168-69.

13. Gibbon's *Journals* illustrate perfectly the process followed. See Chapter 9.

14. See Kerby-Miller, *Memoirs of Martinus Scriblerus*, Notes. Kerby-Miller finds use of these polymaths by Swift, Arbuthnot, Gay, and Pope: Cardanus, the two Scaligers, Scriverius, Barthius, Columesius, Aldrovandus, Peireskius, Valentinus, Allatius, Casaubon, Comenius, Gronovius, Meursius, Pancirollus, and Vossius. Many of these once famous names are now so dead that it is difficult to locate information about them. Bayle's *Dictionary* contains references for most; J. E. Sandys gives limited information for some. But the researcher looking for information on Leo Allatius, for example, will consult recent encyclopaedias and reference works in vain.

15. See Bayle's entry on Barthius.

16. Dr. Johnson read this document on July 22, 1773, but did not find it either an interesting or very good book. *Diary*, p. 159.

17. Jortin, *Miscellaneous Observations*, I, 2-3.

18. Bentley's self-comparison with Scaliger may be inferred from the *Epistola ad Millum* and the Phalaris tracts; Swift makes the open comparison in *The Battle of the Books*, and R. C. Jebb contrasts the two and concludes to the advantage of Bentley. (See *Bentley*, pp. 217-20.) Gibbon compared himself with Scaliger in his *Autobiography*, pp. 136-37, and in his *Journal* (May 23, 1762), he compared himself to Salmasius, Casaubon, and Lipsius, to the detriment of the polyhistors. (See *Journal*, p. 75.) Johnson's infatuation with Grotius was probably due to Grotius' *Defense of the Christian Religion*. (See Boswell, *Life of Johnson*, I, 42.) Johnson gave money to Isaac de Groot, the nephew of Grotius, when he was impoverished, declaring, "Let it not be said that in any lettered country a nephew of Grotius asked a charity and it was refused." (*Diary*, p. 283.) When de Groot was admitted to the Charterhouse as the result of Johnson's petition, the Reverend Vyse wrote to Boswell: "He rejoices at the success it met with, and is lavish in the praise he bestows upon his favorite, Hugo Grotius." *Life*, II, 95.

19. J. C. Scaliger, *Poetics* (New York, 1905); *Iulii Caesaris Scaligeri Poemata* (Apud Petrum Santandreanum, 1591); Erycius Puteanus, *Suada Attica* (Leyden, 1640); Daniel Heinsius, *Laus Asini* (Leyden, 1623). Puteanus' letters were collected in the Harley library, and both Oxford and

291

Notes

Cambridge had additional correspondence and public addresses. Cf. Simar, pp. x-xi.

20. See Gibbon, *Autobiography*, pp. 136.

21. *Scaligeriana Sive Excerpta* has the format of a Suidas anthology, with selections from Scaliger's various works arranged in order. It is a brief work but contains comments on Scaliger's colleagues (Budaeus, Puteanus, Casaubon, Lipsius) derived from letters and essays and complimentary in tone. Entries on Eusebius, Years of the Israelite Passage, date of the Flood are taken from the *Emendatione* and Scaliger's reconstruction of Eusebius' *Chronicon*. There are also passages on the church fathers, historical figures, and Byzantine authors (Stobaeus, Synesius' letters, Planudes, Cedrenus), which were originally contained in Scaliger's chronological compositions.

22. Scaliger, *op.cit.*, Prefatio, gamma 2, delta 2-4, 282, 335, 438.

23. *Ibid.*, delta 1-2, delta 3, 2, 5, 148-149, 206, 335, 434-435, 446.

24. Addison deferred to Vossius in the essay, "On the Usefulness of Medals"; Swift allies him with Temple on the side of the Ancients; Edward Manwaring borrows from him widely in the *Historical and Critical Account of Classic Authors*; see Johnson's *Diary* for Easter Sunday, April 19, 1778 and November 18, 1782.

25. Voss, "Poetics," I.4.14; I.6-7, in *Opera*, III.

26. *Ibid.*, II.3-11.

27. For Comenius' chief commentators, see Note 10 above and the Bibliography of the present work, which lists the most available translations of Comenius' writings. *Johan Amos Comenius, 1592-1670* (Prague, 1958), is a helpful general summary of Comenius' life and work. *The Teacher of Nations*, edited by Joseph Needham (Cambridge, 1942), contains some interesting essays by J. D. Bernal and James B. Conant, as well as other educators, on Comenius' influence.

28. Hoole, *op.cit.*, Preface.

29. Comenius, *The Labyrinth of the World and The Paradise of the Heart*, Edited and translated by Count Lützow (London, 1901), p. 60.

30. *Ibid.*, pp. 78-82, 84.

31. *Ibid.*, pp. 146-48.

32. *Ibid.*, pp. 138, 141-42.

33. *Ibid.*, pp. 93-94, 227-28, 265-70.

34. See Pattison, *Isaac Casaubon*, for a full treatment and evaluation.

35. The most complete account of Casaubon's life is perhaps to be found in the *Dictionary of National Biography*.

36. Cf. Sandys' remarks on Casaubon.

37. See Christopher Dawson, "Gibbon," p. 162; G. M. Young, *Gibbon*, pp. 75-78.

38. Milton's catalog of Salmasius' deficiencies—"landless, homeless, worthless, straw-stuffed scarecrow-knight"—culminated with the spitting out of the ultimate shame: "a sophister and double-dealer, a fine teacher for Dutch youth." Of Holland, Goldsmith wrote, in the *Essay on the Present State of Polite Learning*, that it had no learning or language of its

Notes

own, that Holland borrowed from other nations but was itself empty. Goldsmith, *Works*, III, 487.

   39. Cf. Sandys, II, 319-31 *et passim*.

CHAPTER 8. NEO-CLASSICISM AND THE TRAGIC DRAMA

In addition to the discussions included in standard surveys of English drama and book-length studies of tragic theory and practice, the Neo-Classical tragedy has been the subject of several specific commentaries: C. C. Green's *The Neo-Classic Theory of Tragedy in England During the Eighteenth Century* (1934); R. G. Noyes' *The Neglected Muse: Restoration and Eighteenth Century Tragedy in the Novel, 1740-1780* (1958); and John Loftis' *The Politics of Drama in Augustan England* (1963). Of these, only Green's study has touched on the aspects of tragic drama taken up in this chapter; and his sources, emphases, and conclusions differ considerably from mine. George Steiner's *The Death of Tragedy* includes a limited treatment of the Neo-Classical tragic drama, but his approach does not parallel mine, though he attempts to explain the same phenomenon: the limitations of dramatic tragedy which led to its decline after the mid-seventeenth century. The student of the history of English Neo-Classical drama will find the studies of Nichol Smith, Dobree, Sherburn, *et al.* helpful.

   1. See Green, Noyes, and Steiner as cited above.

   2. See Chapter 3 above for a limited account of the publication and acting of Greek tragedy after 1600. *The London Stage* and the *C.B.E.L.* provide supplementary data.

   3. Thomas Rymer, *A Short View of Tragedy* (London, 1693), A4 obverse; *The Tragedies of the Last Age, Consider'd and examin'd by the Practice of the Ancients, and by the Common sense of all Ages* (London, 1678), p. 6.

   4. Henry H. Adams and Baxter Hathaway, editors, *Dramatic Essays of the Neo-Classic Age*, pp. 102-103, 106, 112-13.

   5. *Ibid.*, pp. 63 ff.

   6. Adams and Hathaway, p. 6.

   7. Adams and Hathaway, pp. 317-18. Note Voltaire's assessment: "I know indeed that the Greek tragic poets, otherwise superior to the English, erred often in mistaking horror for terror and the disgusting and the unbelievable for the tragic and the marvelous. The art was in its infancy at the time of Aeschylus, as at London in the time of Shakespeare. . . ." Pp. 319-20.

   8. Guthrie, *Essay upon English Tragedy*, p. 17.

   9. See Gray's *Correspondence* for 1742.

   10. Manwaring, *An Historical and Critical Account*, pp. 322-32.

   11. Adams and Hathaway, pp. 272 ff.

   12. Guthrie, pp. 18-19.

   13. Pickering, *Reflections upon Theatrical Expression in Tragedy* (London, 1755), pp. 14-15.

Notes

14. Steiner and Loftis include several of the enumerated hypotheses.
15. See Chapter 5.
16. Adams and Hathaway, pp. 17-18, 22.
17. *Ibid.*, pp. 103-106, 123-25, 169.
18. *Ibid.*, pp. 63-67 *passim.*
19. Rymer, *Short View*, pp. 3-4, 11-16; *Tragedies*, p. 15.
20. Dennis, *op.cit.*, pp. 27-32.
21. See *The Tatler*, No. 82; *The Spectator*, No. 39.
22. Adams and Hathaway, p. 272.
23. Guthrie, p. 23.
24. Anonymous, *An Essay on Tragedy, with a Critical Examen of Mahomet and Irene* (London, 1749), pp. 12-13.
25. Hodson, *op.cit.*, pp. 92-93.
26. See Chapter 2 above. Cf. Karl Jaspers, *Tragedy Is Not Enough*, pp. 28-36.
27. See Chapter 4.
28. Jaspers, pp. 49-50. Jaspers is particularly stimulating in his theory of the relationship of the historical and tragic views here and elsewhere.
29. Edith Hamilton, *The Greek Way*, pp. 234-35.
30. Adams and Hathaway, p. 11.
31. *Ibid.*, pp. 72-73.
32. Guthrie, p. 23.
33. Adams and Hathaway, p. 3.
34. *Ibid.*, p. 117.
35. *Ibid.*, p. 169.
36. Rymer, *Tragedies*, pp. 7-8.
37. Adams and Hathaway, p. 162.
38. *Ibid.*, pp. 342-43.
39. Hodson, p. 69.
40. See Rymer, *Short View*, pp. 29-33; Chapter 5.
41. It is not my intention here to attempt to settle the question of whether the Christian and tragic purviews are ultimately irreconcilable or whether there can be written such a thing as a Christian tragedy. from *Paradise Lost*): *Absalom and Achitophel*; the *Davideis*; *The State* the following: Karl Jaspers, *Tragedy Is Not Enough*, pp. 36-40; D. D. Raphael, *The Paradox of Tragedy*, pp. 37-51; Richard B. Sewell, *The Vision of Tragedy*, Chapter V; Cleanth Brooks, editor, *Tragic Themes in Western Literature*; Herbert J. Muller, *The Spirit of Tragedy*; and Richmond Y. Hathorn, *Tragedy, Myth, and Mystery*. My single basic point here is that *as the English Neo-Classicist held them*, they proved incompatible.
42. *Polyeucte* has been praised by some modern critics as passable to good tragic drama; see Steiner, Raphael, Brooks.
43. Adams and Hathaway, pp. 18-19.
44. *Ibid.*, pp. 112-13.
45. Rymer, *Tragedies*, p. 14.
46. See Fielding's preface to *The Tragedy of Tragedies*. Addison's statement appears in *The Spectator*, No. 39.
47. Adams and Hathaway, pp. 112-13.

Notes

48. See Chauncey B. Tinker's essay in Brooks, *op.cit.*, for an opinion on *Samson Agonistes*; compare the views of William Madsen and Joseph Summers in *The Lyric and Dramatic Milton* (1965), pp. 95 ff. The most obvious Neo-Classical uses of Old Testament material are these (aside from *Paradise Lost*): *Absalom and Achitophel*; the *Davideis*; *The State of Innocence*; and *Solomon*. N. B. Prior's introduction to *Solomon*, which again wonders that writers have not utilized Hebrew material more commonly.

49. Compare Peter Drucker's essay in Laurence Michel and Richard Sewell, *Tragedy: Modern Essays in Criticism*. Miguel Unamuno's essay in the same anthology argues that the tragic view depends on the belief that death is the greatest evil.

50. See Chapter 4, Note 9.

51. See the summary of Vossius in Chapter 7. See *The Works of Mr. de St. Evremont*, translated from the French (London, 1700), I, 319 ff., 500-55.

52. This is the thesis of Steiner's *The Death of Tragedy*, q.v.

CHAPTER 9. GIBBON

Gibbon has been fortunate in his editors, if not always in his critics. (Miss) J. E. Norton's *Bibliography of the Works of Edward Gibbon* (Oxford, 1940) is a thorough catalog of Gibbon's complete works, their editions, dates, and descriptions; it also includes commentaries on works provoked by him and excerpts from his critics. Miss Norton's edition of *The Letters of Edward Gibbon* (New York, 1956) in three volumes is equally painstaking and scholarly. D. M. Low's edition of Gibbon's *My Journal, I, II, & III and Ephemerides* (New York, 1929) is a definitive one; and Geoffrey Keynes' synthesis of data from many sources, including Gibbon's own rough catalog of his library, makes *The Library of Edward Gibbon* (London, 1940) a valuable reference work for Gibbonians. J. B. Bury's monumental edition of *The History of the Decline and Fall of the Roman Empire* in seven volumes (London, 1896-1902) is the standard one; but the Modern Library edition (New York) provides a less bulky form of the accurate text and footnotes. Gibbon's *Autobiography* has been conveniently edited by Dero Saunders (New York, 1961) into a highly coherent and readable whole in an edition that scrupulously lists variant readings of the several manuscripts and editions. Only the lesser works of the historian need further attention; and Volume XIII of *The Works of Edward Gibbon*, edited by J. W. McSpadden (New York, 1907), incorporates those in an intelligible manner.

The chapter utilizes some insights from those works about Gibbon that I particularly respect. Gibbon's chief biographers—D. M. Low, G. M. Young—are preeminent among the rest: R. B. Mowat, J. C. Morrison, Peter Quennell. Per Fuglum's exegesis of Gibbon's thought is the most substantial of many examens: by Algernon Cecil, C. V. Wedgwood, E. J. Oliver, J. B. Black, and others. H. L. Bond's study of Gibbon as a literary artist is *sui generis*; its insights are so excellent as to make the reader regret all the more that Mr. Bond did not pursue some of his points as fully as he might have done.

Notes

Appendix (p. 253) gives an abbreviated catalog of Gibbon's library, which I have included for several reasons. It is indicative of the libraries of the age, with their Greek, Latin, patristic, Byzantine, and Renaissance cores. It conveniently identifies the road marks on Gibbon's intellectual journey to Rome. It shows the common intellectual and historical heritage of writers from Dryden to Gibbon. And it directly identifies the works specifically quoted, paraphrased, and absorbed by the masterworks of the eighteenth century.

1. In addition to the critics mentioned above, these writers have dealt with aspects of Gibbon's life and thought: Thomas P. Peardon, Robin G. Collingwood, Shelby T. McCloy, Richard M. Haywood. Complete references for all are given in my bibliography. McCloy's book lists many of Gibbon's contemporary critics; to them may be added the Reverend John Whitaker and George Travis, q.v., in my bibliography.

2. Christopher Dawson, "Gibbon," pp. 161, 180.

3. Compare Dawson's concept of history as an "intelligible order" with Jean Le Clerc's "intelligible World." Cf. Chapter 1 above.

4. These are succinctly presented by Gibbon himself in his *Autobiography* (New York, 1961). Gibbon clearly regarded himself as the embodiment of the Reasonable Man as English Neo-Classicists conceived him.

5. See Gibbon, *Journal*, pp. 97, 147-48; *Essay on the Study of Literature*, XLVI, XLVIII, LIV.

6. Gibbon, *Letters*, I, 124; *Journal*, pp. 116-17; *Autobiography*, pp. 137, 199.

7. Miss Norton's indices to Gibbon's *Letters*—especially Index 1 and Index iii—are a direct guide to Gibbon's Epicureanism. See, particularly, the entries under "Life and Character" and "Pastimes and Pleasures." *Letters*, III, 379 ff.

8. Gibbon, *Journal*, p. 109.

9. *Ibid.*, pp. 136-37.

10. *Autobiography*, p. 27.

11. *Ibid.*, pp. 58-61.

12. *Ibid.*, p. 63.

13. *Ibid.*, pp. 72-73.

14. *Ibid.*, p. 59.

15. See the *Journal*, pp. 5-6, 42, 52, 68, 88-94, 114-17, 136-41, 178.

16. *Autobiography*, pp. 136-37.

17. Boswell, *Life of Johnson*, I, 595.

18. *Autobiography*, p. 66.

19. *Ibid.*, p. 68.

20. *Ibid.*, p. 80.

21. *Letters*, I, 97-100 ff.

22. *Essay*, XIV, XVII, XXXIV, XXXVI-XXXVIII, XL.

23. *Ibid.*, XLVIII-LV *et passim*.

24. *Autobiography*, pp. 165-66, 185.

25. Gibbon, "A Vindication of Some Passages in the Fifteenth and Sixteenth Chapters of The History of the Decline and Fall of the Roman Empire," in *Miscellaneous Works* (ed. J. W. McSpadden), XIII, 186-87, 240.

Notes

26. *Autobiography*, pp. 72-73, 83.

27. *Miscellaneous Works*, XIII, 237-38.

28. *Ibid.*, p. 210.

29. *Ibid.*, pp. 255-56.

30. Gibbon, *The Decline and Fall of the Roman Empire* (New York, 1948), I, 7, 32n., 96n., 129n., 151n., 156, 230, 293, 294, 316n., 328n., 330n., 345n., 403n. See also Volume III of the same edition, pp. 695n., 719-24, and the Appendix, which lists all the Byzantine historians cited in the *History*. I have chosen to allude to this edition rather than J. B. Bury's because of its availability and compactness. Future references will all be to this three-volume edition.

31. *Decline and Fall*, I, 157.

32. *Ibid.*, I, 156, 293.

33. *Miscellaneous Works*, XIII, 214.

34. *Ibid.*, p. 249.

35. *Journal*, pp. 5, 10, 75.

36. *Journal*, pp. 147-48, 163; *Essay*, VIII; *Decline and Fall*, III, 403; *Autobiography*, 129.

37. *Essay*, III; *Decline and Fall*, pp. 717-25 *passim*.

38. *The Library of Edward Gibbon* shows Gibbon's knowledge of the literature of his century; cf. Appendix. In the *History*, he refers to Hume's *Natural History of Religion* (I, 26), Pope's *Iliad* (*loc.cit.*), Wotton's *History of Rome* (I, 76), MacPherson's *Ossian* (I, 113), Hyde, Moyle, and Prideaux (I, 171), Dr. Stukeley's *Carausius* (I, 310n.), Milton's *Paradise Lost* (I, 385n.), Thomas Burnet's *Sacred Theory of the Earth* (I, 392, 406), Rowe's *Tamerlane* (III, 677), Johnson's *Irene* (III, 757), Addison's *Letters from Italy* (III, 867n.) as well as Arbuthnot, Pinkerton, Middleton, and many others.

39. H. L. Bond, *The Literary Art of Edward Gibbon*, pp. 104-105.

40. This phrase, and the value judgment it expresses, are obviously close to Pope's *Essay on Man*:

> Say what the use, were finer optics given,
> T' inspect a mite, not comprehend the heaven?
> Or touch, if tremblingly alive all o'er,
> To smart and agonize at every pore?   (Epistle I. 195-98)

41. *Autobiography*, pp. 206-207.

42. Oliver Goldsmith, *The Roman History* (London, 1769), I, i.

43. *Ibid.*, I, ii-iii.

44. *Essay*, XXVII.

45. Goldsmith, I, iii.

46. Thomas Hearne, *Ductor Historicus*, II, 1-2.

47. For Gibbon's generally disparaging opinion of Augustus and the supposed glories of the Augustan Age, see the *Essay*, LXXX; *Decline and Fall*, I, 54-63, *et passim*. Gibbon's anti-Augustanism was partially the result of the Tory propagandists of the midcentury, partly Gibbon's own limited enthusiasm for the Hanovers, and partly a just assessment of the historical Augustus and his machinations.

48. Cf. *A Bibliography of the Works of Edward Gibbon*, pp. 66-67.

Notes

49. C. V. Wedgwood, *Edward Gibbon*, pp. 32-33.
50. *Decline and Fall*, I, 313; III, 697.
51. *Ibid.*, I, 91-107, 137 ff.
52. *Ibid.*, I, 408.
53. *Ibid.*, I, 188.
54. *Ibid.*, I, 48.
55. *Essay*, VIII, XV.
56. *Decline and Fall*, I, 207.
57. *Letters*, I, 213-14.
58. *Autobiography*, pp. 172-73.
59. *Ibid.*, p. 187.
60. *Decline and Fall*, I, 227, 369.
61. See the *Essay*, III, XIV-XVI; *Decline and Fall*, I, 158, 352, 474n., 757n.
62. *Decline and Fall*, I, 241.
63. *Autobiography*, p. 154.
64. *Ibid.*, p. 195.
65. *Essay*, I; *Decline and Fall*, I, 85, 90, 271, 278-79; III, 862-63, 879-80.

BIBLIOGRAPHY

PRIMARY SOURCES

Adams, George. *The Tragedies of Sophocles, Translated from the Greek, with Notes* . . . To which is prefix'd, a Preface. . . . London, 1729.

Adams, Henry Hitch and Baxter Hathaway. *Dramatic Essays of the Neo-Classic Age.* New York, 1950.

Addison, Joseph. *A Catalogue of the Valuable Library of the Late Celebrated Right Hon. Joseph Addison, Secretary of State &c &c.* London, 1799.

――――. *Cato, a Tragedy As it is Acted at the Theatre-Royal in Drury-Lane by Her Majesty's Servants.* London, 1713.

――――. *A Discourse on Ancient and Modern Learning, Now first published from an Original Manuscript.* Fourth Edition. London, 1739.

――――. *The Letters of Joseph Addison.* Edited by Walter Graham. Oxford: Clarendon Press, 1941.

――――. *The Miscellaneous Works of Joseph Addison.* Edited by A. C. Guthkelch. London, 1914.

――――. *Mr. Addison's Fine Ode to Dr. Thomas Burnet, On His Sacred Theory of the Earth.* Done into English by the Author of a late Tale call'd Coffee. London, 1727.

――――. *The Works of the Right Honourable Joseph Addison, Esq.; In Four Volumes.* London, 1721.

――――. *Works, Edited by Richard Hurd.* Bohn's Standard Library. London, 1906.

Anon. *Cato Examined: Or, Animadversions on the Fable, Plot, Manners, Sentiments, and Diction of the New Tragedy of Cato.* London, 1713.

Anon. *Cicero's Second Oration Against Catiline, Applied to the Present Times: In a Congratulatory Address to the Good People of Augusta, Upon the Flight of Catiline and Others.* London, 1715.

Anon. *An Essay on Tragedy.* London, 1824.

Anon. *An Essay on Tragedy, with a Critical Examen of Mahomet and Irene.* London, 1749.

Anon. *Mr. Addison turn'd Tory: or, The Scene Inverted: Wherein It is made appear that the Whigs have misunderstood that Celebrated Author in his applauded Tragedy, Call'd Cato.* By a Gentleman of Oxford. London, 1713.

Anon. *Observations upon Cato, a Tragedy by Mr. Addison.* In a Letter to * * *. London, 1713.

Anon. *A Short Review of Mr. Hooke's Observations &c concerning the Roman Senate, and the Character of Dionysius of Halicarnassus.* London, 1758.

Anon. *The Temple of Tragedy. A Poetical Essay.* London, 1764.

Appian. *Roman History.* Translated by Horace White. Loeb Classics. 4 vols. London, 1912.

Arbuthnot, John, M.D. *An Account of the State of Learning in the Empire of Lilliput, Together with the History and Character of Bullum, the Emperor's Library-Keeper.* London, 1727.

Bibliography

Arbuthnot, John, M.D. *A Brief Account of Mr. John Ginglicutt's Treatise Concerning the Altercation or Scolding of the Ancients.* London, 1731.
———. *An Essay Concerning the Effects of Air on Human Bodies.* London, 1733.
———. *An Essay Concerning the Nature of Ailments, and the Choice of Them, According to the different Constitutions of Human Bodies.* London, 1731.
———. *An Invitation to Peace: or, Toby's Preliminaries to Nestor Ironsides.* London, 1714.
———. *It Cannot Rain but it Pours: Or, The First Part of London strow'd with Rarities.* London, 1726.
———. *The Miscellaneous Works of the Late Dr. Arbuthnot.* Two volumes. Second edition. Glasgow, 1751.
Arnobius of Sicca. *The Case Against the Pagans.* Translated by G. E. McCracken. Ancient Christian Writers Series, No. 7. 2 vols. Westminster, Maryland, 1949.
Athanasius. "Contra Gentes," "De Incarnatione Verbi Dei," "Life of Saint Anthony," in *The Nicene and Post-Nicene Fathers.* New York, 1892.
Athenagoras. "Embassy," in *The Ante-Nicene Christian Library.* Edited by Alexander Roberts and James Donaldson. Vol. II. Edinburgh, 1867.
Atterbury, Francis. *Maxims, Reflections and Observations, Divine, Moral and Political.* By the Right Reverend Dr. Francis Atterbury. London, 1723.
Basil the Great. "Hexaemeron," in *The Nicene and Post-Nicene Fathers.* New York, 1892.
Bayle, Pierre. *The Dictionary Historical and Critical of Mr. Peter Bayle.* Second edition. London, 1734.
Bentley, Richard. *A Dissertation upon the Epistles of Phalaris.* London, 1699.
———. *Epistola ad Joannem Millium.* Edited by G. P. Goold. Toronto, 1962.
Berkeley, George-Monck. *Literary Relics: Containing Original Letters from Swift et al.* London, 1789.
Blount, Charles. *Janua Scientiarum.* London, 1684.
Bochart, Samuel. *Samuelis Bocharti Opera Omnia.* Fourth edition. Leyden, 1712.
Bodin, Jean. *Method for the Easy Comprehension of History.* Translated by Beatrice Reynolds. Columbia Records of Civilization, No. 37. New York, 1945.
Bolingbroke, Henry St. John Viscount. *A Collection of Political Tracts.* London, 1788.
———. *The Country Journal: or, The Craftsman.* By Caleb D'Anvers, of Gray's Inn, Esq. London, 1735-1738.
———. *Letters and Correspondence, Public and Private.* Four volumes. London, 1798.
———. *Letters on the Study and Use of History.* London, 1870.
———. *Remarks on the History of England.* London, 1788.
———. *The Works of Lord Bolingbroke.* Philadelphia, 1841.

Bibliography

Bossuet, Bishop. *Discours sur L'Histoire Universelle.* Paris: Garnier Frères, n.d.

Boswell, James. *Journals.* Edited by Frederick Pottle *et al.* New York, 1950-64.

———. *The Life of Samuel Johnson.* Edited by George Birkbeck Hill and L. F. Powell. Oxford: Clarendon Press, 1950.

———. *An Ode to Tragedy.* By a Gentleman of Scotland. Edinburgh, 1761.

Boyer, Abel. *The English Theophrastus.* London, 1684.

———. *Letters of Wit, Politicks and Morality.* London, 1701.

Boyle, Charles. *Dr. Bentley's Dissertations on the Epistles of Phalaris, and the Fables of Æsop, Examined by the Honourable Charles Boyle, Esq.* London, 1699.

Burke, Edmund. *The Early Life, Correspondence and writings of the Rt. Hon. Edmund Burke.* Edited by Arthur W. Samuels. Cambridge, 1923.

———. *The Works of the Right Honourable Edmund Burke.* 6 vols. London, 1883.

Burnet, Gilbert. *History of My Own Time.* 2 vols. Oxford: Clarendon Press, 1897.

Burnet, Thomas. *Archeologicae Philosophicae sive doctrina antiqua de rerum originibus.* London, 1692.

———. *Archeologicae Philosophicae: or, The Ancient Doctrine Concerning the Originals of Things.* Faithfully translated into English by Mr. Foxton. London, 1729.

———. *A Re-Survey of the Mosaic System of the Creation. With Rules for the Right Judging of Scripture.* Translated from the Latin by Mr. Foxton. London, 1728.

———. *The Theory of the Earth: containing an Account of the Original of the Earth, and of All the General Changes Which it hath already undergone or is to undergo Till the Consummation of all Things.* Second Edition. London, 1691.

Casaubon, Meric. *Of Credulity and Incredulity: In things Divine & Spiritual.* London, 1670.

———. *A Discourse Concerning Christ and His Incarnation and Exinanition.* London, 1646.

———. *A Letter to Peter du Moulin, etc.* Cambridge, 1669.

———. *The Originall Cause of Temporall Evils.* London, 1645.

———. *A Treatise Concerning Enthusiasme.* London, 1665.

———. *A Treatise of Use and Custom.* London, 1638.

———. *A True & Faithful Relation of What Passed for many Yeers Between Dr. John Dee and Some Spirits.* With a Preface by Meric Casaubon. London, 1659.

———. *The Vindication or Defence of Isaac Casaubon.* London, 1624.

Cato. *Cato Variegatus or Catoes Morall Distichs. Translated and Paraphras'd with variations of Expressing, in English verse.* By Sr. Richard Baker Knight. London, 1636.

Cedrenus, Georgius. *Annales, Sive Historiae Ab Exordio mundi ad Isacium Comnenum usque Compendium.* Gulielmo Xylandro Augustano inter-

Bibliography

prete, qui Annotationes etiam addidit & Tabellas Chronologicas. Basel, 1624.

Chesterfield, Philip Dormer Stanhope Lord. *Letters to His Son.* Edited by O. H. G. Leigh. 2 vols. New York, 1925.

Chevreau, U. *Histoire du Monde.* Paris, 1717.

Cibber, Colley. *An Apology for the Life of Mr. Colley Cibber, Written by Himself.* Edited by R. W. Lowe. Two volumes, London, 1889.

———. *Caesar in Ægypt. A Tragedy. As it is Acted at the Theatre-Royal in Drury-Lane, by His Majesty's Servants.* London, 1725.

———. *The Character and Conduct of Cicero, Considered, From the History of his Life, by the Reverend Dr. Middleton.* London, 1747.

Clarendon, Edward Hyde Lord. *A Brief View and Survey of the Dangerous and pernicious Errors to Church and State, In Mr. Hobbes's Book, Leviathan.* London, 1676.

———. *An Essay on An Active and Contemplative Life: And, Why the one should be preferred before the other.* Glasgow, 1765.

———. *Essays, Moral and Entertaining, by the Right Honourable Edward, Earl of Clarendon.* London, 1819.

———. *The History of the Rebellion and Civil Wars in England.* Oxford: Clarendon Press, 1826.

———. *The Miscellaneous Works of the Right Honourable Edward, Earl of Clarendon.* Second Edition. London, 1751.

Clarke, Samuel. *The Historian's Guide.* London, 1690.

Clayton, Robert, D.D. *A Vindication of the Histories of the Old and New Testament. In Answer to the Objections of the late Lord Bolingbroke. In Two Letters to a Young Nobleman.* New Edition. London, 1753.

Clement of Alexandria. "Exhortation to the Heathen," "The Instructor," "Stromata," in *The Ante-Nicene Christian Library.* Volume IV. Edinburgh, 1867.

Comenius, Johan Amos. *The Analytical Didactic of Comenius (Jan Amos Komenský).* Translated by Vladimir Jelinek. Chicago, 1953.

———. *The Angel of Peace.* Translated by W. A. Morison, Edited by Milos Safranek. Introduction by Matthew Spinka. New York, 1944.

———. *The Gate of Tongues Unlocked and Opened, or else a Seminarie or seed-plot of all Tongues and Sciences . . . brought to light in Latine, English and French . . . By the labour and industry of John Anchoran.* London, 1631.

———. *The Great Didactic.* Translated and edited by M. W. Keatinge. London, 1910.

———. *The Labyrinth of the World and The Paradise of the Heart.* Edited and translated by Count Lützow. London, 1901.

———. *Joh. Amos Comenii Orbis Sensualium Pictus . . . Joh. Amos Comenius' Visible World. Or, a Picture and Nomenclature of all the chief Things there are in the World; and of Mens Employments therein.* By Charles Hoole, M.A. For the use of young Latine Scholars. London, 1685.

———. *The School of Infancy.* Edited and translated by Ernest M. Eller. Chapel Hill, 1956.

Bibliography

Comenius, Johan Amos. *Some Rules for the Conduct of Life, Chiefly done from the Latin of J. A. Comenius.* By the Most Reverend Dr. Edward Synge. London, 1736.

——. *The Way of Light.* Translated by E. T. Campagnac. Liverpool, 1938.

Congreve, William *et al. Letters Upon Several Occasions: Written by Mr. Dryden, Mr. Wycherley, Mr. Congreve, Mr. ——, and Mr. Dennis.* Published by Mr. Dennis. London, 1696.

——. *The Library of William Congreve.* Edited by John Hodges. New York, 1955.

Constantin, Robert. *Lexicon Graecolatinum.* Second Edition. n.p.: Eustathius Vignon, 1592.

Cornelius Nepos. *Lives of Eminent Commanders.* Translated by J. S. Watson. London, 1884.

Cumberland, R. *Sanchoniatho's Phoenician History. Translated from the First Book of Eusebius, De Praeparatione Evangelica.* London, 1720.

Curll, Edmund. "An Apology for Mr. Moyle," in *The Altar of Love,* London, 1727.

Cyprian. *The Writings of Cyprian.* Edited and translated by Alexander Roberts and James Donaldson. *The Ante-Nicene Christian Library.* Edinburgh, 1868.

Daniel, Samuel. *The Collection of the History of England.* Fourth Edition. Continuation by John Trussell, Gent. London, 1650.

Defoe, Daniel. *An Account of the Conduct of Robert Earl of Oxford.* London, 1715.

——. *Atalantis Major.* London, 1711.

——. *Novels and Miscellaneous Works.* Bohn's Standard Library. London, 1893.

——. *The Quarrel of the School-Boys at Athens.* London, 1717.

——. *A True Collection of the Writings of the Author of the True-Born English-man.* Collected by himself. 2 vols. London, 1703.

Dennis, John. *The Advancement and Reformation of Modern Poetry. A Critical Discourse. In Two Parts.* London, 1701.

——. *An Essay on the Genius and Writings of Shakespeare: With Some Letters of Criticism to the Spectator.* By Mr. Dennis. London, 1712.

——. *An Essay upon Publick Spirit; Being a Satyr in Prose upon the Manners and Luxury of the Times, The Chief Sources of our present Parties and Divisions.* London, 1711.

——. *The Impartial Critick: or, Some Observations Upon a Late Book, Entituled A Short View of Tragedy.* London, 1693.

——. *Julius Caesar acquitted, and His Murderers condemn'd . . .* Shewing That it was not Caesar who destroy'd the Roman Liberties, but the Corruptions of the Romans themselves. To which is added A Second Letter, shewing That if ever the Liberties of Great Britain are lost, they will be lost no other way than by the Corruptions of the People of Great Britain themselves. London, 1722.

——. *Original Letters. Familiar, Moral and Critical.* London, 1721.

——. *Remarks upon Cato, a Tragedy.* By Mr. Dennis. London, 1713.

303

Bibliography

Dennis, John. *The Stage Defended, from Scripture, Reason, Experience, and the Common Sense of Mankind, for Two Thousand Years. In a Letter to *****.* By Mr. Dennis. London, 1726.

———. *Vice and Luxury Publick Mischiefs: Or, Remarks on a Book Intituled, The Fable of the Bees.* . . . London, 1724.

Dio Cassius. *Roman History.* Translated by Herbert Foster. 9 vols. Loeb Classics. London, 1914.

Diodorus Siculus. *The Library of History.* Translated by C. H. Oldfather. Loeb Classics. 6 vols. London, 1933.

Diogenes Laertius. *De Vitis, dogm. & apoph. clarorum philosophorum Libri X, Hesychii II.L. De Iisdem philos. & de aliis scriptoribus Liber.* . . . Cologne, 1615.

Dionysius of Halicarnassus. *The Roman Antiquities.* Translated by Earnest Cary. Loeb Classics. 7 vols. Cambridge, Massachusetts, 1937.

Dodd, William, LL.D. *A Commentary on the Books of the Old and New Testament.* In which are inserted the Notes and Collections of John Locke, Esq., and the Right Honourable Edward Earl of Clarendon. 2 vols. London, 1770.

Dryden, John. *The Essays of John Dryden.* Edited by W. P. Ker. Oxford: Clarendon Press, 1926.

Dunton, John *et al. The Athenian Gazette: or Casuistical Mercury.* London, 1691-97.

Eacherd, Laurence, editor. *An Abridgement of Sir Walter Raleigh's History of the World, in Five Books.* By Laurence Eacherd. Published by Phillip Raleigh, Esq., the only Grandson to Sir Walter. London, 1700.

———. *The History of England.* 2 vols. London, 1718.

———. *The History of England, From the First Entrance of Julius Caesar and the Romans, to the Conclusion of the Reign of King James the Second.* . . . London, 1722.

———. *The Roman History From the Building of the City, to the Perfect Settlement of the Empire by Augustus Caesar.* Fourth Edition. 2 vols. London, 1699.

Ephraim Syrus. "Nisibene Hymns," in *The Nicene and Post-Nicene Fathers.* New York, 1892.

Eusebius of Caesaria. *Chronologia.* Paris: Henricus Stephanus, 1512.

———. *The Ecclesiastical History.* Translated by Kirsopp Lake. Loeb Classics. 2 vols. London, 1926.

———. *Eusebius Werke.* Herausgegeben von Josef Karst. Die Griechischen Christlichen Schriftsteller der Ersten Drei Jahrhunderte. Fünfter Band. Leipzig, 1911.

Eutropius. *Abridgement of Roman History.* Translated by John S. Watson. London, 1884.

Falconer, William. *Remarks on the Influence of Climate, Situation, Nature of Country, Population, Nature of Food, and Way of Life, on the Disposition and Temper, Manners and Behaviour, Intellects, Laws and Customs, Forms of Government, and Religion of Mankind.* London, 1781.

Bibliography

Fénelon, François de Salignac. *Reflections upon Learning.* By Monsieur Fénelon, Archbishop of Cambray. Made English from the Paris Edition, by Mr. Ozell. London, 1718.

Feyjoo Y Montenegro. *Essays or Discourses, Selected from the Works of Feyjoo, and Translated from the Spanish,* by John Brett, Esq. 4 vols. London, 1780.

Fielding, Henry. *Fielding's Novels.* Shakespeare Head Press. Oxford: Basil Blackwell, 1926.

———. *Miscellanies.* 3 vols. London, 1743.

Florus, Lucius Annaeus. *Epitome of Roman History.* Translated by E. S. Forster. Loeb Classics. London, 1929.

Francklin, Thomas. *The Centinel.* London, 1757-1758.

Garrick, David. *A Catalogue of the Library . . . of David Garrick, Esq.* London, 1823.

Gay, John. *An Argument Proving from History, Reason, and Scripture, That the Present Mohocks and Hawkubites Are the Gog and Magog mention'd in the Revelations, and therefore That this vain and transitory World will shortly be brought to its final Dissolution.* London, 1712.

———. *Fables.* Second Edition. London, 1728.

———. *Poems on Several Occasions.* 2 vols. London, 1720.

———. *The Poetical, Dramatic, and Miscellaneous Works of John Gay.* In six volumes. To which is prefixed, Dr. Johnson's Biographical and Critical Preface. London, 1795.

———. *The Present State of Wit, in a Letter to a Friend in the Country.* London, 1711.

Gibbon, Edward. *The Autobiography.* Edited by Dero Saunders. New York, 1961.

———. *A Bibliography of the Works of Edward Gibbon.* Edited by J. E. Norton. Oxford: Oxford University Press, 1940.

———. *The Decline and Fall of the Roman Empire.* 3 vols. New York, 1948.

———. *The History of the Decline and Fall of the Roman Empire.* Edited by J. B. Bury. 12 vols. New York, 1906.

———. *The Letters of Edward Gibbon.* Edited by J. E. Norton. 3 vols. New York, 1956.

———. *The Library of Edward Gibbon.* A Catalogue of His Books. With an Introduction by Geoffrey Keynes. London, 1940.

———. *My Journal, I, II, & III and Ephemerides.* Introduction by D. M. Low. New York, 1929.

———. *The Works of Edward Gibbon. Volume 13: Miscellaneous Works.* Edited by J. W. McSpadden. New York, 1907.

Glycas, Michael. *Michaelis Glycae Annales.* Corpus Scriptorum Historiae Byzantinae. Volume XXVII. Bonn, 1836.

Goldsmith, Oliver. *An Enquiry into the Present State of Polite Learning in Europe.* London, 1759.

———. *Essays by Mr. Goldsmith.* London, 1765.

305

Bibliography

Goldsmith, Oliver. *The Grecian History, from the Earliest State to the Death of Alexander the Great.* By Dr. Goldsmith, London, 1774.

——. *The History of England, from the Earliest Times to the Death of George II.* Second Edition, Corrected. 4 vols. London, 1774.

——. *An History of the Earth, and Animated Nature.* By Oliver Goldsmith. In Eight Volumes. London, 1774.

——. *The Life of Henry St. John, Lord Viscount Bolingbroke.* London, 1770.

——. *The Roman History, From the Foundation of the City of Rome, To the Destruction of the Western Empire.* By Dr. Goldsmith. In Two Volumes. London, 1769.

Gray, Thomas. *Correspondence.* Edited by Paget Toynbee and Leonard Whibley. 3 vols. Oxford: Clarendon Press, 1935.

——. *The Poetical Works of Collins and Gray.* Edited by A. L. Poole. London: Oxford University Press, 1937.

Gregory Nazianzen. "Second Theological Oration," "On Pentecost," in *The Nicene and Post Nicene Fathers.* New York, 1892.

Gregory of Nyssa. "Of Virginity," "Against Eunomius," in *The Nicene and Post-Nicene Fathers.* New York, 1892.

Gronovius, Jacob. *Thesaurus Antiquitatum Graecarum.* 13 vols. Amsterdam, 1697-1702.

Grotius, Hugo. *De Jure belli ac pacis.* Amsterdam, 1689.

——. *De veritate religionis christianae.* The Hague, 1729.

——. *Epistolae.* Amsterdam, 1687.

——. *Prolegomena to the Law of War and Peace.* Translated by Francis W. Kelsey. Indianapolis: Bobbs-Merrill, 1957.

Guthrie, William. *An Essay upon English Tragedy.* London, 1747.

——. *A New System of Modern Geography.* Philadelphia, 1794.

Hawkins, John. *The Life of Samuel Johnson, LL.D.* London, 1961.

Hearne, Thomas. *Bibliotheca Hearneiana, Excerpts from the Catalogue of the Library of Thomas Hearne, A.M.* London, 1848.

——. *Ductor Historicus: Or, A Short System of Universal History, And An Introduction to the Study of it.* In Three Books. 2 vols. London, 1714.

——, editor. *Eutropii Breviarium Historiae Romanae.* Oxford, 1723.

——, editor. *T. Livii Patavina Historiarum ab Urbe Condita.* Oxford, 1708.

——, editor. *Thomae Sprotti Chronica.* Oxford, 1719.

Heinsius, Daniel. *Laus Asini.* Leyden, 1623.

Helvicus, Christopher. *The Historical and Chronological Theatre of Christopher Helvicus . . .* Faithfully done into English according to the two best Editions . . . And inlarg'd with Additions all throughout, and continued down to the Present Times. London, 1687.

Herodian. *The History of Herodian, a Greeke Author, treating of the Romayne Emperors, etc.* Translated by Nicholas Smith. London: William Coplande, n.d.

Herodotus. *Histories.* Translated by A. D. Godley. Loeb Classics. 4 vols. London, 1920.

Bibliography

Hervey, James. *Remarks on Lord Bolingbroke's Letters on the Study and Use of History: So far as they relate to the History of the Old Testament.* Dublin, 1752.

Hesychius. *II.L. De Iisdem philos. & de aliis scriptoribus Liber.* . . . Cologne, 1615. (See Diogenes Laertius)

Hippocrates. *Works.* Translated by W. H. S. Jones. Loeb Classics. London, 1923.

Hobbes, Thomas. *Leviathan, or The Matter, Forme, and Power of a Commonwealth Ecclesiastical and Civil.* Edited by Michael Oakeshott. Oxford: Basil Blackwell, 1946.

Hodson, William. *Zoraida: A Tragedy . . . To which is added a postscript, Containing Observations on Tragedy.* London, 1780.

Holinshed, Raphael. *Chronicles of England, Scotland, and Ireland.* 6 vols. London, 1807.

Hughes, John. *To a Lady, with a Tragedy of Cato,* in *Pope's Own Miscellany.* Facsimile. London, 1717.

Hughes, John *et al. Letters by Several Eminent Persons Deceased, Including the Correspondence of John Hughes, Esq., and Several of His Friends.* Published from the Originals. 2 vols. London, 1772.

Hume, David. *Four Dissertations.* London, 1757.

————. *On the Natural History of Religion.* London, 1757.

Irenaeus. "Against Heresies," in *The Ante-Nicene Christian Library.* Volume V. Edinburgh, 1867.

————. *Proof of the Apostolic Preaching.* Translated by Joseph P. Smith, S.J. Westminster, Maryland, 1952.

Isidore of Seville, *Isidori Episcopi Etymologiarum Sive Originum.* Edited by W. M. Lindsay. 2 vols. Oxford: Clarendon Press, 1911.

Jackson, John. *An Address to Deists, Being a Proof of Reveal'd Religion from Miracles and Prophecies.* In Answer to a Book by Peter Annet. London, 1754.

————. *Chronological Antiquities: or, the Antiquities and Chronology of the Most Ancient Kingdoms, from the Creation of the World, for the Space of Five Thousand Years.* London, 1752.

————. *Remarks on Dr. Middleton's Free Enquiry into the Miraculous Powers Supposed to have subsisted in the Christian Church from the Earliest Ages.* London, 1749.

Jerome, Saint. *Die Chronik des Hieronymus, in Eusebius Werke.* Herausgegeben von Rudolf Helm. Die Griechischen Christlichen Schriftsteller der Ersten Drei Jahrhunderte. Siebenter Band. Leipzig, 1913.

————. *Interpretatio Chronicae Eusebii Pamphili, auctore Hieronymo, cum praecedente ejusdem Hieronymi prefatione.* Edited by J. P. Migne Patrologia Latina, Volume 27. Paris, 1846.

Johnson, Samuel. *Julian the Apostate: Being A Short Account of his Life; the Sense of the Primitive Christians about his Succession; And their Behaviour towards him.* London, 1682.

Johnson, Samuel, LL.D. *Diaries, Prayers, and Annals.* Edited by E. L. McAdam, Jr., *et al.* New Haven, 1958.

Johnson, Samuel. *A dictionary of the English language.* . . . By Samuel Johnson. London, 1755.

Bibliography

Johnson, Samuel. *Lives of the English Poets.* Edited by George Birkbeck Hill. 3 vols. Oxford: Clarendon Press, 1905.

——. *Sale Catalogue of Dr. Johnson's Library.* Edited by A. Edward Newton. New York, 1925.

Jortin, John. *Miscellaneous Observations upon Authors, Ancient and Modern.* 2 vols. London, 1731.

Josephus. *The Antiquity of the Jews.* Translated by H. St.J. Thackeray. Loeb Classics. London, 1926.

Justin. *History of the World, extracted from Trogus Pompeius.* Translated by John S. Watson. London, 1884.

Justin Martyr. "First Apology," "Second Dialogue," "The Sole Government of God," in *The Ante-Nicene Christian Library.* Edited by Alexander Roberts and James Donaldson. Volume II, Edinburgh, 1867.

Keill, John. *An Examination of Dr. Burnet's Theory.* London, 1698.

Kennedy, John. *An Examination of the Reverend Mr. Jackson's Chronological Antiquities, in which the Errors and Defects of that elaborate Performance are demonstrated. In a Letter to the Author.* London, 1753.

Kerby-Miller, Charles, editor. *Memoirs of the Extraordinary Life, Works, and Discoveries of Martinus Scriblerus.* New Haven, 1959.

Lactantius. *The Works of Lactantius.* Translated by William Fletcher. 2 vols. *The Ante-Nicene Christian Library.* Edinburgh, 1871.

La Mothe le Vayer, Francis. *Notitia Historicorum Selectorum, or, Animadversions upon the Antient and Famous Greek and Latin Historians. Translated into English, with some Additions.* By W. D. Oxford, 1678.

Law, William. *A Short but Sufficient Confutation Of the Reverend Dr. Warburton's Projected Defence (As he calls it) of Christianity, in His Divine Legation of Moses.* London, 1757.

Le Clerc, Jean. *A Critical Examination of the Reverend Mr. Dean Prideaux's Connection of the Old and New Testament. Made English from the French Original. In two parts.* London, 1722.

——. *Parrhasiana: Or, Thoughts upon Several Subjects; As, Criticism, History, Morality, and Politics.* By Monsieur Le Clerc, under the feigned Name of Theodorus Parrhasi. Done into English by ****. London, 1700.

Lemoine, Abraham. *A Vindication of the Literal Account of the Fall, occasioned by the Objections of the Late Dr. Middleton.* London, 1751.

Lipsius, Justus. *Opera.* 4 vols. Antwerp, 1637.

Livy, Titus. *From the Founding of the City.* Translated by B. O. Foster. Loeb Classics. 13 vols. London, 1925.

Loccenius, Johannus. *Antiquitatum Sueo-Gothicarum, Cum hujus aevi moribus, institutis ac ritibus indigenis pro re nata comparatum Libri Tres.* Stockholm, 1647.

Locke, John. *The Philosophical Works of John Locke.* Edited by J. A. St. John. London, 1901.

Lucan. *The Civil War.* Translated by J. D. Duff. Loeb Classics. London, 1928.

Lycophron. *Alexandra, sive Cassandra.* With commentary by Johannes Tzetzes. Basel, 1546.

Bibliography

Mackaile, Matthew. *Terrae Prodromus Theoricus. Containing a Short Account of Moses Philosophizans. Or the Old (yet New) and True, Scripture Theory of the Earth.* Edinburgh, 1691.

Malebranche, Nicholas de. *Father Malebranche's Treatise Concerning the Search After Truth,* translated by T. Taylor. London, 1694.

Malelas, John. *Joannis Antiocheni Cognomento Malalae Historia Chronica,* Cum Interpret. Edm. Chilmeadi . . . Accedit Epistola Richardi Bentleii Ad. Cl. V. Jo. Millium. Oxford, Sheldon Theatre, 1691.

——. *Ionnis Malalae Chronographia.* Corpus Scriptorum Historiae Byzantinae. Volume XV. Bonn, 1831.

Mandeville, Bernard. *An Enquiry into the Causes of the Frequent Executions at Tyburn: And a Proposal for some Regulations concerning Felons in Prison.* London, 1725.

——. *An Enquiry into the Origin of Honour, and the Usefulness of Christianity in War.* London, 1732.

——. *The Fable of the Bees: Or, Private Vices Publick Benefits.* Containing Several Discourses, to demonstrate That Human Frailties, during the degeneracy of Mankind, may be turn'd to the Advantage of the Civil Society, and made to supply the place of *Moral Virtues.* London, 1714.

——. *The Fable of the Bees.* Edited by F. B. Kaye. 2 vols. Oxford: Clarendon Press, 1924.

——. *Free Thoughts on Religion, The Church, and National Happiness, By B. M.* London, 1720.

——. *A Modest Defence of Publick Stews: Or, An Essay upon Whoring, As it is now practis'd in these Kingdoms.* Written by a Layman. London, 1724.

Manwaring, Edward. *An Historical and Critical Account Of the most Eminent Classic Authors in Poetry and History.* In Three Parts. London, 1737.

M'Dermot, M. *A Philosophical Inquiry into the Source of the Pleasures Derived from Tragic Representations.* London, 1824.

Melanchthon, Philip. *Loci Communes.* Edited and translated by Charles L. Hill. Boston, 1944.

——. *Melanchthons Werke.* Herausgegeben von Robert Stupperich. Band eins. Münster, 1951.

Middleton, Conyers, D.D. *The History of the Life of Marcus Tullius Cicero* in Two Volumes. London, 1741.

——. *A Treatise on the Roman Senate.* In two parts. London, 1747.

Minucius Felix. *Octavius.* Translated by Gerald H. Randall. Loeb Classics. London, 1931.

Minucius Felix and Tertullian. *Those Two Excellent Monuments of Ancient Learning and Piety, Minucius Felix' Octavius, and Tertullian's Apology for the Primitive Christians.* Render'd into English by P.B. London, 1708.

More, Hannah. *The Works of Hannah More.* Bohn's Standard Library. London, 1853.

Bibliography

Moyle, Walter. *The Second Part of an Argument, Shewing, that a Standing Army Is inconsistent with, and absolutely destructive to the Constitution of the English Monarchy.* London, 1697.

——. *The Works of Walter Moyle Esq., None of which were ever before Publish'd.* In Two Volumes. London, 1726.

Origen. "De Principiis," "Contra Celsus," in *The Ante-Nicene Christian Library,* Volumes X, XXIII. Edinburgh, 1867.

Orosius, Paulus. *Seven Books of History Against the Pagans.* Translated by Irving W. Raymond. Columbia University Records of Civilization, No. 26. New York, 1936.

Orrery, John Boyle Earl of. *Remarks on the Life and Writings of Dr. Jonathan Swift.* London, 1752.

Parnell, Thomas. *Poems.* London, 1833.

Paschal Chronicler. *Chronichon Paschale.* Corpus Scriptorum Historiae Byzantinae. Volume XVI. Bonn, 1832.

Penn, J. *A Translation of Ranieri di Calsabigi's Letter to Count Alfieri.* With Notes. London, 1797.

Perizonius, Jacob. *Ægyptiarum Originum et Temporum Antiquissimorum Investigatio in 2 VA.* Utrecht, 1736.

Petavius, Dionysius (Denis Petau). *The History of the World: Or, An Account of Time.* Compiled by the Learned Dionisius Petavius and Continued by Others. London, 1659.

Pezron, Paul. *The Antiquities of Nations; More particularly of the Celtae or Gauls, Taken to be Originally the same People as our Ancient Britains.* Englished by Mr. Jones. London, 1706.

Photius. *Epistolae.* In Greek and Latin, edited with notes by the Rev. Richard Montagu. London, 1651.

——. *The Library of Photius.* By J. H. Freese. Vol. 1. London, 1920.

——. *Myriobiblon.* Rouen: J. Berthelin, 1653.

Pickering, Roger. *Reflections upon Theatrical Expression in Tragedy.* London, 1755.

Pilkington, Laetitia. *Memoirs of Mrs. Laetitia Pilkington, Written by Herself.* London, 1748.

Pinkerton, John. *A Dissertation on the Origin and Progress of the Scythians or Goths.* Edinburgh, 1787.

——. *An Enquiry into the History of Scotland.* New Edition. 2 vols. Edinburgh, 1814.

Pliny. *Natural History.* Translated by H. Rackham. Loeb Classics. London, 1938.

Plutarch. *Lives.* Translated by Bernadotte Perrin. Loeb Classics. 11 vols. London, 1928.

Polybius. *Histories.* Translated by W. R. Paton. Loeb Classics. 6 vols. London, 1922.

Polydore Vergil. *English History.* Edited by Sir Henry Ellis. The Camden Society. London, 1816.

Pope, Alexander. *Correspondence.* Edited by George Sherburn. 5 vols. Oxford: Clarendon Press, 1956.

——. *Miscellanea.* In Two Volumes. [1st ed.] London, 1727.

Bibliography

Pope, Alexander. *The Poems of Alexander Pope*. Twickenham Edition. 6 vols. London, 1939-1962.

————. *Thoughts on Various Subjects*. Dublin, 1737.

————. *The Works of Alexander Pope*. Edited by Whitwell Elwin and W. J. Courthope. London, 1882.

Prideaux, Humphrey. *The Old and New Testament Connected in the History of the Jews*. 3 vols. London, 1716-1718.

Prior, Matthew. *A New Answer to an Argument against a Standing Army*. London, 1697.

————. *The Poetical Works of Matthew Prior*. Edited by Monroe Spears and Bunker Wright. Oxford: Clarendon Press, 1959.

Procopius. *History of the Warres*. London, 1653.

Procopius of Caesaria. *History of the Wars*. Translated by H. B. Dewing. Loeb Classics. 6 vols. London, 1914.

Psellus, Michael. *Sybillina Oracula*. Edited with notes by J. J. Scaliger. Paris, 1599.

Puteanus, Erycius. *Suada Attica*. Leyden, 1615.

Pye, Samuel, M.D. *The Mosaic Theory of the Solar, or Planetary, System*. London, 1766.

————. *Moses and Bolingbroke, A Dialogue. In the Manner of the Right Honourable ******, Author of Dialogues of the Dead*. London, 1765.

Rawlinson, Richard. *Bibliotheca Rawlinsoniana, sive Catalogus Librorum Richardi Rawlinson*. London, 1756.

Reynolds, Sir Joshua. *Portraits by Sir Joshua Reynolds*. Edited by Frederick Hilles. New York, 1952.

Rollin, Charles. *The Method of Teaching and Studying the Belles Lettres, Etc*. Translated into English. In Four Volumes. London, 1734.

Rowe, Nicholas. *Ajax of Sophocles*. Translated by Jackson. Revised by Rowe. London, 1714.

————. *Ulysses*. London, 1704.

————. *The Works of Nicholas Rowe, Esq*. London, 1756.

Russell, William. *The Tragic Muse: A Poem Addressed to Mrs. Siddons*. London, 1783.

Rymer, Thomas. *A Short View of Tragedy*. London, 1693.

————. *The Tragedies of the Last Age, Consider'd and Examin'd by the Practice of the Ancients, and by the Common Sense of all Ages*. London, 1678.

St. Evremond, Charles Seigneur de. *The Works of Mr. St. Evremond*. Translated from the French. London, 1700.

Sarpi, Paolo. *Histoire du Concile de Trente*. Traduite par Pierre-François Le Courayer. Basel, 1738.

Scaliger, Joseph Juste. *De Emendatione Temporum*. Leyden, 1598.

————. *Scaligeriana, Sive Excerpta Ex Ore Josephi Scaligeri*. Per FF.PP. Leyden, 1668.

Scaliger, Julius Caesar. *Iulii Caesaris Scaligeri Poemata*. Apud Petrum Santandreanum, 1591.

————. *Select Translations from Scaliger's Poetics*. By F. M. Padelford. Yale Studies in English, XXVI. New York, 1905.

Bibliography

Sewell, George. *Mr. Sewell's Observations upon Cato, A Tragedy. By Mr. Addison.* In a Letter to ***. To which is added, A Comparison between Cato and Caesar; By Mr. Steele. Third Edition. London, 1714.

Shaftesbury, Anthony Ashley Cooper Third Earl of. *Characteristicks of Men, Manners, Opinions, Times.* Third Edition. 3 vols. London, 1723.

———. *The Life, Unpublished Letters, and Philosophical Regimen of Anthony Earl of Shaftesbury.* Edited by Benjamin Rand. New York, 1900.

———. *The Moralists, A Philosophical Rhapsody.* London, 1709.

———. *Several Letters Written by a Noble Lord to a Young Man at the University.* London, 1726.

Speed, John. *The History of Great Britaine.* Third edition. London, 1650.

Spence, Ferrand. *Miscellanea: or Various Discourses.* London, 1686.

Spingarn, J. E., editor. *Critical Essays of the Seventeenth Century.* 3 vols. Oxford: Clarendon Press, 1908.

Sprat, Thomas. *The Plague of Athens, Which Happened in the Second Year of the Peloponnesian War.* London, 1709.

Sprott, Thomas. *Thomae Sprotti Chronica.* Edited by Thomas Hearne. Oxford, 1719.

Steele, Richard. *The Christian Hero: An Argument Proving that No Principles but those of Religion are sufficient to make a Great Man.* London, 1701.

———. *The Englishman.* Being a Sequel of the *Guardian,* 1713-1714. London: Printed for Sam Buckley, at the Dolphin in Little Britain, n.d.

Steno, Nicolaus. *The Prodromus to a Dissertation Concerning Solids Naturally Contained within Solids.* Englished by H. O. London, 1671.

Stobaeus, John. *Ioannis Stobaei Sententiae.* Aureliae Allobrogum, Apud Francisco Fabrio, Bibliopola Lugdenensi, 1609.

Stow, John. *The Annales, or Generall Chronicle of England,* begun first by maister John Stow, and after him continued and augmented with matters forreyne, and domestique, auncient and moderne, unto the ende of this present year 1614 by Edmond Howes, gentleman. London, 1615.

Strabo, *Geography.* Translated by H. L. Jones. Loeb Classics. 8 vols. London, 1917.

Strauchius, Aegidius. *Breviarium Chronologicum,* Being a Treatise Describing the Terms and Most Celebrated Characters, Periods, and Epocha's us'd in Chronology. By which that Useful Science may easily be attained to. London, 1699.

Stukeley, William. "A Comment on an Ode of Horace," in *Paleographia Sacra: Or, Discourses on the Monuments of Antiquity that Relate to the Sacred History.* London, 1736.

Suetonius. *Lives of the Caesars.* Translated by J. C. Rolfe. Loeb Classics. 2 vols. London, 1951.

Suidas. *Suidae Historica.* Edited by Hieronymus Wolfius. Basel, 1581.

Sulpicius Severus. *Chronicorum, Quae Vulgo Inscribuntur Historia Sacra.* Edited by J. P. Migne. Patrilogiae Cursus Completus, First Series, Volume XX. Paris, 1845.

Swift, Jonathan. *Dean Swift's Library, With a Facsimile of the Original Sales Catalogue.* Edited by Harold Williams. Cambridge, 1932.

Bibliography

Swift, Jonathan. *Journal to Stella*. Edited by Harold Williams. Oxford: Clarendon Press, 1947-48.

————. *The Letters of Jonathan Swift to Charles Ford*. Edited by D. Nichol Smith. Oxford: Clarendon Press, 1935.

————. *The Poems of Jonathan Swift*. Edited by Harold Williams. Oxford: Clarendon Press, 1937.

————. *The Prose Works of Jonathan Swift*. Edited by Herbert Davis. 13 vols. Oxford: Shakespeare Head Press, 1939-1962.

Synesius. *The Essays and Hymns of Synesius of Cyrene*. Translated by Augustine Fitzgerald. 2 vols. London: Oxford University Press, 1930.

————. *A Paradoxe, Proving by reason and example, that Baldnesse is much better than bushie haire, &c.* Englished by Abraham Fleming. London, 1579.

Tacitus, Cornelius. *Annals*. Translated by William Peterson. Loeb Classics. London, 1925.

————. *Germania*. Translated by William Peterson. Loeb Classics. London, 1925.

Tatian. "Address to the Greeks" in *The Ante-Nicene Christian Library*. Volume III. Edinburgh, 1867.

Taylor, Edward. *Cursory Remarks on Tragedy, on Shakespear, and on certain Italian Poets, Principally Tragedians*. London, 1774.

Temple, Sir William. *The Early Essays and Romances of Sir William Temple, Bt.* Edited by G. C. Moore. Oxford, 1930.

————, *Letters Written During His being Ambassador at the Hague*. Published from the Originals by D. Jones, Gen. London, 1699.

————. *The Works of Sir William Temple, Baronet*. 4 vols. London, 1757.

Tertullian. *Apology and De Spectaculis*. Translated by T. R. Glover. Loeb Classics. London, 1931.

Theobald, Lewis. *The Life and Character of Marcus Portius Cato Uticensis*: Collected from the Best Ancient Greek and Latin Authors; And Design'd for the Readers of Cato, A Tragedy. London, 1713.

Theophanes. "Poemata" in *Poetae Christiani Veteres*. 4 vols. Venice, 1501-1504.

————. *Theophanis Chronographia*. Corpus Scriptorum Historiae Byzantinae. Volumes XLI–XLII. Bonn, 1839-41.

Theophilus. "To Autolycus" in *The Ante-Nicene Christian Library*. Volume III. Edinburgh, 1867.

Thucydides. *The History of the Peloponnesian War*. Translated by Richard Crawley. London, 1910.

Travis, George. *Letters to Edward Gibbon, Esq., Author of the History of the Decline and Fall of the Roman Empire*. London, 1794.

Vertot d'Aubeuf, Aubert de. *The History of the Revolutions That Happened in the Government of the Roman Republic*. English'd by Mr. Ozell and others. 2 vols. London, 1720.

————. *On the Characters of Augustus, Horace, and Agrippa*. Edited and translated by George Turnbull. London, 1740.

Vossius, Gerhard Johan. *Gerardi Joannis Vosii Opera in Sex Tomos Divisa*. Amsterdam, 1701.

Bibliography

Walpole, Horace. *Correspondence.* Edited by W. S. Lewis *et al.* New Haven, 1937- .

Warburton, William. *The Works of the Right Reverend William Warburton, D.D.* Twelve volumes. London, 1811.

Warren, Erasmus. *Geologia, or a Discourse Concerning the Earth before a Deluge.* London, 1690.

Whalley, Peter. *An Essay on the Manner of Writing History* (1746). Edited by Keith Stewart. The Augustan Reprint Society, No. 80. Los Angeles, 1960.

Whitaker, John. *Gibbon's History of the Decline and Fall of the Roman Empire Reviewed.* London, 1791.

Wotton, William. *Reflections upon Ancient and Modern Learning.* London, 1694.

Xenophon. *Cyropaedia.* Translated by Walter Miller. Loeb Classics. London, 1914.

———. *Hellenica.* Translated by Carleton Brownson. Loeb Classics. London, 1918.

———. *Memorabilia.* Translated by E. C. Marchant. Loeb Classics. London, 1923.

Zonares, John. *Ioannes Zonarae Annales.* Corpus Scriptorum Historiae Byzantinae. Volumes XLIV, XLV. Bonn, 1841.

Zosimus. *The New History of Count Zosimus, With the Notes of the Oxford Edition.* Introduction by Jean Löwenklau (Leunclavius). London, 1684.

SECONDARY SOURCES

Becker, Carl L. *The Heavenly City of the Eighteenth Century Philosophers.* New Haven, 1932.

Beneš, Eduard. *The Teacher of Nations. Addresses and Essays in Commemoration of the visit to England of the great Czech Educationalist Jan Amos Komenský.* Edited by Joseph Needham. Cambridge, 1942.

Bensly, Edward. "The Library at Moor Park," in *Notes and Queries,* CLIX (1930), 48.

Black, J. B. *The Art of History.* A Study of Four Great Historians of the Eighteenth Century. New York, 1926.

Bond, Harold L. *The Literary Art of Edward Gibbon.* Oxford, 1960.

Born, Lester K., editor. "Introduction" to Desiderius Erasmus, *The Education of a Christian Prince.* New York, 1936.

Bray, René. *La Formation de la Doctrine Classique en France.* Lausanne, 1931.

Brooks, Cleanth, editor. *Tragic Themes in Western Literature.* New Haven, 1955.

Butt, John. *The Augustan Age.* London, 1950.

Carre, Meyrick. *Phases of Thought in England.* Oxford, 1949.

Cecil, Algernon. *Six Oxford Thinkers.* London, 1909.

Clarke, M. L. *Greek Studies in England, 1700-1830.* Cambridge, 1945.

Clifford, James L. and Louis Landa, editors. *Pope and His Contemporaries.* Oxford, 1949.

Bibliography

Cochrane, Charles. *Christianity and Classical Culture*. London, 1944.

Collingwood, Robin G. *The Idea of History*. Oxford, 1946.

Cust, Lionel. *History of the Society of the Dilettanti*. London, 1914.

Dawson, Christopher. "Edward Gibbon," in *Proceedings of the British Academy, 1934*. London, 1934.

Dyson, H. V. D. and John Butt. *Augustans and Romantics*. London, 1940.

Elton, Oliver. *The Augustan Ages*. London, 1899.

Fink, Zera S. *The Classical Republicans*. Evanston, Illinois, 1945.

Fletcher, Harris F. *The Intellectual Development of John Milton*. Urbana, Illinois, 1956.

Foerster, D. M. *Homer in English Criticism. The Historical Approach in the Eighteenth Century*. New Haven, 1947.

Fueter, Eduard. *Geschichte der Neueren Historiographie*. Berlin, 1911.

Fuglum, Per. *Edward Gibbon, His View of Life and Conception of History*. Oslo Studies in English. Oxford, 1953.

Gallaway, Francis. *Reason, Rule, and Revolt in English Classicism*. New York, 1940.

Goldmark, Ruth I. *Studies in the Influence of the Classics on English Literature*. New York, 1918.

Gosse, Sir Edmund. *From Shakespeare to Pope*. Cambridge, 1885.

———. *A History of Eighteenth Century Literature (1660-1780)*. London, 1888.

Green, Clarence C. *The Neo-Classic Theory of Tragedy in England During the Eighteenth Century*. Cambridge, Massachusetts, 1934.

Hamilton, Edith. *The Greek Way*. New York, 1942.

Hans, Nicholas. *New Trends in Education in the Eighteenth Century*. London, 1951.

Harris, Victor. *All Coherence Gone*. Chicago, 1949.

Hathorn, Richmond Y. *Tragedy, Myth, and Mystery*. Bloomington, Indiana, 1962.

Haywood, Richard M. *The Myth of Rome's Fall*. New York, 1958.

Hazard, Paul. *La Crise de la Conscience Européenne (1680-1715)*. Paris, 1935.

Hearnshaw, F. J. C., editor. *The Social and Political Ideas of Some English Thinkers of the Augustan Age*. London, 1928.

Highet, Gilbert. *The Classical Tradition*. London, 1949.

Hooker, Edward N. "Dryden and the Atoms of Epicurus," *E.L.H.*, XXIV (1957), 177-90.

Jack, Ian. *Augustan Satire, 1660-1750*. Oxford, 1952.

Jaeger, Werner. *Paideia*. 3 vols. New York, 1945.

Jaspers, Karl. *Tragedy Is Not Enough*. Translated by Harald Reiche, Harry T. Moore, and Karl Deutsch. London, 1953.

Jebb, R. C. *Bentley*. London, 1882.

Johan Amos Comenius, 1592-1670. Prague, 1958.

Jones, Richard F. *Ancients and Moderns: A Study of the Background of the Battle of the Books*. Saint Louis, 1936.

Larrabee, S. A. *English Bards and Grecian Marbles*. New York, 1943.

Laurie, S. S. *John Amos Comenius, Bishop of the Moravians: His Life and Works*. London, 1881.

315

Bibliography

Proceedings of the Leeds Philosophical and Literary Society: Literary and Historical Section. Volume X, No. III (February 1963). Leeds, 1963.

Levin, Harry. *The Broken Column.* Cambridge, Massachusetts, 1931.

Loftis, John. *The Politics of Drama in Augustan England.* Oxford: Clarendon Press, 1963.

Lovejoy, Arthur O. *Essays in the History of Ideas.* Baltimore, 1948.

———. "The Parallel of Deism and Classicism," *Modern Philology,* XXIX (1932), 281-299.

Low, D. M. *Edward Gibbon, 1737-1794.* London, 1937.

Lucas, F. L. *Tragedy in Relation to Aristotle's Poetics.* London, 1928.

McCloy, Shelby T. *Gibbon's Antagonism to Christianity.* Chapel Hill, North Carolina, 1933.

McCollom, William G. *Tragedy.* New York, 1957.

McKillop, Alan D. *The Background of Thomson's Liberty.* Rice Institute Pamphlets, XXXVIII, No. 2 (July 1951). Houston, Texas, 1951.

———. *The Background of Thomson's Seasons.* Minneapolis, 1942.

Morison, James Cotter. *Gibbon.* New York, 1901.

Mowat, R. B. *Gibbon.* London, 1936.

Muller, Herbert J. *The Spirit of Tragedy.* New York, 1956.

Nadel, George. "Philosophy of History Before Historicism," *History and Theory,* III, No. 3 (1964), 291-315.

Nicoll, Allardyce. *The Theory of Drama.* New York, 1933.

Niebuhr, Reinhold. *Faith and History.* New York, 1949.

Nisard, Charles. *Le triumvirate littéraire au XVIe siècle: Juste Lipse Joseph Scaliger, et Isaac Casaubon.* Paris, 1852.

Noyes, Robert G. *The Neglected Muse: Restoration and Eighteenth-Century Tragedy in the Novel (1740-1780).* Providence, 1958.

Oliver, E. J. *Gibbon and Rome.* London, 1958.

Olson, Elder. *Tragedy and the Theory of Drama.* Detroit, 1961.

Osborn, James M. "Travel Literature and the Rise of Neo-Hellenism in England," *Bulletin of the New York Public Library,* Volume 67, No. 5 (May 1963), 279-300.

Pattison, Mark. *Isaac Casaubon, 1559-1614.* Oxford: Clarendon Press, 1892.

Peardon, Thomas P. *The Transition in English Historical Writing, 1760-1830.* New York, 1933.

Peyre, Henri. *Le Classicisme Français.* New York, 1942.

Quasten, Johannes. *Patrology.* Westminster, Maryland, 1950.

Quennell, Peter. *The Profane Virtues, Four Studies of the Eighteenth Century.* New York, 1945.

Raphael, D. D. *The Paradox of Tragedy.* London, 1960.

Rand, Edward K. *The Building of Eternal Rome.* Cambridge, Massachusetts, 1943.

Rice, Warner G. *Early English Travellers to Greece and the Levant.* Ann Arbor, Michigan, 1933.

Saintsbury, George. *The Peace of the Augustans.* London, 1916.

Sams, Henry W. "Anti-Stoicism in Seventeenth and Early Eighteenth-Century England," *Studies in Philology,* XLI (1944), 65-79.

Sandys, John Edwin. *A History of Classical Scholarship.* Cambridge, Massachusetts, 1906.

Bibliography

Saunders, Jason L. *Justus Lipsius, The Philosophy of Renaissance Stoicism.* New York, 1955.

Sewell, Richard B. *The Vision of Tragedy.* New Haven, 1960.

Sherburn, George. "The Restoration and Eighteenth Century," in *A Literary History of England*, edited by A. C. Baugh. New York, 1948.

Simar, Thomas. *Étude sur Erycius Puteanus (1574-1646).* Paris, 1909.

Spencer, Terence. *Fair Greece Sad Relic.* London, 1954.

Spinka, Mathew. *John Amos Comenius, That Incomparable Moravian.* Chicago, 1943.

Stanford, William Bedell. "Classical Studies in Trinity College, Dublin, Since the Foundations," *Hermathena*, LVII (1941), 3-24.

Steiner, George. *The Death of Tragedy.* London, 1961.

Stephen, Sir Leslie. *History of English Thought in the Eighteenth Century.* London, 1881.

Stern, B. H. *The Rise of Romantic Hellenism in English Literature, 1732-1786.* Menasha, Wisconsin, 1940.

Stromberg, R. N. "History in the Eighteenth Century," *Journal of the History of Ideas*, XII (1951), 295-304.

Summers, Joseph H. editor. *The Lyric and Dramatic Milton.* New York, 1965.

Thompson, James W. *A History of Historical Writing.* New York, 1942.

Thomson, J. A. K. *The Classical Background of English Literature.* London, 1948.

Tillotson, Geoffrey. *Augustan Studies.* London, 1961.

Trickett, Rachel. "The Augustan Pantheon" in *Essays and Studies*, Volume 6 (1953).

Vines, Sherard. *The Course of English Classicism.* New York, 1930.

Wedgwood, Cicely Veronica. *Edward Gibbon.* London, 1955.

Wood, Paul Spencer. "Native Elements in English Neo-Classicism," *Modern Philology*, XXIV (1926), 201-208.

——. "The Opposition to Neo-Classicism in England Between 1660 and 1700," *Publications of the Modern Language Association*, XLIII (1928), 182-97.

INDEX

With few exceptions, all proper names and major topics included in the text itself may be found in the following index, with frequent cross-references between authors, titles, and subjects. The Index does not include secondary authors or works not to be found in the text itself. Only those additional authors and subjects to be found in the Notes and not the text itself are included in the Index. In all other instances the reader may find supplementary information to the items indexed here by consulting the text and the notes to which it refers.

Index

fluence on Gibbon, 217; and the "higher criticism," 226; style compared to Gibbon's, 229; view of women, 231; and Epicurus on language, 275. *See also Spectator*
Aelian (Claudius Aelianus): his *Tactics*, 50; and Attic style, 273
Aeneid, 242. *See also* Virgil
Aeolists, 232
Aeschines, 273
Aeschylus, 15, 168, 176, 244; *Seven Against Thebes*, 73; *Xerxes*, 171; performed, 80; and Bentley, 88; Gray criticizes, 89; and monotheism, 113; Gibbon's knowledge of, 212; Voltaire comments on, 293
Aesop, 70, 125; model for Gay, 53; and the body politic, 56; uses of allegory, 76; his moralism, 87; his authenticity, 125; use of ass as symbol, 145; 17th cent. editions of, 273
Africans: effect of climate on, 47; as Fathers of the Catholic Church, 107
Africanus, Julius: on Nimrod, 135
Agamemnon, 176
Agathias, Dryden's translation of, 74; source for Gibbon, 210
Age of the Enlightenment (epithet), 3ff.; Johnson and, 5; Swift and, 5
Airs, Waters, Places, 47. *See also* Hippocrates
Akenside, Mark: his Hellenic interests, 77
Alaric, 226, 237
Albemarle, Duke of, *see* George Monck
Alcibiades, 68, 92; as tyrant, 52
Alcibiades, see Thomas Otway
Alcmaena, 74
Aldrovandus, Ulysses, 144, 159, 291
Alexander in Persia, 274
Alexander the Great, 26; as subject of opera, 79; in Racine's tragedy, 92; popularity during Restoration period, 92-93; Racine's depiction, 170; favorite of Orrery, 279

Alexander Severus, Emperor of Rome, 233
Alexander's Feast, 80. *See also* Dryden
Alexandrian (epithet), 91
Alexandrian Age: ancient and modern references to, 26
Allatius, Leo, 131, 291; Bentley's use of, 287
All for Love, 165, 168, 191, 243. *See also* Dryden
Alsop, Anthony, 273
ambition: Steele condemns, 189; in Goldsmith's *Roman History*, 224
Ambrose (Saint): cited by Gibbon, 213
America: approach to classicism, 85-86
Americans: colonists' view of George III, 62
Ammianus Marcellinus, 42, 97, 126, 221; Gibbon uses, 210, 215; Gibbon "translates," 237ff.
Amphitrite, 274
Amphitryon: legend of, 74
Amphitryon, 73, 80
Amsterdam, 139
Anabaptists, 158
Anacreon: Prior's interest in, 74; source for imitation, 79; Boswell and mss. at Leyden, 141; Restoration editions of, 273
Anacreontic epigrams: form of, 73
Ananias: Justin Martyr terms "Christian," 113
Ancients, 8, 26, better historians than Moderns, 34ff.; Swift's depiction of, 75; their admiration for Cato, 97ff.; Atterbury on, 106; Shaftesbury on, 123; Corneille on, 170; Lisideius on, 171
Anderson, Adam, 206
Andromeda, 274
angels, 133
Anglo–Saxon literature: studied by Neo-Classicists, 122
Anne, Queen, 5, 87, 93, 115; reign compared to Augustus's by Prior, 22; Swift praises, 66

Index

Index

Index

Index

Index

Index

Index

Moses: an "Ancient," 107; and Plato, 113; Fathers preferred as philosopher, 114ff.; as historian, 115ff.; St. Evremond on, 185; Gibbon on, 249; defended by Warburton, 284-85

Mosheim, Johann Lorenz Von, 214

Motteux, Peter, 81, 274

Moyle, Walter: interest in miracles, 120; and Gibbon on patrology, 212; Gibbon praises, 214; applicability of his *Essays*, 223; on Rome's greatness, 276; his topics, 285

Muratori, Ludovico Antonio: source for Gibbon, 210

Murray, Gilbert, 14

Musaeus: Addison and, 75

Muses, 21; Gay refers to, 23

Myriobiblon, see Photius

mythology: Greek, as source of models, 92; Voss's compilation of Greco–Roman, 151

Narcissus, 74

Natural Order: Fathers use to prove existence of God, 116-17

Neander, 178

Néarque, 185

Negroes, 80

Nembrodus, 133. *See also* Nimrod

Nemesis: Florus's belief in, 46; in Herodotus, 46; Aristotle and, 183; in history, 246

Nemesius, 288

Neo-Augustanism (epithet), 16. *See also* Augustanism

Neo-Classical (epithet): the "new" classical age, 7; term not preferred by British critics, 28

Neo-Classicism:

English: a working definition of term, 30; its supposed ignorance of Greek, 71ff.; Hellenic influences on, 78ff.; and historiography, 78ff.; its historiographical theory, 78ff.; and Epicureanism, 82ff.; its cosmic view, 85, and syntactic studies, 87ff.; and his-torical authority, 91ff.; its neo-Romanism, 91ff.; its Augustan qualities, 93ff.; Cato Uticensis as a symbol of, 95ff.; and paganism, 106; and patristic literature, 107-21; its use of the Fathers, 110ff.; and the existence of God, 117; its similarity to patrism, 117ff.; and Christian ideology, 119-21; its preference for classical to mediaeval culture, 122ff.; its mediaeval studies, 122ff.; and Byzantine culture, 123ff.; its knowledge of Byzantine literature, 124ff.; Byzantine influences on, 127-37; its relation to Humanism, 138ff.; English Neo-Classicism compared to French, 138; some theoretical characteristics, 138; its ties with Holland, 139ff.; and Renaissance scholarship, 143-45; J. J. Scaliger's influence on, 146-48; G. J. Voss's influence and, 148ff.; J. A. Comenius and, 153ff.; its pessimism, 158; as a phase of the literary Renaissance, 163-64; M. Casaubon as architect of, 156ff.; and the failure of tragic drama, 165-92; its dramatic theses, 168ff.; the negative effect of its Hellenism on tragedy, 169ff.; its historical cult and dramatic theory, 174-75; and the "uses" of tragedy, 180ff.; its ideal man, 219; embodied in Gibbon's *History*, 230ff.; and human sexuality, 232; its view of homosexuality, 233-34; and the tragic vision, 250-51; and Gibbon, 251

French: compared to English, 138

Neo-Classicists: compared to Fathers as social critics, 118-19

Neo-Hellenism, 80. *See also* Hellenism

Neo-Romanism: Cato its symbol, 104; compared to Neo-Hellenism, 105; its dependence on Byzantine abstracts, 126

345

addressed by Bentley, 22; Hearne's dedication to, 223

Oxford English Dictionary, 8; citations of "Augustan," 27

Oxford University: classical studies in, 58; its publication of the Fathers, 109; the Neo-Classicists and, 195; Gibbon at, 201-202; Gibbon's and Johnson's opinions of, 213

Ozell, John, 72

Paleographia Sacra, 25
Pan, 274
Pancirollus, 291
Pannonia, 233
Paracelsus, 159
Paradise Lost and *Paradise Regained*, 151, 227. *See also* Milton
Parnell, Thomas: *Battle of the Frogs and the Mice*, 79, 89; *Life of Zoilus*, 89, 125, 127, 131; his imitations of Anacreon, 79; aids Pope, 89; his lexicographical labors, 128; and Bentley, 196; his Homeric commentary, 203
Parrhasiana, 8-9
Parrhasius, Theodore, *see* Jean Le Clerc
Parson Adams: and primitive Christianity, 119
Parthians: Crassus's campaign against, 51
partisanship: deplored in ancient historiography, 54
Partridge, Jeremy, 155
Parvus Cato, 278. *See also Catonic Distiches*
Paschal Chronicle: and Byzantine chronologers, 126; and Divine Right theory, 133; cited by Scaliger, 147
Passion of Sappho, The, 80
Pater, Walter, 14; on Hellenism, 69
patriotism, 104-105. *See also* public spirit
patristic literature: and Neo-Clas-

sicism, 107-21; its categories, 110ff.

Patrists, *see* Fathers

Paul (Saint): and Epicurean doctrine, 84; Malebranche compares to Cato, 106; Milton cites, 108; Seneca's supposed letter to, 282

Pausanius: influence on Swift, 75; English geographers' reliance on, 81; Swift's copy of, 273

Pausanius, 89

Peireskius (Nicholas de Peiresc), 161, 291

Pelagian Heresy, 152

Peleus, 274

Penelope, 274

Pentateuch, 133; Fathers try to correlate with Gentile dates, 114

Pepusch, Christopher, 274

Pepys, Samuel: *Diary*, 139

Percy, Bishop Thomas: and early English literature, 122

Periclean (epithet), 91

Pericles, 52, 92

Perizonius, Jacob, 163

Perrault, Claude, 208

Perseus, 274

Perseus and Andromeda, 80

Persia, 184; decline of, 59; Swift comments on its history, 74; its wars a subject for Restoration drama, 80

Persius (Aulus Persius Flaccus): on luxury, 49; on Cato, 97

Pertinax: as tyrant, 52

Peru, 184, 205

Petavius, Dionysius (Denis Petau), 206, 221

Phaedra, 242

Phaedrus, Gaius Julius: Gibbon studies, 201; the text of, 202; Gibbon cites, 207

Phalaris: as tyrant, 52; Addison and, 75

Phalaris Controversy, 70, 87, 128; Bentley's part in, 88; the question of authenticity, 125; its origins, 150

159, 217; on Stobaeus, 287; Robert, 143
Stephen, Sir Leslie, 13
Stephen of Byzantium, 286
Stern, B.H., 71
Sterne, Laurence: *Tristram Shandy*, 51, 108, 144, 226; and patrology, 283; and doctrine, 119; compared to Gibbon, 196
Stillingfleet, Edward: *Origines sacrae*, 109; and chronology, 78
Stobaeus, John (Johannes), 180; in the *Dunciad*, 124; as source of facts, 127; cited by Voss, 149; preserves Epicurus, 275; praised by H. Stephanus, 287
Stoicism: Lucan makes Cato an example of, 97; Cato as 18th cent. model of, 103; M. Casaubon's furthering of, 157; and English tragic drama, 169; its cosmology and tragedy, 177; and dramatic criticism, 179; Gibbon and, 200; Cato and, 277
Stoics: their ethics, 82; their virtues compared to St. Paul's by Malebranche, 106
Strabo, 81; on luxury, 49; his disinterested judgment, 87; Gray on, 89; Gibbon studies, 212
Strauchius, Aegidius (Giles Strauch), 206, 221
Stukeley, William, 25, 218; and patrists, 283
Suetonius, 42; on tyrants, 52; source for Goldsmith, 224
Suidas, 127, 128; *Suidae Historica*, 129; its effect on etymological studies, 129; in the *Dunciad*, 123; edited by Küster, 125; edited by Porson, 126; as source of facts, 127; Voss uses as guide, 148-49; Gibbon mentions, 215; and Epicurus, 275
Sulla, Lucius Cornelius, 19, 54
Sulpicius Severus, 110, 115, 282; Gibbon disputes, 213
sumptuary laws, 54, 55; Swift advo-

cates, 64. *See also* censor and censorship
Sutton, R., 273
Swift, Deane, 102
Swift, Jonathan, 7, 14, 27, 31, 63, 71, 161, 193
    works: Argument Against Abolishing Christianity, 118; *Battle of the Books*, 74, 131, 150; *Drapier Letters*, 24, 50, 65; *Examiner*, 5, 45, 64, 231; *Further Thoughts on Religion*, 117; *Gulliver's Travels*, 4, 6, 24, 50, 53, 65, 129, 139; *History of the Last Four Years of the Queen*, 54; *Journal to Stella*, 5, 56, 102; *Letter to a Young Wife*, 119; *Mechanical Operation of the Spirit*, 84; *Memoirs of the Change in the Queen's Ministry*, 65; *Mr. Collins' Discourse of Freethinking*, 111; *Modest Proposal*, 50, 232; *Ode to Sancroft*, 102; *Ode to the Athenian Society*, 75; *Of Contests and Dissentions*, 64, 75; *Project for the Advancement of Religion*, 54, 64; *Proposal for Correcting the English Tongue*, 64-65; *Public Spirit of the Whigs*, 65; *Sentiments of a Church of England Man*, 64, 117; *Sermon upon the Excellency of Christianity*, 106; *Tale of a Tub*, 5, 74, 108, 119, 127, 226, 231; *Thoughts on Various Subjects*, 21
    and "reason," 4; a "Perfect Cavil," 6; on classicks, 10; his studies, 18; and Wm. III, 21; on Epicureanism, Socinianism, and the Restoration, 21; on English and Roman corruptions, 24; compares George I to Caesar, 24; commends study of history, 33; his reading in history, 39; his notes toward an English history, 40; attacks modern historiography, 40-41; his library, 42; as conservative Christian, 44; on historians and "nice Judgment," 45;

Index

on language and climate, 48;
owned copy of Polyaenus, 50; on
luxury, 50; on standing armies,
51; compares Marlborough to
Crassus, 51; on regal behavior
and Diodorus, 53; on Censor, 54;
on theater and depravity, 55;
on Irish manufactures, 55; and
exercise, 56; on Golden Age and
Elizabeth I, 60; and English cultural decline, 61ff.; compares
Rome and England, 63ff.; his
sermons, 65; knowledge of Greek
lit., 74-75; his historical pessimism, 78; and Aesop, 79; on
Epicureanism, 82, 84; his language parodies, 87, 128-29, 143;
on Bentley, 88; Plutarch influences, 98; admires Cato, 100ff.;
cites Fathers, 111; and apologetic
lit., 116; on women's education,
119; and doctrine, 120; on Christianity and classicism, 121; as
would-be historian, 122; borrowed Photius's techniques, 131;
his speculations on religion, 135-
36; and Anglo–Dutch relations,
139; and the ass, 145; depicts
G.J. Voss, 148; and Comenius,
154ff.; and the Fall, 158; and M.
Casaubon, 160; his ranging interests, 163; compared to Gibbon,
195ff.; and chronology, 206; Gibbon's use of, 209; his library,
211; his patristic studies, 212; influence on Gibbon, 217; Cato his
ideal, 218; and the historian's
requisites, 228; his style, 229; his
views on faction, 231; on the
Noble Savage, 234; his tragic
view, 250; debt to Dionysius,
271; his Greek collection, 273;
and Epicurus on comets, 275;
compared to Tertullian, 285
Swinburne, Charles Algernon, 14;
Atalanta in Calydon, 69; and
Hellenism, 69
Switzerland: its presses, 32

Sybil, Cumean, 283; the Sybilline
oracles, 144
Sylburg (ius), Friedrich: his lexi-
cography, 143; Swift and, 273
Symposium: Addison borrows love
allegory from, 76. *See also* Plato
Syncellus, George (the Monk), 126;
Gibbon cites, 215
Syncellus, Michael (the Monk), 126
Synesius of Cyrene: *De Providentia*,
133; *De Regno*, 133; *Dion*, 125;
Casaubon's interest in, 125; his
compilations and the Neo–Classi-
cists, 126; Gibbon's admiration
for, 215
Synge, Rev. Edward: his extractions
from Comenius, 153
Syria: its climate and sons, 233
Syrians: as Fathers of the Church,
107
Syrinx, 274

Table Alphabet, 8
Tacitus, Emperor of Rome, 218
Tacitus, Publius Cornelius, 42, 65,
67; *Annals*, 97; *History*, 97;
Whalley criticizes, 38; on tyrants,
52; on German clothing, 55;
Temple praises his style, 108;
source for Gibbon, 210; translated by British historians, 222
Tamerlane, 245
Tarquin Superbus, 52
Tate, Nahum, 191
Tatian: published by Oxford, 109;
condemned all paganism, 112;
praise of Moses as historian, 114;
proof of God in biology, 117
Tatler, The, 5; use of historical
analogies, 45; on Cato, 99; and
editorial favoritism, 143; on
tragic pessimism, 190. *See also*
Spectator
Taverner T (homas): *Cato's Disticks*, 278
Temple, Sir William, 70, 84, 88,
158, 161; *Essays*, 139; *Introduction to the History of England*,

Index

Wood, Paul S., 15-16

Woolston, Rev. Thomas, 120

Wordsworth, William: *Lyrical Ballads*, 6; and Venetian Republic, 164

Wotton, William, 115; *History of Rome*, 222; compares Latin and English, 20; and Epicurus on language, 275

Xenophon, 41, *Hellenica*, 74; *Memorabilia*, 46, 74; on value of history, 43; on Providence and history, 46; on tyrants, 52; Addison cites, 76; use of allegory, 76; his historiographical method, 77; Burnet compared with, 78; as political mentor to Neo-Classicists, 78; cited by Gibbon, 207; Gibbon studies, 241

Xerxes, 243, 274

Xiphilinus, 45; preserves Dio Cassius, 126; Gibbon admires, 215

Xylander, William, 288

Yahoos, 155

Zélide (Belle de Zuylen), 103

Zeno, 176

Zenobia of Palmyra, 236

Zimisces, John, *see* John Zimisces

Zoilus, *see* Parnell

Zonares, John, 126; cited by Voss, 149; Gibbon on, 215

Zosimus, 42, 126; Gibbon criticizes, 215